ROUTLEDGE-CAVENDISH
Core Statutes

Criminal Law

Criminal Law

2007-2008

D.G. Cracknell, LLB, of the Middle Temple, Barrister

Routledge·Cavendish
Taylor & Francis Group
LONDON AND NEW YORK

Sixth edition published 2008 by Routledge-Cavendish
2 Park Square, Milton Park, Abingdon, Oxon, OX14 4RN
Simultaneously published in the USA and Canada
by Routledge-Cavendish
270 Madison Avenue, New York, NY 10016

Routledge-Cavendish is an imprint of the Taylor & Francis Group, an informa business

Previous editions published by Old Bailey Press
First edition   1994
Fifth Edition   2005

Typeset in Garmond

Printed and bound in Great Britain by Cromwell Press, Trowbridge, Wiltshire

British Library Cataloguing in Publication Data
A catalogue record for this book is available from the British Library

Library of Congress Cataloging in Publication Data
A Catalog record for this book has been requested

ISBN10: 0-415-45121-3 (pbk)
ISBN13: 978-0-415-45121-5 (pbk)

Criminal Law
2007-2008

Previously published by Old Bailey Press as the *Cracknell's Statutes* series, Routledge-Cavendish Core Statutes provide a comprehensive series of essential statutory provisions for the core subjects and major options on the LLB or GDL.

Each book in the series

- provides the precise wording of Acts of Parliament and is unnanotated, making it ideal for both course and exam use

- is updated annually to incorporate all of the latest legislation covered in most UK law syllabi

- features consolidated amendments, avoiding the need to cross-refer to amending legislation

- contains both alphabetical and chronological contents listings and is fully indexed

Douglas Cracknell was called to the Bar in 1957 and he is still in practice. Over the years, he has devoted much time to writing and editing textbooks for students and practitioners.

Routledge-Cavendish Core Statutes

New editions available for 2007-2008:

Constitutional and Administrative Law

Contract, Tort and Remedies

Criminal Law

English Legal System

Equity and Trusts

European Union Legislation

CONTENTS

PREFACE

There are relatively few areas of the law in which criminal offences have no place and the great majority of offences are created by Acts of Parliament and regulations made under them. Many statutes, touching upon the criminal law in its widest sense, are concerned with procedure, evidence and civil rights and duties.

Clearly it would be impossible to include all of this statutory material in one volume. Careful selection has been necessary and the statutes, or extracts from them, which have been included in this book are those to which students following most Criminal Law courses will need to refer.

In terms of time, the statutes covered range from the Treason Act 1351 to the Road Safety Act 2006. Relevant provisions of the Identity Cards Act 2006, the Fraud Act 2006 and the Violent Crime Reduction Act 2006, which were in force on 1 June 2007, are amongst those now included.

Amendments – insertions, repeals or substitutions – which were in force on that date have been reflected in the text and the source of any changes is noted at the end of the particular Act.

However, where it seems likely that new legislation, or changes to existing legislation, will be brought into force within the lifetime of this edition, the relevant provisions have been included in an Appendix and attention drawn to them by way of notes in appropriate places in the main text. Certain provisions of the Criminal Justice Act 2003, the Racial and Religious Hatred Act 2006, the Police and Justice Act 2006 and the Road Safety Act 2006 are covered in this way.

Suggestions as to statutes, or statutory provisions, that it would be helpful to include (or which could safely be omitted) would always be most gratefully received.

ALPHABETICAL TABLE OF STATUTES

STATUTES

TREASON ACT 1351
(25 Edw 3 Stat 5 c 2)

Declaration what offences shall be adjudged treason

Item, whereas divers opinions have been before this time in what case treason shall be said, and in what not: the King, at the request of the lords and of the commons, hath made a declaration in the manner as hereafter followeth, that is to say; when a man doth compass or imagine the death of our lord the King, or of our lady his Queen, or of their eldest son and heir; or if a man do violate the King's companion, or the King's eldest daughter unmarried, or the wife of the King's eldest son and heir; or if a man do levy war against our lord the King in his realm, or be adherent to the King's enemies in his realm, giving to them aid and comfort in the realm, or elsewhere, and thereof be probably attainted of open deed by the people of their condition and if a man slea the chancellor, treasurer, or the King's justices of the one bench or the other, justices in eyre, or justices of assise, and all other justices assigned to hear and determine, being in their places, doing their offences: and it is to be understood that in the cases above rehearsed, that ought to be judged treason which extends to our lord the King, and his royal majesty:

As amended by the Forgery Act 1830, s31; 2 & 3 Will 4 c34 (1831–2) s1; 9 Geo 4 c31, s1; 10 Geo 4 c34, s1; Escheat (Procedure) Act 1887, Schedule; Statute Law Revision Act 1948; Criminal Law Act 1967, s10(2), Schedule 3, Pt 1; Criminal Law Act (Northern Ireland) 1967, Schedule 2, Pt 1.

TREASON ACT 1702
(1 Anne Stat 2 c 21)

3 **Endeavouring to hinder the succession to the crown according to the limitations of Stat Limitations stated; and attempting the same by overt act; high treason**

And for the further security of her Majesties person and the succession of the crown in the protestant line and for extinguishing the hopes of the pretended Prince of Wales and all other pretenders and their open and secret abettors be it further enacted by the authority aforesaid that if any person or persons shall endeavour to deprive or hinder any person who shall be the next in succession to the crown for the time being according to the limitations in an Act intituled An Act declaring the rights and liberties of the subject and settling the succession of the crown and according to one other Act intituled An Act for the further limitation of the crown and better securing the rights and liberties of the subject from succeeding after the decease of her Majesty (whom God long preserve) to the imperial crown of this realm and the dominions and territories thereunto belonging according to the limitations in the before mentioned Acts that is to say such issue of her Majesties body as shall from time to time be next in succession to the crown if it shall please God Almighty to bless her Majesty with issue and during the time her Majesty shall have no issue the Princess Sophia Electoress and Dutchess dowager of Hanover and after the decease of the said Princess Sophia the next in succession to the crown for the time being according to the limitation of the said Acts and the same malitiously advisedly and directly shall attempt by any overt act or deed every such offence shall be adjudged high treason and the offender or offenders therein their abettors procurers and comforters knowing the said offence to be done being thereof convicted or attainted according to the laws and statutes of this realm shall be deemed and adjudged traytors and shall be liable to imprisonment for life as in cases of high treason.

As amended by the Statute Law Revision Act 1948; Crime and Disorder Act 1998, s36(2)(c).

VAGRANCY ACT 1824
(5 Geo 4 c 83)

3   Persons [wandering abroad or begging] shall be deemed idle and disorderly persons, and may be imprisoned for one month …

Every person wandering abroad, or placing himself or herself in any public place, street, highway, court, or passage, to beg or gather alms, or causing or procuring or encouraging any child or children so to do; shall be deemed an idle and disorderly person within the true intent and meaning of this Act; and subject to section 70 of the Criminal Justice Act 1982, it shall be lawful for any justice of the peace to commit such offender (being thereof convicted before him by his own view, or by the confession of such offender, or by the evidence on oath of one or more credible witness or witnesses,) to the house of correction for any time not exceeding one calendar month.

[See Appendix, Criminal Justice Act 2003, Schedule 25, para 1, Schedule 32, Pt 2, para 145.]

4   Persons committing certain offences shall be deemed rogues and vagabonds and may be imprisoned for three months …

Every person committing any of the offences hereinbefore mentioned, after having been convicted as an idle and disorderly person; every person wandering abroad and lodging in any barn or outhouse, or in any deserted or unoccupied building, or in the open air, or under a tent, or in any cart or waggon, and not giving a good account of himself or herself; every person wandering abroad, and endeavouring by the exposure of wounds or deformities to obtain or gather alms; every person going about as a gatherer or collector of alms, or endeavouring to procure charitable contributions of any nature or kind, under any false or fraudulent pretence; every person being found in or upon any dwelling house, warehouse, coachhouse, stable, or outhouse, or in any inclosed yard, garden, or area for any unlawful purpose; and every person apprehended as an idle and disorderly person, and violently resisting any constable, or other peace officer so apprehending him or her, and being subsequently convicted of the offence for which he or she shall have been so apprehended; shall be deemed a rogue and vagabond, within the true intent and meaning of this Act; and subject to section 70 of the Criminal Justice Act 1982, it shall be lawful for any justice of the peace to commit such offender (being thereof convicted before him by the confession of such offender, or by the evidence on oath of one or more credible witness or witnesses,) to the house of correction for any time not exceeding three calendar months.

[See Appendix, Criminal Justice Act 2003, Schedule 25, para 2, Schedule 32, Pt 2, para 146.]

5   Certain offenders shall be deemed incorrigible rogues and may be committed for trial at the Crown Court
Every person committing any offence against this Act which shall subject him or her to be dealt with as a rogue and vagabond, such person having been at some former time adjudged so to be, and duly convicted thereof; shall, subject to section 70 of the Criminal Justice Act 1982, be deemed an incorrigible rogue within the true intent and meaning of this Act; and, subject to section 70 of the Criminal Justice Act 1982, it shall be lawful for any justice of the peace to commit such offender (being thereof convicted before him by the confession of such offender, or by the evidence on oath of one or more credible witness or witness,) to the Crown Court either in custody or on bail.

[See Appendix, Criminal Justice Act 2003, Schedule 37, Pt 9.]

NB. See also s70 of the Criminal Justice Act 1982 and s1 of the Vagrancy Act 1935.

As amended by the Statute Law Revision (No 1) Act 1888; Statute Law Revision (No 2) Act 1888; Criminal Justice Act 1925, ss42, 49(4)(5), Schedule 3; National Assurance Act 1948, s62, Schedule 7, Pt I; Criminal Justice Act 1948, ss1(2); 83(3), Schedule 10; Criminal Justice Act 1967, s103(1), Schedule 6, para 1; Theft Act 1968, s33(3), Schedule 3, Pt I; Courts Act 1971, s56(1), Schedule 8, Pt II, para 5(a); Indecent Displays (Control) Act 1981, s5(2), Schedule; Criminal Attempts Act 1981, ss8, 10, Schedule, Pt II; Criminal Justice Act 1982, s77, Schedule 14, para 1, 1(b); Public Order Act 1986, s40(3), Schedule 3; Statute Law (Repeals) Act 1989, Schedule 1, Pt I; Sexual Offences Act 2003, ss139, 140, Schedule 6, para 1, Schedule 7.

LIBEL ACT 1843
(6 & 7 Vict c 96)

4   Publication of libel known to be false
If any person shall maliciously publish any defamatory libel, knowing the same to be false, every such person, being convicted thereof, shall be liable to be imprisoned in the common gaol or house of correction for any term not exceeding two years, and to pay such fine as the court shall award.

5   Publication of libel
If any person shall maliciously publish any defamatory libel, every such person, being convicted thereof, shall be liable to fine or imprisonment, or both, as the Court may award, such imprisonment not to exceed the term of one year.

6   Proceedings upon the trial of an indictment or information for a defamatory libel
On the trial of any indictment or information for a defamatory libel, the defendant having pleaded such plea as hereinafter mentioned, the truth of the matters charged may be inquired into, but shall not amount to a defence, unless it was for the public benefit that the said matters charged should be published; and to entitle the defendant to give evidence of the truth of such matters charged as a defence to such indictment or information it shall be necessary for the defendant, in pleading to the said indictment or information, to allege the truth of the said

matters charged in the manner now required in pleading a justification to an action for defamation, and further to allege that it was for the public benefit that the said matters charged should be published, and the particular fact or facts by reason whereof it was for the public benefit that the said matters charged should be published, to which plea the prosecutor shall be at liberty to reply generally, denying the whole thereof; and if after such plea the defendant shall be convicted on such indictment or information it shall be competent to the court, in pronouncing sentence, to consider whether the guilt of the defendant is aggravated or mitigated by the said plea, and by the evidence given to prove or to disprove the same: Provided always, that the truth of the matters charged in the alleged libel complained of by such indictment or information shall in no case be inquired into without such plea of justification: Provided also, that in addition to such plea it shall be competent to the defendant to plead a plea of not guilty; Provided also, that nothing in this Act contained shall take away or prejudice any defence under the plea of not guilty which it is now competent to the defendant to make under such plea to any action or indictment or information for defamatory words or libel.

7   Evidence to rebut prima facie case of publication by an agent
Whensoever, upon the trial of any indictment or information for the publication of a libel, under the plea of not guilty, evidence shall have been given which shall establish a presumptive case of publication against the defendant by the act of any other person by his authority, it shall be competent to such defendant to prove that such publication was made without his authority, consent, or knowledge, and that the said publication did not arise from want of due care or caution on his part.

As amended by the Statute Law Revision Act 1891.

TREASON FELONY ACT 1848
(11 & 12 Vict c 12)

3   Offences herein mentioned declared to be felonies
If any person whatsoever shall, within the United Kingdom or without, compass, imagine, invent, devise, or intend to deprive or depose our Most Gracious Lady the Queen, from the style, honour, or royal name of the imperial crown of the United Kingdom, or of any other of her Majesty's dominions and countries, or to levy war against her Majesty, within any part of the United Kingdom, in order by force or constraint to compel her to change her measures or counsels, or in order to put any force or constraint upon or in order to intimidate or overawe both Houses or either House of Parliament, or to move or stir any foreigner or stranger with force to invade the United Kingdom or any other of her Majesty's dominions or countries under the obeisance of her Majesty, and such compassings, imaginations, inventions, devices, or intentions, or any of them, shall express, utter, or declare, by publishing any printing or writing, or by any overt act or deed, every person so offending shall be guilty of felony, and being convicted thereof shall be liable, to be transported beyond the seas for the term of his or her natural life.

6   Saving as to 25 Edw 3 stat 5 c2
Provided always, that nothing herein contained shall lessen the force of or in any manner affect any thing enacted by the Treason Act 1351.

7   Indictments for felony valid, though the facts may amount to treason

Provided also, that if the facts or matters alleged in an indictment for any felony under this Act shall amount in law to treason, such indictment shall not by reason thereof be deemed void, erroneous, or defective; and if the facts or matters proved on the trial of any person indicted for any felony under this Act shall amount in law to treason, such person shall not by reason thereof be entitled to be acquitted of such felony; but no person tried for such felony shall be afterwards prosecuted for treason upon the same facts.

As amended by Statute Law Revision Acts 1891 and 1892.

ACCESSORIES AND ABETTORS ACT 1861
(24 & 25 Vict c 94)

8   Abettors in misdemeanours

Whosoever shall aid, abet, counsel, or procure the commission of any indictable offence, whether the same be an offence at common law or by virtue of any Act passed or to be passed, shall be liable to be tried, indicted, and punished as a principal offender.

As amended by the Criminal Law Act 1977, s65(4), Schedule 12.

MALICIOUS DAMAGE ACT 1861
(24 & 25 Vict c 97)

35   Placing wood, etc on railway, taking up rails, etc turning points, showing or hiding signals, etc with intent to obstruct or overthrow any engine, etc

Whosoever shall unlawfully and maliciously put, place, cast, or throw upon or across any railway any wood, stone, or other matter or thing, or shall unlawfully and maliciously take up, remove, or displace any rail, sleeper, or other matter or thing belonging to any railway, or shall unlawfully and maliciously turn, move, or divert any points or other machinery belonging to any railway, or shall unlawfully and maliciously make or show, hide or remove, any signal or light upon or near to any railway, or shall unlawfully and maliciously do or cause to be done any other matter or thing, with intent, in any of the cases aforesaid, to obstruct, upset, overthrow, injure, or destroy any engine, tender, carriage, or truck using such railway, shall be guilty of felony, and being convicted thereof shall be liable, at the discretion of the Court, to be kept in penal servitude for life or to be imprisoned.

36   Obstructing engines or carriages on railways

Whosoever, by any unlawful act, or by any wilful omission or neglect, shall obstruct or cause to be obstructed any engine or carriage using any railway, or shall aid or assist therein, shall be guilty of a misdemeanour, and being convicted thereof shall be liable, at the discretion of the court, to be imprisoned for any term not exceeding two years, with or without hard labour.

58   Malice against owner of property unnecessary

Every punishment and forfeiture by this Act imposed on any person maliciously committing any offence, whether the same be punishable upon indictment or upon summary conviction, shall equally apply and be enforced, whether the offence shall be committed from malice conceived against the owner of the property in respect of which it shall be committed, or otherwise.

As amended by the Statute Law Revision Act 1892; Statute Law Revision (No 2) Act 1893; Criminal Justice Act 1948, s83(3), Schedule 10, Pt I.

OFFENCES AGAINST THE PERSON ACT 1861
(24 & 25 Vict c 100)

4   Conspiring or soliciting to commit murder
Whosoever shall solicit, encourage, persuade or endeavour to persuade, or shall propose to any person, to murder any other person, whether he be a subject of Her Majesty or not, and whether he be within the Queen's dominions or not, shall be guilty of a misdemeanour, and being convicted thereof shall be liable to imprisonment for life

5   Manslaughter
Whosoever shall be convicted of manslaughter shall be liable, at the discretion of the court, to be kept in penal servitude for life.

9   Murder or manslaughter abroad
Where any murder or manslaughter shall be committed on land out of the United Kingdom, whether within the Queen's dominions or without, and whether the person killed were a subject of Her Majesty or not, every offence committed by any subject of Her Majesty in respect of any such case, whether the same shall amount to the offence of murder or of manslaughter, may be dealt with, inquired of, tried, determined, and punished in England or Ireland: Provided, that nothing herein contained shall prevent any person from being tried in any place out of England or Ireland for any murder or manslaughter committed out of England or Ireland, in the same manner as such person might have been tried before the passing of this Act.

16   Threats to kill
A person who without lawful excuse makes to another a threat, intending that that other would fear it would be carried out, to kill that other or a third person shall be guilty of an offence and liable on conviction on indictment to imprisonment for a term not exceeding ten years.

17   Impeding a person endeavouring to save himself or another from shipwreck
Whosoever shall unlawfully and maliciously prevent or impede any person, being on board of or having quitted any ship or vessel which shall be in distress, or wrecked, stranded, or cast on shore, in his endeavour to save his life, or shall unlawfully and maliciously prevent or impede any person in his endeavour to save the life of any such person as in this section first aforesaid, shall be guilty of felony, and being convicted thereof shall be liable to be kept in penal servitude for life.

18   Shooting or attempting to shoot, or wounding, with intent to do grievous bodily harm, or to resist apprehension
Whosoever shall unlawfully and maliciously by any means whatsoever wound or cause any grievous bodily harm to any person with intent to do some grievous bodily harm to any person, or with intent to resist or prevent the lawful apprehension or detainer of any person, shall be guilty of felony, and being convicted thereof shall be liable, to be kept in penal servitude for life.

20   Inflicting bodily injury, with or without weapon
Whosoever shall unlawfully and maliciously wound or inflict any grievous bodily harm upon any other person, either with or without any weapon or instrument, shall be guilty of a misdemeanour, and being convicted thereof shall be liable to be kept in penal servitude.

21   Attempting to choke, etc in order to commit or assist in the committing of any indictable offence
Whosoever shall, by any means whatsoever, attempt to choke, suffocate, or strangle any other person, or shall by any means calculated to choke, suffocate, or strangle, attempt to render any other person insensible, unconscious, or incapable of resistance, with intent in any of such cases thereby to enable himself or any other person to commit, or with intent in any of such cases thereby to assist any other person in committing any indictable offence, shall be guilty of felony, and being convicted thereof shall be liable to be kept in penal servitude for life.

22   Using chloroform, etc to commit or assist in the committing of any indictable offence
Whosoever shall unlawfully apply or administer to or cause to be taken by, or attempt to apply or administer to or attempt to cause to be administered to or taken by, any person, any chloroform, laudanum, or other stupefying or overpowering drug, matter, or thing, with intent in any of such cases thereby to enable himself or any other person to commit, or with intent in any such cases thereby to assist any other person in committing, any indictable offence, shall be guilty of felony, and being convicted thereof shall be liable to be kept in penal servitude for life.

23   Maliciously administering poison, etc so as to endanger life or inflict grievous bodily harm
Whosoever shall unlawfully and maliciously administer to or cause to be administered to or taken by any other person any poison or other destructive or noxious thing, so as thereby to endanger the life of such person, or so as thereby to inflict upon such person any grievous bodily harm, shall be guilty of felony, and being convicted thereof shall be liable to be kept in penal servitude for any term not exceeding ten years.

24   Maliciously administering poison, etc with intent to injure, aggrieve, or annoy any other person
Whosoever shall unlawfully and maliciously administer to or cause to be administered to or taken by any other person, any poison or other destructive or noxious thing, with intent to injure, aggrieve, or annoy such person, shall be guilty of a misdemeanour, and being convicted thereof shall be liable to be kept in penal servitude.

25   Person charged with felony under s23 may be found guilty of misdemeanour under s24
If, upon the trial of any person for any felony in the last but one preceding section mentioned, the jury shall not be satisfied that such person is guilty thereof, but shall be satisfied that he is guilty of any misdemeanour in the last preceding section mentioned, then and in every such case the jury may acquit the accused of such felony, and find him guilty of such misdemeanour, and thereupon he shall be liable to be punished in the same manner as if convicted upon an indictment for such misdemeanour.

32   Placing wood, etc on railway, taking up rails, turning points, showing or hiding signals, etc with intent to endanger passengers
Whosoever shall unlawfully and maliciously put or throw upon or across any railway any wood, stone, or other matter or thing, or shall unlawfully and maliciously take up, remove, or displace

any rail, sleeper, or other matter or thing belonging to any railway, or shall unlawfully and maliciously turn, move, or divert any points or other machinery belonging to any railway, or shall unlawfully and maliciously make or show, hide or remove, any signal or light upon or near to any railway, or shall unlawfully and maliciously do or cause to be done any other matter or thing, with intent, in any of the cases aforesaid, to endanger the safety of any person travelling or being upon such railway, shall be guilty of felony, and being convicted thereof shall be liable, at the discretion of the court to be kept in penal servitude for life or to be imprisoned.

33   Casting stone, etc upon a railway carriage, with intent to endanger the safety of any person therein, or in any part of the same train

Whosoever shall unlawfully and maliciously throw, or cause to fall or strike, at, against, into, or upon any engine, tender, carriage, or truck used upon any railway, any wood, stone, or other matter or thing, with intent to injury or endanger the safety of any person being in or upon such engine, tender, carriage, or truck, or in or upon any other engine, tender, carriage, or truck of any train of which such first-mentioned engine, tender, carriage, or truck shall form part, shall be guilty of felony, and being convicted thereof shall be liable to be kept in penal servitude for life.

35   Drivers of carriages injuring persons by furious driving

Whosoever, having the charge of any carriage or vehicle, shall by wanton or furious driving or racing, or other wilful misconduct, or by wilful neglect, do or cause to be done any bodily harm to any person whatsoever, shall be guilty of a misdemeanour, and being convicted thereof shall be liable, at the discretion of the court, to be imprisoned for any term not exceeding two years, with or without hard labour.

36   Obstructing or assaulting a clergyman or other minister in the discharge of his duties in place of worship or burial place, or on his way thither

Whosoever shall, by threats or force, obstruct or prevent or endeavour to obstruct or prevent, any clergyman or other minister in or from celebrating divine service or otherwise officiating in any church, chapel, meeting house, or other place of divine worship, or in or from the performance of his duty in the lawful burial of the dead in any churchyard or other burial place, or shall strike or offer any violence to, or shall, upon any civil process, or under the pretence of executing any civil process, arrest any clergyman or other minister who is engaged in, or to the knowledge of the offender is about to engage in, any of the rites or duties in this section aforesaid, or who to the knowledge of the offender shall be going to perform the same or returning from the performance thereof, shall be guilty of a misdemeanour, and being convicted thereof shall be liable, at the discretion of the court, to be imprisoned for any term not exceeding two years, with or without hard labour.

38   Assault with intent to [resist or prevent arrest]

Whosoever shall assault any person with intent to resist or prevent the lawful apprehension or detainer of himself or of any other person for any offence, shall be guilty of a misdemeanour, and being convicted thereof shall be liable, at the discretion of the court, to be imprisoned for any term not exceeding two years, with or without hard labour.

47   Assault occasioning bodily harm – common assault

Whosoever shall be convicted upon an indictment of any assault occasioning actual bodily harm shall be liable to be kept in penal servitude.

57   Bigamy

Whosoever, being married, shall marry any other person during the life of the former husband or wife, whether the second marriage shall have taken place in England or Ireland or elsewhere, shall be guilty of felony, and being convicted thereof shall be liable to be kept in penal servitude for any term not exceeding seven years: Provided, that nothing in this section contained shall extend to any second marriage contracted elsewhere than in England and Ireland by any other than a subject of Her Majesty, or to any person marrying a second time whose husband or wife shall have been continually absent from such person for the space of seven years then last past, and shall not have been known as such person to be living within that time, or shall extend to any person who, at the time of such second marriage, shall have been divorced from the bond of the first marriage, or to any person whose former marriage shall have been declared void by the sentence of any court of competent jurisdiction.

58   Administering drugs or using instruments to procure abortion
Every woman, being with child, who, with intent to procure her own miscarriage, shall unlawfully administer to herself any poison or other noxious thing, or shall unlawfully use any instrument or other means whatsoever with the like intent, and whosoever, with intent to procure the miscarriage of any woman, whether she be or be not with child, shall unlawfully administer to her or cause to be taken by her any poison or other noxious thing, or shall unlawfully use any instrument or other means whatsoever with the like intent, shall be guilty of felony, and being convicted thereof shall be liable to be kept in penal servitude for life.

59   Procuring drugs, etc to cause abortion
Whosoever shall unlawfully supply or procure any poison or other noxious thing, or any instrument or thing whatsoever, knowing that the same is intended to be unlawfully used or employed with intent to procure the miscarriage of any woman, whether she be or not with child, shall be guilty of a misdemeanour, and being convicted thereof shall be liable to be kept in penal servitude.

60   Concealing the birth of a child
If any woman shall be delivered of a child, every person who shall, by any secret disposition of the dead body of the said child, whether such child died before, at, or after its birth, endeavour to conceal the birth thereof, shall be guilty of a misdemeanour, and being convicted thereof shall be liable, at the discretion of the court, to be imprisoned for any term not exceeding two years, with or without hard labour.

64   Making or having gunpowder, etc with intent to commit or enable any person to commit any felony mentioned in this Act
Whosoever shall knowingly have in his possession, or make or manufacture, any gunpowder, explosive substance, or any dangerous or noxious thing, or any machine, engine, instrument, or thing, with intent by means thereof to commit, or for the purpose of enabling any other person to commit, any of the felonies in this Act mentioned shall be guilty of a misdemeanour, and being convicted thereof shall be liable, at the discretion of the court, to be imprisoned for any term not exceeding two years.

As amended by the Statute Law Revision Act 1892; Statute Law Revision (No 2) Act 1893; Criminal Justice Act 1925, s49 Schedule 3; Criminal Justice Act 1948, s83(3), Schedule 10, Part I; Police Act 1964, s64(3), Schedule 10, Part I; Criminal Law Act 1967, s10(2), Schedule 2, para 13(1), Schedule 3, Part III; Criminal Law Act 1977, ss5(10) (a), (b), s65(4), (5), Schedules 12, 13; Criminal Justice Act 1988, s170(2), Schedule 16.

EXPLOSIVE SUBSTANCES ACT 1883
(46 & 47 Vict c 3)

2   Causing explosion likely to endanger life or property

A person who in the United Kingdom or (being a citizen of the United Kingdom and Colonies) in the Republic of Ireland unlawfully and maliciously causes by any explosive substance an explosion of a nature likely to endanger life or to cause serious injury to property shall, whether any injury to person or property has been actually caused or not, be guilty of an offence and on conviction on indictment shall be liable to imprisonment for life.

3   Attempt to cause explosion, or for making or keeping explosive with intent to endanger life or property

(1) A person who in the United Kingdom or a dependency or (being a citizen of the United Kingdom and Colonies) elsewhere unlawfully and maliciously –

    (a)   does any act with intent to cause, or conspires to cause, by an explosive substance an explosion of a nature likely to endanger life or cause serious injury to property; whether in the United Kingdom or elsewhere; or

    (b)   makes or has in his possession or under his control an explosive substance with intent by means thereof to endanger life, or cause serious injury to property, whether in the United Kingdom or elsewhere, or to enable any other person so to do,

shall, whether any explosion does or not take place, and whether any injury to person or property is actually caused or not, be guilty of an offence and on conviction on indictment shall be liable to imprisonment for life, and the explosive substance shall be forfeited.

(2) In this section 'dependency' means the Channel Islands, the Isle of Man and any colony, other than a colony for whose external relations a country other than the United Kingdom is responsible.

4   Making or possession of explosive under suspicious circumstances

(1) Any person who makes or knowingly has in his possession or under his control any explosive substance, under such circumstances as to give rise to a reasonable suspicion that he is not making it or does not have it in his possession or under his control for a lawful object, shall, unless he can show that he made it or had it in his possession or under his control for a lawful object, be guilty of felony, and, on conviction, shall be liable to penal servitude for a term not exceeding fourteen years, or to imprisonment for a term not exceeding two years with or without hard labour, and the explosive substance shall be forfeited.

As amended by the Criminal Jurisdiction Act 1975, s7(1), (3); Criminal Law Act 1977, s65(4), Schedule 12; Terrorism Act 2006, s17(5).

TRIAL OF LUNATICS ACT 1883
(46 & 47 Vict c 38)

2   Special verdict where accused found guilty, but insane at date of act or omission charged …

(1) Where in any indictment or information any act or omission is charged against any person as an offence, and it is given in evidence on the trial of such person for that offence that he was insane, so as not to be responsible, according to law, for his actions at the time when the act was

done or omission made, then, if it appears to the jury before whom such person is tried that he did the act or made the omission charged, but was insane as aforesaid at the time when he did or made the same, the jury shall return a special verdict that the accused is not guilty by reason of insanity.

As amended by the Criminal Procedure (Insanity) Act 1964, s1.

PUBLIC MEETING ACT 1908
(8 Edw 7 c 66)

1   Penalty on endeavour to break up public meeting
(1) Any person who at a lawful public meeting acts in a disorderly manner for the purpose of preventing the transaction of the business for which the meeting was called together shall be guilty of an offence and shall on summary conviction be liable to imprisonment for a term not exceeding six months or to a fine not exceeding level 5 on the standard scale or to both.
(2) Any person who incites others to commit an offence under this section shall be guilty of a like offence.
(3) If any constable reasonably suspects any person of committing an offence under the foregoing provisions of this section, he may if requested so to do by the chairman of the meeting require that person to declare to him immediately his name and address and, if that person refuses or fails so to declare his name and address or gives a false name and address he shall be guilty of an offence under this subsection and liable on summary conviction thereof to a fine not exceeding level 1 on the standard scale.
(4) This section does not apply as respects meetings to which section 97 of the Representation of the People Act 1983 applies.

As amended by the Public Order Act 1936, s6; Representation of the People Act 1949, s175(1), Schedule 9; Public Order Act 1963 s1(2); Criminal Law Act 1977 ss15(1)(a), 30, Schedule 1; Representation of the People Act 1983, s206, Schedule 8, para 1; Police and Criminal Evidence Act 1984, ss26(1), 119(2), Schedule 7, Part I.

PERJURY ACT 1911
(1 & 2 Geo 5 c 6)

1   Perjury
(1) If any person lawfully sworn as a witness or as an interpreter in a judicial proceedings wilfully makes a statement material in that proceeding, which he knows to be false or does not believe to be true, he shall be guilty of perjury, and shall, on conviction thereof on indictment, be liable to penal servitude for a term not exceeding seven years, or to imprisonment with or without hard labour for a term not exceeding two years, or to a fine or to both such penal servitude or imprisonment and fine.
(2) The expression 'judicial proceeding' includes a proceeding before any court, tribunal, or person having by law power to hear, receive, and examine evidence on oath.
(3) Where a statement made for the purposes of a judicial proceeding is not made before the tribunal itself, but is made on oath before a person authorised by law to administer an oath to

the person who makes the statement, and to record or authenticate the statement, it shall, for the purposes of this section, be treated as having been made in a judicial proceeding.

(4) A statement made by a person lawfully sworn in England for the purposes of a judicial proceeding –

    (a) in another part of His Majesty's dominions; or

    (b) in a British tribunal lawfully constituted in any place by sea or land outside His Majesty's dominions; or

    (c) in a tribunal of any foreign state,

shall, for the purposes of this section, be treated as a statement made in a judicial proceeding in England.

(5) Where, for the purposes of a judicial proceeding in England, a person is lawfully sworn under the authority of an Act of Parliament –

    (a) in any other part of His Majesty's dominions; or

    (b) before a British tribunal or a British officer in a foreign country, or within the jurisdiction of the Admiralty of England;

a statement made by such person so sworn as aforesaid (unless the Act of Parliament under which it was made otherwise specifically provides) shall be treated for the purposes of this section as having been made in the judicial proceedings in England for the purposes whereof it was made.

(6) The question whether a statement on which perjury is assigned was material is a question of law to be determined by the court of trial.

1A   False unsworn statement under Evidence (Proceedings in Other Jurisdictions) Act 1975

If any person, in giving any testimony (either orally or in writing) otherwise than on oath, where required to do so by an order under section 2 of the Evidence (Proceedings in Other Jurisdictions) Act 1975, makes a statement –

    (a) which he knows to be false in a material particular, or

    (b) which is false in a material particular and which he does not believe to be true,

he shall be guilty of an offence and shall be liable on conviction on indictment to imprisonment for a term not exceeding two years or a fine or both.

2   False statements on oath made otherwise than in a judicial proceeding

If any person –

(1) being required or authorised by law to make any statement on oath for any purpose, and being lawfully sworn (otherwise than in a judicial proceeding) wilfully makes a statement which is material for that purpose and which he knows to be false or does not believe to be true; or

(2) wilfully uses any false affidavit for the purposes of the Bills of Sale Act 1878, as amended by any subsequent enactment,

he shall be guilty of a misdemeanour, and, on conviction thereof on indictment shall be liable to penal servitude for a term not exceeding seven years or to imprisonment, with or without hard labour, for a term not exceeding two years, or to a fine or to both such penal servitude or imprisonment and fine.

3   False statements, etc with reference to marriage

(1) If any person –

    (a) for the purpose of procuring a marriage, or a certificate or licence for marriage, knowingly and wilfully makes a false oath, or makes or signs a false declaration, notice or certificate required under any Act of Parliament for the time being in force relating to marriage; or

    (b) knowingly and wilfully makes, or knowingly and wilfully causes to be made, for the purpose of being inserted in any register of marriage, a false statement as to any particular required by law to be known and registered relating to any marriage; or

    (c) forbids the issue of any certificate or licence for marriage by falsely representing himself to be a person whose consent to the marriage is required by law knowing such representation to be false; or

    (d) with respect to a declaration made under section 16(1A) or 27B(2) of the Marriage Act 1949 –

        (i) enters a caveat under subsection (2) of the said section 16, or

        (ii) makes a statement mentioned in subsection(4) of the said 27B, which he knows to be false in a material particular,

he shall be guilty of a misdemeanour, and, on conviction thereof on indictment, shall be liable to penal servitude for a term not exceeding seven years or to imprisonment, with or without hard labour, for a term not exceeding two years, or to a fine or to both such penal servitude or imprisonment and fine and on summary conviction thereof shall be liable to a penalty not exceeding the prescribed sum.

(2) No prosecution for knowingly and wilfully making a false declaration for the purpose of procuring any marriage out of the district in which the parties or one of them dwell shall take place after the expiration of eighteen months from the solemnisation of the marriage to which the declaration refers.

4   False statements, etc as to births or deaths

(1) If any person –

    (a) wilfully makes any false answer to any question put to him by any registrar of births or deaths relating to the particulars required to be registered concerning any birth or death, or wilfully gives to any such registrar any false information concerning any birth or death or the cause of any death; or

    (b) wilfully makes any false certificate or declaration under or for the purposes of any Act relating to the registration of births or deaths, or, knowing any such certificate or declaration to be false,uses the same as true or gives or sends the same as true to any person; or

    (c) wilfully makes, gives or uses any false statement or declaration as to a child born alive as having been still-born, or as to the body of a deceased person or a still-born child in any coffin, or falsely pretends that any child born alive was still-born; or

    (d) makes any false statement with intent to have the same inserted in any register of births or deaths;

he shall be guilty of a misdemeanour and shall be liable –

        (i) on conviction thereof on indictment, to penal servitude for a term not exceeding seven years, or to imprisonment, with or without hard labour, for a term not exceeding two years, or to a fine instead of either of the said punishments; and

        (ii) on summary conviction thereof, to a penalty not exceeding the prescribed sum.

(2) A prosecution on indictment for an offence against this section shall not be commenced more than three years after the commission of the offence.

5   False statutory declarations and other false statements without oath

If any person knowingly and wilfully makes (otherwise than on oath) a statement false in a material particular and the statement is made –

    (a) in a statutory declaration; or

    (b) in an abstract, account, balance sheet, book, certificate, declaration, entry, estimate, inventory, notice, report, return, or other document which he is authorised or required to make, attest or verify, by any public general Act of Parliament for the time being in force; or

    (c) in any oral declaration or oral answer which he is required to make by, under, or in pursuance of any public general Act of Parliament for the time being in force,

he shall be guilty of misdemeanour and shall be liable on conviction thereof on indictment to imprisonment, with or without hard labour, for any term not exceeding two years, or to a fine or to both such imprisonment and fine.

6   False declarations, etc to obtain registration, etc for carrying on a vocation

If any person –

    (a) procures or attempts to procure himself to be registered on any register or roll kept under or in pursuance of any public general Act of Parliament for the time being in force of persons qualified by law to practise any vocation or calling; or

    (b) procures or attempts to procure a certificate of the registration of any person on any such register or roll as aforesaid,

by wilfully making or producing or causing to be made or produced either verbally or in writing, any declaration, certificate, or representation which he knows to be false or fraudulent, he shall be guilty of misdemeanour and shall be liable on conviction thereof on indictment to imprisonment for any term not exceeding twelve months, or to a fine, or to both such imprisonment and fine.

7   Aiders, abettors, suborners, etc

(1) Every person who aids, abets, counsels, procures, or suborns another person to commit an offence against this Act shall be liable to be proceeded against, indicted, tried and punished as if he were a principal offender.

(2) Every person who incites another person to commit an offence against this Act shall be guilty of a misdemeanour, and, on conviction thereof on indictment, shall be liable to imprisonment, or to a fine, or to both such imprisonment and fine.

15   Interpretation, etc

(1) For the purposes of this Act, the forms and ceremonies used in administering an oath are immaterial, if the court or person before whom the oath is taken has power to administer an oath for the purpose of verifying the statements in question, and if the oath has been administered in a form and with ceremonies which the person taking the oath has accepted without objection, or has declared to be binding on him.

(2) In this Act –

The expression 'oath' includes 'affirmation' and 'declaration' and the expression 'swear' includes 'affirm' and 'declare'; and

The expression 'statutory declaration' means a declaration made by virtue of the Statutory Declarations Act 1835, or of any Act, Order in Council, rule or regulation applying or extending the provisions thereof.

As amended by the Criminal Justice Act 1925, s28(1); Criminal Law Act 1967, s10(2), Schedule 3 Part III; Evidence (Proceedings in Other Jurisdictions) Act 1975, s8(1), Schedule 1; Administration of Justice Act 1977, ss8(3), 32(4), Schedule 5, Part III; Magistrates' Courts Act 1980, s32(2); Marriage (Prohibited Degrees of Relationship) Act 1986 s4.

OFFICIAL SECRETS ACT 1911
(1 & 2 Geo 5 c 28)

1   Penalties for spying

(1) If any person for any purpose prejudicial to the safety or interests of the State –

    (a) approaches, inspects, passes over, or is in the neighbourhood of, or enters any prohibited place within the meaning of this Act; or

    (b) makes any sketch, plan, model, or note which is calculated to be or might be or is intended to be directly or indirectly useful to an enemy; or

    (c) obtains, collects, records, or publishes, or communicates to any other person any secret official code word, or pass word, or any sketch, plan, model, article or note, or other document or information which is calculated to be or might be or is intended to be directly or indirectly useful to an enemy;

he shall be guilty of felony.

(2) On a prosecution under this section, it shall not be necessary to show that the accused person was guilty of any particular act tending to show a purpose prejudicial to the safety or interests of the State, and, notwithstanding that no such act is proved against him, he may be convicted if, from the circumstances of the case, or his conduct, or his known character as proved, it appears that his purpose was a purpose prejudicial to the safety or interests of the State; and if any sketch, plan, model, article, note, document, or information relating to or used in any prohibited place within the meaning of this Act, or anything in such a place or any secret official code word or pass word, is made, obtained, collected, recorded, published, or communicated by any person other than a person acting under lawful authority, it shall be deemed to have been made, obtained, collected, recorded, published or communicated for a purpose prejudicial to the safety or interests of the State unless the contrary is proved.

3   Definition of prohibited place

For the purposes of this Act, the expression 'prohibited place' means –

    (a) any work of defence, arsenal, naval or air force establishment or station, factory, dockyard, mine, minefield, camp, ship, or aircraft belonging to or occupied by or on behalf of His Majesty, or any telegraph, telephone, wireless or signal station, or office so belonging or occupied, and any place belonging to or occupied by or on behalf of His Majesty and used for the purpose of building, repairing, making or storing any munitions of war, or any sketches, plans, models, or documents relating thereto, or for the purpose of getting any metals, oil, or minerals of use in time of war; and

    (b) any place not belonging to His Majesty where any munitions of war, or any sketches, models, plans or documents relating thereto, are being made, repaired, gotten, or stored under contract with, or with any person on behalf of, His Majesty, or otherwise on behalf of His Majesty; and

    (c) any place belonging to or used for the purposes of His Majesty which is for the time being declared by order of a Secretary of State to be a prohibited place for the purposes of this section on the ground that information with respect thereto, or damage thereto, would be useful to an enemy; and

    (d) any railway, road, way, or channel, or other means of communication by land or water (including any works or structures being part thereof or connected therewith), or any place used for gas, water, or electricity works or other works for purposes of a public character,or any place where any munitions of war, or any sketches, models, plans or documents relating thereto, are being made, repaired, or stored otherwise than on behalf of His Majesty, which is for the time being declared by order of a Secretary of State to be a prohibited place for the purposes of this section, on the ground that information with respect thereto, or the destruction or obstruction thereof, or interference therewith, would be useful to an enemy.

7   Penalty for harbouring spies

If any person knowingly harbours any person whom he knows, or has reasonable grounds for supposing, to be a person who is about to commit or has committed an offence under this Act, or knowingly permits to meet or assemble in any premises in his occupation or under his control any such persons, or if any person having harboured any such person, or permitted to meet or assemble in any premises in his occupation or under his control any such persons, wilfully omits or refuses to disclose to a superintendent of police any information which it is in his power to give in relation to any such person he shall be guilty of a misdemeanour.

As amended by the Official Secrets Act 1920, ss10, 11(2), Schedules 1, 2.

OFFICIAL SECRETS ACT 1920
(10 & 11 Geo 5 c 75)

1   Unauthorised use of uniforms; falsification of reports, forgery, personation, and false documents

(1) If any person for the purpose of gaining admission, or of assisting any other person to gain admission, to a prohibited place, within the meaning of the Official Secrets Act 1911 (hereinafter referred to as 'the principal Act'), or for any other purpose prejudicial to the safety or interests of the State within the meaning of the said Act –

(a) uses or wears, without lawful authority, any naval, military, air-force, police, or other official uniform, or any uniform so nearly resembling the same as to be calculated to deceive, or falsely represent himself to be a person who is or has been entitled to use or wear any such uniform; or

(b) orally, or in writing in any declaration or application, or in any document signed by him or on his behalf, knowingly makes or connives at the making of any false statement or any omission; or

(c) tampers with any passport or any naval, military, air-force, police, or official pass, permit, certificate, licence, or other document of a similar character (hereinafter in this section referred to as an official document), or has in his possession any forged, altered, or irregular official document; or

(d) personates, or falsely represents himself to be a person holding, or in the employment of a person holding office under His Majesty, or to be or not to be a person to whom an official document or secret official code word, or pass word, has been duly issued or communicated, or with intent to obtain an official document, secret official code word or pass word, whether for himself or any other person, knowingly makes any false statement; or

(e) uses, or has in his possession or under his control, without the authority of the Government Department or the authority concerned, any die, seal, or stamp of or belonging to, or used, made or provided by any Government Department, or by any diplomatic, naval, military, or air force authority appointed by or acting under the authority of His Majesty, or any die, seal or stamp so nearly resembling any such die,

> seal or stamp as to be calculated to deceive, or counterfeits any such die, seal or stamp, or uses, or has in his possession, or under his control, any such counterfeited die, seal or stamp;

he shall be guilty of a misdemeanour.

(2) If any person –

> (a) retains for any purpose prejudicial to the safety or interests of the State any official document, whether or not completed or issued for use, when he has no right to retain it or when it is contrary to his duty to retain it, or fails to comply with any directions issued by any Government Department or any person authorised by such department with regard to the return or disposal thereof; or
>
> (b) allows any other person to have possession of any official document issued for his use alone, or communicates any secret official code word or pass word so issued, or, without lawful authority or excuse, has in his possession any official document or secret official code word or pass word issued for the use of some person other than himself, or on obtaining possession of any official document by finding or otherwise, neglects or fails to restore it to the person or authority by whom or for whose use it was issued, or to a police constable; or
>
> (c) without lawful authority or excuse, manufactures or sells, or has in his possession for sale any such die, seal or stamp as aforesaid;

he shall be guilty of a misdemeanour.

(3) In the case of any prosecution under this section involving the proof of a purpose prejudicial to the safety or interests of the State, subsection (2) of section one of the principal Act shall apply in like manner as it applies to prosecutions under that section.

3   Interfering with officers of the police or members of His Majesty's forces

No person in the vicinity of any prohibited place shall obstruct, knowingly mislead or otherwise interfere with or impede, the chief officer or a superintendent or other officer of police, or any member of His Majesty's forces engaged on guard, sentry, patrol, or other similar duty in relation to the prohibited place, and, if any person acts in contravention of, or fails to comply with, this provision, he shall be guilty of a misdemeanour.

6   Duty of giving information as to commission of offences

(1) Where a chief officer of police is satisfied that there is reasonable ground for suspecting that an offence under section 1 of the principal Act has been committed and for believing that any person is able to furnish information as to the offence or suspected offence, he may apply to a Secretary of State for permission to exercise the powers conferred by this subsection and, if such permission is granted, he may authorise a superintendent of police, or any police officer not below the rank of inspector, to require the person believed to be able to furnish information to give any information in his power relating to the offence or suspected offence, and, if so required and on tender of his reasonable expenses, to attend at such reasonable time and place as may be specified by the superintendent or other officer; and if a person required in pursuance of such an authorisation to give information, or to attend as aforesaid, fails to comply with any such requirement or knowingly gives false information, he shall be guilty of a misdemeanour.

(2) Where a chief officer of police has reasonable grounds to believe that the case is one of great emergency and that in the interest of the State immediate action is necessary, he may exercise the powers conferred by the last foregoing subsection without applying for or being granted the permission of a Secretary of State, but if he does so shall forthwith report the circumstances to the Secretary of State.

(3) References in this section to a chief officer of police shall be construed as including references

to any other officer of police expressly authorised by a chief officer of police to act on his behalf for the purposes of this section when by reason of illness, absence, or other cause he is unable to do so.

7   Attempts, incitements, etc

Any person who attempts to commit any offence under the principal Act or this Act, or solicits or incites or endeavours to persuade another person to commit an offence, or aids or abets and does any act preparatory to the commission of an offence under the principal Act or this Act, shall be guilty of a felony or a misdemeanour or a summary offence according as the offence in question is a felony, a misdemeanour or a summary offence, and on conviction shall be liable to the same punishment, and to be proceeded against in the same manner, as if he had committed the offence.

As amended by the Official Secrets Act 1939, s1; Forgery and Counterfeiting Act 1981, s30, Schedule, Part I.

INFANT LIFE (PRESERVATION) ACT 1929
(19 & 29 Geo 5 c 34)

1   Punishment for child destruction

(1) Subject as hereinafter in this subsection provided, any person who, with intent to destroy the life of a child capable of being born alive, by any wilful act causes a child to die before it has an existence independent of its mother, shall be guilty of felony, to wit, of child destruction, and shall be liable on conviction thereof on indictment to penal servitude for life:

Provided that no person shall be found guilty of an offence under this section unless it is proved that the act which caused the death of the child was not done in good faith for the purpose only of preserving the life of the mother.

(2) For the purposes of this Act, evidence that a woman had at any material time been pregnant for a period of twenty-eight weeks or more shall be prima facie proof that she was at that time pregnant of a child capable of being born alive.

2   Prosecution of offences

(2) Where upon the trial of any person for the murder or manslaughter of any child, or for infanticide, or for an offence under section 58 of the Offences against the Person Act 1861 (which relates to administering drugs or using instruments to procure abortion), the jury are of opinion that the person charged is not guilty of murder, manslaughter or infanticide, or of an offence under the said section 58, as the case may be, but that he is shown by the evidence to be guilty of the felony of child destruction, the jury may find him guilty of that felony, and thereupon the person convicted shall be liable to be punished as if he had been convicted upon an indictment for child destruction.

(3) Where upon the trial of any person for the felony of child destruction the jury are of opinion that the person charged is not guilty of that felony, but that he is shown by the evidence to be guilty of an offence under the said section 58 of the Offences against the Person Act 1861, the jury may find him guilty of that offence, and thereupon the person convicted shall be liable to be punished as if he had been convicted upon an indictment under that section.

As amended by the Criminal Law Act 1967, s10(2), Schedule 3, Pt II; Police and Criminal Evidence Act 1984, s119(2), Schedule 7, Part V.

CHILDREN AND YOUNG PERSONS ACT 1933
(23 Geo 5 c 12)

1   Cruelty to persons under sixteen

(1) If any person who has attained the age of sixteen years and has responsibility for any child or young person under that age, wilfully assaults, ill-treats, neglects, abandons, or exposes him, or causes or procures him to be assaulted, ill-treated, neglected, abandoned, or exposed, in a manner likely to cause him unnecessary suffering or injury to health (including injury to or loss of sight or hearing, or limb, or organ of the body, and any mental derangement), that person shall be guilty of a misdemeanour, and shall be liable –

    (a)   on conviction on indictment, to a fine, or alternatively, or in addition thereto, to imprisonment for any term not exceeding ten years;

    (b)   on summary conviction, to a fine not exceeding the prescribed sum, or alternatively, or in addition thereto, to imprisonment for any term not exceeding six months.

(2) For the purposes of this section –

    (a)   a parent or other person legally liable to maintain a child or young person, or the legal guardian of a child or young person, shall be deemed to have neglected him in a manner likely to cause injury to his health if he has failed to provide adequate food, clothing, medical aid or lodging for him, or if, having been unable otherwise to provide such food, clothing, medical aid or lodging, he has failed to take steps to procure it to be provided under the enactments applicable in that behalf;

    (b)   where it is proved that the death of an infant under three years of age was caused by suffocation (not being suffocation caused by disease or the presence of any foreign body in the throat or air passages of the infant) while the infant was in bed with some other person who has attained the age of sixteen years, that other person shall, if he was, when he went to bed, under the influence of drink, be deemed to have neglected the infant in a manner likely to cause injury to its health.

(3) A person may be convicted of an offence under this section –

    (a)   notwithstanding that actual suffering or injury to health, or the likelihood of actual suffering or injury to health was obviated by the action of another person;

    (b)   notwithstanding the death of the child or young person in question.

38   Evidence of child of tender years

(2) If any child whose evidence is received unsworn in any proceedings for an offence by virtue of section 52 of the Criminal Justice Act 1991 wilfully gives false evidence in such circumstances that he would, if the evidence had been given on oath, have been guilty of perjury, he shall be liable on summary conviction to be dealt with as if he had been summarily convicted of an indictable offence punishable in the case of an adult with imprisonment.

50   Age of criminal responsibility

It shall be conclusively presumed that no child under the age of ten years can be guilty of any offence.

As amended by the National Assistance (Adaptation of Enactments) Regulations 1950, the Children and Young Persons Act 1963, ss16(1), 64(1), (3), Schedule 3, para 1, Schedule 5; Murder (Abolition of Death Penalty) Act 1965, s1(5), (4); Criminal Law Act 1967, s10, Schedule 2, para 13(1), Schedule 3, Part III; Children Act 1975, s108(1)(b), Schedule 4, Part III; Magistrates' Courts Act 1980, s32(2); Criminal Justice Act 1988, ss34(1), 45, 170(2), Schedule 16; Children Act 1989, s108(4), (5), Schedule 12, para 2, Schedule 13, para 2; Criminal Justice Act 1991, s100, Schedule 11, para 1; Criminal Justice and Public Order Act 1994, s16; Children Act 2004, ss58(5), 64, Schedule 5, Pt 5.

INCITEMENT TO DISAFFECTION ACT 1934
(24 & 25 Geo 5 c 56)

1   Penalty on persons endeavouring to seduce members of His Majesty's forces from their duty or allegiance

If any person maliciously and advisedly endeavours to seduce any members of His Majesty's forces from his duty or allegiance to His Majesty, he shall be guilty of an offence under this Act.

VAGRANCY ACT 1935
(25 & 26 Geo 5 c 20)

1   Amendment of 5 Geo 4 c 38, s4

(1) So much of section 4 of the Vagrancy Act 1824, as enacts that a person wandering abroad and lodging in any barn or outhouse, or in any deserted or unoccupied building, or in the open air, or under a tent, or in any cart or waggon, not having any visible means of subsistence, and not giving a good account of himself, shall be deemed a rogue and vagabond within the meaning of that Act, shall have effect subject to the following provisions of this section.

(3) A person wandering abroad and lodging as aforesaid shall not be deemed by virtue of the said enactment a rogue and vagabond within the meaning of the said Act unless it is proved either –

    (a)   that, in relation to the occasion on which he lodged as aforesaid, he had been directed to a reasonably accessible place of shelter and failed to apply for, or refused, accommodation there;

    (b)   that he is a person who persistently wanders abroad and, notwithstanding that a place of shelter is reasonably accessible, lodges or attempts to lodge as aforesaid; or

    (c)   that by, or in the course of, lodging as aforesaid he caused damage to property, infection with vermin, or other offensive consequence, or that he lodged as aforesaid in such circumstances as to appear to be likely so to do.

In this subsection the expression 'a place to shelter' means a place where provision is regularly made for giving (free of charge) accommodation for the night to such persons as apply therefor.

(4) The reference in the said enactment to a person lodging under a tent or in a cart or waggon shall not be deemed to include a person lodging under a tent or in a cart or waggon with or in which he travels.

As amended by the Statute Law Revision Act 1950.

INFANTICIDE ACT 1938
(1 & 2 Geo 6 c 36)

1   Offence of infanticide

(1) Where a woman by any wilful act or omission causes the death of her child being a child under the age of twelve months, but at the time of the act or omission the balance of her mind was disturbed by reason of her not having fully recovered from the effect of giving birth to the child or by reason of the effect of lactation consequent upon the birth of the child, then, notwithstanding that the circumstances were such that but for this Act the offence would have

amounted to murder, she shall be guilty of felony, to wit of infanticide, and may for such offence be dealt with and punished as if she had been guilty of the offence of manslaughter of the child.

(2) Where upon the trial of a woman for the murder of her child, being a child under the age of twelve months, the jury are of opinion that she by any wilful act or omission caused its death, but that at the time of the act or omission the balance of her mind was disturbed by reason of her not having fully recovered from the effect of giving birth to the child or by reason of the effect of lactation consequent upon the birth of the child, then the jury may, notwithstanding that the circumstances were such that but for the provisions of this Act they might have returned a verdict of murder, return in lieu thereof a verdict of infanticide

(3) Nothing in this Act shall affect the power of the jury upon an indictment for the murder of a child to return a verdict of manslaughter, or a verdict of guilty but insane.

As amended by the Criminal Law Act 1967, s10(2), Schedule 3, Part III.

PREVENTION OF CRIME ACT 1953
(1 & 2 Eliz 2 c 14)

1   Prohibition of the carrying of offensive weapons without lawful authority or reasonable excuse

(1) Any person who without lawful authority or reasonable excuse, the proof whereof shall lie on him, has with him in any public place any offensive weapon shall be guilty of an offence, and shall be liable –

   (a)   on summary conviction, to imprisonment for a term not exceeding six months or a fine not exceeding the prescribed sum, or both;

   (b)   on conviction on indictment, to imprisonment for a term not exceeding four years or a fine or both.

(2) Where any person is convicted of an offence under subsection (1) of this section the court may make an order for the forfeiture or disposal of any weapon in respect of which the offence was committed.

(4) In this section 'public place' includes any highway and any other premises or place to which at the material time the public have or are permitted to have access, whether on payment or otherwise; and 'offensive weapon' means any article made or adapted for use for causing injury to the person, or intended by the person having it with him for such use by him or by some other person.

As amended by the Criminal Law Act 1977, s32(1); Magistrates' Courts Act 1980, s32(2); Police and Criminal Evidence Act 1984, ss26(1), 119(2), Schedule 7, Part I; Public Order Act 1986, s40(2), Schedule 2, para 2; Criminal Justice Act 1988, s46(1), (3); Offensive Weapons Act 1996, s2(1), (4).

SEXUAL OFFENCES ACT 1956
(4 & 5 Eliz 2 c 69)

33   Keeping a brothel

It is an offence for a person to keep a brothel, or to manage, or act or assist in the management of, a brothel.

33A   Keeping a brothel used for prostitution

(1) It is an offence for a person to keep, or to manage, or act or assist in the management of, a brothel to which people resort for practices involving prostitution (whether or not also for other practices).

(2) In this section 'prostitution' has the meaning given by section 51(2) of the Sexual Offences Act 2003.

34   Landlord letting premises for use as brothel

It is an offence for the lessor or landlord of any premises or his agent to let the whole or part of the premises with the knowledge that it is to be used, in whole or in part, as a brothel, or, where the whole or part of the premises is used as a brothel, to be wilfully a party to that use continuing.

35   Tenant permitting premises to be used as brothel

(1) It is an offence for the tenant or occupier, or person in charge, of any premises knowingly to permit the whole or part of the premises to be used as a brothel.

(2) Where the tenant or occupier of any premises is convicted (whether under this section or, for an offence committed before the commencement of this Act, under section 13 of the Criminal Law Amendment Act 1885) of knowingly permitting the whole or part of the premises to be used as a brothel, the First Schedule of this Act shall apply to enlarge the rights of the lessor or landlord with respect to the assignment or determination of the lease or other contract under which the premises are held by the person convicted.

(3) Where the tenant or occupier of any premises is so convicted, or was so convicted under the said section 13 before the commencement of this Act, and either –

   (a)   the lessor or landlord, after having the conviction brought to his notice, fails or failed to exercise his statutory rights in relation to the lease or contract under which the premises are or were held by the person convicted; or

   (b)   the lessor or landlord, after exercising his statutory rights so as to determine that lease or contract, grants or granted a new lease or enters or entered into a new contract of tenancy of the premises to, with or for the benefit of the same person, without having all reasonable provisions to prevent the recurrence of the offence inserted in the new lease or contract;

then, if subsequently an offence under this section is committed in respect of the premises during the subsistence of the lease or contract referred to in paragraph (a) of this subsection or (where paragraph (b) applies) during the subsistence of the new lease or contract, the lessor landlord shall be deemed to be a party to that offence unless he shows that he took all reasonable steps to prevent the recurrence of the offence.

Reference in this subsection to the statutory rights of a lessor or landlord refer to his rights under the First Schedule to this Act or under subsection (1) of section 5 of the Criminal Law Amendment Act 1912 (the provision replaced for England and Wales by that Schedule).

36   Tenant permitting premises to be used for prostitution

It is an offence for the tenant or occupier of any premises knowingly to permit the whole or part of the premises to be used for the purposes of habitual prostitution (whether any prostitute involved is male or female).

As amended by the Sexual Offences Act 2003, ss55(1), (2), 56, Schedule 1, para 1.

HOMICIDE ACT 1957
(5 & 6 Eliz 2 c 11)

1   Abolition of 'constructive malice'

(1) Where a person kills another in the course or furtherance of some other offence, the killing shall not amount to murder unless done with the same malice aforethought (express or implied) as is required for a killing to amount to murder when not done in the course or furtherance of another offence.

(2) For the purpose of the foregoing subsection, a killing done in the course or for the purpose of resisting an officer of justice, or of resisting or avoiding or preventing a lawful arrest, or of affecting or assisting an escape or rescue from legal custody, shall be treated as a killing in the course or furtherance of an offence.

2   Persons suffering from diminished responsibility

(1) Where a person kills or is a party to a killing of another, he shall not be convicted of murder if he was suffering from such abnormality of mind (whether arising from a condition of arrested or retarded development or mind or any inherent causes or induced by disease or injury) as substantially impaired his mental responsibility for his acts and omissions in doing or being a party to the killing.

(2) On a charge of murder, it shall be for the defence to prove that the person charged is by virtue of this section not liable to be convicted of murder.

(3) A person who but for this section would be liable, whether as principal or as accessory, to be convicted of murder shall be liable instead to be convicted of manslaughter.

(4) The fact that one party to a killing is by virtue of this section not liable to be convicted of murder shall not affect the question whether the killing amounted to murder in the case of any other party to it.

3   Provocation

Where on a charge of murder there is evidence on which the jury can find that the person charged was provoked (whether by things done or by things said or by both together) to lose his self-control, the question whether the provocation was enough to make a reasonable man do as he did shall be left to be determined by the jury; and in determining that question the jury shall take into account everything both done and said according to the effect which, in their opinion, it would have on a reasonable man.

4   Suicide pacts

(1) It shall be manslaughter, and shall not be murder, for a person acting in pursuance of a suicide pact between him and another to kill the other or be a party to the other being killed by a third person.

(2) Where it is shown that a person charged with the murder of another killed the other or was a party to his being killed, it shall be for the defence to prove that the person charged was acting in pursuance of a suicide pact between him and the other.

(3) For the purposes of this section 'suicide pact' means a common agreement between two or more persons having for its object the death of all of them, whether or not each is to take his own life, but nothing done by a person who enters into a suicide pact shall be treated as done by him in pursuance of the pact unless it is done while he has the settled intention of dying in pursuance of the pact.

As amended by the Suicide Act 1961, s3(2), Schedule 2.

RESTRICTION OF OFFENSIVE WEAPONS ACT 1959
(7 & 8 Eliz 2 c 37)

1   Penalties for offences in connection with dangerous weapons
(1) Any person who manufactures, sells or hires or offers for sale or hire, or exposes or has in his possession for the purpose of sale or hire, or lends or gives to any other person –
  (a) any knife which has a blade which opens automatically by hand pressure applied to a button, spring or other device in or attached to the handle of the knife, sometimes known as a 'flick knife' or 'flick gun'; or
  (b) any knife which has a blade which is released from the handle or sheath thereof by the force of gravity or the application of centrifugal force and which, when released, is locked in place by means of a button, spring, lever, or other device, sometimes known as a 'gravity knife',
shall be guilty of an offence and shall be liable on summary conviction to imprisonment for a term not exceeding six months or to a fine not exceeding level 5 on the standard scale or to both such imprisonment and fine.
(2) The importation of any such knife as is described in the foregoing subsection is hereby prohibited.

As amended by the Restriction of Offensive Weapons Act 1961, s1; Criminal Justice Act 1988, s46(2), (3).

STREET OFFENCES ACT 1959
(7 & 8 Eliz 2 c 57)

1   Loitering or soliciting for purposes of prostitution
(1) It shall be an offence for a common prostitute (whether male or female) to loiter or solicit in a street or public place for the purpose of prostitution.
(2) A person guilty of an offence under this section shall be liable, on summary conviction, to a fine of an amount not exceeding level 2 on the standard scale or, for an offence committed after a previous conviction, to a fine of an amount not exceeding level 3 on that scale.
(4) For the purposes of this section 'street' includes any bridge, road, lane, footway, subway, square, court, alley or passage, whether a thoroughfare or not, which is for the time being open to the public; and the doorways and entrances of premises abutting on a street (as hereinbefore defined), and any ground adjoining and open to a street, shall be treated as forming part of the street.

As amended by the Criminal Justice Act 1982, s71; Sexual Offences Act 2003, s56, Schedule 1, para 2; Serious Organised Crime and Police Act 2005, s111, Schedule 7, Pt 1, para 14, Schedule 17, Pt 2.

OBSCENE PUBLICATIONS ACT 1959
(7 & 8 Eliz 2 c 66)

1   Test of obscenity
(1) For the purposes of this Act an article shall be deemed to be obscene if its effect or (where

the article comprises two or more distinct items) the effect of any one of its items, is, if taken as a whole, such as to tend to deprave and corrupt persons who are likely, having regard to all relevant circumstances, to read, see or hear the matter contained or embodied in it.

(2) In this Act 'article' means any description of article containing or embodying matter to be read or looked at or both, any sound record, and any film or other record of a picture or pictures.

(3) For the purposes of this Act a person publishes an article who –

  (a) distributes, circulates, sells, lets on hire, gives, or lends it or who offers it for sale or for letting on hire; or

  (b) in the case of an article containing or embodying matter to be looked at or a record, shows, plays or projects it, or, where the matter is data stored electronically, transmits that data.

(4) For the purposes of this Act a person also publishes an article to the extent that any matter recorded on it is included by him in a programme included in a programme service.

(5) Where the inclusion of any matter in a programme so included would, if that matter were recorded matter, constitute the publication of an obscene article for the purposes of this Act by virtue of subsection (4) above, this Act shall have effect in relation to the inclusion of that matter in that programme as if it were recorded matter.

(6) In this section 'programme' and 'programme service' have the same meaning as in the Broadcasting Act 1990.

2   Prohibition of publication of obscene matter

(1) Subject as hereinafter provided, any person who, whether for gain or not, publishes an obscene article or who has an obscene article for publication for gain (whether gain to himself or gain to another) shall be liable –

  (a) on summary conviction to a fine not exceeding the prescribed sum or to imprisonment for a term not exceeding six months;

  (b) on conviction on indictment to a fine or to imprisonment for a term not exceeding three years or both.

(3) A prosecution for an offence against this section shall not be commenced more than two years after the commission of the offence.

(3A) Proceedings for an offence under this section shall not be instituted except by or with the consent of the Director of Public Prosecutions in any case where the article in question is a moving picture film of a width of not less than sixteen millimetres and the relevant publication or the only other publication which followed or could reasonably have been expected to follow from the relevant publication took place or (as the case may be) was to take place in the course of an exhibition of a film and in this subsection 'the relevant publication' means –

  (a) in the case of any proceedings under this section for publishing an obscene article, the publication in respect of which the defendant would be charged if the proceedings were brought; and

  (b) in the case of any proceedings under this section for having an obscene article for publication for gain, the publication which, if the proceedings were brought, the defendant would be alleged to have had in contemplation.

(4) A person publishing an article shall not be proceeded against for an offence at common law consisting of the publication of any matter contained or embodied in the article where it is of the essence of the offence that the matter is obscene.

(4A) Without prejudice to subsection (4) above, a person shall not be proceeded against for an offence at common law –

  (a) in respect of an exhibition of a film or anything said or done in the course of an exhibition of a film, where it is of the essence of the common law offence that the exhibition or, as the case may be, what was said or done was obscene, indecent, offensive, disgusting or injurious to morality; or

(b) in respect of an agreement to give an exhibition of a film or to cause anything to be said or done in the course of such an exhibition where the common law offence consists of conspiring to corrupt public morals or to do any act contrary to public morals or decency.

(5) A person shall not be convicted of an offence against this section if he proves that he had not examined the article in respect of which he is charged and had no reasonable cause to suspect that it was such that his publication of it would make him liable to be convicted of an offence against this section.

(6) In any proceedings against a person under this section the question whether an article is obscene shall be determined without regard to any publication by another person unless it could reasonably have been expected that the publication by the other person would follow from publication by the person charged.

(7) In this section 'exhibition of a film' has the meaning given in paragraph 15 of Schedule 1 to the Licensing Act 2003.

3 Powers of search and seizure

(1) If a justice of the peace is satisfied by information on oath that there is reasonable ground for suspecting that, in any premises or on any stall or vehicle, being premises or a stall or vehicle specified in the information, obscene articles are, or are from time to time, kept for publication for gain, the justice may issue a warrant under his hand empowering any constable to enter (if need be by force) and search the premises, or to search the stall or vehicle, and to seize and remove any articles found therein or thereon which the constable has reason to believe to be obscene articles and to be kept for publication for gain.

(2) A warrant under the foregoing subsection shall, if any obscene articles are seized under the warrant, also empower the seizure and removal of any documents found in the premises or, as the case may be, on the stall or vehicle which relate to a trade or business carried on at the premises or from the stall or vehicle.

(3) Subject to subsection 3A of this section any articles seized under subsection (1) of this section shall be brought before a justice of the peace acting in the local justice area in which the articles were seized, who may thereupon issue a summons to the occupier of the premises or, as the case may be, the user of the stall or vehicle to appear on a day specified in the summons before a magistrates' court acting in that local justice area to show cause why the articles or any of them should not be forfeited; and if the court is satisfied, as respects any of the articles, that at the time when they were seized they were obscene articles kept for publication for gain, the court shall order those articles to be forfeited:

Provided that if the person summoned does not appear, the court shall not make an order unless service of the summons is proved.

Provided also that this subsection does not apply in relation to any article seized under subsection (1) of this section which is returned to the occupier of the premises or, as the case may be, to the user of the stall or vehicle in or on which it was found.

(3A) Without prejudice to the duty of a court to make an order for the forfeiture of an article where section 1(4) of the Obscene Publications Act 1964 applies (orders made on conviction), in a case where by virtue of subsection (3A) of section 2 of this Act proceedings under the said section 2 for having an article for publication for gain could not be instituted except by or with the consent of the Director of Public Prosecutions, no order for the forfeiture of the article shall be made under this section unless the warrant under which the article was seized was issued on an information laid by or on behalf of the Director of Public Prosecutions.

(4) In addition to the person summoned, any other person being the owner, author or maker of any of the articles brought before the court, or any other person through whose hands they had passed before being seized, shall be entitled to appear before the court on the day specified in the summons to show cause why they should not be forfeited.

(5) Where an order is made under this section for the forfeiture of any articles, any person who appeared, or was entitled to appear, to show cause against the making of the order may appeal to the Crown Court; and no such order shall take effect until the expiration of the period within which the notice of appeal to the Crown Court may be given against the order or, if before the expiration thereof notice of appeal is duly given or application is made for the statement of a case for the opinion of the High Court, until the final determination or abandonment of the proceedings on the appeal or case.

(6) If as respects any articles brought before it the court does not order forfeiture, the court may if it thinks fit order the person on whose information the warrant for the seizure of the articles was issued to pay such costs as the court thinks reasonable to any person who has appeared before the court to show cause why those articles should not be forfeited; and costs ordered to be paid under this subsection shall be enforceable as a civil debt.

(7) For the purposes of this section the question whether an article is obscene shall be determined on the assumption that copies of it would be published in any manner likely having regard to the circumstances in which it was found, but in no other manner.

4   Defence of public good

(1) Subject to subsection 1A of this section a person shall not be convicted of an offence against section 2 of this Act, and an order for forfeiture shall not be made under the foregoing section, if it is proved that publication of the article in question is justified as being for the public good on the ground that it is in the interests of science, literature, art or learning, or of other objects of general concern.

(1A) Subsection (1) of this section shall not apply where the article in question is a moving picture film or soundtrack, but –

   (a) a person shall not be convicted of an offence against section 2 of this Act in relation to any such film or soundtrack, and

   (b) an order for forfeiture of any such film or soundtrack shall not be made under section 3 of this Act,

if it is proved that publication of the film or soundtrack is justified as being for the public good on the ground that it is in the interests of drama, opera, ballet or any other art, or of literature or learning.

(2) It is hereby declared that the opinion of experts as to the literary, artistic, scientific or other merits of an article may be admitted in any proceedings under this Act either to establish or to negative the said ground.

(3) In this section 'moving picture soundtrack' means any sound record designed for playing with a moving picture film, whether incorporated with the film or not.

As amended by the Obscene Publications Act 1964, s1(1); Courts Act 1971, s56(2), Schedule 8 para 37, Schedule 9 Part I; Criminal Law Act 1977, s53(1), (5), (6), (7), 65(4), Schedule 12, 65(5) Schedule 13; Magistrates' Courts Act 1980, s32(2); Police and Criminal Evidence Act 1984, s119(2), Schedule 7, Part I; Cinemas Act 1985, s24(1), Schedule 2, para 6; Broadcasting Act 1990, ss162; 203(3), Schedule 21; Criminal Justice and Public Order Act 1994, s168(1), Schedule 9, para 3; Courts Act 2003, s109(1), (3), Schedule 8, para 106, Schedule 10; Licensing Act 2003, s198, Schedule 6, para 28.

SUICIDE ACT 1961
(9 & 10 Eliz 2 c 60)

1   Suicide to cease to be a crime
The rule of law whereby it is a crime for a person to commit suicide is hereby abrogated.

2   Criminal liability for complicity in another's suicide
(1) A person who aids, abets, counsels or procures the suicide of another, or an attempt by another to commit suicide, shall be liable on conviction on indictment to imprisonment for a term not exceeding fourteen years.
(2) If on the trial of an indictment for murder or manslaughter it is proved that the accused aided, abetted, counselled or procured the suicide of the person in question, the jury may find him guilty of that offence. ...
(4) No proceedings shall be instituted for an offence under this section except by or with the consent of the Director of Public Prosecutions.

As amended by the Criminal Law Act 1967, s10(2), Schedule 3, Pt II; Criminal Jurisdiction Act 1975, s14(5), Schedule 6, Pt I.

OBSCENE PUBLICATIONS ACT 1964
(1964 c 74)

1   Obscene articles intended for publication for gain ...
(2) For the purpose of any proceedings for an offence against the said section 2 [of the Obscene Publications Act 1959] a person shall be deemed to have an article for publication for gain if with a view to such publication he had the article in his ownership, possession or control.
(3) In proceedings brought against a person under the said section 2 for having an obscene article for publication for gain the following provisions shall apply in place of subsections (5) and (6) of that section, that is to say –

   (a)   he shall not be convicted of that offence if he proves that he had not examined the article and had no reasonable cause to suspect that it was such that his having it would make him liable to be convicted of an offence against that section; and

   (b)   the question whether the article is obscene shall be determined by reference to such publication for gain of the article as in the circumstances it may reasonably be inferred he had in contemplation and to any further publication that could reasonably be expected to follow from it, but not to any other publication.

(4) Where articles are seized under section 3 of the Obscene Publications Act 1959 (which provides for the seizure and forfeiture of obscene articles kept for publication for gain), and a person is convicted under section 2 of that Act of having them for publication for gain, the Court on his conviction shall order the forfeiture of those articles:
Provided that an order made by virtue of this subsection (including an order so made on appeal) shall not take effect until the expiration of the ordinary time within which an appeal in the matter of the proceedings in which the order was made may be instituted or, where such an appeal is duly instituted, until the appeal is finally decided or abandoned; and for this purpose –

   (a)   an application for a case to be stated or for leave to appeal shall be treated as the institution of an appeal; and

    (b) where a decision on appeal is subject to a further appeal, the appeal shall not be deemed to be finally decided until the expiration of the ordinary time within which a further appeal may be instituted or, where a further appeal is duly instituted, until the further appeal is finally decided or abandoned.

(5) References in section 3 of the Obscene Publications Act 1959 and this section to publication for gain shall apply to any publication with a view to gain, whether the gain is to accrue by way of consideration for the publication or in any other way.

2　Negatives, etc for production of obscene articles

(1) The Obscene Publications Act 1959 (as amended by this Act) shall apply in relation to anything which is intended to be used, either alone or as one of a set, for the reproduction or manufacture therefrom of articles containing or embodying matter to be read, looked at or listened to, as if it were an article containing or embodying that matter so far as that matter is to be derived from it or from the set.

(2) For the purposes of the Obscene Publications Act 1959 (as so amended) an article shall be deemed to be had or kept for publication if it is had or kept for the reproduction or manufacture therefrom of articles for publication; and the question whether an article so had or kept is obscene shall –

    (a) for purposes of section 2 of the Act be determined in accordance with section 1(3)(b) above as if any reference there to publication of the article were a reference to publication of articles reproduced or manufactured from it; and

    (b) for purposes of section 3 of the Act be determined on the assumption that articles reproduced or manufactured from it would be published in any manner likely having regard to the circumstances in which it was found, but in no other manner.

CRIMINAL PROCEDURE (INSANITY) ACT 1964
(1964 c 84)

1　Acquittal on grounds of insanity

The special verdict required by section 2 of the Trial of Lunatics Act 1883 (hereinafter referred to as a 'special verdict') shall be that the accused is not guilty by reason of insanity.

4　Finding of unfitness to plead

(1) This section applies where on the trial of a person the question arises (at the instance of the defence or otherwise) whether the accused is under a disability, that is to say, under any disability such that apart from this Act it would constitute a bar to his being tried.

(2) If, having regard to the nature of the supposed disability, the court are of opinion that it is expedient to do so and in the interests of the accused, they may postpone consideration of the question of fitness to be tried until any time up to the opening of the case for the defence.

(3) If, before the question of fitness to be tried falls to be determined, the jury return a verdict of acquittal on the count or each of the counts on which the accused is being tried, that question shall not be determined.

(4) Subject to subsection (2) and (3) above, the question of fitness to be tried shall be determined as soon as it arises.

(5) The question of fitness to be tried shall be determined by the court without a jury.

(6) The court shall not make a determination under subsection (5) above except on the written

or oral evidence of two or more registered medical practitioners at least one of whom is duly approved.

4A   Finding that the accused did the act or made the omission charged against him
(1) This section applies where in accordance with section 4(5) above it is determined by a court that the accused is under a disability.
(2) The trial shall not proceed or further proceed but it shall be determined by a jury –
>   (a) on the evidence (if any) already given in the trial; and
>   (b) on such evidence as may be adduced or further adduced by the prosecution, or adduced by a person appointed by the court under this section to put the case for the defence,

whether they are satisfied, as respects the count or each of the counts on which the accused was to be or was being tried, that he did the act or made the omission charged against him as the offence.
(3) If as respects that count or any of those counts the jury are satisfied as mentioned in subsection (2) above, they shall make a finding that the accused did the act or made the omission charged against him.
(4) If as respects that count or any of those counts the jury are not so satisfied, they shall return a verdict of acquittal as if on the count in question the trial had proceeded to a conclusion.
(5) Where the question of disability was determined after arraignment of the accused, the determination under subsection (2) is to be made by the jury by whom he was being tried.

5   Powers to deal with persons not guilty by reason of insanity or unfit to plead, etc
(1) This section applies where –
>   (a) a special verdict is returned that the accused is not guilty by reason of insanity; or
>   (b) findings have been made that the accused is under a disability and that he did the act or made the omission charged against him.
(2) The court shall make in respect of the accused –
>   (a) a hospital order (with or without a restriction order);
>   (b) a supervision order; or
>   (c) an order for his absolute discharge.
(3) Where –
>   (a) the offence to which the special verdict or the findings relate is an offence the sentence for which is fixed by law, and
>   (b) the court have power to make a hospital order,

the court shall make a hospital order with a restriction order (whether or not they would have power to make a restriction order apart from this subsection).
(4) In this section –
>   'hospital order' has the meaning given in section 37 of the Mental Health Act 1983;
>   'restriction order' has the meaning given to it by section 41 of that Act;
>   'supervision order' has the meaning given in Part 1 of Schedule 1A to this Act.

6   Evidence by prosecution of insanity or diminished responsibility
Where on a trial for murder the accused contends –
>   (a) that at the time of the alleged offence he was insane so as not to be responsible according to law for his actions; or
>   (b) that at that time he was suffering from such abnormality of mind as is specified in subsection (1) of section 2 of the Homicide Act 1957 (diminished responsibility),

the court shall allow the prosecution to adduce or elicit evidence tending to prove the other of those contentions, and may give directions as to the stage of the proceedings at which the prosecution may adduce such evidence.

As amended by the Criminal Procedure (Insanity and Unfitness to Plead) Act 1991, ss2, 3, 8(1), (3), Schedule 4; Domestic Violence, Crime and Victims Act 2004, ss22, 24(1).

MURDER (ABOLITION OF DEATH PENALTY) ACT 1965
(1965 c 71)

1   Abolition of death penalty for murder
(1) No person shall suffer death for murder, and a person convicted of murder shall be sentenced to imprisonment for life.
(3) For the purpose of any proceedings on or subsequent to a person's trial on a charge of capital murder that charge and any plea or finding of guilty of capital murder shall be treated as being or having been a charge, or a plea or finding of guilty, of murder only; and if at the commencement of this Act a person is under sentence of death for murder, the sentence shall have effect as a sentence of imprisonment for life.
(4) In the foregoing subsections any reference to murder shall include an offence of or corresponding to murder under s70 of the Army Act 1955 or of the Air Force Act 1955 or under section 42 of the Naval Discipline Act 1957, and any reference to capital murder shall be construed accordingly ...

As amended by the Powers of Criminal Courts (Sentencing) Act 2000, s165(4), Schedule 12, Pt I; Criminal Justice Act 2003, s332, Schedule 37, Pt 8.

CRIMINAL LAW ACT 1967
(1967 c 58)

1   Abolition of distinction between felony and misdemeanour
(1) All distinctions between felony and misdemeanour are hereby abolished.
(2) Subject to the provisions of this Act, on all matters on which a distinction has previously been made between felony and misdemeanour, including mode of trial, the law and practice in relation to all offences cognisable under the law of England and Wales (including piracy) shall be the law and practice applicable at the commencement of this Act in relation to misdemeanour.

3   Use of force in making arrest, etc
(1) A person may use such force as is reasonable in the circumstances in the prevention of crime, or in effecting or assisting in the lawful arrest of offenders or suspected offenders or of persons unlawfully at large.
(2) Subsection (1) above shall replace the rules of the common law on the questions when force used for a purpose mentioned in the subsection is justified by that purpose.

4   Penalties for assisting offenders
(1) Where a person has committed a relevant offence, any other person who, knowing or believing him to be guilty of the offence or of some other relevant offence, does without lawful authority

or reasonable excuse any act with intent to impede his apprehension or prosecution shall be guilty of an offence.

(1A) In this section and section 5 below, 'relevant offence' means –

    (a) an offence for which the sentence is fixed by law,

    (b) an offence for which a person of 18 years or over (not previously convicted) may be sentenced to imprisonment for a term of five years (or might be so sentenced but for the restrictions imposed by section 33 of the Magistrates' Courts Act 1980).

(2) If on the trial of an indictment for a relevant offence the jury are satisfied that the offence charged (or some other offence of which the accused might on that charge be found guilty) was committed, but find the accused not guilty of it, they may find him guilty of any offence under subsection (1) above of which they are satisfied that he is guilty in relation to the offence charged (or that other offence).

(3) A person committing an offence under subsection (1) above with intent to impede another person's apprehension or prosecution shall on conviction on indictment be liable to imprisonment according to the gravity of the other person's offence, as follows –

    (a) if that offence is one for which the sentence is fixed by law, he shall be liable to imprisonment for not more than ten years;

    (b) if it is one for which a person (not previously convicted) may be sentenced to imprisonment for a term of fourteen years, he shall be liable to imprisonment for not more than seven years;

    (c) if it is not one included above but is one for which a person (not previously convicted) may be sentenced to imprisonment for a term of ten years, he shall be liable to imprisonment for not more than five years;

    (d) in any other case, he shall be liable to imprisonment for not more than three years.

(4) No proceedings shall be instituted for an offence under subsection (1) above except by or with the consent of the Director of Public Prosecutions.

5   Penalties for concealing offences or giving false information

(1) Where a person has committed a relevant offence, any other person who, knowing or believing that the offence or some other relevant offence has been committed, and that he has information which might be of material assistance in securing the prosecution or conviction of an offender for it, accepts or agrees to accept for not disclosing that information any consideration other than the making of good or loss or injury caused by the offence, or the making of reasonable compensation for that loss or injury, shall be liable on conviction on indictment to imprisonment for not more than two years.

(2) Where a person causes any wasteful employment of the police by knowingly making to any person a false report tending to show that an offence has been committed, or to give rise to apprehension for the safety of any persons or property, or tending to show that he has information material to any police inquiry, he shall be liable on summary conviction to imprisonment for not more than six months or to a fine of not more than level 4 on the standard scale or to both.

(3) No proceedings shall be instituted for an offence under this section except by or with the consent of the Director of Public Prosecutions.

(5) The compounding of an offence other than treason shall not be an offence otherwise than under this section.

6   Trial of offences

(1) Where a person is arraigned on an indictment –

    (a) he shall in all cases be entitled to make a plea of not guilty in addition to any demurrer or special plea;

(b) he may plead not guilty of the offence specifically charged in the indictment but guilty of another offence of which he might be found guilty on that indictment;

(c) if he stands mute of malice or will not answer directly to the indictment, the court may order a plea of not guilty to be entered on his behalf, and he shall then be treated as having pleaded not guilty.

(2) On an indictment for murder a person found not guilty of murder may be found guilty –

(a) of manslaughter, or of causing grievous bodily harm with intent to do so; or

(b) of any offence of which he may be found guilty under an enactment specifically so providing, or under section 4(2) of this Act; or

(c) of an attempt to commit murder, or of an attempt to commit any other offence of which he might be found guilty;

but may not be found guilty of any offence not included above.

(3) Where, on a person's trial on indictment for any offence except treason or murder, the jury find him not guilty of the offence specifically charged in the indictment, but the allegations in the indictment amount to or include (expressly or by implication) an allegation of another offence falling within the jurisdiction of the court of trial, the jury may find him guilty of that other offence or of an offence of which he could be found guilty on an indictment specifically charging that other offence.

(3A) For the purposes of subsection (3) above an offence falls within the jurisdiction of the court of trial if it is an offence to which section 40 of the Criminal Justice Act 1988 applies (power to join in indictment count for common assault, etc), even if a count charging the offence is not included in the indictment.

(3B) A person convicted of an offence by virtue of subsection (3A) may only be dealt with for it in a manner in which a magistrates' court could have dealt with him.

(4) For purposes of subsection (3) above any allegation of an offence shall be taken as including an allegation of attempting to commit that offence; and where a person is charged on indictment with attempting to commit an offence or with any assault or other act preliminary to an offence, but not with the completed offence, then (subject to the discretion of the court to discharge the jury or otherwise act with a view to the preferment of an indictment for the completed offence) he may be convicted of the offence charged notwithstanding that he is shown to be guilty of the completed offence.

(5) Where a person arraigned on an indictment pleads not guilty of an offence charged in the indictment but guilty of some offence of which he might be found guilty on that charge, and he is convicted on that plea of guilty without trial for the offence of which he had pleaded not guilty, then (whether or not the two offences are separately charged in distinct counts) his conviction of the one offence shall be an acquittal of the other.

(6) Any power to bring proceedings for an offence by criminal information in the High Court is hereby abolished.

(7) Subsections (1) to (3) above shall apply to an indictment containing more than one count as if each count were a separate indictment.

[See Appendix, Criminal Justice Act 2003, Schedule 36, Pt 4, para 41.]

13   Abolition of certain offences, and consequential repeals

(1) The following offences are hereby abolished, that is to say –

(a) any distinct offence under the common law in England and Wales of maintenance (including champerty, but not embracery), challenging to fight, eavesdropping or being a common barrator, a common scold or a common night walker; and

(b) any offence under an enactment mentioned in Part I of Schedule 4 to this Act, to the extent to which the offence depends on any section or part of a section included in the third column of that Schedule.

As amended by the Criminal Jurisdiction Act 1975, s14(5), Schedule 6, Pt I; Criminal Justice Act 1982, ss38, 46; Police and Criminal Evidence Act 1984, s119(1), Schedule 6, Part I, para 17; Criminal Justice Act 2003, s331, Schedule 36, Pt 4, para 41; Domestic Violence, Crime and Victims Act 2004, s11; Serious Organised Crime and Police Act 2005, s111, Schedule 7, Pt 3, para 40.

SEXUAL OFFENCES ACT 1967
(1967 c 60)

6   Premises resorted to for homosexual practices

Premises shall be treated for purposes of sections 33 to 35 of the Act of 1956 as a brothel if people resort to it for the purpose of lewd homosexual practices in circumstances in which resort thereto for lewd heterosexual practices would have led to its being treated as a brothel for the purposes of those sections.

CRIMINAL JUSTICE ACT 1967
(1967 c 80)

8   Proof of criminal intent

A court or jury, in determining whether a person has committed an offence, –

(a) shall not be bound in law to infer that he intended or foresaw a result of his actions by reason only of its being a natural and probable consequence of those actions; but

(b) shall decide whether he did intend or foresee that result by reference to all the evidence, drawing such inferences from the evidence as appear proper in the circumstances.

ABORTION ACT 1967
(1967 c 87)

1   Medical termination of pregnancy

(1) Subject to the provisions of this section, a person shall not be guilty of an offence under the law relating to abortion when a pregnancy is terminated by a registered medical practitioner if two registered medical practitioners are of the opinion, formed in good faith –

(a) that the pregnancy has not exceeded its twenty-fourth week and that the continuance of the pregnancy would involve risk, greater than if the pregnancy were terminated, of injury to the physical or mental health of the pregnant woman or any existing children of her family; or

(b) that the termination is necessary to prevent grave permanent injury to the physical or mental health of the pregnant woman; or

(c) that the continuance of the pregnancy would involve risk to the life of the pregnant woman, greater than if the pregnancy were terminated; or

(d) that there is a substantial risk that if the child were born it would suffer form such physical or mental abnormalities as to be seriously handicapped.

(2) In determining whether the continuance of a pregnancy would involve such risk of injury to health as is mentioned in paragraph (a) or (b) of subsection (1) of this section, account may be taken of the pregnant woman's actual or reasonably foreseeable environment.

(3) Except as provided by subsection (4) of this section, any treatment for the termination of pregnancy must be carried out in a hospital vested in the Secretary of State for the purposes of his functions under the National Health Service Act 2006 or the National Health Service (Scotland) Act 1978, or in a hospital vested in a Primary Care Trust or National Health Service trust or an NHS foundation trust, or in a place approved for the purposes of this section by the Secretary of State.

(3A) The power under subsection (3) of this section to approve a place includes power, in relation to treatment consisting primarily in the use of such medicines as may be specified in the approval and carried out in such manner as may be so specified, to approve a class of places'.

(4) Subsection (3) of this section, and so much of subsection (1) as relates to the opinion of two registered medical practitioners, shall not apply to the termination of a pregnancy by a registered medical practitioner in a case where he is of the opinion, formed in good faith, that the termination is immediately necessary to save the life or to prevent grave permanent injury to the physical or mental health of the pregnant woman.

4 Conscientious objection to participation in treatment

(1) Subject to subsection (2) of this section, no person shall be under any duty, whether by contract or by any statutory or other legal requirement, to participate in any treatment authorised by this Act to which he has a conscientious objection: Provided that in any legal proceedings the burden of proof of conscientious objection shall rest on the person claiming to rely on it.

(2) Nothing in subsection (1) of this section shall affect any duty to participate in treatment which is necessary to save the life or to prevent grave permanent injury to the physical or mental health of a pregnant woman. …

5 Supplementary provisions

(1) No offence under the Infant Life (Preservation) Act 1929 shall be committed by a registered medical practitioner who terminates a pregnancy in accordance with the provisions of this Act.

(2) For the purposes of the law relating to abortion, anything done with intent to procure a woman's miscarriage (or, in the case of a woman carrying more than one foetus, her miscarriage of any foetus) is unlawfully done unless authorised by section 1 of this Act and, in the case of a woman carrying more than one foetus, anything done with intent to procure her miscarriage of any foetus is authorised by that section if –

    (a)   the ground for termination for the pregnancy specified in subsection (1)(d) of that section applies in relation to any foetus and the thing is done for the purpose of procuring the miscarriage of that foetus, or

    (b)   any of the other grounds for termination of the pregnancy specified in that section applies.

6 Interpretation

In this Act, the following expressions have meanings hereby assisgned to them –

    'the law relating to abortion' means sections 58 and 59 of the Offences Against the Person Act 1861, and any rule of law relating to the procurement of abortion.

As amended by the Health Service Act 1980 ss1, 2, 25(4), Schedule 1, para 17(1), Schedule 7; Human Fertilisation and Embryology Act 1990, s37 (1), (2), (4), (5); National Health Service and Community Care Act 1990, s66(1),Schedule 9, para 8; Health Act 1999 (Supplementary, Consequential, etc Provisions) Order 2000, art 3(1), Schedule 1, para 6; Health and Social Care (Community Health and Standards) Act

2003, s34, Schedule 4, paras 9, 10; National Health Service (Consequential Provisions) Act 2006, s2, Schedule 1, para 30.

CRIMINAL APPEAL ACT 1968
(1968 c 19)

1   Right of appeal
(1) Subject to subsection (3) below, a person convicted of an offence on indictment may appeal to the Court of Appeal against his conviction.
(2) An appeal under this section lies only –
    (a) with the leave of the Court of Appeal; or
    (b) if the judge of the court of trial grants a certificate that the case is fit for appeal.
(3) Where a person is convicted before the Crown Court of a scheduled offence it shall not be open to him to appeal to the Court of Appeal against the conviction on the ground that the decision of the court which sent him to the Crown Court for trial as to the value involved was mistaken.
(4) In subsection (3) above 'scheduled offence' and 'the value involved' have the same meanings as they have in section 22 of the Magistrates' Courts Act 1980 (certain offences against property to be tried summarily if value of property or damage is small).

2   Grounds for allowing an appeal under s1
(1) Subject to the provisions of this Act, the Court of Appeal –
    (a) shall allow an appeal against conviction if they think that the conviction is unsafe; and
    (b) shall dismiss such an appeal in any other case.
(2) In the case of an appeal against conviction the court shall, if they allow the appeal, quash the conviction.
(3) An order of the Court of Appeal quashing a conviction shall, except when under section 7 below the appellant is ordered to be retried, operate as a direction to the court of trial to enter, instead of the record of conviction, a judgment and verdict of acquittal.

3   Power to substitute conviction of alternative offence
(1) This section applies on an appeal against conviction, where the appellant has been convicted of an offence to which he did not plead guilty and the jury could on the indictment have found him guilty of some other offence, and on the finding of the jury it appears to the Court of Appeal that the jury must have been satisfied of facts which proved him guilty of the other offence.
(2) The court may, instead of allowing or dismissing the appeal, substitute for the verdict found by the jury a verdict of guilty of the other offence, and pass such sentence in substitution for the sentence passed at the trial as may be authorised by law for the other offence, not being a sentence of greater severity.

3A   Power to substitute conviction of alternative offence after guilty plea
(1) This section applies on an appeal against conviction where –
    (a) an appellant has been convicted of an offence to which he pleaded guilty,
    (b) if he had not so pleaded, he could on the indictment have pleaded, or been found, guilty of some other offence, and
    (c) it appears to the Court of Appeal that the plea of guilty indicates an admission by the appellant of facts which prove him guilty of the other offence.

(2) The Court of Appeal may, instead of allowing or dismissing the appeal, substitute for the appellant's plea of guilty a plea of guilty of the other offence and pass such sentence in substitution for the sentence passed at the trial as may be authorised by law for the other offence, not being a sentence of greater severity.

4 Sentence when appeal allowed on part of an indictment

(1) This section applies where, on an appeal against conviction on an indictment containing two or more counts, the Court of Appeal allow the appeal in respect of part of the indictment.

(2) Except as provided by subsection (3) below, the court may in respect of any count on which the appellant remains convicted pass such sentence, in substitution for any sentence passed thereon at the trial, as they think proper and is authorised by law for the offence of which he remains convicted on that count.

(3) The court shall not under this section pass any sentence such that the appellant's sentence on the indictment as a whole will, in consequence of the appeal, be of greater severity than the sentence (taken as a whole) which was passed at the trial for all offences of which he was convicted on the indictment.

5 Disposal of appeal against conviction on special verdict

(1) This section applies on an appeal against conviction in a case where the jury have found a special verdict.

(2) If the Court of Appeal consider that a wrong conclusion has been arrived at by the court of trial on the effect of the jury's verdict they may, instead of allowing the appeal, order such conclusion to be recorded as appears to them to be in law required by the verdict, and pass such sentence in substitution for the sentence passed at the trial as may be authorised by law.

6 Substitution of finding of insanity or findings of unfitness to plead, etc

(1) This section applies where, on an appeal against conviction, the Court of Appeal, on the written or oral evidence of two or more registered medical practitioners at least one of whom is duly approved, are of opinion –
    (a) that the proper verdict would have been one of not guilty by reason of insanity; or
    (b) that the case is not one where there should have been a verdict of acquittal, but there should have been findings that the accused was under a disability and that he did the act or made the omission charged against him.

(2) The Court of Appeal shall make in respect of the accused –
    (a) a hospital order (with or without a restriction order);
    (b) a supervision order; or
    (c) an order for his absolute discharge.

(3) Where –
    (a) the offence to which the appeal relates is an offence the sentence for which is fixed by law, and
    (b) the court have power to make a hospital order,
the court shall make a hospital order with a restriction order (whether or not they would have power to make a restriction order apart from this subsection).

(4) Section 5A of the Criminal Procedure (Insanity) Act 1964 ('the 1964 Act') applies in relation to this section as it applies in relation to section 5 of that Act.

(5) Where the Court of Appeal make an interim hospital order by virtue of this section –
    (a) the power of renewing or terminating it and of dealing with the appellant on its termination shall be exercisable by the court below and not by the Court of Appeal; and

(b) the court below shall be treated for the purposes of section 38(7) of the Mental Health
Act 1983 (absconding offenders) as the court that made the order.

(6) Where the Court of Appeal make a supervision order by virtue of this section, any power of
revoking or amending it shall be exercisable as if the order had been made by the court below.

(7) In this section –

'hospital order' has the meaning given in section 37 of the Mental Health Act 1983;
'interim hospital order' has the meaning given in section 38 of that Act;
'restriction order' has the meaning given to it by section 41 of that Act;
'supervision order' has the meaning given in Part 1 of Schedule 1A to the 1964 Act.

7   Power to order retrial

(1) Where the Court of Appeal allow an appeal against conviction and it appears to the court that
the interests of justice so require, they may order the appellant to be retried.

(2) A person shall not under this section be ordered to be retried for any offence other than –

(a) the offence of which he was convicted at the original trial and in respect of which his
appeal is allowed as mentioned in subsection (1) above;

(b) an offence of which he could have been convicted at the original trial on an indictment
for the first-mentioned offence; or

(c) an offence charged in an alternative count of the indictment in respect of which no
verdict was given in consequence his being convicted of the first-mentioned offence.

12   Appeal against verdict of not guilty by reason of insanity

A person in whose case there is returned a verdict of not guilty by reason of insanity may appeal
to the Court of Appeal against the verdict –

(a) with the leave of the Court of Appeal; or

(b) if the judge of the court of trial grants a certificate that the case is fit for appeal.

13   Disposal of appeal under s12

(1) Subject to the provisions of this section, the Court of Appeal –

(a) shall allow an appeal under section 12 of this Act if they think that the verdict is unsafe;
and

(b) shall dismiss such an appeal in any other case.

(3) Where apart from this subsection –

(a) an appeal under section 12 of this Act would fall to be allowed; and

(b) none of the grounds for allowing it relates to the question of the insanity of the accused,

the Court of Appeal may dismiss the appeal if they are of opinion that, but for the insanity of
the accused, the proper verdict would have been that he was guilty of an offence other than the
offence charged.

(4) Where an appeal under section 12 of this Act is allowed, the following provisions apply:

(a) if the ground, or one of the grounds, for allowing the appeal is that the finding of the
jury as to the insanity of the accused ought not to stand and the Court of Appeal are
of opinion that the proper verdict would have been that he was guilty of an offence
(whether the offence charged or any other offence of which the jury could have found
him guilty), the court –

(i)   shall substitute for the verdict of not guilty by reason of insanity a verdict of guilty
of that offence; and

(ii) shall, subject to subsection (5) below, have the like powers of punishing or
otherwise dealing with the appellant, and other powers, as the court of trial would
have had if the jury had come to the substituted verdict; and

(b) in any other case, the Court of Appeal shall substitute for the verdict of the jury a verdict of acquittal.

(5) The Court of Appeal shall not by virtue of subsection (4)(a) above sentence any person to death; but where under that paragraph they substitute a verdict of guilty of an offence for which apart from this subsection they would be required to sentence the appellant to death, their sentence shall (whatever the circumstances) be one of imprisonment for life.

(6) An order of the Court of Appeal allowing an appeal in accordance with this section shall operate as a direction to the court of trial to amend the record to conform with the order.

14   Substitution of findings of unfitness to plead, etc

(1) This section applies where, on an appeal under section 12 of this Act, the Court of Appeal, on the written or oral evidence of two or more registered medical practitioners at least one of whom is duly approved, are of opinion that –

(a) the case is not one where there should have been a verdict of acquittal; but

(b) there should have been findings that the accused was under a disability and that he did the act or made the omission charged against him.

(2) The Court of Appeal shall make in respect of the accused –

(a) a hospital order (with or without a restriction order);

(b) a supervision order; or

(c) an order for his absolute discharge.

(3) Where –

(a) the offence to which the appeal relates is an offence the sentence for which is fixed by law, and

(b) the court have power to make a hospital order,

the court shall make a hospital order with a restriction order (whether or not they would have power to make a restriction order apart from this subsection).

(4) Section 5A of the Criminal Procedure (Insanity) Act 1964 ('the 1964 Act') applies in relation to this section as it applies in relation to section 5 of that Act.

(5) Where the Court of Appeal make an interim hospital order by virtue of this section –

(a) the power of renewing or terminating it and of dealing with the appellant on its termination shall be exercisable by the court below and not by the Court of Appeal; and

(b) the court below shall be treated for the purposes of section 38(7) of the Mental Health Act 1983 (absconding offenders) as the court that made the order.

(6) Where the Court of Appeal make a supervision order by virtue of this section, any power of revoking or amending it shall be exercisable as if the order had been made by the court below.

(7) In this section –

'hospital order' has the meaning given in section 37 of the Mental Health Act 1983;

'interim hospital order' has the meaning given in section 38 of that Act;

'restriction order' has the meaning given to it by section 41 of that Act;

'supervision order' has the meaning given in Part 1 of Schedule 1A to the 1964 Act.

15   Right of appeal against finding of disability

(1) Where there has been a determination under section 4 of the Criminal Procedure (Insanity) Act 1964 of the question of a person's fitness to be tried, and there have been findings that he is under disability and that he did the act or made the omission charged against him, the person may appeal to the Court of Appeal against either or both of those findings.

(2) An appeal under this section lies only –

(a) with the leave of the Court of Appeal; or

(b) if the judge of the court of trial grants a certificate that the case is fit for appeal.

16 Disposal of appeal under s15

(1) The Court of Appeal –

(a) shall allow an appeal under section 15 of this Act against a finding if they think that the finding is unsafe; and

(b) shall dismiss such an appeal in any other case.

(3) Where the Court of Appeal allow an appeal under section 15 of this Act against a finding that the appellant is under a disability –

(a) the appellant may be tried accordingly for the offence with which he was charged; and

(b) the court may, subject to section 25 of the Criminal Justice and Public Order Act 1994 [no bail for defendants charged with or convicted of homicide or rape after previous conviction of such offences], make such orders as appear to them necessary or expedient pending any such trial for this custody, release on bail or continued detention under the Mental Health Act 1983;

and Schedule 3 to this Act has effect for applying provisions in Part IIIof that Act to persons in whose case an order is made by the court under this subsection.

(4) Where, otherwise than in a case falling within subsection (3) above, the Court of Appeal allow an appeal under section 15 of this Act against a finding that the appellant did the act or made the omission charged against him, the court shall, in addition to quashing the finding, direct a verdict of acquittal to be recorded (but not a verdict of not guilty by reason of insanity).

16A Right of appeal against hospital order, etc

(1) A person in whose case the Crown Court –

(a) makes a hospital order or interim hospital order by virtue of section 5 or 5A [Orders made under or by virtue of section 5] of the Criminal Procedure (Insanity) Act 1964, or

(b) makes a supervision order under section 5 of that Act,

may appeal to the Court of Appeal against the order.

(2) An appeal under this section lies only –

(a) with the leave of the Court of Appeal; or

(b) if the judge of the court of trial grants a certificate that the case is fit for appeal.

16B Disposal of appeal under s16A

(1) If on an appeal under section 16A of this Act the Court of Appeal consider that the appellant should be dealt with differently from the way in which the court below dealt with him –

(a) they may quash any order which is the subject of the appeal; and

(b) they may make such order, whether by substitution for the original order or by variation of or addition to it, as they think appropriate for the case and as the court below had power to make.

(2) The fact that an appeal is pending against an interim hospital order under the Mental Health Act 1983 shall not affect the power of the court below to renew or terminate the order or deal with the appellant on its termination.

(3) Where the Court of Appeal make an interim hospital order by virtue of this section –

(a) the power of renewing or terminating it and of dealing with the appellant on its termination shall be exercisable by the court below and not by the Court of Appeal; and

    (b) the court below shall be treated for the purposes of section 38(7) of the said Act of 1983 (absconding offenders) as the court that made the order.

(4) The fact that an appeal is pending against a supervision order under section 5 of the Criminal Procedure (Insanity) Act 1964 shall not affect the power of the court below to revoke the order, or of a magistrates' court to revoke or amend it.

(5) Where the Court of Appeal make a supervision order by virtue of this section, the power of revoking or amending it shall be exercisable as if the order had been made by the court below.

20   Disposal of groundless appeal or application for leave to appeal

If it appears to the registrar that a notice of appeal or application for leave to appeal does not show any substantial ground of appeal, he may refer the appeal or application for leave to the Court for summary determination; and where the case is so referred the Court may, if they consider that the appeal of application for leave is frivolous or vexatious, and can be determined without adjourning it for a full hearing, dismiss the appeal or application for leave summarily, without calling on anyone to attend the hearing or to appear for the Crown thereon.

23A Power to order investigations

(1) On an appeal against conviction or an application for leave to appeal against conviction the Court of Appeal may direct the Criminal Cases Review Commission to investigate and report to the Court on any matter if it appears to the Court that –

    (a) in the case of an appeal, the matter is relevant to the determination of the appeal and ought, if possible, to be resolved before the appeal is determined;

    (aa) in the case of an application for leave to appeal, the matter is relevant to the determination of the application and ought, if possible, to be resolved before the application is determined;

    (b) an investigation of the matter by the Commission is likely to result in the Court being able to resolve it; and

    (c) the matter cannot be resolved by the Court without an investigation by the Commission. ...

(4) Where the Commission have reported to the Court of Appeal on any matter which they have been directed under subsection (1) above to investigate, the Court –

    (a) shall notify the appellant and the respondent that the Commission have reported; and

    (b) may make available to the appellant and the respondent the report of the Commission and any statements, opinions and reports which accompanied it.

(5) In this section 'respondent' includes a person who will be a respondent if leave to appeal is granted.

33   Right of appeal to House of Lords

(1) An appeal lies to the House of Lords, at the instance of the defendant or the prosecutor, from any decision of the Court of Appeal on an appeal to that court under Part I of this Act or Part 9 of the Criminal Justice Act 2003 or section 9 (preparatory hearings) of the Criminal Justice Act 1987 or section 35 of the Criminal Procedure and Investigations Act 1996 or section 47 of the Criminal Justice Act 2003.

(1A) In subsection (1) above the references to the prosecutor includes a reference to the Director of Assets Recovery Agency in a case where (and to the extent that) he is a party to the appeal to the Court of Appeal.

(1B) An appeal lies to the House of Lords, at the instance of the acquitted person or the prosecutor, from any decision of the Court of Appeal on an application under section 76(1) or (2) of the Criminal Justice Act 2003 (retrial for serious offences).

(2) The appeal lies only with the leave of the Court of Appeal or the House of Lords; and leave shall not be granted unless it is certified by the Court of Appeal that a point of law of general public importance is involved in the decision and it appears to the Court of Appeal or the House of Lords (as the case may be) that the point is one which ought to be considered by that House.
(3) Except as provided by this Part of this Act and section 13 of the Administration of Justice Act 1960 (appeal in cases of contempt of court), no appeal shall lie from any decision of the criminal division of the Court of Appeal.
(4) In relation to an appeal under subsection (1B), references in this Part to a defendant are references to the acquitted person.

44A Appeals in cases of death
(1) Where a person has died –
    (a) any relevant appeal which might have been begun by him had he remained alive may be begun by a person approved by the Court of Appeal; and
    (b) where any relevant appeal was begun by him while he was alive or is begun in relation to his case by virtue of paragraph (a) above or by a reference by the Criminal Cases Review Commission, any further step which might have been taken by him in connection with the appeal if he were alive may be taken by a person so approved.
(2) In this section 'relevant appeal' means –
    (a) an appeal under section 1, 9 [appeal against sentence following conviction on indictment], 12 or 15 of this Act; or
    (b) an appeal under section 33 of this Act from any decision of the Court of Appeal on an appeal under any of those sections.
(3) Approval for the purposes of this section may only be given to –
    (a) the widow or widower or surviving civil partner of the dead person;
    (b) a person who is the personal representative (within the meaning of section 55(1)(xi) of the Administration of Estates Act 1925) of the dead person; or
    (c) any other person appearing to the Court of Appeal to have, by reason of a family or similar relationship with the dead person, a substantial financial or other interest in the determination of a relevant appeal relating to him.
(4) Except in the case of an appeal begun by a reference by the Criminal Cases Review Commission, an application for such approval may not be made after the end of the period of one year beginning with the date of death. ...

49 Saving for prerogative of mercy
Nothing in this Act is to be taken as affecting Her Majesty's prerogative of mercy.

50 Meaning of 'sentence'
(1) In this Act 'sentence', in relation to an offence, includes any order made by a court when dealing with an offender including, in particular –
    (a) a hospital order under Part III of the Mental Health Act 1983, with or without a restriction order;
    (b) an interim hospital order under that Part;
    (bb) a hospital direction and a limitation direction under that Part;
    (c) a recommendation for deportation;
    (ca) a confiscation order under Part 2 of the Proceeds of Crime Act 2002;
    (cb) an order which varies a confiscation order made under Part 2 of the Proceeds of Crime Act 2002 if the varying order is made under section 21, 22 or 29 of that Act (but not otherwise);

    (d) a confiscation order under the Drug Trafficking Act 1994 other than one made by the High Court;

    (e) a confiscation order under Part VI of the Criminal Justice Act 1988;

    (f) an order varying a confiscation order of a kind which is included by virtue of paragraph (d) or (e) above;

    (g) an order made by the Crown Court varying a confiscation order which was made by the High Court by virtue of section 19 of the Act of 1994; and

    (h) a declaration of relevance, within the meaning of section 23 of the Football Spectators Act 1989; and

    (i) an order under section 129(2) of the Licensing Act 2003 (forfeiture or suspension of personal licence).

(1A) Section 14 of the Powers of Criminal Courts (Sentencing) Act 2000 (under which a conviction of an offence for which an order for conditional or absolute discharge is made is deemed not to be a conviction except for certain purposes) shall not prevent an appeal under this Act, whether against conviction or otherwise.

(2) Any power of the criminal division of the Court of Appeal to pass a sentence includes a power to make a recommendation for deportation in cases where the court from which the appeal lies had power to make such a recommendation.

(3) An order under section 17 of the Access to Justice Act 1999 is not a sentence for the purposes of this Act.

As amended by the Bail Act 1976, s12(1), Schedule 2, para 39; Criminal Law Act 1977, s44; Magistrates' Courts Act 1980 s154(1), Schedule 7, para 71; Supreme Court Act 1981, s152(1), Schedule 5; Criminal Justice Act 1982, s66(1); Mental Health Act 1983, s148(1), Schedule 4, para 23(f); Criminal Justice Act 1987, s15, Schedule 2, para 3; Criminal Justice Act 1988, ss43(1), (2), 157, 170(2), Schedule 16; Criminal Procedure (Insanity and Unfitness to Plead) Act 1991, ss4(1), (2), 7, 8(2), (3), Schedule 3, paras 2, 3, 4, Schedule 4; Criminal Justice Act 1991, ss100, 101(2), Schedule 11, para 4, Schedule 13; Criminal Justice Act 1993, s79(13), Schedule 1, Pt I, para 1; Criminal Justice and Public Order Act 1994, s168(2), Schedule 10, para 21; Drug Trafficking Act 1994, s65(1), Schedule 1, para 2; Criminal Appeal Act 1995, ss1(1), (3), (5), 2(1), (3), (5), 5(1), 7(1), 29(1), Schedule 2, para 4(1), (2); Criminal Procedure and Investigations Act 1996, s36(1)(a); Crime (Sentences) Act 1997, s55(1), Schedule 4, para 6(1)(a); Access to Justice Act 1999, s24, Schedule 4, para 3; Powers of Criminal Courts (Sentencing) Act 2000, s165(1), Schedule 9, para 30; Proceeds of Crime Act 2002, s456, Schedule 11, para 4; Licensing Act 2003, s198, Schedule 6, paras 38, 42; Criminal Justice Act 2003, ss41, 68(1), 81(1)–(3), 313(1)–(4), (6), 316, 331, Schedule 3, para 44(1), (2) Schedule 36, Pt 4, para 44; Civil Partnership Act 2004, s261(1), Schedule 27, para 26; Domestic Violence, Crime and Victims Act 2004, ss24(3), 25, 58(1), Schedule 10, para 4; Violent Crime Reduction Act 2006, s52(2), Schedule 3, Pt 2, para 14(1), (2)(a).

FIREARMS ACT 1968
(1968 c 27)

1   Requirement of firearm certificate

(1) Subject to any exemption under this Act, it is an offence for a person –

    (a) to have in his possession, or to purchase or acquire, a firearm to which this section applies without holding a firearm certificate in force at the time, or otherwise than as authorised by such a certificate;

    (b) to have in his possession, or to purchase or acquire, any ammunition to which this section applies without holding a firearm certificate in force at the time, or otherwise than as authorised by such a certificate, or in quantities in excess of those so authorised.

(2) It is an offence for a person to fail to comply with a condition subject to which a firearm certificate is held by him.

(3) This section applies to every firearm except –

    (a) a shot gun within the meaning of this Act, that is to say a smooth-bore gun (not being an air gun) which –

        (i) has a barrel not less than 24 inches in length and does not have any barrel with a bore exceeding 2 inches in diameter;

        (ii) either has no magazine or has a non-detachable magazine incapable of holding more than two cartridges; and

        (iii) is not a revolver gun; and

    (b) an air weapon (that is to say, an air rifle, air gun or air pistol which does not fall within section 5(1) and which is not of a type declared by rules made by the Secretary of State under section 53 of this Act to be specially dangerous)

(3A) A gun which has been adapted to have such a magazine as is mentioned in subsection (3)(a)(ii) above shall not be regarded as falling within that provision unless the magazine bears a mark approved by the Secretary of State for denoting that fact and that mark has been made, and the adaptation has been certified in writing as having been carried out in a manner approved by him, either by one of the two companies mentioned in section 58(1) of this Act or by such other person as may be approved by him for that purpose.

(4) This section applies to any ammunition for a firearm, except the following articles, namely –

    (a) cartridges containing five or more shot, none of which exceeds .36 inch in diameter;

    (b) ammunition for an air gun, air rifle or air pistol; and

    (c) blank cartridges not more than one inch in diameter measured immediately in front of the rim or cannelure of the base of the cartridge.

2   Requirement of certificate for possession of shot guns

(1) Subject to any exemption under this Act, it is an offence for a person to have in his possession, or to purchase or acquire, a shot gun without holding a certificate under this Act authorising him to possess shot guns.

(2) It is an offence for a person to fail to comply with a condition subject to which a shot gun certificate is held by him.

3   Business and other transactions with firearms and ammunition

(1) A person commits an offence if, by way of trade or business, he –

    (a) manufactures, sells, transfers, repairs, tests or proves any firearm or ammunition to which section 1 of this Act applies, or a shot gun; or

    (b) exposes for sale or transfer, or has in his possession for sale, transfer, repair, test or proof any such firearm or ammunition, or a shot gun,

without being registered under this Act as a firearms dealer.

(2) It is an offence for a person to sell or transfer to any other person in the United Kingdom, other than a registered firearms dealer, any firearm or ammunition to which section 1 of this Act applies, or a shot gun, unless that other produces a firearm certificate authorising him to purchase or acquire it or, as the case may be, his shot gun certificate, or shows that he is by virtue of this Act entitled to purchase or acquire it without holding a certificate.

(3) It is an offence for a person to undertake the repair, test or proof of a firearm or ammunition to which section 1 of this Act applies, or of a shot gun, for any other person in the United Kingdom other than a registered firearms dealer as such, unless that other produces or causes to be produced a firearm certificate authorising him to have possession of the firearm or ammunition

or, as the case may be, his shot gun certificate, or shows that he is by virtue of this Act entitled to have possession of it without holding a certificate.

(4) Subsections (1) to (3) above have effect subject to any exemption under subsequent provisions of this Part of this Act.

(5) A person commits an offence if, with a view to purchasing or acquiring, or procuring the repair, test or proof of, any firearm or ammunition to which section 1 of this Act applies, or a shot gun, he produces a false certificate or a certificate in which any false entry has been made, or personates a person to whom a certificate has been granted, or knowingly or recklessly makes a statement false in any material particular.

(6) It is an offence for a pawnbroker to take in pawn any firearm or ammunition to which section 1 of this Act applies, or a shot gun.

4 Conversion of weapons

(1) Subject to this section, it is an offence to shorten the barrel of a shot gun to a length less than 24 inches.

(2) It is not an offence under subsection (1) above for a registered firearms dealer to shorten the barrel of a shot gun for the sole purpose of replacing a defective part of the barrel so as to produce a barrel not less than 24 inches in length.

(3) It is an offence for a person other than a registered firearms dealer to convert into a firearm anything which, though having the appearance of being a firearm, is so constructed as to be incapable of discharging any missile through its barrel.

(4) A person who commits an offence under section 1 of this Act by having in his possession, or purchasing or acquiring, a shot gun which has been shortened contrary to subsection (1) above or a firearm which has been converted as mentioned in subsection (3) above (whether by a registered firearms dealer or not), without holding a firearm certificate authorising him to have it in his possession, or to purchase or acquire it, shall be treated for the purposes of provisions of this Act relating to the punishment of offences as committing that offence in an aggravated form.

5 Weapons subject to general prohibition

(1) A person commits an offence if, without the authority of the Defence Council …, he has in his possession, or purchases or acquires, or manufactures, sells or transfers –

(a) any firearm which is so designed or adapted that two or more missiles can be successively discharged without repeated pressure on the trigger;

(ab) any self-loading or pump-action rifled gun other than one which is chambered for .22 rim-fire cartridges;

(aba) any firearm which either has a barrel less than 30 centimetres in length or is less than 60 centimetres in length overall, other than an air weapon, a muzzle-loading gun or a firearm designed as signalling apparatus;

(ac) any self-loading or pump-action smooth-bore gun which is not an air weapon or chambered for .22 rim-fire cartridges and either has a barrel less than 24 inches in length or is less than 40 inches in length overall;

(ad) any smooth-bore revolver gun other than one which is chambered for 9mm rim-fire cartridges or a muzzle-loading gun;

(ae) any rocket launcher, or any mortar, for projecting a stabilised missile, other than a launcher or mortar designed for line-throwing or pyrotechnic purposes or as signalling apparatus;

(af) any air rifle, air gun or air pistol which uses, or is designed or adapted for use with, a self-contained gas cartridge system;

(b) any weapon of whatever description designed or adapted for the discharge of any noxious liquid, gas or other thing; and

(c) any cartridge with a bullet designed to explode on or immediately before impact, any ammunition containing or designed or adapted to contain any such noxious thing as is mentioned in paragraph (b) above and, if capable of being used with a firearm of any description, any grenade, bomb (or other like missile), or rocket or shell designed to explode as aforesaid.

(1A) Subject to section 5A of this Act, a person commits an offence if, without the authority of the Secretary of State …, he has in his possession, or purchases or acquires or sells or transfers –

(a) any firearm which is disguised as another object;

(b) any rocket or ammunition not falling within paragraph (c) of subsection (1) of this section which consists in or incorporates a missile designed to explode on or immediately before impact and is for military use;

(c) any launcher or other projecting apparatus not falling within paragraph (ae) of that subsection which is designed to be used with any rocket or ammunition falling within paragraph (b) above or with ammunition which would fall within that paragraph but for its being ammunition falling within paragraph (c) of that subsection;

(d) any ammunition for military use which consists in or incorporates a missile designed so that a substance contained in the missile will ignite on or immediately before impact;

(e) any ammunition for military use which consists in or incorporates a missile designed, on account of its having a jacket and hard-core, to penetrate armour plating, armour screening or body armour;

(f) any ammunition which incorporates a missile designed or adapted to expand on impact;

(g) anything which is designed to be projected as a missile from any weapon and is designed to be, or has been, incorporated in –

(i) any ammunition falling within any of the preceding paragraphs; or

(ii) any ammunition which would fall within any of those paragraphs but for it being specified in subsection (1) of this section.

(2) The weapons and ammunition specified in subsections (1) and (1A) of this section (including, in the case of ammunition, any missiles falling within subsection (1A)(g) of this section) are referred to in this Act as 'prohibited weapons' and 'prohibited ammunition' respectively.

(3) An authority given to a person by the Defence Council … under this section shall be in writing and be subject to conditions specified therein.

(4) The conditions of the authority shall include such as the Defence Council …, having regard to the circumstances of each particular case, think fit to impose for the purpose of securing that the prohibited weapon or ammunition to which the authority relates will not endanger the public safety or the peace.

(5) It is an offence for a person to whom an authority is given under this section to fail to comply with any condition of the authority.

(6) The Defence Council may at any time, if they think fit, revoke an authority given to a person under this section by notice in writing requiring him to deliver up the authority to such person as may be specified in the notice within twenty-one days from the date of the notice; and it is an offence for him to fail to comply with that requirement.

(7) For the purposes of this section and section 5A of this Act –

(a) any rocket or ammunition which is designed to be capable of being used with a military weapon shall be taken to be for military use;

(b) references to a missile designed so that a substance contained in the missile will ignite on or immediately before impact include references to any missile containing a substance that ignites on exposure to air; and

(c) references to a missile's expanding on impact include references to its deforming in any predictable manner on or immediately after impact.

(8) For the purposes of subsection (1)(aba) and (ac) above, any detachable, folding, retractable or other movable butt-stock shall be disregarded in measuring the length of any firearm.

(9) Any reference in this section to a muzzle-loading gun is a reference to a gun which is designed to be loaded at the muzzle end of the barrel or chamber with a loose charge and a separate ball (or other missile).

5A   Exemptions from requirement of authority under s5

(1) Subject to subsection (2) below, the authority of the Secretary of State ... shall not be required by virtue of subsection (1A) of section 5 of this Act for any person to have in his possession, or to purchase, acquire, sell or transfer, any prohibited weapon or ammunition if he is authorised by a certificate under this Act to possess, purchase or acquire that weapon or ammunition subject to a condition that he does so only for the purpose of it being kept or exhibited as part of a collection.

(2) No sale or transfer may be made under subsection (1) above except to a person who –

(a) produces the authority of the Secretary of State ... under section 5 of this Act for his purchase or acquisition; or

(b) shows that he is, under this section or a licence under the Schedule to the Firearms (Amendment) Act 1988 (museums etc) entitled to make the purchase or acquisition without the authority of the Secretary of State ... .

(3) The authority of the Secretary of State ... shall not be required by virtue of subsection (1A) of section 5 of this Act for any person to have in his possession, or to purchase or acquire, any prohibited weapon or ammunition if his possession, purchase or acquisition is exclusively in connection with the carrying on of activities in respect of which –

(a) that person; or

(b) the person on whose behalf he has possession, or makes the purchase or acquisition, is recognised, for the purposes of the law of another member State relating to firearms, as a collector of firearms or a body concerned in the cultural or historical aspects of weapons.

(4) The authority of the Secretary of State ... shall not be required by virtue of subsection (1A) of section 5 of this Act for any person to have in his possession, or to purchase or acquire, or to sell or transfer, any expanding ammunition or the missile for any such ammunition if –

(a) he is authorised by a firearm certificate or visitor's firearm permit to possess, or purchase or acquire, any expanding ammunition; and

(b) the certificate or permit is subject to a condition restricting the use of any expanding ammunition to use in connection with any one or more of the following, namely –

(i) the lawful shooting of deer;

(ii) the shooting of vermin or, in the course of carrying on activities in connection with the management of any estate, other wildlife;

(iii) the humane killing of animals;

(iv) the shooting of animals for the protection of other animals or humans.

(5) The authority of the Secretary of State ... shall not be required by virtue of subsection (1A) of section 5 of this Act for any person to have in his possession any expanding ammunition or the missile for any such ammunition if –

(a) he is entitled under section 10 of this Act, to have a slaughtering instrument and the ammunition for it in his possession; and

    (b) the ammunition or missile in question is designed to be capable of being used with a slaughtering instrument.

(6) The authority of the Secretary of State … shall not be required by virtue of subsection (1A) of section 5 of this Act for the sale or transfer of any expanding ammunition or the missile for any such ammunition to any person who produces a certificate by virtue of which he is authorised under subsection (4) above to purchase or acquire it without the authority of the Secretary of State ….

(7) The authority of the Secretary of State … shall not be required by virtue of subsection (1A) of section 5 of this Act for a person carrying on the business of a firearms dealer, or any servant of his, to have in his possession, or to purchase, acquire, sell or transfer, any expanding ammunition or the missile for any such ammunition in the ordinary course of that business.

(8) In this section –

    (a) references to expanding ammunition are references to any ammunition which incorporates a missile which is designed to expand on impact; and

    (b) references to the missile for any such ammunition are references to anything which, in relation to any such ammunition, falls within section 5(1A)(g) of this Act.

16   Possession of firearm with intent to injure

It is an offence for a person to have in his possession any firearm or ammunition with intent by means thereof to endanger life or to enable another person by means thereof to endanger life whether any injury has been caused or not.

16A Possession of firearm with intent to cause fear of violence

It is an offence for a person to have in his possession any firearm or imitation firearm with intent –

    (a) by means thereof to cause, or

    (b) to enable another person by means thereof to cause,

any person to believe that unlawful violence will be used against him or another person.

17   Use of firearm to resist arrest

(1) It is an offence for a person to make or attempt to make any use whatsoever of a firearm or imitation firearm with intent to resist or prevent the lawful arrest or detention of himself or another person.

(2) If a person, at the time of his committing or being arrested for an offence specified in Schedule 1 to this Act, has in his possession a firearm or imitation firearm, he shall be guilty of an offence under this subsection unless he shows that he had it in his possession for a lawful object.

(4) For purposes of this section, the definition of 'firearm' in section 57(1) of this Act shall apply without paragraphs (b) and (c) of that subsection, and 'imitation firearm' shall be construed accordingly. …

18   Carrying firearm with criminal intent

(1) It is an offence for a person to have with him a firearm or imitation firearm with intent to commit an indictable offence, or to resist arrest or prevent the arrest of another, in either case while he has the firearm or imitation firearm with him.

(2) In proceedings for an offence under this section proof that the accused had a firearm or imitation firearm with him and intended to commit an offence or to resist or prevent arrest, is evidence that he intended to have it with him while doing so. …

19   Carrying firearm in a public place

A person commits an offence if, without lawful authority or reasonable excuse (the proof whereof lies on him) he has with him in a public place –

- (a)   a loaded shot gun;
- (b)   an air weapon (whether loaded or not);
- (c)   any other firearm (whether loaded or not) together with ammunition suitable for use in that firearm, or
- (d)   an imitation firearm.

20   Trespassing with firearm

(1) A person commits an offence if, while he has a firearm or imitation firearm with him, he enters or is in any building or part of a building as a trespasser and without reasonable excuse (the proof whereof lies on him).

(2) A person commits an offence if, while he has a firearm or imitation firearm with him, he enters or is on any land as a trespasser and without reasonable excuse (the proof whereof lies on him).

(3) In subsection (2) of this section the expression 'land' includes land covered with water.

21   Possession of firearms by persons previously convicted of crime

(1) A person who has been sentenced to custody for life or to preventive detention, or to imprisonment or to corrective training for a term of three years or more or to youth custody or detention in a young offender institution for such a term, or who has been sentenced to be detained for such a term in a young offenders institution in Scotland, shall not at any time have a firearm or ammunition in his possession.

(2) A person who has been sentenced to imprisonment for a term of three months or more but less than three years or to youth custody or detention in a young offender institution for such a term, or who has been sentenced to be detained for such a term in a detention centre or in a young offenders institution in Scotland or who has been subject to a secure training order or a detention and training order, shall not at any time before the expiration of the period of five years from the date of his release have a firearm or ammunition in his possession.

(2A) For the purposes of subsection (2) above, 'the date of his release' means –

- (a)   in the case of a person sentenced to imprisonment with an order under section 47(1) of the Criminal Law Act 1977 (prison sentence partly served and partly suspended), the date on which he completes service of so much of the sentence as was by that order required to be served in prison;
- (b)   in the case of a person who has been subject to a secure training order –
  - (i)   the date on which he is released from detention under the order;
  - (ii)   the date on which he is released from detention ordered under section 4 of the Criminal Justice and Public Order Act 1994; or
  - (iii)   the date halfway through the total period specified by the court in making the order,

whichever is the later.

- (c)   in the case of a person who has been subject to a detention and training order –
  - (i)   the date on which he is released from detention under the order,
  - (ii)   the date on which he is released from detention ordered under section 104 of the Powers of Criminal Courts (Sentencing) Act 2000; or
  - (iii)   the date of the half-way point of the term of the order whichever is the later.

(d) in the case of a person who has been subject to a sentence of imprisonment to which an intermittent custody order under section 183(1)(b) of the Criminal Justice Act 2003 relates, the date of his final release.

(2B) A person who is serving a sentence of imprisonment to which an intermittent custody order under section 183 of the Criminal Justice Act 2003 relates shall not during any licence period specified for the purposes of subsection (1)(b)(i) of that section have a firearm or ammunition in his possession.

(3) A person who –

(a) is the holder of a licence issued under section 53 of the Children and Young Persons Act 1933 or section 57 of the Children and Young Persons (Scotland) Act 1937 (which sections provide for the detention of children and young persons convicted of serious crime, but enable them to be discharged on licence by the Secretary of State); or

(b) is subject to a recognisance to keep the peace or to be of good behaviour, a condition of which is that he shall not possess, use or carry a firearm, or is subject to a community order containing a requirement that he shall not possess, use or carry a firearm; or

(c) has, in Scotland, been ordained to find caution a condition of which is that he shall not possess, use or carry a firearm;

shall not, at any time during which he holds the licence or is so subject or has been so ordained, have a firearm or ammunition in his possession.

(3ZA) In subsection (3)(b) above, 'community order' means –

(a) a community order within the meaning of Part 12 of the Criminal Justice Act 2003 made in England and Wales, or

(b) a probation order made in Scotland.

(3A) Where by section 19 of the Firearms Act (Northern Ireland) 1969, or by any other enactment for the time being in force in Northern Ireland and corresponding to this section, a person is prohibited in Northern Ireland from having a firearm or ammunition in his possession, he shall also be so prohibited in Great Britain at any time when to have it in his possession in Northern Ireland would be a contravention of the said section 19 or corresponding enactment.

(4) It is an offence for a person to contravene any of the foregoing provisions of this section.

(5) It is an offence for a person to sell or transfer a firearm or ammunition to, or to repair, test or prove a firearm or ammunition for, a person whom he knows or has reasonable ground for believing to be prohibited by this section from having a firearm or ammunition in his possession.

(6) A person prohibited under subsection (1), (2), (2B), (3) or (3A) of this section from having in his possession a firearm or ammunition may apply to the Crown Court or, in Scotland, in accordance with Act of Sederunt to the sheriff for a removal of the prohibition; and if the application is granted that prohibition shall not then apply to him.

(7) Schedule 3 to this Act shall have effect with respect to the courts with jurisdiction to entertain an application under this section and to the procedure appertaining thereto.

22 Acquisition and possession of firearms by minors

(1) It is an offence for a person under the age of seventeen to purchase or hire any firearm or ammunition.

(1A) Where a person under the age of eighteen is entitled, as the holder of a certificate under this Act, to have a firearm in his possession, it is an offence for that person to use that firearm for a purpose not authorised by the European weapons directive.

(2) It is an offence for a person under the age of fourteen to have in his possession any firearm or ammunition to which section 1 of this Act or section 15 of the Firearms (Amendment) Act

1988 applies, except in circumstances where under section 11(1), (3) or (4) of this Act he is entitled to have possession of it without holding a firearm certificate.

(3) It is an offence for a person under the age of fifteen to have with him an assembled shot gun except while under the supervision of a person of or over the age of twenty-one, or while the shot gun is so covered with a securely fastened gun cover that it cannot be fired.

(4) Subject to section 23 below, it is an offence for a person under the age of seventeen to have with him an air weapon or ammunition for an air weapon.

23 Exceptions from s22(4)

(1) It is not an offence under section 22(4) of this Act for a person to have with him an air weapon or ammunition while he is under the supervision of a person of or over the age of twenty-one; but where a person has with him an air weapon on any premises in circumstances where he would be prohibited from having it with him but for this subsection, it is an offence –

    (a) for him to use it for firing any missile beyond those premises; or

    (b) for the person under whose supervision he is to allow him so to use it.

(2) It is not an offence under section 22(4) of this Act for a person to have with him an air weapon or ammunition at a time when –

    (a) being a member of a rifle club or miniature rifle club for the time being approved by the Secretary of State for the purposes of this section or section 15 of the Firearms (Amendment) Act 1988, he is engaged as such a member in connection with target shooting; or

    (b) he is using the weapon or ammunition at a shooting gallery where the only firearms used are either air weapons or miniature rifles not exceeding .23 inch calibre.

(3) It is not an offence under section 22(4) of this Act for a person of or over the age of fourteen to have with im an air weapon or ammunition on private premises with the consent of the occupier.

(4) But where a person has with him an air weapon on premises in circumstances where he would be prohibited from having it with him but for subsection (3), it is an ofence for him to use it for firing any missile beyond those premises.

24 Supplying firearms to minors

(1) It is an offence to sell or let on hire any firearm or ammunition to a person under the age of seventeen.

(2) It is an offence –

    (a) to make a gift of or lend any firearm or ammunition to which section 1 of this Act applies to a person under the age of fourteen; or

    (b) to part with the possession of any such firearm or ammunition to a person under that age, except in circumstances where that person is entitled under section 11(1), (3) or (4) of this Act or section 15 of the Firearms (Amendment) Act 1988 to have possession thereof without holding a firearm certificate.

(3) It is an offence to make a gift of a shot gun or ammunition for a shot gun to a person under the age of fifteen.

(4) It is an offence –

    (a) to make a gift of an air weapon or ammunition for an air weapon to a person under the age of seventeen; or

    (b) to part with the possession of an air weapon or ammunition for an air weapon to a person under the age of seventeen except where by virtue of section 23 of this Act the person is not prohibited from having it with him.

(5) In proceedings for an offence under any provision of this section it is a defence to prove that

the person charged with the offence believed the other person to be of or over the age mentioned in that provision and had reasonable ground for the belief.

25   Supplying firearm to person drunk or insane

It is an offence for a person to sell or transfer any firearm or ammunition to, or to repair, prove or test any firearm or ammunition for, another person whom he knows or has reasonable cause for believing to be drunk or of unsound mind.

57   Interpretation

(1) In this Act, the expression 'firearm' means a lethal barrelled weapon of any description from which any shot, bullet or other missile can be discharged and includes –

    (a)   any prohibited weapon, whether it is such a lethal weapon as aforesaid or not; and

    (b)   any component part of such a lethal or prohibited weapon; and

    (c)   any accessory to any such weapon designed or adapted to diminish the noise or flash caused by firing the weapon;

and so much of section 1 of this Act as excludes any description of firearm from the category of firearms to which that section applies shall be construed as also excluding component parts of, and accessories to, firearms of that description.

(2) In this Act, the expression 'ammunition' means ammunition for any firearm and includes grenades, bombs and other like missiles, whether capable of use with a firearm or not, and also includes prohibited ammunition.

(2A) In this Act 'self-loading' and 'pump-action' in relation to any weapon mean respectively that it is designed or adapted (otherwise than as mentioned in section 5(1)(a)) so that it is automatically reloaded or that it is so designed or adapted that it is reloaded by the manual operation of the fore-end or forestock of the weapon.

(2B) In this Act 'revolver', in relation to a smooth-bore gun, means a gun containing a series of chambers which revolve when the gun is fired. ...

SCHEDULE 1

OFFENCES TO WHICH SECTION 17(2) APPLIES

1. Offences under section 1 of the Criminal Damage Act 1971.

2. Offences under any of the following provisions of the Offences Against the Person Act 1861 –
    sections 20 to 22 (inflicting bodily injury; garrotting; criminal use of stupefying drugs);
    section 30 (laying explosive to buildings, etc);
    section 32 (endangering railway passengers by tampering with track);
    section 38 (assault with intent to commit felony or resist arrest);
    section 47 (criminal assaults);

2A. Offences under Part 1 of the Child Abduction Act 1984 (abduction of children)

4. Theft, robbery, burglary, blackmail, and any offence under section 12(1) (taking of motor vehicle or other conveyance without owner's consent) of the Theft Act 1968.

5. Offences under section 89(1) of the Police Act 1996 or section 41 of the Police (Scotland) Act 1967 (assaulting constable in execution of his duty).

5A. An offence under section 90(1) of the Criminal Justice Act 1991 (assaulting prisoner custody officer).

5B. An offence under section 13(1) of the Criminal Justice and Public Order Act 1994 (assaulting secure training centre custody officer).

6. Offences under any of the following provisions of the Sexual Offences Act 2003 –

   (a) section 1 (rape);
   (b) section 2 (assault by penetration);
   (c) section 4 (causing a person to engage in sexual activity without consent), where the activity caused involved penetration within subsection (4)(a) to (d) of that section;
   (d) section 5 (rape of a child under 13);
   (e) section 6 (assault of a child under 13 by penetration);
   (f) section 8 (causing or inciting a child under 13 to engage in sexual activity), where an activity involving penetration within subsection (3)(a) to (d) of that section was caused;
   (g) section 30 (sexual activity with a person with a mental disorder impeding choice), where the touching involved penetration within subsection (3)(a) to (d) of that section;
   (h) section 31 (causing or inciting a person, with a mental disorder impeding choice, to engage in sexual activity), where an activity involving penetration within subsection (3)(a) to (d) of that section was caused.

8. Aiding and abetting the commission of any offence specified in paragraphs 1 to 6 of this Schedule.

9. Attempting to commit any offence so specified.

NB. Section 1(3) of the Firearms (Amendment) Act 1997 (substitution of 'rifled gun' for 'rifle' in s5(1)(ab) of this Act) does not have effect in relation to weapons prohibited by s5(1)(aba): Firearms (Amendment) Act 1997 (Commencement) (No 2) Order 1997, art 5.

For the position where a person was in possession of a weapon within s5(1)(af) when the insertion of that provision came into force (20 January 2004), see s39(4), (5) of the Anti-social Behaviour Act 2003.

As amended by the Theft Act 1968, s33(2), Schedule 2, Part III; Criminal Damage Act 1971, s11(7), (8), Schedule, Part I; Courts Act 1971, s56(2), Schedule 9, Part II; Criminal Justice Act 1972, s29; Criminal Justice Act 1982, s77, Schedule 14, para 24; Criminal Justice and Public Order Act 1994, s168(2), Schedule 10, para 24(1), (2)(b); Child Abduction Act 1984, s11(2); Criminal Justice Act 1988, s123(6), Schedule 8, Part I, para 6, s170(2), Schedule 16; Firearms (Amendment) Act 1988, ss1(1), (2), (3), 2, 23(1) (4), 25(1), (2); Firearms Acts (Amendment) Regulations 1992, regs 3, 4(1); Firearms (Amendment) Act 1994, ss1(1), 2(1); Criminal Justice and Public Order Act 1994, s168(1), Schedule 9, para 8; Police Act 1996, s103(1), Schedule 7, Pt II, para 16; Firearms (Amendment) Act 1997, ss1(1)–(6), (9), 9, 10, 52, Schedule 2, paras 1, 2(1), 3, Schedule 3; Firearms (Amendment) (No 2) Act 1997, s2(7), Schedule; Crime and Disorder Act 1998, s119, Schedule 8, para 14(1), (2); Powers of Criminal Courts (Sentencing) Act 2000, s165(1), Schedule 9, para 31; Anti-social Behaviour Act 2003, ss37(1), 38(1)–(4), 39(1)–(3); Criminal Justice Act 2003, s304, Schedule 32, Pt 1, paras 11, 12; Sexual Offences Act 2003, s139, Schedule 6, para 16.

THEFT ACT 1968

(1968 c 60)

1   Basic definition of theft

(1) A person is guilty of theft if he dishonestly appropriates property belonging to another with

the intention of permanently depriving the other of it; and 'thief' and 'steal' shall be construed accordingly.

(2) It is immaterial whether the appropriation is made with a view to gain, or is made for the thief's own benefit.

(3) The five following sections of this Act shall have effect as regards the interpretation and operation of this section (and, except as otherwise provided by this Act, shall apply only for purposes of this section).

2 'Dishonestly'

(1) A person's appropriation of property belonging to another is not to be regarded as dishonest –

   (a) if he appropriates the property in the belief that he has in law the right to deprive the other of it, on behalf of himself or of a third person; or

   (b) if he appropriates the property in the belief that he would have the other's consent if the other knew of the appropriation and the circumstances of it; or

   (c) (except where the property came to him as trustee or personal representative) if he appropriates the property in the belief that the person to whom the property belongs cannot be discovered by taking reasonable steps.

(2) A person's appropriation of property belonging to another may be dishonest notwithstanding that he is willing to pay for the property.

3 'Appropriates'

(1) Any assumption by a person of the rights of an owner amounts to an appropriation, and this includes, where he has come by the property (innocently or not) without stealing it, any later assumption of a right to it by keeping or dealing with it as owner.

(2) Where property or a right or interest in property is or purports to be transferred for value to a person acting in good faith, no later assumption by him of rights which he believed himself to be acquiring shall, by reason of any defect in the transferor's title, amount to theft of the property.

4 'Property'

(1) 'Property' includes money and all other property, real or personal, including things in action and other intangible property.

(2) A person cannot steal land, or things forming part of land and severed from it by him or by his directions, except in the following cases, that is to say –

   (a) when he is a trustee or personal representative, or is authorised by power of attorney, or as liquidator of a company; or otherwise, to sell or dispose of land belonging to another, and he appropriates the land or anything forming part of it by dealing with it in breach of the confidence reposed in him; or

   (b) when he is not in possession of the land and appropriates anything forming part of the land by severing it or causing it to be severed, or after it has been severed; or

   (c) when, being in possession of the land under a tenancy, he appropriates the whole or part of any fixture or structure let to be used with the land.

For purposes of this subsection 'land' does not include incorporeal hereditaments, 'tenancy' means a tenancy for years or any less period and includes an agreement for such a tenancy, but a person who after the end of a tenancy remains in possession as statutory tenant or otherwise is to be treated as having possession under the tenancy, and 'let' shall be construed accordingly.

(3) A person who picks mushrooms growing wild on any land, or who picks flowers, fruit or foliage from a plant growing wild on any land, does not (although not in possession of the land) steal what he picks, unless he does it for reward or for sale or other commercial purpose.

For purposes of this subsection 'mushroom' includes any fungus, and 'plant' includes any shrub or tree.

(4) Wild creatures, tamed or untamed, shall be regarded as property; but a person cannot steal a wild creature not tamed nor ordinarily kept in captivity, or the carcass of any such creature, unless either it has been reduced into possession by or on behalf of another person and possession of it has not since been lost or abandoned, or another person is in course of reducing it into possession.

5 'Belonging to another'

(1) Property shall be regarded as belonging to any person having possession or control of it, or having in it any proprietary right or interest (not being an equitable interest arising only from an agreement to transfer or grant an interest).

(2) Where property is subject to a trust, the persons to whom it belongs shall be regarded as including any person having a right to enforce the trust, and an intention to defeat the trust shall be regarded accordingly as an intention to deprive of the property any person having that right.

(3) Where a person receives property from or on account of another, and is under an obligation to the other to retain and deal with that property or its proceeds in a particular way, the property or proceeds shall be regarded (as against him) as belonging to the other.

(4) Where a person gets property by another's mistake, and is under an obligation to make restoration (in whole or in part) of the property or its proceeds or of the value thereof, then to the extent of that obligation the property or proceeds shall be regarded (as against him) as belonging to the person entitled to restoration, and an intention not to make restoration shall be regarded accordingly as an intention to deprive that person of the property or proceeds.

(5) Property of a corporation sole shall be regarded as belonging to the corporation notwithstanding a vacancy in the corporation.

6 'With the intention of permanently depriving the other of it'

(1) A person appropriating property belonging to another without meaning the other permanently to lose the thing itself is nevertheless to be regarded as having the intention of permanently depriving the other of it if his intention is to treat the thing as his own to dispose of regardless of the other's rights; and a borrowing or lending of it may amount to so treating it if, but only if, the borrowing or lending is for a period and in circumstances making it equivalent to an outright taking or disposal.

(2) Without prejudice to the generality of subsection (1) above, where a person, having possession or control (lawfully or not) of property belonging to another, parts with the property under a condition as to its return which he may not be able to perform, this (if done for purposes of his own and without the other's authority) amounts to treating the property as his own to dispose of regardless of the other's rights.

7 Theft

A person guilty of theft shall on conviction on indictment be liable to imprisonment for a term not exceeding seven years.

8 Robbery

(1) A person is guilty of robbery if he steals, and immediately before or at the time of doing so, and in order to do so, he uses force on any person or puts or seeks to put any person in fear of being then and there subjected to force.

(2) A person guilty of robbery, or of an assault with intent to rob, shall on conviction on indictment be liable to imprisonment for life.

9   Burglary

(1) A person is guilty of burglary if –

(a) he enters any building or part of a building as a trespasser and with intent to commit any such offence as is mentioned in subsection (2) below; or

(b) having entered any building or part of a building as a trespasser he steals or attempts to steal anything in the building or that part of it or inflicts or attempts to inflict on any person therein any grievous bodily harm.

(2) The offences referred to in subsection (1)(a) above are offences of stealing anything in the building or part of a building in question, of inflicting on any person therein any grievous bodily harm therein, and of doing unlawful damage to the building or anything therein.

(3) A person guilty of burglary shall on conviction on indictment be liable to imprisonment for a term not exceeding –

(a) where the offence was committed in respect of a building or part of a building which is a dwelling, fourteen years;

(b) in any other case, ten years.

(4) References in subsections (1) and (2) above to a building, and the reference in subsection (3) above to a building which is a dwelling, shall apply also to an inhabited vehicle or vessel, and shall apply to any such vehicle or vessel at times when the person having a habitation in it is not there as well as at times when he is.

10   Aggravated burglary

(1) A person is guilty of aggravated burglary if he commits any burglary and at the time has with him any firearm or imitation firearm, any weapon of offence, or any explosive; and for this purpose –

(a) 'firearm' includes an airgun or air pistol, and 'imitation firearm' means anything which has the appearance of being a firearm, whether capable of being discharged or not; and

(b) 'weapon of offence' means any article made or adapted for use for causing injury to or incapacitating a person, or intended by the person having it with him for such use; and

(c) 'explosive' means any article manufactured for the purpose of producing a practical effect by explosion, or intended by the person having it with him for that purpose.

(2) A person guilty of aggravated burglary shall on conviction on indictment be liable to imprisonment for life.

11   Removal of articles from places open to the public

(1) Subject to subsections (2) and (3) below, where the public have access to a building in order to view the building or part of it, or a collection or part of a collection housed in it, any person who without lawful authority removes from the building or its grounds the whole or part of any article displayed or kept for display to the public in the building or that part of it or in its grounds shall be guilty of an offence.

For this purpose 'collection' includes a collection got together for a temporary purpose, but references in this section to a collection do not apply to a collection made or exhibited for the purpose of effecting sales or other commercial dealings.

(2) It is immaterial for purposes of subsection (1) above, that the public's access to a building is limited to a particular period or particular occasion; but where anything removed from a building or its grounds is there otherwise than as forming part of, or being on loan for exhibition with, a collection intended for permanent exhibition to the public, the person removing it does not thereby commit an offence under this section unless he removes it on a day when the public have access to the building as mentioned in subsection (1) above.

(3) A person does not commit an offence under this section if he believes that he has lawful authority for the removal of the thing in question or that he would have it if the person entitled to give it knew of the removal of the circumstances of it.

(4) A person guilty of an offence under this section shall, on conviction on indictment be liable to imprisonment for a term not exceeding five years.

12   Taking motor vehicle or other conveyance without authority

(1) Subject to subsections (5) and (6) below, a person shall be guilty of an offence if, without having the consent of the owner or other lawful authority, he takes any conveyance for his own or another's use or, knowing that any conveyance has been taken without such authority, drives it or allows himself to be carried in or on it.

(2) A person guilty of an offence under subsection (1) above shall be liable on summary conviction to fine not exceeding level 5 on the standard scale, to imprisonment for a term not exceeding six months, or to both.

(4) If on the trial of an indictment for theft the jury are not satisfied that the accused committed theft, but it is proved that the accused committed an offence under subsection (1) above, the jury may find him guilty of the offence under subsection (1) and if he is found guilty of it, he shall be liable as he would have been liable under subsection (2) above on summary conviction.

(4A) Proceedings for an offence under subsection (1) above (but not proceedings of a kind falling within subsection (4) above) in relation to a mechanically propelled vehicle –

(a) shall not be commenced after the end of the period of three years beginning with the day on which the offence was committed; but

(b) subject to that, may be commenced at any time within the period of six months beginning with the relevant day.

(4B) In subsection (4A)(b) above 'the relevant day' means –

(a) in the case of a prosecution for an offence under subsection (1) above by a public prosecutor, the day on which sufficient evidence to justify the proceedings came to the knowledge of any person responsible for deciding whether to commence any such prosecution;

(b) in the case of a prosecution for an offence under subsection (1) above which is commenced by a person other than a public prosecutor after the discontinuance of a prosecution falling within paragraph (a) above which relates to the same facts, the day on which sufficient evidence to justify the proceedings came to the knowledge of the person who has decided to commence the prosecution or (if later) the discontinuance of the other prosecutions;

(c) in the case of any other prosecution for an offence under subsection (1) above, the day on which sufficient evidence to justify the proceedings came to the knowledge of the person who has decided to commence the prosecution.

(4C) For the purposes of subsection (4A)(b) above a certificate of a person responsible for deciding whether to commence a prosecution of a kind mentioned in subsection (4B)(a) above as to the date on which such evidence as is mentioned in the certificate came to the knowledge of any person responsible for deciding whether to commence any such prosecution shall be conclusive evidence of that fact.

(5) Subsection (1) above shall not apply in relation to pedal cycles; but, subject to subsection (6) below, a person who, without having the consent of the owner or other lawful authority, takes a pedal cycle for his own or another's use, or rides a pedal cycle knowing it to have been taken without such authority, shall on summary conviction be liable to a fine not exceeding level 3 on the standard scale.

(6) A person does not commit an offence under this section by anything done in the belief that he has lawful authority to do it or that he would have the owner's consent if the owner knew of his doing it and the circumstances of it.

(7) For purposes of this section –

    (a) 'conveyance' means any conveyance constructed or adapted for the carriage of a person or person whether by land, water or air, except that it does not include a conveyance constructed or adapted for use only under the control of a person not carried in or on it, and 'drive' shall be construed accordingly; and

    (b) 'owner', in relation to a conveyance which is the subject of a hiring agreement or hire-purchase agreement, means the person in possession of the conveyance under that agreement.

12A Aggravated vehicle-taking

(1) Subject to subsection (3) below, a person is guilty of aggravated taking of a vehicle if –

    (a) he commits an offence under section 12(1) above (in this section referred to as a 'basic offence') in relation to a mechanically propelled vehicle; and

    (b) it is proved that, at any time after the vehicle was unlawfully taken (whether by him or another) and before it was recovered, the vehicle was driven, or injury or damage was caused, in one or more of the circumstances set out in paragraphs (a) to (d) of subsection (2) below.

(2) The circumstances referred to in subsection (1)(b) above are –

    (a) that the vehicle was driven dangerously on a road or other public place;

    (b) that, owing to the driving of the vehicle, an accident occurred by which injury was caused to any person;

    (c) that, owing to the driving of the vehicle, an accident occurred by which damage was caused to any property, other than the vehicle;

    (d) that damage was caused to the vehicle.

(3) A person is not guilty of an offence under this section if he proves that, as regards any such proven driving, injury or damage as is referred to in subsection (1)(b) above, either –

    (a) the driving, accident or damage referred to in subsection (2) above occurred before he committed the basic offence; or

    (b) he was neither in nor on nor in the immediate vicinity of the vehicle when that driving, accident or damage occurred.

(4) A person guilty of an offence under this section shall be liable on conviction on indictment to imprisonment for a term not exceeding two years or, if it is proved that, in circumstances falling within subsection (2)(b) above, the accident caused the death of the person concerned, fourteen years.

(5) If a person who is charged with an offence under this section is found not guilty of that offence but it is proved that he committed a basic offence, he may be convicted of the basic offence.

(6) If by virtue of subsection (5) above a person is convicted of a basic offence before the Crown Court, that court shall have the same powers and duties as a magistrates' court would have had on convicting him of such an offence.

(7) For the purposes of this section a vehicle is driven dangerously if –

    (a) it is driven in a way which falls far below what would be expected of a competent and careful driver; and

    (b) it would be obvious to a competent and careful driver that driving the vehicle in that way would be dangerous.

(8) For the purposes of this section a vehicle is recovered when it is restored to its owner or to other lawful possession or custody; and in this subsection 'owner' has the same meaning as in section 12 above.

13   Abstracting of electricity

A person who dishonestly uses without due authority, or dishonestly causes to be wasted or diverted, any electricity shall on conviction on indictment be liable to imprisonment for a term not exceeding five years.

14   Extension to thefts from mails outside England and Wales, and robbery, etc on such a theft

(1) Where a person –

    (a) steals or attempts to steal any mail bag or postal packet in the course of transmission as such between places in different jurisdictions in the British postal area, or any of the contents of such a mail bag or postal packet; or

    (b) in stealing or with intent to steal any such mail bag or postal packet or any of its contents, commits any robbery, attempted robbery or assault with intent to rob;

then, notwithstanding that he does so outside England and Wales, he shall be guilty of committing or attempting to commit the offence against this Act as if he had done so in England or Wales, and he shall accordingly be liable to be prosecuted, tried and punished in England and Wales without proof that the offence was committed there.

(2) In subsection (1) above the reference to different jurisdictions in the British postal area is to be construed as referring to the several jurisdictions of England and Wales, of Scotland, of Northern Ireland, of the Isle of Man and of the Channel Islands.

17   False accounting

(1) Where a person dishonestly, with a view to gain for himself or another or with intent to cause loss to another –

    (a) destroys, defaces, conceals or falsifies any account or any record or document made or required for any accounting purpose; or

    (b) in furnishing information for any purpose produces or makes use of any account, or any such record or document as aforesaid, which to his knowledge is or may be misleading, false or deceptive in a material particular;

he shall, on conviction on indictment, be liable to imprisonment for a term not exceeding seven years.

(2) For purposes of this section a person who makes or concurs in making in an account or other document an entry which is or may be misleading, false or deceptive in a material particular, or who omits or concurs in omitting a material particular from an account or other document, is to be treated as falsifying the account or document.

18   Liability of company officers for certain offences by company

(1) Where an offence committed by a body corporate under section 17 of this Act is proved to have been committed with the consent or connivance of any director, manager, secretary or other similar officer of the body corporate or any person who was purporting to act in any such capacity, he as well as the body corporate shall be guilty of that offence, and shall be liable to be proceeded against and punished accordingly.

(2) Where the affairs of a body corporate are managed by its members, this section shall apply in relation to the acts and defaults of a member in connection with his functions of management as if he were a director of the body corporate.

19   False statements by company directors, etc

(1) Where an officer of a body corporate or unincorporated association (or person purporting to act as such), with intent to deceive members or creditors of the body corporate or association about its affairs, publishes or concurs in publishing a written statement or account which to his knowledge is or may be misleading, false or deceptive in a material particular, he shall on conviction on indictment be liable to imprisonment for a term not exceeding seven years.

(2) For purposes of this section a person who has entered into a security for the benefit of a body corporate or association is to be treated as a creditor of it.

(3) Where the affairs of a body corporate or association are managed by its members, this section shall apply to any statement which a member publishes or concurs in publishing in connection with his functions of management as if he were an officer of the body corporate or association.

20   Suppression, etc of documents

(1) A person who dishonestly, with a view to gain for himself or another or with intent to cause loss to another, destroys, defaces or conceals any valuable security, any will or other testamentary document or any original document of or belonging to, or filed or deposited in, any court of justice or any government department shall on conviction on indictment be liable to imprisonment for a term not exceeding seven years.

(3) For purposes of this section 'valuable security' means any document creating, transferring, surrendering or releasing any right to, in or over property, or authorising the payment of money or delivery of any property, or evidencing the creation, transfer, surrender or release of any such right, or the payment of money or delivery of any property, or the satisfaction of any obligation.

21   Blackmail

(1) A person is guilty of blackmail if, with a view to gain for himself or another or with intent to cause loss to another, he makes any unwarranted demand with menaces; and for this purpose this demand with menaces is unwarranted unless the person making it does so in belief –

> (a) that he has reasonable grounds for making the demand; and
>
> (b) that the use of the menaces is a proper means of reinforcing the demand.

(2) The nature of the act or omission demanded is immaterial, and it is also immaterial whether the menaces relate to action to be taken by the person making the demand.

(3) A person guilty of blackmail shall on conviction on indictment be liable to imprisonment for a term not exceeding fourteen years.

22   Handling stolen goods

(1) A person handles stolen goods if (otherwise than in the course of the stealing) knowing or believing them to be stolen goods he dishonestly receives the goods or dishonestly undertakes or assists in their retention, removal, disposal or realisation by or for the benefit of another person, or if he arranges to do so.

(2) A person guilty of handling stolen goods shall on conviction on indictment be liable to imprisonment for a term not exceeding fourteen years.

23   Advertising rewards for return of goods stolen or lost

Where any public advertisement of a reward for the return of any goods which have been stolen or lost uses any words to the effect that no question will be asked, or that the person producing the goods will be safe from apprehension or inquiry, or that any money paid for the purchase of the goods or advanced by way of loan on them will be repaid, the person advertising the reward and any person who prints or publishes the advertisement shall on summary conviction be liable to a fine not exceeding level 3 on the standard scale.

24 Scope of offences relating to stolen goods

(1) The provisions of this Act relating to goods which have been stolen shall apply whether the stealing occurred in England or Wales or elsewhere, and whether it occurred before or after the commencement of this Act, provided that the stealing (if not an offence under this Act) amounted to an offence where and at the time when the goods were stolen; and references to stolen goods shall be construed accordingly.

(2) For purposes of those provisions references to stolen goods shall include, in addition to the goods originally stolen and parts of them (whether in their original state or not) –

    (a) any other goods which directly or indirectly represent or have at any time represented the stolen goods in the hands of the thief as being the proceeds of any disposal or realisation of the whole or part of the goods stolen or of goods so representing the stolen goods; and

    (b) any other goods which directly or indirectly represent or have at any time represented the stolen goods in the hands of a handler of the stolen goods or any part of them as being the proceeds of any disposal or realisation of the whole or part of the stolen goods handled by him or of goods so representing them.

(3) But no goods shall be regarded as having continued to be stolen goods after they have been restored to the person from whom they were stolen or to other lawful possession or custody, or after that person or any other person claiming through him have otherwise ceased as regards those goods to have any right to restitution in respect of the theft.

(4) For purposes of the provisions of this Act relating to goods which have been stolen (including subsections (1) to (3) above) goods obtained in England or Wales or elsewhere either by blackmail or, subject to subsection (5) below, by fraud (within the meaning of the Fraud Act 2006) shall be regarded as stolen; 'steal', 'theft' and 'thief' shall be construed accordingly.

(5) Subsection (1) above applies in relation to goods obtained by fraud as if –

    (a) the reference to the commencement of this Act were a reference to the commencement of the Fraud Act 2006, and

    (b) the reference to an offence under this Act were a reference to an offence under section 1 of that Act.

24A Dishonestly retaining a wrongful credit

(1) A person is guilty of an offence if –

    (a) a wrongful credit has been made to an account kept by him or in respect of which he has any right or interest;

    (b) he knows or believes that the credit is wrongful; and

    (c) he dishonestly fails to take such steps as are reasonable in the circumstances to secure that the credit is cancelled.

(2) References to a credit are to a credit of an amount of money.

(2A) A credit to an account is wrongful to the extent that it derives from –

    (a) theft;

    (b) blackmail;

    (c) fraud (contrary to section 1 of the Fraud Act 2006); or

    (d) stolen goods.

(5) In determining whether a credit to an account is wrongful, it is immaterial (in particular) whether the account is overdrawn before or after the credit is made.

(6) A person guilty of an offence under this section shall be liable on conviction on indictment to imprisonment for a term not exceeding ten years.

(7) Subsection (8) below applies for purposes of provisions of this Act relating to stolen goods (including subsection (2A) above).

(8) References to stolen goods include money which is dishonestly withdrawn from an account to which a wrongful credit has been made, but only to the extent that the money derives from the credit.

(9) 'Account' means an account kept with –

   (a) a bank;

   (b) a person carrying on a business which falls within subsection (10) below; or

   (c) an issuer of electronic money (as defined for the purposes of Part 2 of the Financial Services and Markets Act 2000).

(10) A business falls within this subsection if –

   (a) in the course of the business money received by way of deposit is lent to others; or

   (b) any other activity of the business is financed, wholly or to any material extent, out of the capital of or the interest on money received by way of deposit.

(11) References in subsection (10) above to a deposit must be read with

   (a) section 22 of the Financial Services and Markets Act 2000;

   (b) any relevant order under that section; and

   (c) Schedule 2 to that Act;

but any restriction on the meaning of deposit which arises from the identity of the person making it is to be disregarded.

(12) For the purposes of subsection (10) above –

   (a) all the activities which a person carries on by way of business shall be regarded as a single business carried on by him; and

   (b) 'money' includes money expressed in a currency other than sterling.

25   Going equipped for stealing, etc

(1) A person shall be guilty of an offence if, when not at his place of abode, he has with him any article for use in the course of or in connection with any burglary or theft.

(2) A person guilty of an offence under this section shall on conviction on indictment be liable to imprisonment for a term not exceeding three years.

(3) Where a person is charged with an offence under this section, proof that he had with him any article made or adapted for use in committing a burglary or theft shall be evidence that he had it with him for such use.

(5) For purposes of this section an offence under section 12(1) of this Act of taking a conveyance shall be treated as theft.

26   Search for stolen goods

(1) If it is made to appear by information on oath before a justice of the peace that there is reasonable cause to believe that any person has in his custody or possession or on his premises any stolen goods, the justice may grant a warrant to search for and seize the same; but no warrant to search for stolen goods shall be addressed to a person other than a constable except under the authority of an enactment expressly so providing.

(3) Where under this section a person is authorised to search premises for stolen goods, he may enter and search the premises accordingly, and may seize any goods he believes to be stolen goods.

(5) This section is to be construed in accordance with section 24 of this Act.

30   Spouses and civil partners

(1) This Act shall apply in relation to the parties to a marriage, and to property belonging to the

wife or husband whether or not by reason of an interest derived from the marriage, as it would apply if they were not married and any such interest subsisted independently of the marriage.

(2) Subject to subsection (4) below, a person shall have the same right to bring proceedings against that person's wife or husband for any offence (whether under this Act or otherwise) as if they were not married, and a person bringing any such proceedings shall be competent to give evidence for the prosecution at every stage of the proceedings.

(4) Proceedings shall not be instituted against a person for any offence of stealing or doing unlawful damage to property which at the time of the offence belongs to that person's wife or husband or civil partner, or for any attempt, incitement or conspiracy to commit such an offence, unless the proceedings are instituted by or with the consent of the Director of Public Prosecutions: Provided that –

    (a) this subsection shall not apply to proceedings against a person for an offence –

        (i) if that person is charged with committing the offence jointly with the wife or husband or civil partner;

        (ii) if by virtue of any judicial decree or order (wherever made) that person and the wife or husband are at the time of the offence under no obligation to cohabit; or

        (iii) an order (wherever made) is in force providing for the separation of that person and his or her civil partner.

(5) Notwithstanding section 6 of the Prosecution of Offences Act 1979 subsection (4) of this section shall apply –

    (a) to an arrest (if without warrant) made by the wife or husband or civil partner, and

    (b) to a warrant of arrest issued on an information laid by the wife or husband or civil partner.

32   Effect on existing law and construction of references to offences

(1) The following offences are hereby abolished for all purposes not relating to offences committed before the commencement of this Act, that is to say –

    (a) any offence at common law of larceny, robbery, burglary, receiving stolen property, obtaining property by threats, extortion by colour of office or franchise, false accounting by public officers, concealment of treasure trove and, except as regards offences relating to the public revenue, cheating; and

    (b) any offences under an enactment mentioned in Part I of Schedule 3 to this Act, to the extent to which the offence depends on any section or part of a section included in column 3 of that Schedule;

but so that the provisions in Schedule 1 to this Act (which preserve with modifications certain offences under the Larceny Act 1861 of taking or killing deer and taking or destroying fish) shall have effect as there set out.

(2) Except as regards offences committed before the commencement of this Act, and except in so far as the context otherwise requires, –

    (a) references in any enactment passed before this Act to an offence abolished by this Act shall, subject to any express amendment or repeal made by this Act, have effect as references to the corresponding offence under this Act, and in any such enactment the expression 'receive' (when it relates to an offence of receiving) shall mean handle, and 'receiver' shall be construed accordingly; and

    (b) without prejudice to paragraph (a) above, references in any enactment, whenever passed, to theft or stealing (including references to stolen goods), and references to robbery, blackmail, burglary, aggravated burglary or handling stolen goods, shall be construed in accordance with the provisions of this Act including those of section 24.

34 Interpretation

(1) Sections 4(1) and 5(1) of this Act shall apply generally for purposes of this Act as they apply for purposes of section 1.

(2) For purposes of this Act –

    (a) 'gain' and 'loss' are to be construed as extending only to gain or loss in money or other property, but as extending to any such gain or loss whether temporary or permanent; and –

        (i) 'gain' includes a gain by keeping what one has, as well as a gain by getting what one has not; and

        (ii) 'loss' includes a loss by not getting what one might get, as well as a loss by parting with what one has;

    (b) 'goods', except in so far as the context otherwise requires, includes money and every other description of property except land, and includes things severed from the land by stealing; and

    (c) 'mail bag' and 'postal packet' have the meanings given by section 125(1) of the Postal Services Act 2000.

SCHEDULE 1

Taking or destroying fish

2. (1) Subject to subparagraph (2) below, a person who unlawfully takes or destroys, or attempts to take or destroy, any fish in water which is private property or in which there is any private right of fishery shall on summary conviction be liable to imprisonment for a term not exceeding three months or to a fine not exceeding level 3 on the standard scale or to both.

(2) Subparagraph (1) above shall not apply to taking or destroying fish by angling in the daytime (that is to say, in the period beginning one hour before sunrise and ending one hour after sunset); but a person who by angling in the daytime unlawfully takes or destroys, or attempts to take or destroy, any fish in water which is private property or in which there is any private right of fishery shall on summary conviction be liable to a fine not exceeding level 1 on the standard scale.

(3) The court by which a person is convicted of an offence under this paragraph may order the forfeiture of anything which, at the time of the offence, he had with him for use for taking or destroying fish.

NB. The amending provisions of the Serious Organised Crime and Police Act 2005 shown below were not in force on 1 September 2005.

As amended by the Criminal Jurisdiction Act 1975, s14(4), Schedule 5, para 2; Theft Act 1978 s5(5); Prosecution of Offences Act 1979, s11(1), Schedule 1; Criminal Justice Act 1982, ss35, 38, 46; Criminal Justice Act 1988, s37(1); Criminal Justice Act 1991, s26(1), (2); Aggravated Vehicle-Taking Act 1992, s1(1); Criminal Justice and Public Order Act 1994, s168(2), Schedule 10, para 26; Theft (Amendment) Act 1996, ss1(1), 2(1); Financial Services and Markets Act 2000 (Consequential Amendments and Repeals) Order 2001, art 278(1)–(3); Vehicles (Crime) Act 2001, s37; Postal Services Act 2000 (Consequential Modifications) Order 2003, art 3, Schedule 1, para 1, Schedule 2; Criminal Justice Act 2003, s285(1); Sexual Offences Act 2003, ss139, 140, Schedule 6, para 17, Schedule 7; Civil Partnership Act 2004, s261(1), (4), Schedule 27, para 27, Schedule 30; Serious Organised Crime and Police Act 2005, s111, Schedule 7, Pt 1, Schedule 17, Pt 2; Fraud Act 2006, s14(1), (3), Schedule 1, paras 1(a)(iv), 4–8, Schedule 3.

COINAGE ACT 1971
(1971 c 24)

9   Prohibition of coins and tokens not issued by authority

(1) No piece of gold, silver, copper, or bronze, or of any metal or mixed metal, of any value whatever, shall be made or issued except with the authority of the Treasury, as a coin or a token for money, or as purporting that the holder thereof is entitled to demand any value denoted thereon.

(2) Every person who acts in contravention of this section shall be liable on summary conviction to a fine not exceeding level 2 on the standard scale.

10   Restrictions on melting or breaking of metal coins

(1) No person shall, except under the authority of a licence granted by the Treasury melt down or break up any metal coin which is for the time being current in the United Kingdom or which, having been current there, has at any time after 16 May 1969 ceased to be so.

(2) Any person who contravenes subsection (1) of this section shall be liable –

     (a) on summary conviction, to a fine not exceeding the prescribed sum;

     (b) on conviction on indictment, to a fine or to imprisonment for a term not exceeding two years, or both.

(3) If any condition attached to a licence granted under subsection (1) of this section is contravened or not complied with, the person to whom the licence was granted shall be liable on summary conviction to a fine not exceeding level 5 on the standard scale unless he proves that the contravention or non-compliance occurred without his consent or connivance and that he exercised all due diligence to prevent it.

(4) The court by or before which any person is convicted of an offence under this section may, whether or not it imposes any other punishment, order the articles in respect of which the offence was committed to be forfeited to Her Majesty.

(5) Where an offence under this section committed by a body corporate is proved to have been committed with the consent or connivance of, or to be attributable to any neglect on the part of, any director, manager, secretary or other similar officer of the body corporate or any person who was purporting to act in any such capacity, he as well as the body corporate shall be guilty of that offence and shall be liable to be proceeded against and punished accordingly.

As amended by the Government Trading Funds Act 1973, s7(4); Magistrates' Courts Act 1980, s32(2); Criminal Justice Act 1982, ss37, 46.

UNSOLICITED GOODS AND SERVICES ACT 1971
(1971 c 30)

2   Demands and threats regarding payment

(1) A person who, not having reasonable cause to believe there is a right to payment, in the course of any trade or business makes a demand for payment, or asserts a present or prospective right to payment, for what he knows are unsolicited goods sent (after the commencement of this Act) to another person with a view to his acquiring them for the purposes of his trade or business, shall be guilty of an offence and on summary conviction shall be liable to a fine not exceeding level 4 on the standard scale.

(2) A person who, not having reasonable cause to believe there is a right to payment, in the course of any trade or business and with a view to obtaining any payment for what he knows are unsolicited goods sent as aforesaid –

(a) threatens to bring any legal proceedings; or

(b) places or causes to be placed the name of any person on a list of defaulters or debtors or threatens to do so; or

(c) invokes or causes to be invoked any other collection procedure or threatens to do so,

shall be guilty of an offence and shall be liable on summary conviction to a fine not exceeding level 5 on the standard scale.

3   Directory entries

(1) A person ('the purchaser') shall not be liable to make any payment, and shall be entitled to recover any payment made by him, by way of charge for including or arranging for the inclusion in a directory of an entry relating to that person or his trade or business, unless –

(a) there has been signed by the purchaser or on his behalf an order complying with this section,

(b) there has been signed by the purchaser or on his behalf a note complying with this section of his agreement to the charge and before the note was signed, a copy of it was supplied, for retention by him, to him or a person acting on his behalf,

(c) there has been transmitted by the purchaser or a person acting on his behalf an electronic communication which includes a statement that the purchaser agrees to the charge and the relevant condition is satisfied in relation to that communication, or

(d) the charges arise under a contract in relation to which the conditions in section 3B(1) (renewed and extended contracts) are met.

(2) A person shall be guilty of an offence punishable on summary conviction with a fine not exceeding the prescribed sum if, in a case where a payment in respect of a charge would be recoverable from him in accordance with the terms of subsection (1) above, he demands payment, or asserts a present or prospective right to payment, of the charge or any part of it, without knowing or having reasonable cause to believe that –

(a) the entry to which the charge relates was ordered in accordance with this section,

(b) a proper note of the agreement has been duly signed, or

(c) the requirements set out in subsection (1)(c) or (d) above have been met.

(3) For the purpose of this section –

(a) an order for an entry in a directory must be made by means of an order form or other stationery belonging to the purchaser, which may be sent electronically but which must bear his name and address (or one or more of his addresses); and

(b) the note of a person's agreement to a charge must –

(i) specify the particulars set out in Part 1 of the Schedule to the Regulatory Reform (Unsolicited Goods and Services Act 1971) (Directory Entries and Demands for Payment) Order 2005, and

(ii) give reasonable particulars of the entry in respect of which the charge would be payable.

(3A) In relation to an electronic communication which includes a statement that the purchaser agrees to a charge for including or arranging the inclusion in a directory of any entry, the relevant condition is that –

(a) before the electronic communication was transmitted the information referred to in subsection (3B) below was communicated to the purchaser, and

(b) the electronic communication can readily be produced and retained in a visible and legible form.

(3B) That information is –

    (a) the following particulars –

        (i)   the amount of the charge;

        (ii) the name of the directory or proposed directory;

        (iii) the name of the person producing the directory;

        (iv) the geographic address at which that person is established;

        (v)   if the directory is or is to be available in printed form, the proposed date of publication of the directory or of the issue in which the entry is to be included;

        (vi) if the directory or the issue in which the entry is to be included is to be put on sale, the price at which it is to be offered for sale and the minimum number of copies which are to be available for sale;

        (vii) if the directory or the issue in which the entry is to be included is to be distributed free of charge (whether or not it is also to be put on sale), the minimum number of copies which are to be so distributed;

        (viii) if the directory is or is to be available in a form other than in printed form, adequate details of how it may be accessed; and

    (b) reasonable particulars of the entry in respect of which the charge would be payable.

(3C) In this section 'electronic communication' has the same meaning as in the Electronic Communications Act 2000.

(4) Nothing in this section shall apply to a payment due under a contract entered into before the commencement of this Act, or entered into by the acceptance of an offer made before that commencement.

3B   Renewed and extended contracts

(1) The conditions referred to in section 3(1)(d) above are met in relation to a contract ('the new contract') if –

    (a) a person ('the purchaser') has entered into an earlier contract ('the earlier contract') for including or arranging for the inclusion in a particular issue or version of a directory ('the earlier directory') of an entry ('the earlier entry') relating to him or his trade or business;

    (b) the purchaser was liable to make a payment by way of a charge arising under the earlier contract for including or arranging for the inclusion of the earlier entry in the earlier directory;

    (c) the new contract is a contract for including or arranging for the inclusion in a later issue or version of a directory ('the later directory') of an entry ('the later entry') relating to the purchaser or his trade or business;

    (d) the form, content and distribution of the later directory is materially the same as the form, content and distribution of the earlier directory;

    (e) the form and content of the later entry is materially the same as the form and content of the earlier entry;

    (f) if the later directory is published other than in electronic form –

        (i)   the earlier directory was the last, or the last but one, issue or version of the directory to be published before the later directory, and

        (ii) the date of publication of the later directory is not more than 13 months after the date of publication of the earlier directory;

    (g) if the later directory is published in electronic form, the first date on which the new contract requires the later entry to be published is not more than the relevant period after the last date on which the earlier contract required the earlier entry to be published;

(h) if it was a term of the earlier contract that the purchaser renew or extend the contract –

   (i) before the start of the new contract the relevant publisher has given notice in writing to the purchaser containing the information set out in Part 3 of the Schedule to the Regulatory Reform (Unsolicited Goods and Services Act 1971) (Directory Entries and Demands for Payment) Order 2005; and

   (ii) the purchaser has not written to the relevant publisher withdrawing his agreement to the renewal or extension of the earlier contract within the period of 21 days starting when he receives the notice referred to in sub-paragraph (i); and

(i) if the parties to the earlier contract and the new contract are different –

   (i) the parties to both contracts have entered into a novation agreement in respect of the earlier contract; or

   (ii) the relevant publisher has given the purchaser the information set out in Part 4 of the Schedule to the Regulatory Reform (Unsolicited Goods and Services Act 1971) (Directory Entries and Demands for Payment) Order 2005.

(2) For the purposes of subsection (1)(d) and (e), the form, content or distribution of the later directory, or the form or content of the later entry, shall be taken to be materially the same as that of the earlier directory or the earlier entry (as the case may be), if a reasonable person in the position of the purchaser would –

(a) view the two as being materially the same; or

(b) view that of the later directory or the later entry as being an improvement on that of the earlier directory or the earlier entry.

(3) For the purposes of subsection (1)(g) 'the relevant period' means the period of 13 months or (if shorter) the period of time between the first and last dates on which the earlier contract required the earlier entry to be published.

(4) For the purposes of subsection (1)(h) and (i) 'the relevant publisher' is the person with whom the purchaser has entered into the new contract.

(5) The information referred to in subsection (1)(i)(ii) must be given to the purchaser prior to the conclusion of the new contract.

4 Unsolicited publications

(1) A person shall be guilty of an offence if he sends or causes to be sent to another person any book, magazine or leaflet (or advertising material for any such publication) which he knows or ought reasonably to know is unsolicited and which describes or illustrates human sexual techniques.

(2) A person found guilty of an offence under this section shall be liable on summary conviction to a fine not exceeding level 5 on the standard scale.

(3) A prosecution for an offence under this section shall not in England and Wales be instituted except by, or with the consent of, the Director of Public Prosecutions.

6 Interpretation

(1) In this Act, unless the context or subject matter otherwise requires, –

'acquire' includes hire;

'send' includes deliver, and 'sender' shall be construed accordingly;

'unsolicited' means, in relation to goods sent to any person, that they are sent without any prior request made by him or on his behalf. ...

As amended by the Unsolicited Goods and Services (Amendment) Act 1975, ss1, 4(4); Magistrates' Courts Act 1980, s32(2); Criminal Justice Act 1982, ss38, 46; Consumer Protection (Distance Selling) Regulations 2000, reg 22(1), (3); Unsolicited Goods and Services Act 1971 (Electronic Communications) Order 2001, arts 2, 4–6; Unsolicited Goods and Services Act 1971 (Electronic Commerce) (Amendment) Regulations 2005, reg 2; Regulatory Reform (Unsolicited Goods and Services Act 1971) (Directory Entries and Demands for Payment) Order 2005, art 2.

MISUSE OF DRUGS ACT 1971
(1971 c 38)

4   Restriction of production and supply of controlled drugs

(1) Subject to any regulations under section 7 of this Act for the time being in force, it shall not be lawful for a person –
  (a)   to produce a controlled drug; or
  (b)   to supply or offer to supply a controlled drug to another.

(2) Subject to section 28 of this Act, it is an offence for a person –
  (a)   to produce a controlled drug in contravention of subsection (1) above; or
  (b)   to be concerned in the production of such a drug in contravention of that subsection by another.

(3) Subject to section 28 of this Act, it is an offence for a person –
  (a)   to supply or offer to supply a controlled drug to another in contravention of subsection (1) above; or
  (b)   to be concerned in the supplying of such a drug to another in contravention of that subsection; or
  (c)   to be concerned in the making to another in contravention of that subsection of an offer to supply such a drug.

4A   Aggravation of offence of supply of controlled drug

(1) This section applies if –
  (a)   a court is considering the seriousness of an offence under section 4(3) of this Act, and
  (b)   at the time the offence was committed the offender had attained the age of 18.

(2) If either of the following conditions is met the court –
  (a)   must treat the fact that the condition is met as an aggravating factor (that is to say, a factor that increases the seriousness of the offence), and
  (b)   must state in open court that the offence is so aggravated.

(3) The first condition is that the offence was committed on or in the vicinity of school premises at a relevant time.

(4) The second condition is that in connection with the commission of the offence the offender used a courier who, at the time the offence was committed, was under the age of 18.

(5) In subsection (3), a relevant time is –
  (a)   any time when the school premises are in use by persons under the age of 18;
  (b)   one hour before the start and one hour after the end of any such time.

(6) For the purposes of subsection (4), a person uses a courier in connection with an offence under section 4(3) of this Act if he causes or permits another person (the courier) –
  (a)   to deliver a controlled drug to a third person, or
  (b)   to deliver a drug related consideration to himself or a third person.

(7) For the purposes of subsection (6), a drug related consideration is a consideration of any description which –

(a) is obtained in connection with the supply of a controlled drug, or

(b) is intended to be used in connection with obtaining a controlled drug.

(8) In this section –

'school premises' means land used for the purposes of a school excluding any land occupied solely as a dwelling by a person employed at the school; and

'school' has the same meaning –

(a) in England and Wales, as in section 4 of the Education Act 1996 …

5 Restriction of possession of controlled drugs

(1) Subject to any regulations under section 7 of this Act for the time being in force it shall not be lawful for a person to have a controlled drug in his possession.

(2) Subject to section 28 of this Act and to subsection (4) below, it is an offence for a person to have a controlled drug in his possession in contravention of subsection (1) above.

(3) Subject to section 28 of this Act, it is an offence for a person to have a controlled drug in his possession, whether lawfully or not, with intent to supply it to another in contravention of section 4(1) of this Act.

(4) In any proceedings for an offence under subsection (2) above in which it is proved that the accused had a controlled drug in his possession, it shall be a defence for him to prove –

(a) that, knowing or suspecting it to be a controlled drug, he took possession of it for the purpose of preventing another from committing or continuing to commit an offence in connection with that drug and that as soon as possible after taking possession of it he took all such steps as were reasonably open to him to destroy the drug or to deliver it into the custody of a person lawfully entitled to take custody of it; or

(b) that, knowing or suspecting it to be a controlled drug, he took possession of it for the purpose of delivering it into the custody of a person lawfully entitled to take custody of it and that as soon as possible after taking possession of it he took all such steps as were reasonably open to him to deliver it into the custody of such a person.

(4A) In any proceedings for an offence under subsection (3) above, if it is proved that the accused had an amount of a controlled drug in his possession which is not less than the prescribed amount, the court or jury must assume that he had the drug in his possession with the intent to supply it as mentioned in subsection (3).

(4B) Subsection (4A) above does not apply if evidence is adduced which is sufficient to raise an issue that the accused may not have had the drug in his possession with that intent.

(4C) Regulations under subsection (4A) above have effect only in relation to proceedings for an offence committed after the regulations come into force.

(6) Nothing in subsection (4) above shall prejudice any defence which it is open to a person charged with an offence under this section to raise apart from that subsection.

6 Restrictions of cultivation of cannabis plant

(1) Subject to any regulations under section 7 of this Act for the time being in force, it shall not be lawful for a person to cultivate any plants of the genus Cannabis.

(2) Subject to section 28 of this Act, it is an offence to cultivate any such plant in contravention of subsection (1) above.

8 Occupiers, etc of premises to be punishable for permitting certain activities to take place there

A person commits an offence if, being the occupier or concerned in the management of any premises, he knowingly permits or suffers any of the following activities to take place on those premises, that is to say –

    (a) producing or attempting to produce a controlled drug in contravention of section 4(1) of this Act;

    (b) supplying or attempting to supply a controlled drug to another in contravention of section 4(1) of this Act, or offering to supply a controlled drug to another in contravention of section 4(1);

    (c) preparing opium for smoking;

    (d) smoking cannabis, cannabis resin or prepared opium.

9   Prohibition of certain activities, etc relating to opium

Subject to section 28 of this Act, it is an offence for a person –

    (a) to smoke or otherwise use prepared opium; or

    (b) to frequent a place used for the purpose of opium smoking; or

    (c) to have in his possession –

        (i) any pipes or other utensils made or adapted for use in connection with the smoking of opium, being pipes or utensils which have been used by him or with his knowledge and permission in that connection or which he intends to use or permit others to use in that connection; or

        (ii) any utensils which have been used by him or with his knowledge and permission in connection with the preparation of opium for smoking.

9A   Prohibition of supply, etc of articles for administering or preparing controlled drugs

(1) A person who supplies or offers to supply any article which may be used or adapted to be used (whether by itself or in combination with another article or other articles) in the administration by any person of a controlled drug to himself or another, believing that the article (or the article as adapted) is to be so used in circumstances where the administration is unlawful, is guilty of an offence.

(2) It is not an offence under subsection (1) above to supply or offer to supply a hypodermic syringe, or any part of one.

(3) A person who supplies or offers to supply any article which may be used to prepare a controlled drug for administration by any person to himself or another believing that the article is to be so used in circumstances where the administration is unlawful is guilty of an offence.

(4) For the purposes of this section, any administration of a controlled drug is unlawful except –

    (a) the administration by any person of a controlled drug to another in circumstances where the administration of the drug is not unlawful under section 4(1) of this Act, or

    (b) the administration by any person of a controlled drug to himself in circumstances where having the controlled drug in his possession is not unlawful under section 5(1) of this Act.

(5) In this section, references to administration by any person of a controlled drug to himself include a reference to his administering it to himself with the assistance of another.

28   Proof of lack of knowledge, etc to be a defence in proceedings for certain offences

(1) This section applies to offences under any of the following provisions of this Act, that is to say section 4(2) and (3), section 5(2) and (3), section 6(2) and section 9.

(2) Subject to subsection (3) below, in any proceedings for an offence to which this section applies it shall be a defence for the accused to prove that he neither knew of nor suspected nor had reason

to suspect the existence of some fact alleged by the prosecution which it is necessary for the prosecution to prove if he is to be convicted of the offence charged.

(3) Where in any proceedings for an offence to which this section applies it is necessary, if the accused is to be convicted of the offence charged, for the prosecution to prove that some substance or product involved in the alleged offence was the controlled drug which the prosecution alleges it to have been, and it is proved that the substance or product in question was that controlled drug, the accused –

> (a) shall not be acquitted of the offence charged by reason only of proving that he neither knew nor suspected nor had reason to suspect that the substance or product in question was the particular controlled drug alleged; but
>
> (b) shall be acquitted thereof –
>> (i) if he proves that he neither believed nor suspected nor had reason to suspect that the substance or product in question was a controlled drug; or
>> (ii) if he proves that he believed the substance or product in question to be a controlled drug, or a controlled drug of a description, such that, if it had in fact been that controlled drug or a controlled drug of that description, he would not at the material time have been committing any offence to which this section applies.

(4) Nothing in this section shall prejudice any defence which it is open to a person charged with an offence to which this section applies to raise apart from this section.

As amended by the Criminal Attempts Act 1981, s10, Schedule, Part I; Drug Trafficking Offences Act 1986, s34(1); Drugs Act 2005, ss1, 2.

CRIMINAL DAMAGE ACT 1971
(1971 c 48)

1 Destroying or damaging property

(1) A person who without lawful excuse destroys or damages any property belonging to another intending to destroy or damage any such property or being reckless as to whether any such property would be destroyed or damaged shall be guilty of an offence.

(2) A person who without lawful excuse destroys or damages any property, whether belonging to himself or another –

> (a) intending to destroy or damage any property or being reckless as to whether any property would be destroyed or damaged; and
>
> (b) intending by the destruction or damage to endanger the life of another or being reckless as to whether the life of another would be thereby endangered;

shall be guilty of an offence.

(3) An offence committed under this section by destroying or damaging property by fire shall be charged as arson.

2 Threats to destroy or damage property

A person who without lawful excuse makes to another a threat, intending that that other would fear it would be carried out –

> (a) to destroy or damage any property belonging to that other or a third person; or
>
> (b) to destroy or damage his own property in a way which he knows is likely to endanger the life of that other or a third person;

shall be guilty of an offence.

3   Possessing anything with intent to destroy or damage property

A person who has anything in his custody or under his control intending without lawful excuse to use it or cause or permit another to use it –

(a)   to destroy or damage any property belonging to some other person; or

(b)   to destroy or damage his own or the user's property in a way which he knows is likely to endanger the life of some other person;

shall be guilty of an offence.

4   Punishment of offences

(1) A person guilty of arson under section 1 above or of an offence under section 1(2) above (whether arson or not) shall on conviction on indictment be liable to imprisonment for life.

(2) A person guilty of any other offence under this Act shall on conviction on indictment be liable to imprisonment for a term not exceeding ten years.

5   'Without lawful excuse'

(1) This section applies to any offence under section 1(1) above and any offence under section 2 or 3 above other than one involving a threat by the person charged to destroy or damage property in a way which he knows is likely to endanger the life of another or involving an intent by the person charged to use or cause or permit the use of something in his custody or under his control so to destroy or damage property.

(2) A person charged with an offence to which this section applies shall, whether or not he would be treated for those purposes as having a lawful excuse apart from this subsection, be treated for those purposes as having a lawful excuse –

(a)   if at the time of the act or acts alleged to constitute the offence he believed that the person or persons whom he believed to be entitled to consent to the destruction of or damage to the property in question had so consented, or would have so consented to it if he or they had known of the destruction or damage and its circumstances, or

(b)   if he destroyed or damaged or threatened to destroy or damage the property in question or, in the case of a charge of an offence under section 3 above, intended to use or cause or permit the use of something to destroy or damage it, in order to protect property belonging to himself or another or a right or interest in property which was or which he believed to be vested in himself or another, and at the time of the act or acts alleged to constitute the offence he believed –

(i)   that the property, right or interest was in immediate need of protection; and

(ii) that the means of protection adopted or proposed to be adopted were or would be reasonable having regard to all the circumstances.

(3) For the purposes of this section it is immaterial whether a belief is justified or not if it is honestly held.

(4) For the purposes of subsection (2) above a right or interest in property includes any right or privilege in or over land, whether created by grant, licence or otherwise.

(5) This section shall not be construed as casting doubt on any defence recognised by law as a defence to criminal charges.

10   Interpretation

(1) In this Act 'property' means property of a tangible nature, whether real or personal, including money and –

(a)   including wild creatures which have been tamed or are ordinarily kept in captivity, and any other wild creatures or their carcasses if, but only if, they have been reduced into possession which has not been lost or abandoned or are in the course of being reduced into possession; but

    (b) not including mushrooms growing wild on any land or flowers, fruit or foliage of a plant growing wild in any land.

For the purposes of this subsection 'mushroom' includes any fungus and 'plant' includes any shrub or tree.

(2) Property shall be treated for the purposes of this Act as belonging to any person –

    (a) having the custody or control of it;

    (b) having in it any proprietary right or interest (not being an equitable interest arising only from an agreement to transfer or grant an interest); or

    (c) having a charge on it.

(3) Where property is subject to a trust, the persons to whom it belongs shall be so treated as including any person having a right to enforce the trust.

(4) Property of a corporation sole shall be so treated as belonging to the corporation notwithstanding a vacancy in the corporation.

SEX DISCRIMINATION ACT 1975

(1975 c 65)

37   Discriminatory practices

(1) In this section 'discriminatory practice' means –

    (a) the application of a provision, criterion or practice which results in an act of discrimination which is unlawful by virtue of any provision of Part 2 or 3 taken with section 1(2)(b) or 3(1)(b) or which would be likely to result in such an act of discrimination if the persons to whom it is applied were not all of one sex, or

    (b) the application of a requirement or condition which results in an act of discrimination which is unlawful by virtue of any provisions of Part 3 taken with section 1(1)(b) or which would be likely to result in such an act of discrimination if the persons to whom it is applied were not all of one sex.

(2) A person acts in contravention of this section if and so long as –

    (a) he applies a discriminatory practice, or

    (b) he operates practices or other arrangements which in any circumstances would call for the application by him of a discriminatory practice.

(3) Proceedings in respect of a contravention of this section shall be brought only by the Commission in accordance with sections 67 to 71 of this Act.

38   Discriminatory advertisements

(1) It is unlawful to publish or cause to be published an advertisement which indicates, or might reasonably be understood as indicating, an intention by a person to do any act which is or might be unlawful by virtue of Part II or III.

(2) Subsection (1) does not apply to an advertisement if the intended act would not in fact be unlawful.

(3) For the purposes of subsection (1), use of a job description with a sexual connotation (such as 'waiter', 'salesgirl', 'postman' or 'stewardess') shall be taken to indicate an intention to discriminate, unless the advertisement contains an indication to the contrary.

(4) The publisher of an advertisement made unlawful by subsection (1) shall not be subject to any liability under that subsection in respect of the publication of the advertisement if he proves –

    (a) that the advertisement was published in reliance on a statement made to him by the person who caused it to be published to the effect that, by reason of the operation of subsection (2), the publication would not be unlawful, and

    (b) that it was reasonable for him to rely on the statement.

(5) A person who knowingly or recklessly makes a statement such as is referred to in subsection (4) which in a material respect is false or misleading commits an offence, and shall be liable on summary conviction to a fine not exceeding level 5 on the standard scale.

39   Instructions to discriminate

It is unlawful for a person –

    (a) who has authority over another person, or

    (b) in accordance with whose wishes that other person is accustomed to act,

to instruct him to do any act which is unlawful by virtue of Part II or III, or procure or attempt to procure the doing by him of any such act.

40   Pressure to discriminate

(1) It is unlawful to induce, or attempt to induce, a person to do any act which contravenes Part II or III by –

    (a) providing or offering to provide him with any benefit, or

    (b) subjecting or threatening to subject him to any detriment.

(2) An offer or threat is not prevented from falling within subsection (1) because it is not made directly to the person in question, if it is made in such a way that he is likely to hear of it.

41   Liability of employers and principals

(1) Anything done by a person in the course of his employment shall be treated for the purposes of this Act as done by his employer as well as by him, whether or not it was done with the employer's knowledge or approval.

(2) Anything done by a person as agent for another person with the authority (whether express or implied, and whether precedent or subsequent) of that other person shall be treated for the purpose of this Act as done by that other person as well as by him.

(3) In proceedings brought under this Act against any person in respect of an act alleged to have been done by an employee of his it shall be a defence for that person to prove that he took such steps as were reasonably practicable to prevent the employee from doing that act, or from doing in the course of his employment acts of that description.

42   Aiding unlawful acts

(1) A person who knowingly aids another person to do an act made unlawful by this Act shall be treated for the purpose of this Act as himself doing an unlawful act of the like description.

(2) For the purposes of subsection (1) an employee or agent for whose act the employer or principal is liable under section 41 (or would be so liable but for section 41 (3)) shall be deemed to aid the doing of the act by the employer or principal.

(3) A person does not under this section knowingly aid another to do an unlawful act if –

    (a) he acts in reliance on a statement made to him by that other person that, by reason of any provision of this Act, the act which he aids would not be unlawful, and

    (b) it is reasonable for him to rely on the statement.

(4) A person who knowingly or recklessly makes a statement such as is referred to in subsection

(3)(a) which in a material respect is false or misleading commits an offence, and shall be liable on summary conviction to a fine not exceeding level 5 on the standard scale.

As amended by the Criminal Justice Act 1982, ss38, 46; Sex Discrimination (Indirect Discrimination and Burden of Proof) Regulations 2001, reg 8(2).

CRIMINAL LAW ACT 1977
(1977 c 45)

1   The offence of conspiracy
(1) Subject to the following provisions of this Part of this Act, if a person agrees with any other person or persons that a course of conduct shall be pursued which, if the agreement is carried out in accordance with their intentions, either –
> (a)   will necessarily amount to or involve the commission of any offence or offences by one or more of the parties to the agreement, or
> (b)   would do so but for the existence of facts which render the commission of the offence or any of the offences impossible,

he is guilty of conspiracy to commit the offence or offences in question.
(2) Where liability for any offence may be incurred without knowledge on the part of the person committing it of any particular fact or circumstance necessary for the commission of the offence, a person shall nevertheless not be guilty of conspiracy to commit that offence by virtue of subsection (1) above unless he and at least one other party to the agreement intend or know that that fact or circumstance shall or will exist at the time when the conduct constituting the offence is to take place.
(4) In this Part of this Act 'offence' means an offence triable in England and Wales.

1A   Conspiracy to commit offences outside the United Kingdom.
(1) Where each of the following conditions is satisfied in the case of an agreement, this Part of this Act has effect in relation to the agreement as it has effect in relation to an agreement falling within section 1(1) above.
(2) The first condition is that the pursuit of the agreed course of conduct would at some stage involve –
> (a)   an act by one or more of the parties, or
> (b)   the happening of some other event,

intended to take place in a country or territory outside the United Kingdom.
(3) The second condition is that that act or other event constitutes an offence under the law in force in that country or territory
(4) The third condition is that the agreement would fall within section 1(1) above as an agreement relating to the commission of an offence but for the fact that the offence would not be an offence triable in England and Wales if committed in accordance with the parties' intentions
(5) The fourth condition is that –
> (a)   a party to the agreement, or a party's agent, did anything in England and Wales in relation to the agreement before its formation, or
> (b)   a party to the agreement became a party in England and Wales (by joining it either in person or through an agent), or
> (c)   a party to the agreement, or a party's agent, did or omitted anything in England and Wales in pursuance of the agreement.

(6) In the application of this Part of this Act to an agreement in the case of which each of the above conditions is satisfied, a reference to an offence is to be read as a reference to what would be the offence in question but for the fact that it is not an offence triable in England and Wales.

(7) Conduct punishable under the law in force in any country or territory is an offence under that law for the purposes of this section, however it is described in that law.

(8) Subject to subsection (9) below, the second condition is to be taken to be satisfied unless, not later than rules of court may provide, the defence serve on the prosecution a notice

    (a) stating that, on the facts as alleged with respect to the agreed course of conduct, the condition is not in their opinion satisfied,

    (b) showing their grounds for that opinion, and

    (c) requiring the prosecution to show that it is satisfied.

(9) The court may permit the defence to require the prosecution to show that the second condition is satisfied without the prior service of a notice under subsection (8) above.

(10) In the Crown Court the question whether the second condition is satisfied shall be decided by the judge alone, and shall be treated as a question of law for the purposes of

    (a) section 9(3) of the Criminal Justice Act 1987 (preparatory hearing in fraud cases), and

    (b) section 31(3) of the Criminal Procedure and Investigations Act 1996 (preparatory hearing in other cases).

(11) Any act done by means of a message (however communicated) is to be treated for the purposes of the fourth condition as done in England and Wales if the message is sent or received in England and Wales.

(12) In any proceedings in respect of an offence triable by virtue of this section, it is immaterial to guilt whether or not the accused was a British citizen at the time of any act or other event proof of which is required for conviction of the offence.

(13) References in any enactment, instrument or document (except those in this Part of this Act) to an offence of conspiracy to commit an offence include an offence triable in England and Wales as such a conspiracy by virtue of this section (without prejudice to subsection (6) above).

(14) Nothing in this section

    (a) applies to an agreement entered into before the day on which the Criminal Justice (Terrorism and Conspiracy) Act 1998 was passed, or

    (b) imposes criminal liability on any person acting on behalf of, or holding office under, the Crown.

2   Exemptions from liability for conspiracy

(1) A person shall not by virtue of section 1 above be guilty of conspiracy to commit any offence if he is an intended victim of that offence.

(2) A person shall not by virtue of section 1 above be guilty of conspiracy to commit any offence or offences if the only other person or persons with whom he agrees are (both initially and at all times during the currency of the agreement) persons of any one or more of the following descriptions, that is to say –

    (a) his spouse or civil partner;

    (b) a person under the age of criminal responsibility; and

    (c) an intended victim of that offence or of each of those offences.

(3) A person is under the age of criminal responsibility for the purposes of subsection (2)(b) above so long as it is conclusively presumed, by virtue of section 50 of the Children and Young Persons Act 1933, that he cannot be guilty of any offence.

3   Penalties for conspiracy

(1) A person guilty by virtue of section 1 above of conspiracy to commit any offence or offences shall be liable on conviction on indictment –

    (a) in a case falling within subsection (2) or (3) below, to imprisonment for a term related in accordance with that subsection to the gravity of the offence or offences in question (referred to below in this section as the relevant offence or offences); and

    (b) in any other case, to a fine.

Paragraph (b) above shall not be taken as prejudicing the application of section 163 of the Criminal Justice Act 2003 (general power of court to fine offender convicted on indictment) in a case falling within subsection (2) or (3) below.

(2) Where the relevant offence or any of the relevant offences is an offence of any of the following descriptions, that is to say –

    (a) murder, or any other offence the sentence for which is fixed by law;

    (b) an offence for which a sentence extending to imprisonment for life is provided; or

    (c) an indictable offence punishable with imprisonment for which no maximum term of imprisonment is provided,

the person convicted shall be liable to imprisonment for life.

(3) Where in a case other than one to which subsection (2) above applies the relevant offence or any of the relevant offences is punishable with imprisonment, the person convicted shall be liable to imprisonment for a term not exceeding the maximum term provided for that offence or (where more than one such offence is in question) for any one of those offences (taking the longer or the longest term as the limit for the purposes of this section where the terms provided differ).

In the case of an offence triable either way the references above in this subsection to the maximum term provided for that offence are references to the maximum term so provided on conviction on indictment.

4   Restrictions on the institution of proceedings for conspiracy

(1) Subject to subsection (2) below proceedings under section 1 above for conspiracy to commit any offence or offences shall not be instituted against any person except by or with the consent of the Director of Public Prosecutions if the offence or (as the case may be) each of the offences in question is a summary offence.

(2) In relation to the institution of proceedings under section 1 above for conspiracy to commit –

    (a) an offence which is subject to a prohibition by or under any enactment on the institution of proceedings otherwise than by, or on behalf or with the consent of, the Attorney General, or

    (b) two or more offences of which at least one is subject to such a prohibition,

subsection (1) above shall have effect with the substitution of a reference to the Attorney General for the reference to the Director of Public Prosecutions.

(3) Any prohibition by or under any enactment on the institution of proceedings for any offence which is not a summary offence otherwise than by, or on behalf or with the consent of, the Director of Public Prosecutions or any other person shall apply also in relation to proceedings under section 1 above for conspiracy to commit that offence.

(4) Where –

    (a) an offence has been committed in pursuance of any agreement; and

    (b) proceedings may not be instituted for that offence because any time limit applicable to the institution of any such proceedings has expired,

proceedings under section 1 above for conspiracy to commit that offence shall not be instituted against any person on the basis of that agreement.

(5) Subject to subsection (6) below, no proceedings for an offence triable by virtue of section 1A above may be instituted except by or with the consent of the Attorney General.

(6) The Secretary of State may by order provide that subsection (5) above shall not apply, or shall not apply to any case of a description specified in the order. ...

5   Abolitions, savings, transitional provisions, consequential amendment and repeals

(1) Subject to the following provisions of this section, the offence of conspiracy at common law is hereby abolished.

(2) Subsection (1) above shall not affect the offence of conspiracy at common law so far as relates to conspiracy to defraud.

(3) Subsection (1) above shall not affect the offence of conspiracy at common law if and in so far as it may be committed by entering into an agreement to engage in conduct which –

    (a)   tends to corrupt public morals or outrages public decency; but

    (b)   would not amount to or involve the commission of an offence if carried out by a single person otherwise than in pursuance of an agreement. ...

(6) The rules laid down by sections 1 and 2 above shall apply for determining whether a person is guilty of an offence of conspiracy under any enactment other than section 1 above, but conduct which is an offence under any such other enactment shall not also be an offence under section 1 above.

(7) Incitement to commit the offence of conspiracy (whether the conspiracy incited would be an offence at common law or under section 1 above or any other enactment) shall cease to be offences.

(8) The fact that the person or persons who, so far as appears from the indictment on which any person has been convicted of conspiracy, were the only other parties to the agreement on which his conviction was based, have been acquitted of conspiracy by reference to that agreement (whether after being tried with the person convicted or separately) shall not be a ground for quashing his conviction unless under all the circumstances of the case his conviction is inconsistent with the acquittal of the other person or persons in question.

(9) Any rule of law or practice inconsistent with the provisions of subsection (8) above is hereby abolished. ...

6   Violence for securing entry

(1) Subject to the following provisions of this section, any person who, without lawful authority, uses or threatens violence for the purpose of securing entry into any premises for himself or for any other person is guilty of an offence, provided that –

    (a)   there is someone present on those premises at the time who is opposed to the entry which the violence is intended to secure; and

    (b)   the person using or threatening the violence knows that this is the case.

(1A) Subsection (1) above does not apply to a person who is a displaced residential occupier or a protected intending occupier of the premises in question or who is acting on behalf of such an occupier; and if the accused adduces sufficient evidence that he was, or was acting on behalf of, such an occupier he shall be presumed to be, or to be acting on behalf of, such an occupier unless the contrary is proved by the prosecution.

(2) Subject to subsection (1A) above, the fact that a person has any interest in or right to possession or occupation of any premises shall not for the purposes of subsection (1) above constitute lawful authority for the use or threat of violence by him or anyone else for the purpose of securing his entry into those premises.

(4) It is immaterial for the purposes of this section –

    (a) whether the violence in question is directed against the person or against property; and

    (b) whether the entry which the violence is intended to secure is for the purpose of acquiring possession of the premises in question or for any other purpose.

(5) A person guilty of an offence under this section shall be liable on summary conviction to imprisonment for a term not exceeding six months or to a fine not exceeding level 5 on the standard scale or to both.

(7) Section 12 below contains provisions which apply for determining when any person is to be regarded for the purposes of this Part of this Act as a displaced residential occupier of any premises or of any access to any premises and section 12A below contains provisions which apply for determining when any person is to be regarded for the purposes of this Part of this Act as a protected intending occupier of any premises or of any access to any premises.

7   Adverse occupation of residential premises

(1) Subject to the following provisions of this section and to section 12A(9) below, any person who is on any premises as a trespasser after having entered as such is guilty of an offence if he fails to leave those premises on being required to do so by or on behalf of –

    (a) a displaced residential occupier of the premises; or

    (b) an individual who is a protected intending occupier of the premises.

(2) In any proceedings for an offence under this section it shall be a defence for the accused to prove that he believed that the person requiring him to leave the premises was not a displaced residential occupier or protected intending occupier of the premises or a person acting on behalf of a displaced residential occupier or protected intending occupier.

(3) In any proceedings for an offence under this section it shall be a defence for the accused to prove –

    (a) that the premises in question are or form part of premises used mainly for non-residential purposes; and

    (b) hat he was not on any part of the premises used wholly or mainly for residential purposes.

(4) Any reference in the preceding provisions of this section to any premises includes a reference to any access to them, whether or not any such access itself constitutes premises, within the meaning of this Part of this Act.

(5) A person guilty of an offence under this section shall be liable on summary conviction to imprisonment for a term not exceeding six months or to a fine not exceeding level 5 on the standard scale or to both.

(7) Section 12 below contains provisions which apply for determining when any person is to be regarded for the purposes of this Part of this Act as a displaced residential occupier of any premises or of any access to any premises and section 12A below contains provisions which apply for determining when any person is to be regarded for the purposes of this Part of this Act as a protected intending occupier of any premises or of any access to any premises.

8   Trespassing with a weapon of offence

(1) A person who is on any premises as a trespasser, after having entered as such, is guilty of an offence if, without lawful authority or reasonable excuse, he has with him on the premises any weapon of offence.

(2) In subsection (1) above 'weapon of offence' means any article made or adapted for use for causing injury to or incapacitating a person, or intended by the person having it with him for such use.

(3) A person guilty of an offence under this section shall be liable on summary conviction to imprisonment for a term not exceeding three months or to a fine not exceeding level 5 on the standard scale or both.

12   Supplementary provisions

(1) In this Part of this Act –

    (a) 'premises' means any building, any part of a building under separate occupation, any land ancillary to a building, the site comprising any building or buildings together with any land ancillary thereto, and (for the purposes only of sections 10 and 11 above) any other place; and

    (b) 'access' means, in relation to any premises, any part of any site or building within which those premises are situated which constitutes an ordinary means of access to those premises (whether or not that is its sole or primary use).

(2) References in this section to a building shall apply also to any structure other than a movable one, and to any movable structure, vehicle or vessel designed or adapted for use for residential purposes; and for the purposes of subsection (1) above –

    (a) part of a building is under separate occupation if anyone is in occupation or entitled to occupation of that part as distinct from the whole; and

    (b) land is ancillary to a building if it is adjacent to it and used (or intended for use) in connection with the occupation of that building or any part of it.

(3) Subject to subsection (4) below, any person who was occupying any premises as a residence immediately before being excluded from occupation by anyone who entered those premises, or any access to those premises, as a trespasser is a displaced residential occupier of the premises for the purposes of this Part of this Act so long as he continues to be excluded from occupation of the premises by the original trespasser or by any subsequent trespasser.

(4) A person who was himself occupying the premises in question as a trespasser immediately before being excluded from occupation shall not by virtue of subsection (3) above be a displaced residential occupier of the premises for the purposes of this Part of this Act.

(5) A person who by virtue of subsection (3) above is a displaced residential occupier of any premises shall be regarded for the purposes of this Part of this Act as a displaced residential occupier also of any access to those premises.

(6) Anyone who enters or is on or in occupation of any premises by virtue of –

    (a) any title derived from a trespasser; or

    (b) any licence or consent given by a trespasser or by a person deriving title from a trespasser,

shall himself be treated as a trespasser for the purposes of this Part of this Act (without prejudice to whether or not he would be a trespasser apart from this provision); and references in this Part of this Act to a person's entering or being on or occupying any premises as a trespasser shall be construed accordingly.

(7) Anyone who is on any premises as a trespasser shall not cease to be a trespasser for the purposes of this Part of this Act by virtue of being allowed time to leave the premises, nor shall anyone cease to be a displaced residential occupier of any premises by virtue of any such allowance of time to a trespasser.

(8) No rule of law ousting the jurisdiction of magistrates' courts to try offences where a dispute of title to property is involved shall preclude magistrates' courts from trying offences under this Part of this Act.

12A Protected intending occupiers: supplementary provisions

(1) For the purposes of this Part of this Act an individual is a protected intending occupier of any premises at any time if at that time he falls within subsection (2), (4) or (6) below.

(2) An individual is a protected intending occupier of any premises if –

    (a) he has in those premises a freehold interest or a leasehold interest with not less than two years still to run;

    (b he requires the premises for his own occupation as a residence;

    (c) he is excluded from occupation of the premises by a person who entered them, or any access to them, as a trespasser; and

    (d) he or a person acting on his behalf holds a written statement –

        (i) which specifies his interest in the premises;

        (ii) which states that he requires the premises for occupation as a residence for himself; and

        (iii) with respect to which the requirements in subsection (3) below are fulfilled.

(3) The requirements referred to in subsection (2)(d)(iii) above are –

    (a) that the statement is signed by the person whose interest is specified in it in the presence of a justice of the peace or commissioner for oaths; and

    (b) that the justice of the peace or commissioner for oaths has subscribed his name as a witness to the signature.

(4) An individual is also a protected intending occupier of any premises if –

    (a) he has a tenancy of those premises (other than a tenancy falling within subsection (2)(a) above or (6)(a) below) or a licence to occupy those premises granted by a person with a freehold interest or a leasehold interest with not less than two years still to run in the premises;

    (b) he requires the premises for his own occupation as a residence;

    (c) he is excluded from occupation of the premises by a person who entered them, or any access to them, as a trespasser; and

    (d) he or a person acting on his behalf holds a written statement –

        (i) which states that he has been granted a tenancy of those premises or a licence to occupy those premises;

        (ii) which specifies the interest in the premises of the person who granted that tenancy or licence to occupy ('the landlord');

        (iii) which states that he requires the premises for occupation as a residence for himself; and

        (iv) ith respect to which the requirements in subsection (5) below are fulfilled.

(5) The requirements referred to in subsection (4)(d)(iv) above are –

    (a) that the statement is signed by the landlord and by the tenant or licensee in the presence of a justice of the peace or commissioner for oaths;

    (b) that the justice of the peace or commissioner for oaths has subscribed his name as a witness to the signatures.

(6) An individual is also a protected intending occupier of any premises if –

    (a) he has a tenancy of those premises (other than a tenancy falling within subsection (2)(a) or (4)(a) above) or a licence to occupy those premises granted by an authority to which this subsection applies;

    (b) he requires the premises for his own occupation as a residence;

    (c) he is excluded from occupation of the premises by a person who entered the premises, or any access to them, as a trespasser; and

(d)   there has been issued to him by or on behalf of the authority referred to in paragraph
      (a) above a certificate stating that –
      (i)   he has been granted a tenancy of those premises or a licence to occupy those
            premises as a residence by the authority; and
      (ii) the authority which granted that tenancy or licence to occupy is one to which this
            subsection applies, being of a description specified in the certificate.

(7) Subsection (6) above applies to the following authorities –

(a)   any body mentioned in section 14 of the Rent Act 1977 (landlord's interest belonging
      to local authority etc);
(b)   the Housing Corporation; and
(d)   a registered social landlord within the meaning of the Housing Act 1985 (see section
      5(4) and (5) of that Act).

(7A) Subsection (6) also applies to the Secretary of State if the tenancy or licence is granted by
him under Part III of the Housing Associations Act 1985.

(8) A person is guilty of an offence if he makes a statement for the purposes of subsection (2)(d)
or (4)(d) above which he knows to be false in a material particular or if he recklessly makes such
a statement which is false in a material particular.

(9) In any proceedings for an offence under section 7 of this Act where the accused was requested
to leave the premises by a person claiming to be or to act on behalf of a protected intending
occupier of the premises –

(a)   it shall be a defence for the accused to prove that, although asked to do so by the
       accused at the time the accused was requested to leave, that person failed at that time
       to produce to the accused such a statement as is referred to in subsection (2)(d) or
       (4)(d) above or such a certificate as is referred to in subsection (6)(d) above; and
(b)   any document purporting to be a certificate under subsection (6)(d) above shall be
       received in evidence and, unless the contrary is proved, shall be deemed to have been
       issued by or on behalf of the authority stated in the certificate.

(10) A person guilty of an offence under subsection (8) above shall be liable on summary
conviction to imprisonment for a term not exceeding six months or to a fine not exceeding level
5 on the standard scale or to both.

(11) A person who is a protected intending occupier of any premises shall be regarded for the
purposes of this Part of this Act as a protected intending occupier also of any access to those
premises.

51   Bomb hoaxes

(1) A person who –

(a)   places any article in any place whatever; or
(b)   dispatches any article by post, rail or any other means whatever of sending things from
      one place to another,

with the intention (in either case) of inducing in some other person a belief that it is likely to
explode or ignite and thereby cause personal injury or damage to property is guilty of an offence.
In this subsection 'article' includes substance.

(2) A person who communicates any information which he knows or believes to be false to
another person with the intention of inducing in him or any other person a false belief that a
bomb or other thing liable to explode or ignite is present in any place or location whatever is
guilty of an offence.

(3) For a person to be guilty of an offence under subsection (1) or (2) above it is not necessary

for him to have any particular person in mind as the person in whom he intends to induce the belief mentioned in that subsection.

(4) A person guilty of an offence under this section shall be liable –

    (a) on summary conviction, to imprisonment for a term not exceeding six months or to a fine not exceeding the prescribed sum, or both;

    (b) on conviction on indictment, to imprisonment for a term not exceeding seven years.

As amended by the Magistrates' Courts Act 1980, s32(2); Criminal Attempts Act 1981, ss5, 10, Schedule, Pt I; Criminal Justice Act 1982, ss38, 46; Housing (Consequential Provisions) Act 1985, s4, Schedule 2, para 36; Criminal Justice Act 1987, s12(2); Housing Act 1988, s140(1), Schedule 17, Part II, para 101; Computer Misuse Act 1990, s7(1)(2); Criminal Justice Act 1991, s26(4); Trade Union and Labour Relations (Consolidation) Act 1992, s300(1), Schedule 1; Criminal Justice Act 1993, s5(1); Criminal Justice and Public Order Act 1994, ss72, 73, 74, 168(3), Schedule 11; Housing Act 1996 (Consequential Provisions) Order 1996, art 5, Schedule 2, para 8; Government of Wales Act 1998, ss140(1), 152, Schedule 16, para 3, Schedule 18, Pt VI; Criminal Justice (Terrorism and Conspiracy) Act 1998, ss5, 9, Schedule 1, Pt II, para 4, Schedule 2, Pt II; Criminal Justice Act 2003, s304, Schedule 32, Pt 1, para 24; Civil Partnership Act 2004, s261(1), Schedule 27, para 56; Serious Organised Crime and Police Act 2005, s111, Schedule 7, para 19(1)–(4), Schedule 17, Pt 2.

THEFT ACT 1978
(1978 c 31)

3   Making off without payment

(1) Subject to subsection (3) below, a person who, knowing that payment on the spot for any goods supplied or service done is required or expected from him, dishonestly makes off without having paid as required or expected and with intent to avoid payment of the amount due shall be guilty of an offence.

(2) For purposes of this section 'payment on the spot' includes payment at the time of collecting goods on which work has been done or in respect of which service has been provided.

(3) Subsection (1) above shall not apply where the supply of the goods or the doing of the service is contrary to law, or where the service done is such that payment is not legally enforceable.

4   Punishments

(1) Offences under this Act shall be punishable either on conviction on indictment or on summary conviction.

(2) A person convicted on indictment shall be liable –

    (b) for an offence under section 3 of this Act, to imprisonment for a term not exceeding two years.

(3) A person convicted summarily of any offence under this Act shall be liable –

    (a) to imprisonment for a term not exceeding six months; or

    (b) to a fine not exceeding the prescribed sum for the purposes of section 32 of the Magistrates' Courts Act 1980 (punishment on summary conviction of offences triable either way: £5,000 or other sum substituted by order under that Act),

or to both.

5   Supplementary
(2) Sections 30(1) (husband and wife), 31(1) (effect on civil proceedings) and 34 (interpretation) of the Theft Act 1968, so far as they are applicable in relation to this Act, shall apply as they apply in relation to that Act. ...

As amended by the Magistrates' Courts Act 1980, s154(1), Schedule 7, para 170, Criminal Justice Act 1991, s17(2)(c); Theft (Amendment) Act 1996, s4(1); Serious Organised Crime and Police Act 2005, s111, Schedule 7, Pt 1, para 20, Schedule 17, Pt 2; Fraud Act 2006, s14(1), (3), Schedule 1, para 1(b), 14, 15, Schedule 3.

MAGISTRATES' COURTS ACT 1980
(1980 c 43)

32   Penalties on summary conviction for offences triable either way
(1) On summary conviction of any of the offences triable either way listed in Schedule 1 to this Act a person shall be liable to imprisonment for a term not exceeding six months or to a fine not exceeding the prescribed sum or both, except that –
   (a) a magistrates' court shall not have power to impose imprisonment for an offence so listed if the Crown Court would not have that power in the case of an adult convicted of it on indictment;
   (b) on summary conviction of an offence consisting in the incitement to commit an offence triable either way a person shall not be liable to any greater penalty than he would be liable to on summary conviction of the last-mentioned offence.
(2) For any offence triable either way which is not listed in Schedule 1 to this Act, being an offence under a relevant enactment, the maximum fine which may be imposed on summary conviction shall by virtue of this subsection be the prescribed sum unless the offence is one for which by virtue of an enactment other than this subsection a larger fine may be imposed on summary conviction.
(3) Where, by virtue of any relevant enactment, a person summarily convicted of an offence triable either way would, apart from this section, be liable to a maximum fine of one amount in the case of a first conviction and of a different amount in the case of a second or subsequent conviction, subsection (2) above shall apply irrespective of whether the conviction is a first, second or subsequent one.
(9) In this section –
   'fine' includes a pecuniary penalty but does not include a pecuniary forfeiture or pecuniary compensation;
   'the prescribed sum' means £5,000 or such sum as is for the time being substituted in this definition by an order in force under section 143(1) below;
   'relevant enactment' means an enactment contained in the Criminal Law Act 1977 or in any Act passed before, or in the same Session as, that Act.

[See Appendix, Criminal Justice Act 2003, s282(1).]

33   Maximum penalties on summary conviction in pursuance of section 22
(1) Where in pursuance of subsection (2) of section 22 above a magistrates' court proceeds to the summary trial of an information, then, if the accused is summarily convicted of the offence –
   (a) subject to subsection (3) below the court shall not have power to impose on him in respect of that offence imprisonment for more than three months or a fine greater than level 4 on the standard scale; and

(b) section 3 of the Powers of Criminal Courts (Sentencing) Act 2000 (committal to
Crown Court for sentencing) shall not apply as regards that offence.

(2) In subsection (1) above 'fine' includes a pecuniary penalty but does not include a pecuniary
forfeiture or pecuniary compensation.

(3) Paragraph (a) of subsection (1) above does not apply to an offence under section 12A of the
Theft Act 1968 (aggravated vehicle-taking).

[See Appendix, Criminal Justice Act 2003, Schedule 3, paras 1, 13, Schedule 32, Pt 1, paras 25,
27, Schedule 37, Pt 4.]

44   Aiders and abettors

(1) A person who aids, abets, counsels or procures the commission by another person of a
summary offence shall be guilty of the like offence and may be tried (whether or not he is charged
as a principal) either by a court having jurisdiction to try that other person or by a court having
by virtue of his own offence jurisdiction to try him.

(2) Any offence consisting in aiding, abetting, counselling or procuring the commission of an
offence triable either way (other than an offence listed in Schedule 1 to this Act) shall by virtue
of this subsection be triable either way.

45   Incitement

(1) Any offence consisting in the incitement to commit a summary offence shall be triable only
summarily.

(2) Subsection (1) above is without prejudice to any other enactment by virtue of which any
offence is triable only summarily.

(3) On conviction of an offence consisting in the incitement to commit a summary offence a
person shall be liable to the same penalties as he would be liable to on conviction of the last-
mentioned offence.

132   Minimum term

A magistrates' court shall not impose imprisonment for less than 5 days.

*As amended by the Criminal Justice Act 1991, ss17(2)(a), (b), (c), 68, 101(2), Schedule 4, Pt II, Schedule
8, para 6(1)(c), Schedule 13; Aggravated Vehicle-Taking Act 1992, s2(3); Powers of Criminal Courts
(Sentencing) Act 2000, s165(1), Schedule 9, para 65.*

HIGHWAYS ACT 1980

(1980 c 66)

131   Penalty for damaging highway, etc

(1) If a person, without lawful authority or excuse –

(a) makes a ditch or excavation in a highway which consists of or comprises a carriageway, or

(b) removes any soil or turf from any part of a highway, except for the purpose of improving
the highway and with the consent of the highway authority for the highway, or

(c) deposits anything whatsoever on a highway so as to damage the highway, or

(d) lights any fire, or discharges any firearm or firework, within 50 feet from the centre of
a highway which consists of or comprises a carriageway, and in consequence thereof
the highway is damaged,

he is guilty of an offence.

(2) If a person without lawful authority or excuse pulls down or obliterates a traffic sign placed on or over a highway, or a milestone or direction post (not being a traffic sign) so placed, he is guilty of an offence; but it is a defence in any proceedings under this subsection to show that the traffic sign, milestone or post was not lawfully so placed.

(3) A person guilty of an offence under this section is liable to a fine not exceeding level 3 on the standard scale.

131A   Disturbance of surface of certain highways

(1) A person who, without lawful authority or excuse, so disturbs the surface of –

    (a) a footpath,

    (b) a bridleway, or

    (c) any other highway which consists of or comprises a carriageway other than a made-up carriageway,

as to render it inconvenient for the exercise of the public right of way is guilty of an offence and liable to a fine not exceeding level 3 on the standard scale.

(2) Proceedings for an offence under this section shall be brought only by the highway authority or the council of the non-metropolitan district, parish or community in which the offence is committed; and, without prejudice to section 130 (protection of public rights) above, it is the duty of the highway authority to ensure that where desirable in the public interest such proceedings are brought.

132   Unauthorised marks on highways

(1) A person who, without either the consent of the highway authority for the highway in question or an authorisation given by or under an enactment or a reasonable excuse, paints or otherwise inscribes or affixes any picture, letter, sign or other mark upon the surface of a highway or upon any tree, structure or works on or in a highway is guilty of an offence and liable to a fine not exceeding level 4 on the standard scale.

(2) The highway authority for a highway may, without prejudice to their powers apart from this subsection and whether or not proceedings in respect of the matter have been taken in pursuance of subsection (1) above, remove any picture, letter, sign or other mark which has, without either the consent of the authority or an authorisation given by or under an enactment, been painted or otherwise inscribed or affixed upon the surface of the highway or upon any tree, structure or works on or in the highway.

137   Penalty for wilful obstruction

(1) If a person, without lawful authority or excuse, in any way wilfully obstructs the free passage along a highway he is guilty of an offence and liable to a fine not exceeding level 3 on the standard scale.

138   Penalty for erecting building, etc in highway

If a person, without lawful authority or excuse, erects a building or fence, or plants a hedge, in a highway which consists of or comprises a carriageway he is guilty of an offence and liable to a fine not exceeding level 3 on the standard scale.

148   Penalty for depositing things or pitching booths, etc on highway

If, without lawful authority or excuse –

    (a) a person deposits on a made-up carriageway any dung, compost or other material for dressing land, or any rubbish, or

    (b) a person deposits on any highway that consists of or comprises a made-up carriageway any dung, compost or other material for dressing land, or any rubbish, within 15 feet from the centre of that carriageway, or

(c)   a person deposits any thing whatsoever on a highway to the interruption of any user of the highway, or

(d)   a hawker or other itinerant trader pitches a booth, stall or stand, or encamps, on a highway,

he is guilty of an offence and liable to a fine not exceeding level 3 of the standard scale.

155   Penalties in connection with straying animals

(1) If any horses, cattle, sheep, goats or swine are at any time found straying or lying on or at the side of a highway their keeper is guilty of an offence; but this subsection does not apply in relation to a part of a highway passing over any common, waste or unenclosed ground. In this section 'keeper', in relation to any animals, means a person in whose possession they are.

(2) A person guilty of an offence under this section is liable to a fine not exceeding level 3 on the standard scale.

(3) A person guilty of an offence under this section is also liable to pay the reasonable expenses of removing any animal so found straying or lying to the premises of their keeper, or to the common pound, or to such other place as may have been provided for the purpose, and any person who incurs such expenses is entitled to recover them summarily as a civil debt. For the purposes of this subsection 'expenses', in a case where an animal has been removed to the common pound, includes the usual fees and charges of the authorised keeper of the pound.

(4) If a person, without lawful authority or excuse, releases any animal seized for the purpose of being impounded under this section from the pound or other place where it is impounded, or on the way to or from any such place, or damages any such place, he is guilty of an offence and liable to a fine not exceeding level 2 on the standard scale.

(5) Nothing in this section prejudices or affects any right of pasture on the side of a highway.

161   Penalties for causing certain kinds of danger or annoyance

(1) If a person, without lawful authority or excuse, deposits any thing whatsoever on a highway in consequence of which a user of the highway is injured or endangered, that person is guilty of an offence and liable to a fine not exceeding level 3 on the standard scale.

(2) If a person, without lawful authority or excuse –

(a)   lights any fire on or over a highway which consists of or comprises a carriageway; or

(b)   discharges any firearm or firework within 50 feet of the centre of such a highway,

and in consequence a user of the highway is injured, interrupted or endangered, that person is guilty of an offence and liable to a fine not exceeding level 3 on the standard scale.

(3) If a person plays at football or any other game on a highway to the annoyance of a user of the highway he is guilty of an offence and liable to a fine not exceeding level 1 on the standard scale.

(4) If a person, without lawful authority or excuse, allows any filth, dirt, lime or other offensive matter or thing to run or flow on to a highway from any adjoining premises, he is guilty of an offence and liable to a fine not exceeding level 1 on the standard scale.

161A   Danger or annoyance caused by fires lit otherwise than on highways

(1) If a person –

(a)   lights a fire on any land not forming part of a highway which consists of or comprises a carriageway; or

(b)   directs or permits a fire to be lit on any such land,

and in consequence a user of any highway which consists of or comprises a carriageway is injured, interrupted or endangered by, or by smoke from, that fire or any other fire caused by that fire, that person is guilty of an offence and liable to a fine not exceeding level 5 on the standard scale.

(2) In any proceedings for an offence under this section it shall be a defence for the accused to prove –

- (a) that at the time the fire was lit he was satisfied on reasonable grounds that it was unlikely that users of any highway consisting of or comprising a carriageway would be injured, interrupted or endangered by, or by smoke from, that fire or any other fire caused by that fire; and
- (b) either –
  - (i) that both before and after the fire was lit he did all he reasonably could to prevent users of any such highway from being so injured, interrupted or endangered, or
  - (ii) that he had a reasonable excuse for not doing so.

162 Penalty for placing rope, etc across highway

A person who for any purpose places any rope, wire or other apparatus across a highway in such a manner as to be likely to cause danger to persons using the highway is, unless he proves that he had taken all necessary means to give adequate warning of the danger, guilty of an offence and liable to a fine not exceeding level 3 on the standard scale.

163 Prevention of water falling on or flowing on to highway

(1) A competent authority may, by notice to the occupier of premises adjoining a highway, require him within 28 days from the date of service of the notice to construct or erect and thereafter to maintain such channels, gutters or downpipes as may be necessary to prevent –

- (a) water from the roof or any other part of the premises falling upon persons using the highway, or
- (b) so far as is reasonably practicable, surface water from the premises flowing on to, or over, the footway of the highway.

For the purposes of this section the competent authorities, in relation to any highway, are the highway authority and also (where they are not the highway authority) the local authority for the area in which the highway is situated.

(2) A notice under subsection (1) above may, at the option of the authority, be served on the owner of the premises in question instead of on the occupier or may be served on both the owner and the occupier of the premises.

(3) A person aggrieved by a requirement under this section may appeal to a magistrates' court.

(4) Subject to any order made on appeal, if a person on whom a notice is served under this section fails to comply with the requirement of the notice within the period specified in subsection (1) above he is guilty of an offence and liable to a fine not exceeding level 1 on the standard scale; and if the offence is continued after conviction he is guilty of a further offence and liable to a fine not exceeding £2 for each day on which the offence is so continued.

As amended by the Criminal Justice Act 1982, ss38, 46; Highways (Amendment) Act 1986, s1(2)(3); Rights of Way Act 1990, s1(2).

FORGERY AND COUNTERFEITING ACT 1981
(1981 c 45)

PART I

1   The offence of forgery
A person is guilty of forgery if he makes a false instrument, with the intention that he or another shall use it to induce somebody to accept it as genuine, and by reason of so accepting it to do or not to do some act to his own or any other person's prejudice.

2   The offence of copying a false instrument
It is an offence for a person to make a copy of an instrument which is, and which he knows or believes to be, a false instrument, with the intention that he or another shall use it to induce somebody to accept it as a copy of a genuine instrument, and by reason of so accepting it to do or not to do some act to his own or any other person's prejudice.

3   The offence of using a false instrument
It is an offence for a person to use an instrument which is, and which he knows or believes to be, false, with the intention of inducing somebody to accept it as genuine, and by reason of so accepting it to do or not to do some act to his own or any other person's prejudice.

4   The offence of using a copy of a false instrument
It is an offence for a person to use a copy of an instrument which is, and which he knows or believes to be, a false instrument, with the intention of inducing somebody to accept it as a copy of a genuine instrument, and by reason of so accepting it to do or not to do some act to his own or any other person's prejudice.

5   Offences relating to money orders, share certificates, passports, etc
(1) It is an offence for a person to have in his custody or under his control an instrument to which this section applies which is, and which he knows or believes to be, false, with the intention that he or another shall use it to induce somebody to accept it as genuine, and by reason of so accepting it to do or not to do some act to his own or any other person's prejudice.
(2) It is an offence for a person to have in his custody or under his control, without lawful authority or excuse, an instrument to which this section applies which is, and which he knows or believes to be, false.
(3) It is an offence for a person to make or to have in his custody or under his control a machine or implement, or paper or any other material, which to his knowledge is or has been specially designed or adapted for the making of an instrument to which this section applies, with the intention that he or another shall make an instrument to which this section applies which is false and that he or another shall use the instrument to induce somebody to accept it as genuine, and by reason of so accepting it to do or not to do some act to his own or any other person's prejudice.
(4) It is an offence for a person to make or to have in his custody or under his control any such machine, implement, paper or material, without lawful authority or excuse.
(5) The instruments to which this section applies are –
    (a)   money orders;
    (b)   postal orders;
    (c)   United Kingdom postage stamps;
    (d)   Inland Revenue stamps;

(e)   share certificates;

(g)   cheques and other bills of exchange;

(h)   travellers' cheques;

(ha) bankers' drafts;

(hb) promissory notes;

(j)   cheque cards;

(ja) debit cards;

(k)   credit cards;

(l)   certified copies relating to an entry in a register of births, adoptions, marriages, civil partnerships or deaths and issued by the Registrar General, the Registrar General for Northern Ireland, a registration officer or a person lawfully authorised to issue certified copies relating to such entries; and

(m)   certificates relating to entries in such registers.

(6) In subsection (5)(e) above 'share certificate' means an instrument entitling or evidencing the title of a person to a share or interest –

(a)   in any public stock, annuity, fund or debt of any government or state, including a state which forms part of another state; or

(b)   in any stock, fund or debt of a body (whether corporate or unincorporated) established in the United Kingdom or elsewhere.

(7) An instrument is also an instrument to which this section applies if it is a monetary instrument specified for the purposes of this section by an order made by the Secretary of State. …

6   Penalties for offences under Part I

(1) A person guilty of an offence under this Part of this Act shall be liable on summary conviction –

(a)   to a fine not exceeding the statutory maximum; or

(b)   to imprisonment for a term not exceeding six months; or

(c)   to both.

(2) A person guilty of an offence to which this subsection applies shall be liable on conviction on indictment to imprisonment for a term not exceeding ten years.

(3) The offences to which subsection (2) above applies are offences under the following provisions of this Part of this Act –

(a)   section 1;

(b)   section 2;

(c)   section 3;

(d)   section 5;

(e)   section 5(1); and

(f)   section 5(3).

(4) A person guilty of an offence under section 5(2) or (4) above shall be liable on conviction on indictment to imprisonment for a term not exceeding two years.

8   Meaning of 'instrument'

(1) Subject to subsection (2) below, in this Part of this Act 'instrument' means –

(a)   any document, whether of a formal or informal character;

(b)   any stamp issued or sold by a postal operator;

(c)   any Inland Revenue stamp; and

(d)   any disc, tape, sound track or other device on or in which information is recorded or stored by mechanical, electronic or other means.

(2) A currency note within the meaning of Part II of this Act is not an instrument for the purposes of this Part of this Act.

(3) A mark denoting payment of postage which a postal operator authorises to be used instead of an adhesive stamp is to be treated for the purposes of this Part of this Act as if it were a stamp issued by the postal operator concerned.

(3A) In this section 'postal operator' has the same meaning as in the Postal Services Act 2000.

(4) In this Part of this Act 'Inland Revenue stamp' means a stamp as defined in section 27 of the Stamp Duties Management Act 1891.

9   Meaning of 'false' and 'making'

(1) An instrument is false for the purposes of this Part of this Act –

    (a) if it purports to have been made in the form in which it is made by a person who did not in fact make it in that form; or

    (b) if it purports to have been made in the form in which it is made on the authority of a person who did not in fact authorise its making in that form; or

    (c) if it purports to have been made in the terms in which it is made by a person who did not in fact make it in those terms; or

    (d) if it purports to have been made in the terms in which it is made on the authority of a person who did not in fact authorise its making in those terms; or

    (e) if it purports to have been altered in any respect by a person who did not in fact alter it in that respect; or

    (f) if it purports to have been altered in any respect on the authority of a person who did not in fact authorise the alteration in that respect; or

    (g) if it purports to have been made or altered on a date on which, or at a place at which, or otherwise in circumstances in which, it was not in fact made or altered; or

    (h) if it purports to have been made or altered by an existing person but he did not in fact exist.

(2) A person is to be treated for the purposes of this Part of this Act as making a false instrument if he alters an instrument so as to make it false in any respect (whether or not it is false in some other respect apart from that alteration).

10   Meaning of 'prejudice' and 'induce'

(1) Subject to subsections (2) and (4) below, for the purposes of this Part of this Act an act or omission intended to be induced is to a person's prejudice if, and only if, it is one which, if it occurs –

    (a) will result –

        (i) in his temporary or permanent loss of property; or

        (ii) in his being deprived of an opportunity to earn remuneration or greater remuneration; or

        (iii) in his being deprived of an opportunity to gain a financial advantage otherwise than by way of remuneration; or

    (b) will result in somebody being given an opportunity –

        (i) to earn remuneration or greater remuneration from him; or

        (ii) to gain a financial advantage from him otherwise than by way of remuneration; or

    (c) will be the result of his having accepted a false instrument as genuine, or a copy of a false instrument as a copy of a genuine one, in connection with his performance of any duty.

(2) An act which a person has an enforceable duty to do and an omission to do an act which a person is not entitled to do shall be disregarded for the purposes of this Part of this Act.

(3) In this Part of this Act references to inducing somebody to accept a false instrument as genuine, or a copy of a false instrument as a copy of a genuine one, include references to inducing a machine to respond to the instrument or copy as if it were a genuine instrument or, as the case may be, a copy of a genuine one.

(4) Where subsection (3) above applies, the act or omission intended to be induced by the machine responding to the instrument or copy shall be treated as an act or omission to a person's prejudice.

(5) In this section 'loss' includes not getting what one might get as well as parting with what one has.

13   Abolition of offence of forgery at common law

The offence of forgery at common law is hereby abolished for all purposes not relating to offences committed before the commencement of this Act.

PART II

14   Offences of counterfeiting notes and coins

(1) It is an offence for a person to make a counterfeit of a currency note or of a protected coin, intending that he or another shall pass or tender it as genuine.

(2) It is an offence for a person to make a counterfeit of a currency note or of a protected coin without lawful authority or excuse.

15   Offences of passing, etc counterfeit notes and coins

(1) It is an offence for a person –

  (a) to pass or tender as genuine any thing which is, and which he knows or believes to be, a counterfeit of a currency note or of a protected coin; or

  (b) to deliver to another any thing which is, and which he knows or believes to be, such a counterfeit, intending that the person to whom it is delivered or another shall pass or tender it as genuine.

(2) It is an offence for a person to deliver to another, without lawful authority or excuse, any thing which is, and which he knows or believes to be, a counterfeit of a currency note or of a protected coin.

16   Offences involving the custody or control of counterfeit notes and coins

(1) It is an offence for a person to have in his custody or under his control any thing which is, and which he knows or believes to be, a counterfeit of a currency note or of a protected coin, intending either to pass or tender it as genuine or to deliver it to another with the intention that he or another shall pass or tender it as genuine.

(2) It is an offence for a person to have in his custody or under his control, without lawful authority or excuse, any thing which is, and which he knows or believes to be, a counterfeit of a currency note or of a protected coin.

(3) It is immaterial for the purposes of subsections (1) and (2) above that a coin or note is not in a fit state to be passed or tendered or that the making or counterfeiting of a coin or note has not been finished or perfected.

17 Offences involving the making or custody or control of counterfeiting materials and implements

(1) It is an offence for a person to make, or to have in his custody or under his control, any thing which he intends to use, or to permit any other person to use, for the purpose of making a counterfeit of a currency note or of a protected coin with the intention that it be passed or tendered as genuine.

(2) It is an offence for a person without lawful authority or excuse –

(a) to make; or

(b) to have in his custody or under his control,

any thing which, to his knowledge, is or has been specially designed or adapted for the making of a counterfeit of a currency note.

(3) Subject to subsection (4) below, it is an offence for a person to make, or to have in his custody or under his control, any implement which, to his knowledge, is capable of imparting to any thing a resemblance –

(a) to the whole or part of either side of a protected coin; or

(b) to the whole or part of the reverse of the image on either side of a protected coin.

(4) It shall be defence for a person charged with an offence under subsection (3) above to show –

(a) that he made the implement or, as the case may be, had it in his custody or under his control, with the written consent of the Treasury; or

(b) that he had lawful authority otherwise than by virtue of paragraph (a) above, or a lawful excuse, for making it or having it in his custody or under his control.

18 The offence of reproducing British currency notes

(1) It is an offence for any person, unless the relevant authority has previously consented in writing, to reproduce on any substance whatsoever, and whether or not on the correct scale, any British currency note or any part of a British currency note.

(2) In this section –

'British currency note' means any note which –

(a) has been lawfully issued in England and Wales, Scotland or Northern Ireland; and

(b) is or has been customarily used as money in the country where it was issued; and

(c) is payable on demand; and

'the relevant authority', in relation to a British currency note of any particular description, means the authority empowered by law to issue notes of that description.

19 Offences of making, etc imitation British coins

(1) It is an offence for a person –

(a) to make an imitation British coin in connection with a scheme intended to promote the sale of any product or the making of contracts for the supply of any service; or

(b) to sell or distribute imitation British coins in connection with any such scheme, or to have imitation British coins in his custody or under his control with a view to such sale or distribution,

unless the Treasury have previously consented in writing to the sale or distribution of such imitation British coins in connection with that scheme.

(2) In this section –

'British coin' means any coin which is legal tender in any part of the United Kingdom; and

'imitation British coin' means any thing which resembles a British coin in shape, size and the substance of which it is made.

20   Prohibition of importation of counterfeit notes and coins
The importation, landing or unloading of a counterfeit of a currency note or of a protected coin without the consent of the Treasury is hereby prohibited.

21   Prohibition of exportation of counterfeit notes and coins
(1) The exportation of a counterfeit of a currency note or of a protected coin without the consent of the Treasury is hereby prohibited.

(2) A counterfeit of a currency note or of a protected coin which is removed to the Isle of Man from the United Kingdom shall be deemed to be exported from the United Kingdom –
  (a) for the purposes of this section; and
  (b) for the purposes of the customs and excise Acts, in their application to the prohibition imposed by this section. ...

22   Penalties for offences under Part II
(1) A person guilty of an offence to which this subsection applies shall be liable –
  (a) on summary conviction –
      (i)   to a fine not exceeding the statutory maximum; or
      (ii) to imprisonment for a term not exceeding six months; or
      (iii) to both; or
  (b) on conviction on indictment –
      (i)   to a fine; or
      (ii) to imprisonment for a term not exceeding ten years; or
      (iii) to both.

(2) The offences to which subsection (1) above applies are offences under the following provisions of this Part of this Act –
  (a) section 14(1);
  (b) section 15(1);
  (c) section 16(1); and
  (d) section 17(1).

(3) A person guilty of an offence to which this subsection applies shall be liable –
  (a) on summary conviction –
      (i)   to a fine not exceeding the statutory maximum; or
      (ii) to imprisonment for a term not exceeding six months; or
      (iii) to both; and
  (b) on conviction on indictment –
      (i)   to a fine; or
      (ii) to imprisonment for a term not exceeding two years; or
      (iii) to both.

(4) The offences to which subsection (3) above applies are offences under the following provisions of this Part of this Act –
  (a) section 14(2);
  (b) section 15(2);
  (c) section 16(2);
  (d) section 17(2); and
  (e) section 17(3).

(5) A person guilty of an offence under section 18 or 19 above shall be liable –
  (a) on summary conviction, to a fine not exceeding the statutory maximum; and
  (b) on conviction on indictment, to a fine.

27   Meaning of 'currency note' and 'protected coin'

(1) In this Part of this Act –

'currency note' means –

(a) any note which –

(i) has been lawfully issued in England and Wales, Scotland, Northern Ireland, any of the Channel Islands, the Isle of Man or the Republic of Ireland; and

(ii) is or has been customarily used as money in the country where it was issued; and

(iii) is payable on demand; or

(b) any note which –

(i) has been lawfully issued in some country other than those mentioned in paragraph (a)(i) above; and

(ii) is customarily used as money in that country; and

'protected coin' means any coin which –

(a) is customarily used as money in any country; or

(b) is specified in an order made by the Treasury for the purposes of this Part of this Act.

(2) The power to make an order conferred on the Treasury by subsection (1) above shall be exercisable by statutory instrument.

(3) A statutory instrument containing such an order shall be laid before Parliament after being made.

28   Meaning of 'counterfeit'

(1) For the purposes of this Part of this Act a thing is a counterfeit of a currency note or of a protected coin –

(a) if it is not a currency note or a protected coin but resembles a currency note or protected coin (whether on one side only or on both) to such an extent that it is reasonably capable of passing for a currency note or protected coin of that description; or

(b) if it is a currency note or protected coin which has been so altered that it is reasonably capable of passing for a currency note or protected coin of some other description.

(2) For the purposes of this Part of this Act –

(a) a thing consisting of one side only of a currency note, with or without the addition of other material, is a counterfeit of such a note;

(b) a thing consisting –

(i) of parts of two or more currency notes; or

(ii) of parts of a currency note, or of parts of two or more currency notes, with the addition of other material,

is capable of being a counterfeit of a currency note.

(3) References in this Part of this Act to passing or tendering a counterfeit of a currency note or a protected coin are not to be construed as confined to passing or tendering it as legal tender.

As amended by the Fines and Penalties (Northern Ireland) Order 1984, art 19(1), Schedule 6, paras 20, 21, Schedule 7; Criminal Justice Act 1991, s17(2)(c); Statute Law (Repeals) Act 1993; Postal Services Act 2000 (Consequential Modifications No 1) Order 2001, art 3(1), Schedule 1, para 50; Crime (International Co-operation) Act 2003, s88; Civil Partnership Act 2004, s261(1), Schedule 27, para 67; Asylum and Immigration (Treatment of Claimants, etc) Act 2004, s3(1), (3); Identity Cards Act 2006, s44(2), Schedule 2.

CRIMINAL ATTEMPTS ACT 1981
(1981 c 47)

1   Attempting to commit an offence

(1) If, with intent to commit an offence to which this section applies, a person does an act which is more than merely preparatory to the commission of the offence, he is guilty of attempting to commit the offence.

(1A) Subject to section 8 of the Computer Misuse Act 1990 (relevance of external law), if this subsection applies to an act, what the person doing it had in view shall be treated as an offence to which this section applies.

(1B) Subsection (1A) above applies to an act if –

   (a) it is done in England and Wales; and

   (b) it would fall within subsection (1) above as more than merely preparatory to the commission of an offence under section 3 of the Computer Misuse Act 1990 but for the fact that the offence, if completed, would not be an offence triable in England and Wales.

(2) A person may be guilty of attempting to commit an offence to which this section applies even though the facts are such that the commission of the offence is impossible.

(3) In any case where –

   (a) apart from this subsection a person's intention would not be regarded as having amounted to an intent to commit an offence; but

   (b) if the facts of the case had been as he believed them to be, his intention would be so regarded,

then, for the purposes of subsection (1) above, he shall be regarded as having had an intent to commit that offence.

(4) This section applies to any offence which, if it were completed, would be triable in England and Wales as an indictable offence, other than –

   (a) conspiracy (at common law or under section 1 of the Criminal Law Act 1977 or any other enactment);

   (b) aiding, abetting, counselling, procuring or suborning the commission of an offence;

   (c) offences under section 4(1) (assisting offenders) or 5(1) (accepting or agreeing to accept consideration for not disclosing information about an arrestable offence) of the Criminal law Act 1967.

1A   Extended jurisdiction in relation to certain attempts

(1) If this section applies to an act, what the person doing the act had in view shall be treated as an offence to which section 1(1) above applies.

(2) This section applies to an act if –

   (a)   it is done in England and Wales, and

   (b) it would fall within section 1(1) above as more than merely preparatory to the commission of a Group A offence but for the fact that that offence, if completed, would not be an offence triable in England and Wales.

(3) In this section 'Group A offence' has the same meaning as in Part I of the Criminal Justice Act 1993.

(4) Subsection (1) above is subject to the provisions of section 6 of the Act of 1993 (relevance of external law).

(5) Where a person does any act to which this section applies, the offence which he commits shall for all purposes be treated as the offence of attempting to commit the relevant Group A offence.

2   Application of procedural and other provisions to offences under s1

(1) Any provision to which this section applies shall have effect with respect to an offence under section 1 above of attempting to commit an offence as it has effect with respect to the offence attempted.

(2) This section applies to provisions of any of the following descriptions made by or under any enactment (whenever passed) –

(a)   provisions whereby proceedings may not be instituted or carried on otherwise than by, or on behalf or with the consent of, any person (including any provisions which also make other exceptions to the prohibition);

(b)   provisions conferring power to institute proceedings;

(c)   provisions as to the venue of proceedings;

(d)   provisions whereby proceedings may not be instituted after the expiration of a time limit;

(e)   provisions conferring a power of arrest or search;

(f)   provisions conferring a power of seizure and detention of property;

(g)   provisions whereby a person may not be convicted or committed for trial on the uncorroborated evidence of one witness (including any provision requiring the evidence of not less than two credible witnesses);

(h)   provisions conferring a power of forfeiture, including any power to deal with anything liable to be forfeited;

(i)   provisions whereby, if an offence committed by a body corporate is proved to have been committed with the consent or connivance of another person, that person also is guilty of the offence.

[See Appendix, Criminal Justice Act 2003, Schedule 3, para 52, Schedule 37, Pt 4.]

3   Offences of attempt under other enactments

(1) Subsections (2) to (5) below shall have effect, subject to subsection (6) below and to any inconsistent provision in any other enactment, for the purpose of determining whether a person is guilty of an attempt under a special statutory provision.

(2) For the purposes of this Act an attempt under a special statutory provision is an offence which –

(a)   is created by an enactment other than section 1 above, including an enactment passed after this Act; and

(b)   is expressed as an offence of attempting to commit another offence (in this section referred to as 'the relevant full offence').

(3) A person is guilty of an attempt under a special statutory provision if, with intent to commit the relevant full offence, he does an act which is more than merely preparatory to the commission of that offence.

(4) A person may be guilty of an attempt under a special statutory provision even though the facts are such that the commission of the relevant full offence is impossible.

(5) In any case where –

(a)   apart from this subsection a person's intention would not be regarded as having amounted to an intent to commit the relevant full offence; but

(b)   if the facts of the case had been as he believed them to be, his intention would be so regarded,

then, for the purposes of subsection (3) above, he shall be regarded as having had an intent to commit that offence.

(6) Subsections (2) to (5) above shall not have effect in relation to an act done before the commencement of this Act.

4   Trial and penalties

(1) A person guilty by virtue of section 1 above of attempting to commit an offence shall –

    (a) if the offence attempted is murder or any other offence the sentence for which is fixed by law, be liable on conviction on indictment to imprisonment for life; and

    (b) if the offence attempted is indictable but does not fall within paragraph (a) above, be liable on conviction on indictment to any penalty to which he would have been liable on conviction on indictment of that offence; and

    (c) if the offence attempted is triable either way, be liable on summary conviction to any penalty to which he would have been liable on summary conviction of that offence.

(2) In any case in which a court may proceed to summary trial of an information charging a person with an offence and an information charging him with an offence under section 1 above of attempting to commit it or an attempt under a special statutory provision, the court may, without his consent, try the informations together.

(3) Where, in proceedings against a person for an offence under section 1 above, there is evidence sufficient in law to support a finding that he did not act falling within subsection (1) of that section, the question whether or not this act fell within that subsection is a question of fact.

(4) Where, in proceedings against a person for an attempt under a special statutory provision, there is evidence sufficient in law to support a finding that he did an act falling within subsection (3) of section 3 above, the question whether or not his act fell within that subsection is a question of fact.

(5) Subsection (1) above shall have effect –

    (b) notwithstanding anything –

        (i) in section 32(1) (no limit to fine on conviction on indictment) of the Criminal Law Act 1977; or

        (ii) in section 78(1) and (2) (maximum of six months' imprisonment on summary conviction unless express provision made to the contrary) of the Powers of Criminal Courts (Sentencing) Act 2000.

[See Appendix, Criminal Justice Act 2003, Schedule 23, Pt 1, para 33.]

6   Effect of Part I on common law

(1) The offence of attempt at common law and any offence at common law of procuring materials for crime are hereby abolished for all purposes not relating to acts done before the commencement of this Act.

(2) Except as regards offences committed before the commencement of this Act, references in any enactment passed before this Act which fall to be construed as references to the offence of attempt at common law shall be construed as references to the offence under section 1 above.

8   Abolition of offence of loitering, etc with intent

The provisions of section 4 of the Vagrancy Act 1824 which apply to suspected persons and reputed thieves frequenting or loitering about the places described in that section with the intent there specified shall cease to have effect.

9   Interference with vehicles

(1) A person is guilty of the offence of vehicle interference if he interferes with a motor vehicle or trailer or with anything carried in or on a motor vehicle or trailer with the intention that an offence specified in subsection (2) below shall be committed by himself or some other person.

(2) The offences mentioned in subsection (1) above are –
- (a) theft of the motor vehicle or trailer or part of it;
- (b) theft of anything carried in or on the motor vehicle or trailer; and
- (c) an offence under section 12(1) of the Theft Act 1968 (taking and driving away without consent);

and, if it is shown that a person accused of an offence under this section intended that one of those offences should be committed, it is immaterial that it cannot be shown which it was.

(3) A person guilty of an offence under this section shall be liable on summary conviction to imprisonment for a term not exceeding three months or to a fine not exceeding level 4 on the standard scale or to both.

(5) In this section 'motor vehicle' and 'trailer' have the meanings assigned to them by section 185(1) of the Road Traffic Act 1988.

[See Appendix, Criminal Justice Act 2003, Schedule 26, para 28.]

As amended by the Criminal Justice Act 1982, ss38, 46; Road Traffic (Consequential Provisions) Act 1988, s4, Schedule 3, para 23; Computer Misuse Act 1990, s7(3); Criminal Justice Act 1993, s5(2); Powers of Criminal Courts (Sentencing) Act 2000, s165(1), Schedule 9, para 62; Sexual Offences Act 2003, s140, Schedule 7.

TAKING OF HOSTAGES ACT 1982
(1982 c 28)

1   Hostage-taking

(1) A person, whatever his nationality, who, in the United Kingdom or elsewhere, –
- (a) detains any other person ('the hostage'), and
- (b) in order to compel a State, international governmental organisation or person to do or abstain from doing any act, threatens to kill, injure or continue to detain the hostage,

commits an offence.

(2) A person guilty of an offence under this Act shall be liable, on conviction on indictment, to imprisonment for life.

FIREARMS ACT 1982
(1982 c 31)

1   Control of imitation firearms readily convertible into firearms to which section 1 of the 1968 Act applies

(1) This Act applies to an imitation firearm if –
- (a) it has the appearance of being a firearm to which section 1 of the 1968 Act (firearms requiring a firearm certificate) applies; and
- (b) it is so construed or adapted as to be readily convertible into a firearm to which that section applies.

(2) Subject to section 2(2) of this Act and the following provisions of this section, the 1968 Act shall apply in relation to an imitation firearm to which this Act applies as it applies in relation to a firearm to which section 1 of that Act applies.

(3) Subject to the modifications in subsection (4) below, any expression given a meaning for the purposes of the 1968 Act has the same meaning in this Act.

(4) For the purposes of this section and the 1968 Act, as it applies by virtue of this section –

    (a)   the definition of air weapon in section 1(3)(b) of that Act (air weapons excepted from requirement of firearm certificate) shall have effect without the exclusion of any type declared by rules made by the Secretary of State under section 53 of that Act to be specially dangerous; and

    (b)   the definition of firearm in sections 57(1) of that Act shall have effect without paragraphs (b) and (c) of that subsection (component parts and accessories).

(5) In any proceedings brought by virtue of this section for an offence under the 1968 Act involving an imitation firearm to which this Act applies, it shall be a defence for the accused to show that he did not know and had no reason to suspect that the imitation firearm was so constructed or adapted as to be readily convertible into a firearm to which section 1 of that Act applies.

(6) For the purposes of this section an imitation firearm shall be regarded as readily convertible into a firearm to which section 1 of the 1968 Act applies if –

    (a)   it can be so converted without any special skill on the part of the person converting it in the construction or adaptation of firearms of any description; and

    (b)   the work involved in converting it does not require equipment or tools other than such as are in common use by persons carrying out works of construction and maintenance in their own homes.

2   Provisions supplementary to section 1

(1) Subject to subsection (2) below, references in the 1968 Act, and in any order made under section 6 of that Act (orders prohibiting movement of firearms or ammunition) before this Act comes into force –

    (a)   to firearms (without qualification); or

    (b)   to firearms to which section 1 of that Act applies;

shall be read as including imitation firearms to which this Act applies.

(2) The following provisions of the 1968 Act do not apply by virtue of this Act to an imitation firearm to which this Act applies, that is to say –

    (a)   section 4(3) and (4) (offence to convert anything having appearance of firearm into a firearm and aggravated offence under section 1 involving a converted firearm); and

    (b)   the provisions of that Act which relate to, or to the enforcement of control over, the manner in which a firearm is used or the circumstances in which it is carried;

but without prejudice, in the case of the provisions mentioned in paragraph (b) above, to the application to such an imitation firearm of such of those provisions as apply to imitation firearms apart from this Act.

(3) The provisions referred to in subsection (2)(b) are sections 16 to 20 and section 47.

AVIATION SECURITY ACT 1982
(1982 c 36)

1   Hijacking

(1) A person on board an aircraft in flight who unlawfully, by the use of force or by threats of any kind, seizes the aircraft or exercises control of it commits the offence of hijacking, whatever

his nationality, whatever the State in which the aircraft is registered and whether the aircraft is in the United Kingdom or elsewhere, but subject to subsection (2) below.

(2) If –

  (a) the aircraft is used in military, customs or police service, or
  (b) both the place of take-off and the place of landing are in the territory of the State in which the aircraft is registered,

subsection (1) above shall not apply unless –

  (i)   the person seizing or exercising control of the aircraft is a United Kingdom national; or
  (ii) his act is committed in the United Kingdom; or
  (iii) the aircraft is registered in the United Kingdom or is used in the military or customs service of the United Kingdom or in the service of any police force in the United Kingdom.

(3) A person who commits the offence of hijacking shall be liable, on conviction on indictment, to imprisonment for life.

(4) If the Secretary of State by order made by statutory instrument declares –

  (a) that any two or more States named in the order have established an organisation or agency which operates aircraft; and
  (b) that one of those States has been designated as exercising, for aircraft so operated, the powers of the State of registration,

the State declared under paragraph (b) of this subsection shall be deemed for the purposes of this section to be the State in which any aircraft so operated is registered; but in relation to such an aircraft subsection (2)(b) above shall have effect as if it referred to the territory of any one of the States named in the order.

(5) For the purposes of this section the territorial waters of any State shall be treated as part of its territory.

2   Destroying, damaging or endangering safety of aircraft

(1) It shall, subject to subsection (4) below, be an offence for any person unlawfully and intentionally–

  (a) to destroy an aircraft in service or so to damage such an aircraft as to render it incapable of flight or as to be likely to endanger its safety in flight; or
  (b) to commit on board an aircraft in flight any act of violence which is likely to endanger the safety of the aircraft.

(2) It shall also, subject to subsection (4) below, be an offence for any person unlawfully and intentionally to place, or cause to be placed, on an aircraft in service any device or substance which is likely to destroy the aircraft, or is likely so to damage it as to render it incapable of flight or as to be likely to endanger its safety in flight; but nothing in this subsection shall be construed as limiting the circumstances in which the commission of any act –

  (a) may constitute an offence under subsection (1) above, or
  (b) may constitute attempting or conspiring to commit, or aiding, abetting, counselling or procuring, or being art and part in, the commission of such an offence.

(3) Except as provided by subsection (4) below, subsections (1) and (2) above shall apply whether any such act as is therein mentioned is committed in the United Kingdom or elsewhere, whatever the nationality of the person committing the act and whatever the State in which the aircraft is registered.

(4) Subsections (1) and (2) above shall not apply to any act committed in relation to an aircraft used in military, customs or police service unless –

(a)   the act is committed in the United Kingdom, or

(b)   where the act is committed outside the United Kingdom, the person committing it is a United Kingdom national.

(5) A person who commits an offence under this section shall be liable, on conviction on indictment, to imprisonment for life.

(6) In this section 'unlawfully' –

(a)   in relation to the commission of an act in the United Kingdom, means so as (apart from this Act) to constitute an offence under the law of the part of the United Kingdom in which the act is committed, and

(b)   in relation to the commission of an act outside the United Kingdom, means so that the commission of the act would (apart from this Act) have been an offence under the law of England and Wales if it had been committed in England and Wales or of Scotland if it had been committed in Scotland.

(7) In this section 'act of violence' means –

(a)   any act done in the United Kingdom which constitutes the offence of murder, attempted murder, manslaughter, culpable homicide or assault or an offence under sections 18, 20, 21, 22, 23, 24, 28 or 29 of the Offences against the Person Act 1861 or under section 2 of the Explosive Substances Act 1883, and

(b)   any act done outside the United Kingdom which, if done in the United Kingdom, would constitute such an offence as is mentioned in paragraph (a) above.

3   Other acts endangering or likely to endanger safety of aircraft

(1) It shall, subject to subsection (5) and (6) below, be an offence for any person unlawfully and intentionally to destroy or damage any property to which this subsection applies, or to interfere with the operation of any such property, where the destruction, damage or interference is likely to endanger the safety of aircraft in flight.

(2) Subsection (1) above applies to any property used for the provision of air navigation facilities, including any land, building or ship so used, and including any apparatus or equipment so used, whether it is on board an aircraft or elsewhere.

(3) It shall also, subject to subsections (4) and (5) below, be an offence for a person intentionally to communicate any information which is false, misleading or deceptive in a material particular, where the communication of the information endangers the safety of an aircraft or is likely to endanger the safety of aircraft in flight.

(4) It shall be a defence for a person charged with an offence under subsection (3) above to prove –

(a)   that he believed, and had reasonable grounds for believing, that the information was true; or

(b)   that, when he communicated the information, he was lawfully employed to perform duties which consisted of or included the communication of information and that he communicated the information in good faith in the performance of those duties.

(5) Subsections (1) and (3) above shall not apply to the commission of any act unless either the act is committed in the United Kingdom, or, where it is committed outside the United Kingdom –

(a)   the person committing it is a United Kingdom national; or

(b)   the commission of the act endangers or is likely to endanger the safety in flight of a civil aircraft registered in the United Kingdom or chartered by demise to a lessee whose principal place of business, or (if he has no place of business) whose permanent residence, is in the United Kingdom; or

(c)   the act is committed on board a civil aircraft which is so registered or so chartered; or

    (d) the act is committed on board a civil aircraft which lands in the United Kingdom with
        the person who committed the act still on board.

(6) Subsection (1) above shall also not apply to any act committed outside the United Kingdom
and so committed in relation to property which is situated outside the United Kingdom and is
not used for the provision of air navigation facilities in connection with international air
navigation, unless the person committing the act is a United Kingdom national.

(7) A person who commits an offence under this section shall be liable, on conviction on
indictment, to imprisonment for life.

(8) In this section 'civil aircraft' means any aircraft other than an aircraft used in military, customs
or police service and 'unlawfully' has the same meaning as in section 2 of this Act.

4   Offences in relation to certain dangerous articles

(1) It shall be an offence for any person without lawful authority or reasonable excuse (the proof
of which shall lie on him) to have with him –

    (a) in any aircraft registered in the United Kingdom, whether at a time when the aircraft
        is in the United Kingdom or not, or

    (b) in any other aircraft at a time when it is in, or in flight over, the United Kingdom, or

    (c) in any part of an aerodrome in the United Kingdom, or

    (d) in any air navigation installation in the United Kingdom which does not form part of
        an aerodrome,

any article to which this section applies.

(2) This section applies to the following articles, that is to say –

    (a) any firearm, or any article having the appearance of being a firearm, whether capable
        of being discharged or not;

    (b) any explosive, any article manufactured or adapted (whether in the form of a bomb,
        grenade or otherwise) so as to have the appearance of being an explosive, whether it is
        capable of producing a practical effect by explosion or not, or any article marked or
        labelled so as to indicate that it is or contains an explosive; and

    (c) any article (not falling within either of the preceding paragraphs) made or adapted for
        use for causing injury to or incapacitating a person or for destroying or damaging
        property, or intended by the person having it with him for such use, whether by him
        or by any other person.

(3) For the purposes of this section a person who is for the time being in an aircraft, or in part
of an aerodrome, shall be treated as having with him in the aircraft, or in that part of the
aerodrome, as the case may be, an article to which this section applies if –

    (a) where he is in an aircraft, or an article in which it is contained, is in the aircraft and
        has been caused (whether by him or by any other person) to be brought there as being,
        or as forming part of, his baggage on a flight in the aircraft or has been caused by him
        to be brought there as being, or as forming part of, any other property to be carried
        on such a flight, or

    (b) where he is in part of an aerodrome (otherwise than in an aircraft), the article, or an
        article in which it is contained, is in that or any other part of the aerodrome and has
        been caused (whether by him or by any other person) to be brought into the aerodrome
        as being, or as forming part of, his baggage on a flight from that aerodrome or has
        been caused by him to be brought there as being, or as forming part of, any other
        property to be carried on such a flight on which he is also to be carried,

notwithstanding that the circumstances may be such that (apart from this subsection) he would not be regarded as having the article with him in the aircraft or in a part of the aerodrome, as the case may be.

(4) A person guilty of an offence under this section shall be liable –

    (a) on summary conviction, to a fine not exceeding the statutory maximum or to imprisonment for a term not exceeding three months or to both;

    (b) on conviction on indictment, to a fine or to imprisonment for a term not exceeding five years or to both.

(5) Nothing in subsection (3) above shall be construed as limiting the circumstances in which a person would, apart from that subsection, be regarded as having an article with him as mentioned in subsection (1) above.

8   Prosecution of offences and proceedings

(1) Proceedings for an offence under any of the preceding provisions of this Part of this Act (other than sections 4 and 7) shall not be instituted –

    (a) in England and Wales, except by, or with the consent of, the Attorney General …

38   Interpretation, etc …

(3) For the purposes of this Act –

    (a) the period during which an aircraft is in flight shall be deemed to include any period from the moment when all its external doors are closed following embarkation until the moment when any such door is opened for disembarkation, and, in the case of a forced landing, any period until the competent authorities take over responsibility for the aircraft and for persons and property on board; and

    (b) an aircraft shall be taken to be in service during the whole of the period which begins with the pre-flight preparation of the aircraft for a flight and ends 24 hours after the aircraft lands having completed that flight, and also at any time (not falling within that period) while, in accordance with the preceding paragraph, the aircraft is in flight,

and anything done on board an aircraft while in flight over any part of the United Kingdom shall be treated as done in that part of the United Kingdom. …

CRIMINAL JUSTICE ACT 1982
(1982 c 48)

37   The standard scale of fines for summary offences

(1) There shall be a standard scale of fines for summary offences, which shall be known as 'the standard scale'.

(2) The standard scale is shown below –

Level on the scale	Amount of fine
1	£200
2	£500
3	£1,000
4	£2,500
5	£5,000

(3) Where any enactment (whether contained in an Act passed before or after this Act) provides –

    (a) that a person convicted of a summary offence shall be liable on conviction to a fine or a maximum fine by reference to a specified level on the standard scale; or

    (b) confers power by subordinate instrument to make a person liable on conviction of a summary offence (whether or not created by the instrument) to a fine or maximum fine by reference to a specified level on the standard scale,

it is to be construed as referring to the standard scale for which this section provides as that standard scale has effect from time to time by virtue either of this section or of an order under section 143 of the Magistrates' Courts Act 1980.

70   Vagrancy offences

(1) Where a person is convicted –

    (a) under section 3 or 4 of the Vagrancy Act 1824, of wandering abroad, or placing himself in any public place, street, highway, court, or passage, to beg or gather alms; or

    (b) under section 4 of that Act, –

        (i) of wandering abroad and lodging in any barn or outhouse, or in any deserted or unoccupied building, or in the open air, or under a tent, or in any cart or waggon, and not giving a good account of himself; or

       (ii) of wandering abroad, and endeavouring by the exposure of wounds and deformities to obtain or gather alms,

the court shall not have power to sentence him to imprisonment but shall have the same power to fine him as if this section had not been enacted.

(2) If a person deemed a rogue and vagabond by virtue of section 4 of the Vagrancy Act 1824 is thereafter guilty of an offence mentioned in subsection (1) above, he shall be convicted of that offence under section 4 of that Act and accordingly –

    (a) shall not be deemed an incorrigible rogue; and

    (b) shall not be committed to the Crown Court,

by reason only of that conviction.

(3) This section applies to offences committed before as well as after it comes into effect.

[See Appendix, Criminal Justice Act 2003, Schedule 37, Pt 9.]

As amended by the Criminal Justice Act 1991, ss17(1), 101(1), Schedule 12, para 6.

REPRESENTATION OF THE PEOPLE ACT 1983
(1983 c 2)

97   Disturbances at election meetings

(1) A person who at a lawful public meeting to which this section applies acts, or incites others to act, in a disorderly manner for the purpose of preventing the transaction of the business for which the meeting was called together shall be guilty of an illegal practice.

(2) This section applies to –

    (a) a political meeting held in any constituency between the date of the issue of a writ for the return of a Member of Parliament for the constituency and the date at which a return to the writ is made;

    (b) a meeting held with reference to a local government election in the electoral area for that election in the period beginning with the last date on which notice of the election may be published in accordance with rules made under section 36 or, in Scotland, section 42 above and ending with the day of election.

(3) If a constable reasonably suspects any person of committing an offence under subsection (1) above, he may if requested so to do by the chairman of the meeting require that person to declare to him immediately his name and address and, if that person refuses or fails so to declare his name and address or gives a false name and address, he shall be liable on summary conviction to a fine not exceeding level 1 on the standard scale.

As amended by the Police and Criminal Evidence Act 1984, ss26(1), 119(2), Schedule 7, Part I; Representation of the People Act 1985, s24, Schedule 4, para 39.

CHILD ABDUCTION ACT 1984
(1984 c 37)

1 Offences of abduction of child by parent, etc

(1) Subject to subsections (5) and (8) below, a person connected with a child under the age of sixteen commits an offence if he takes or sends the child out of the United Kingdom without the appropriate consent.

(2) A person is connected with a child for the purposes of this section if –
   (a) he is a parent or guardian of the child; or
   (b) in the case of a child whose parents were not married to each other at the time of his birth, there are reasonable grounds for believing that he is the father of the child; or
   (c) he is a guardian of the child;
   (ca) he is a special guardian of the child; or
   (d) he is a person in whose favour a residence order is in force with respect to the child; or
   (e) he has custody of the child.

(3) In this section 'the appropriate consent', in relation to a child, means –
   (a) the consent of each of the following –
      (i) the child's mother;
      (ii) the child's father, if he has parental responsibility for him;
      (iii) any guardian of the child;
      (iiia) any special guardian of the child;
      (iv) any person in whose favour a residence order is in force with respect to the child;
      (v) any person who has custody of the child; or
   (b) the leave of the court granted under or by virtue of any provision of Part II of the Children Act 1989; or
   (c) if any person has custody of the child, the leave of the court which awarded custody to him.

(4) A person does not commit an offence under this section by taking or sending a child out of the United Kingdom without obtaining the appropriate consent if –
   (a) he is a person in whose favour there is a residence order in force with respect to the child, and he takes or sends the child out of the United Kingdom for a period of less than one month; or
   (b) he is a special guardian of the child and he takes or sends the child out of the United Kingdom for a period of less than three months.

(4A) Subsection (4) above does not apply if the person taking or sending the child out of the United Kingdom does so in breach of an order under Part II of the Children Act 1989.

(5) A person does not commit an offence under this section by doing anything without the consent of another person whose consent is required under the foregoing provisions if –

- (a) he does it in the belief that the other person –
  - (i) has consented;
  - (ia) who is a special guardian of the child; or
  - (ii) would consent if he was aware of all the relevant circumstances; or
- (b) he has taken all reasonable steps to communicate with the other person but has been unable to communicate with him; or
- (c) the other person has unreasonably refused to consent.

(5A) Subsection (5)(c) above does not apply if –

- (a) the person who refused to consent is a person–
  - (i) in whose favour there is a residence order in force with respect to the child;
  - (ia) who is a special guardian of the child; or
  - (ii) who has custody of the child; or
- (b) the person taking or sending the child out of the United Kingdom is, by so acting, in breach of an order made by a court in the United Kingdom.

(6) Where, in proceedings for an offence under this section, there is sufficient evidence to raise an issue as to the application of subsection (5) above, it shall be for the prosecution to prove that that subsection does not apply.

(7) For the purposes of this section –

- (a) 'guardian of a child', 'special guardian', 'residence order' and 'parental responsibility' have the same meaning as in the Children Act 1989; and
- (b) a person shall be treated as having custody of a child if there is in force an order of a court in the United Kingdom awarding him (whether solely or jointly with another person) custody, legal custody or care and control of the child.

(8) This section shall have effect subject to the provisions of the Schedule to this Act in relation to a child who is in the care of a local authority, detained in a place of safety, remanded to a local authority accommodation or the subject of proceedings or an order relating to adoption.

2   Offence of abduction of child by other persons

(1) Subject to subsection (3) below, a person, other than one mentioned in subsection (2) below commits an offence if, without lawful authority or reasonable excuse, he takes or detains a child under the age of sixteen –

- (a) so as to remove him from the lawful control of any person having lawful control of the child; or
- (b) so as to keep him out of the lawful control of any person entitled to lawful control of the child.

(2) The persons are –

- (a) where the father and mother of the child in question were married to each other at the time of his birth, the child's father and mother;
- (b) where the father and mother of the child in question were not married to each other at the time of his birth, the child's mother; and
- (c) any other person mentioned in section 1(2)(c) to (e) above.

(3) In proceedings against any person for an offence under this section, it shall be a defence for that person to prove –

- (a) where the father and mother of the child in question were not married to each other at the time of his birth –

(i)   that he is the child's father; or

(ii) that, at the time of the alleged offence, he believed, on reasonable grounds, that he was the child's father; or

(b) hat, at the time of the alleged offence, he believed that the child had attained the age of sixteen.

3   Construction of references to taking, sending and detaining

For the purposes of this Part of this Act –

(a) a person shall be regarded as taking a child if he causes or induces the child to accompany him or any other person or causes the child to be taken;

(b) a person shall be regarded as sending a child if he causes the child to be sent;

(c) a person shall be regarded as detaining a child if he causes the child to be detained or induces the child to remain with him or any other person; and

(d) references to a child's parents and to a child whose parents were (or were not) married to each other at the time of his birth shall be construed in accordance with section 1 of the Family Law Reform Act 1987 (which extends their meaning).

4   Penalties and prosecutions

(1) A person guilty of an offence under this Part of this Act shall be liable –

(a) on summary conviction, to imprisonment for a term not exceeding six months or to a fine not exceeding the statutory maximum, or to both such imprisonment and fine;

(b) on conviction on indictment, to imprisonment for a term not exceeding seven years.

(2) No prosecution for an offence under section 1 above shall be instituted except by or with the consent of the Director of Public Prosecutions.

5   Restriction on prosecutions for offence of kidnapping

Except by or with the consent of the Director of Public Prosecutions no prosecution shall be instituted for an offence of kidnapping if it was committed –

(a) against a child under the age of sixteen; and

(b) by a person connected with the child, within the meaning of section 1 above.

As amended by the Family Law Act 1986, s65; Children Act 1989, s108(4), (7), Schedule 12, paras 37(1)–(5), 38, 39, Schedule 15; Adoption and Children Act 2002, s139(1), Schedule 3, para 42.

POLICE AND CRIMINAL EVIDENCE ACT 1984

(1984 c 60)

24   Arrest without warrant: constables

(1) A constable may arrest without a warrant –

(a) anyone who is about to commit an offence;

(b) anyone who is in the act of committing an offence;

(c) anyone whom he has reasonable grounds for suspecting to be about to commit an offence;

(d) anyone whom he has reasonable grounds for suspecting to be committing an offence.

(2) If a constable has reasonable grounds for suspecting that an offence has been committed, he may arrest without a warrant anyone whom he has reasonable grounds to suspect of being guilty of it.

(3) If an offence has been committed, a constable may arrest without a warrant –

(a)   anyone who is guilty of the offence;

(b)   anyone whom he has reasonable grounds for suspecting to be guilty of it.

(4) But the power of summary arrest conferred by subsection (1), (2) or (3) is exercisable only if the constable has reasonable grounds for believing that for any of the reasons mentioned in subsection (5) it is necessary to arrest the person in question.

(5) The reasons are –

(a)   to enable the name of the person in question to be ascertained (in the case where the constable does not know, and cannot readily ascertain, the person's name, or has reasonable grounds for doubting whether a name given by the person as his name is his real name);

(b)   correspondingly as regards the person's address;

(c)   to prevent the person in question –

(i)   causing physical injury to himself or any other person;

(ii)   suffering physical injury;

(iii) causing loss of or damage to property;

(iv) committing an offence against public decency (subject to subsection (6)); or

(v)   causing an unlawful obstruction of the highway;

(d)   to protect a child or other vulnerable person from the person in question;

(e)   to allow the prompt and effective investigation of the offence or of the conduct of the person in question;

(f)   to prevent any prosecution for the offence from being hindered by the disappearance of the person in question.

(6) Subsection (5)(c)(iv) applies only where members of the public going about their normal business cannot reasonably be expected to avoid the person in question.

24A   Arrest without warrant: other persons

(1) A person other than a constable may arrest without a warrant –

(a)   anyone who is in the act of committing an indictable offence;

(b)   anyone whom he has reasonable grounds for suspecting to be committing an indictable offence.

(2) Where an indictable offence has been committed, a person other than a constable may arrest without a warrant –

(a)   anyone who is guilty of the offence;

(b)   anyone whom he has reasonable grounds for suspecting to be guilty of it.

(3) But the power of summary arrest conferred by subsection (1) or (2) is exercisable only if –

(a)   the person making the arrest has reasonable grounds for believing that for any of the reasons mentioned in subsection (4) it is necessary to arrest the person in question; and

(b)   it appears to the person making the arrest that it is not reasonably practicable for a constable to make it instead.

(4) The reasons are to prevent the person in question –

(a)   causing physical injury to himself or any other person;

(b)   suffering physical injury;

(c)   causing loss of or damage to property; or

(d)   making off before a constable can assume responsibility for him.

28   Information to be given on arrest

(1) Subject to subsection (5) below, where a person is arrested, otherwise than by being informed that he is under arrest, the arrest is not lawful unless the person arrested is informed that he is under arrest as soon as is practicable after his arrest.

(2) Where a person is arrested by a constable, subsection (1) above applies regardless of whether the fact of the arrest is obvious.

(3) Subject to subsection (5) below, no arrest is lawful unless the person arrested is informed of the ground for the arrest at the time of, or as soon as is practicable after, the arrest.

(4) Where a person is arrested by a constable, subsection (3) above applies regardless of whether the ground for the arrest is obvious.

(5) Nothing in this section is to be taken to require a person to be informed –

    (a) that he is under arrest; or

    (b) of the ground for the arrest,

if it was not reasonably practicable for him to be so informed by reason of his having escaped from arrest before the information could be given.

117 Power of constable to use reasonable force

Where any provision of this Act –

    (a) confers a power on a constable; and

    (b) does not provide that the power may only be exercised with the consent of some person, other than a police officer,

the officer may use reasonable force, if necessary, in the exercise of the power.

As amended by the Serious Organised Crime and Police Act 2005, ss110(1), (2), (4), 111, 174(2), Schedule 7, Pt 1, para 24(1), (3), Schedule 17, Pt 2.].

INTOXICATING SUBSTANCES (SUPPLY) ACT 1985
(1985 c 26)

1   Offence of supply of intoxicating substance

(1) It is an offence for a person to supply or offer to supply a substance other than a controlled drug –

    (a) to a person under the age of eighteen whom he knows, or has reasonable cause to believe, to be under that age; or

    (b) to a person –

        (i)   who is acting on behalf of a person under that age; and

        (ii) whom he knows, or has reasonable cause to believe, to be so acting,

if he knows or has reasonable cause to believe that the substance is, or its fumes are, likely to be inhaled by the person under the age of eighteen for the purpose of causing intoxication.

(2) In proceedings against any person for an offence under subsection (1) above it is a defence for him to show that at the time he made the supply or offer he was under the age of eighteen and was acting otherwise than in the course or furtherance of a business.

(3) A person guilty of an offence under this section shall be liable on summary conviction to imprisonment for a term not exceeding six months or to a fine not exceeding level 5 on the standard scale, or to both.

(4) In this section 'controlled drug' has the same meaning as in the Misuse of Drugs Act 1971.

SEXUAL OFFENCES ACT 1985
(1985 c 44)

1 Kerb-crawling

(1) A person commits an offence if he solicits another person (or different persons) for the purpose of prostitution –

    (a)   from a motor vehicle while it is in a street or public place; or

    (b)   in a street or public place while in the immediate vicinity of a motor vehicle that he has just got out of or off,

persistently or in such manner or in such circumstances as to be likely to cause annoyance to the person (or any of the persons) solicited, or nuisance to other persons in the neighbourhood.

(2) A person guilty of an offence under this section shall be liable on summary conviction to a fine not exceeding level 3 on the standard scale.

(3) In this section 'motor vehicle' has the same meaning as in the Road Traffic Act 1988.

2 Persistent soliciting

(1) A person commits an offence if in a street or public place he persistently solicits another person (or different persons) for the purpose of prostitution.

(2) A person guilty of an offence under this section shall be liable on summary conviction to a fine not exceeding level 3 on the standard scale.

As amended by the Road Traffic (Consequential Provisions) Act 1988, s4, Schedule 3, para 29; Sexual Offences Act 2003, s56, Schedule 1, para 4.

SPORTING EVENTS (CONTROL OF ALCOHOL, ETC) ACT 1985
(1985 c 57)

1 Offences in connection with alcohol on coaches and trains

(1) This section applies to a vehicle which –

    (a)   is a public service vehicle or railway passenger vehicle, and

    (b)   s being used for the principal purpose of carrying passengers for the whole or part of a journey to or from a designated sporting event.

(2) A person who knowingly causes or permits alcohol to be carried on a vehicle to which this section applies is guilty of an offence –

    (a)   if the vehicle is a public service vehicle and he is the operator of the vehicle or the servant or agent of the operator, or

    (b)   if the vehicle is a hired vehicle and he is the person to whom it is hired or the servant or agent of that person.

(3) A person who has alcohol in his possession while on a vehicle to which this section applies is guilty of offence.

(4) A person who is drunk on a vehicle to which this section applies is guilty of an offence.

(5) In this section 'public service vehicle' and 'operator' have the same meaning as in the Public Passenger Vehicles Act 1981.

1A   Alcohol on certain other vehicles

(1) This section applies to a motor vehicle which –

(a) is not a public service vehicle but is adapted to carry more than 8 passengers, and

(b) is being used for the principal purpose of carrying two or more passengers for the whole or part of a journey to or from a designated sporting event.

(2) A person who knowingly causes or permits alcohol to be carried on a motor vehicle to which this section applies is guilty of an offence –

(a) if he its driver, or

(b) if he is not its driver but is its keeper, the servant or agent of its keeper, a person to whom it is made available (by hire, loan or otherwise) by its keeper or the keeper's servant or agent, or the servant or agent of a person to whom it is so made available.

(3) A person who has alcohol in his possession while on a motor vehicle to which this section applies is guilty of an offence.

(4) A person who is drunk on a motor vehicle to which this section applies is guilty of an offence.

(5) In this section –

'keeper', in relation to a vehicle, means the person having the duty to take out a licence for it under the Vehicle Excise and Registration Act 1994,

'motor vehicle' means a mechanically propelled vehicle intended or adapted for use on roads, and

'public service vehicle' has the same meaning as in the Public Passenger Vehicles Act 1981.

2   Offences in connection with alcohol, containers, etc at sports grounds

(1) A person who has alcohol or an article to which this section applies in his possession –

(a) at any time during the period of a designated sporting event when he is in any area of a designated sports ground from which the event may be directly viewed, or

(b) while entering or trying to enter a designated sports ground at any time during a period of a designated sporting event at that ground,

is guilty of an offence.

(2) A person who is drunk in a designated sports ground at any time during the period of a designated sporting event at that ground or is drunk while entering or trying to enter such a ground at any time during the period of a designated sporting event at that ground is guilty of an offence.

(3) This section applies to any article capable of causing injury to a person struck by it, being –

(a) a bottle, can or other portable container (including such an article when crushed or broken) which –

(i)   is for holding any drink, and

(ii) is of a kind which, when empty, is normally discarded or returned to, or left to be recovered by, the supplier, or

(b) part of an article falling within paragraph (a) above;

but does not apply to anything that is for holding any medicinal product (within the meaning of the Medicines Act 1968) or any veterinary medicinal product (within the meaning of the Veterinary Medicines Regulations 2006).

2A   Fireworks, etc

(1) A person is guilty of an offence if he has an article or substance to which this section applies in his possession –

(a) at any time during the period of a designated sporting event when he is in any area of a designated sports ground from which the event may be directly viewed, or

    (b) while entering or trying to enter a designated sports ground at any time during the period of a designated sporting event at the ground.

(2) It is a defence for the accused to prove that he had possession with lawful authority.

(3) This section applies to any article or substance whose main purpose is the emission of a flare for purposes of illuminating or signalling (as opposed to igniting or heating) or the emission of smoke or a visible gas; and in particular it applies to distress flares, fog signals, and pellets and capsules intended to be used as fumigators or for testing pipes, but not to matches, cigarette lighters or heaters.

(4) This section also applies to any article which is a firework.

7   Powers of enforcement

(1) A constable may, at any time during the period of a designated sporting event at any designated sports ground, enter any part of the ground for the purpose of enforcing the provisions of this Act.

(2) A constable may search a person he has reasonable grounds to suspect is committing or has committed an offence under this Act.

(3) A constable may stop a public service vehicle (within the meaning of section 1 of this Act) or a motor vehicle to which section 1A of this Act applies and may search such a vehicle or a railway passenger vehicle if he has reasonable grounds to suspect that an offence under that section is being or has been committed in respect of the vehicle.

8   Penalties for offences

A person guilty of an offence under this Act shall be liable on summary conviction –

    (a) in the case of an offence under section 1(2) or 1A(2), to a fine not exceeding level 4 on the standard scale,

    (b) in the case of an offence under section 1(3), 1A(3), 2(1) or 2A(1), to a fine not exceeding level 3 on the standard scale or to imprisonment for a term not exceeding three months or both,

    (c) in the case of an offence under section 1(4), 1A(4) or 2(2), to a fine not exceeding level 2 on the standard scale.

9   Interpretation

(1) The following provisions shall have effect for the interpretation of this Act.

(2) 'Designated sports ground' means any place –

    (a) used (wholly or partly) for sporting events where accommodation is provided for spectators, and

    (b) for the time being designated, or of a class designated, by order made by the Secretary of State;

and an order under this subsection may include provision for determining for the purposes of this Act the outer limit of any designated sports ground.

(3) 'Designated sporting event' –

    (a) means a sporting event or proposed sporting event for the time being designated, or of a class designated, by order made by the Secretary of State, and

    (b) includes a designated sporting event within the meaning of Part V of the Criminal Justice (Scotland) Act 1980;

and an order under this subsection may apply to events or proposed events outside Great Britain as well as those in England and Wales.

(4) The period of a designated sporting event is the period beginning two hours before the start

of the event or (if earlier) two hours before the time at which it is advertised to start and ending one hour after the end of the event, but –

    (a)   where an event advertised to start at a particular time on a particular day is postponed to a later day, the period includes the period in the day on which it is advertised to take place beginning two hours before and ending one hour after that time, and

    (b)   where an event advertised to start at a particular time on a particular day does not take place, the period is the period referred to in paragraph (a) above.

(6) This Act does not apply to any sporting event or proposed sporting event –

    (a)   where all competitors are to take part otherwise than for reward, and

    (b)   to which all spectators are to be admitted free of charge.

(7) An expression used in this Act and in the Licensing Act 2003 has the same meaning in this Act as in that Act.

(8) Any power to make an order under this section shall be exercisable by statutory instrument subject to annulment in pursuance of a resolution of either House of Parliament.

As amended by the Public Order Act 1986, s40(1), (3), Schedule 1, Part 1, paras 1, 2, 3, 5, 6, 7; Schedule 3; Vehicle Excise and Registration Act 1994, s63, Schedule 3, para 20; Licensing Act 2003, ss198, 199, Schedule 6, paras 96–98, 100(a); Serious Organised Crime and Police Act 2005, s111, Schedule 7, Pt 1, para 25, Schedule 17, Pt 2; Veterinary Medicines Regulations 2006, reg 44(3), Schedule 9, Pt 1, para 5.

PUBLIC ORDER ACT 1986
(1986 c 64)

PART I

NEW OFFENCES

1   Riot

(1) Where 12 or more persons who are present together use or threaten unlawful violence for a common purpose and the conduct of them (taken together) is such as would cause a person of reasonable firmness present at the scene to fear for his personal safety, each of the persons using unlawful violence for the common purpose is guilty of riot.

(2) It is immaterial whether or not the 12 or more use or threaten unlawful violence simultaneously.

(3) The common purpose may be inferred from conduct.

(4) No person of reasonable firmness need actually be, or be likely to be, present at the scene.

(5) Riot may be committed in private as well as in public places.

(6) A person guilty of riot is liable on conviction on indictment to imprisonment for a term not exceeding ten years or a fine or both.

2   Violent disorder

(1) Where three or more persons who are present together use or threaten unlawful violence and the conduct of them (taken together) is such as would cause a person of reasonable firmness present at the scene to fear for his personal safety, each of the persons using or threatening unlawful violence is guilty of violent disorder.

(2) It is immaterial whether or not the three or more use or threaten unlawful violence simultaneously.

(3) No person of reasonable firmness need actually be, or be likely to be, present at the scene.

(4) Violent disorder may be committed in private as well as in public places.

(5) A person guilty of violent disorder is liable on conviction on indictment to imprisonment for a term not exceeding five years or a fine or both, or on summary conviction to imprisonment for a term not exceeding six months or a fine not exceeding the statutory maximum or both.

3 Affray

(1) A person is guilty of affray if he uses or threatens unlawful violence towards another and his conduct is such as would cause a person of reasonable firmness present at the scene to fear for his personal safety.

(2) Where two or more persons use or threaten the unlawful violence, it is the conduct of them taken together that must be considered for the purposes of subsection (1).

(3) For the purposes of this section a threat cannot be made by the use of words alone.

(4) No person of reasonable firmness need actually be, or be likely to be, present at the scene.

(5) Affray may be committed in private as well as in public places.

(7) A person guilty of affray is liable on conviction on indictment to imprisonment for a term not exceeding three years or a fine or both, or on summary conviction to imprisonment for a term not exceeding six months or a fine not exceeding the statutory maximum or both.

4 Fear or provocation of violence

(1) A person is guilty of an offence if he –

    (a) uses towards another person threatening, abusive or insulting words or behaviour, or

    (b) distributes or displays to another person any writing, sign or other visible representation which is threatening, abusive or insulting,

with intent to cause that person to believe that immediate unlawful violence will be used against him or another by any person, or to provoke the immediate use of unlawful violence by that person or another, or whereby that person is likely to believe that such violence will be used or it is likely that such violence will be provoked.

(2) An offence under this section may be committed in a public or a private place, except that no offence is committed where the words or behaviour are used, or the writing, sign or other visible representation is distributed or displayed, by a person inside a dwelling and the other person is also inside that or another dwelling.

(4) A person guilty of an offence under this section is liable on summary conviction to imprisonment for a term not exceeding six months or a fine not exceeding level 5 on the standard scale or both.

4A Intentional harassment, alarm or distress

(1) A person is guilty of an offence if, with intent to cause a person harassment, alarm or distress, he –

    (a) uses threatening, abusive or insulting words or behaviour, or disorderly behaviour, or

    (b) displays any writing, sign or other visible representation which is threatening, abusive or insulting,

thereby causing that or another person harassment, alarm or distress.

(2) An offence under this section may be committed in a public or a private place, except that no offence is committed where the words or behaviour are used, or the writing, sign or other visible representation is displayed, by a person inside a dwelling and the person who is harassed, alarmed or distressed is also inside that or another dwelling.

(3) It is a defence for the accused to prove –

    (a) that he was inside a dwelling and had no reason to believe that the words or behaviour used, or the writing, sign or other visible representation displayed, would be heard or seen by a person outside that or any other dwelling, or

(b)   that his conduct was reasonable.

(5) A person guilty of an offence under this section is liable on summary conviction to imprisonment for a term not exceeding 6 months or a fine not exceeding level 5 on the standard scale or both.

5   Harassment, alarm or distress

(1) A person is guilty of an offence if he –

(a)   uses threatening, abusive or insulting words or behaviour, or disorderly behaviour, or

(b)   displays any writing, sign or other visible representation which is threatening, abusive or insulting,

within the hearing or sight of a person likely to be caused harassment, alarm or distress thereby.

(2) An offence under this section may be committed in a public or a private place, except that no offence is committed where the words or behaviour are used, or the writing, sign or other visible representation is displayed, by a person inside a dwelling and the other person is also inside that or another dwelling.

(3) It is a defence for the accused to prove –

(a)   that he had no reason to believe that there was any person within hearing or sight who was likely to be caused harassment, alarm or distress, or

(b)   that he was inside a dwelling and had no reason to believe that the words or behaviour used, or the writing, sign or other visible representation displayed, would be heard or seen by a person outside that or any other dwelling, or

(c)   that his conduct was reasonable.

(6) A person guilty of an offence under this section is liable on summary conviction to a fine not exceeding level 3 on the standard scale.

6   Mental element: miscellaneous

(1) A person is guilty of riot only if he intends to use violence or is aware that his conduct may be violent.

(2) A person is guilty of violent disorder or affray only if he intends to use or threaten violence or is aware that his conduct may be violent or threaten violence.

(3) A person is guilty of an offence under section 4 only if he intends his words or behaviour, or the writing, sign or other visible representation, to be threatening, abusive or insulting, or is aware that it may be threatening, abusive or insulting.

(4) A person is guilty of an offence under section 5 only if he intends his words or behaviour, or the writing, sign or other visible representation, to be threatening, abusive or insulting, or is aware that it may be threatening, abusive or insulting or (as the case may be) he intends his behaviour to be or is aware that it may be disorderly.

(5) For the purposes of this section a person whose awareness is impaired by intoxication shall be taken to be aware of that of which he would be aware if not intoxicated, unless he shows either that his intoxication was not self-induced or that it was caused solely by the taking or administration of a substance in the course of medical treatment.

(6) In subsection (5) 'intoxication' means any intoxication, whether caused by drink, drugs or other means, or by a combination of means.

(7) Subsections (1) and (2) do not affect the determination for the purposes of riot or violent disorder of the number of persons who use or threaten violence.

7   Procedure: miscellaneous

(1) No prosecution for an offence of riot or incitement to riot may be instituted except by or with the consent of the Director of Public Prosecutions.

(2) For the purposes of the rules against charging more than one offence in the same count or information, each of sections 1 to 5 creates one offence.

(3) If on the trial on indictment of a person charged with violent disorder or affray the jury find him not guilty of the offence charged, they may (without prejudice to section 6(3) of the Criminal Law Act 1967) find him guilty of an offence under section 4.

(4) The Crown Court has the same powers and duties in relation to a person who is by virtue of subsection (3) convicted before it of an offence under section 4 as a magistrates' court would have on convicting him of the offence.

8   Interpretation

In this Part –

    'dwelling' means any structure or part of a structure occupied as a person's home or as other living accommodation (whether the occupation is separate or shared with others) but does not include any part not so occupied, and for this purpose 'structure' includes a tent, caravan, vehicle, vessel or other temporary or movable structure;

    'violence' means any violent conduct, so that –

    (a) except in the context of affray, it includes violent conduct towards property as well as violent conduct towards persons, and

    (b) it is not restricted to conduct causing or intended to cause injury or damage but includes any other violent conduct (for example, throwing at or towards a person a missile of a kind capable of causing injury which does not hit or falls short).

9   Offences abolished

(1) The common law offences of riot, rout, unlawful assembly and affray are abolished. …

PART II

PROCESSIONS AND ASSEMBLIES

11   Advance notice of public processions

(1) Written notice shall be given in accordance with this section of any proposal to hold a public procession intended –

    (a) to demonstrate support for or opposition to the views or actions of any person or body of persons,

    (b) to publicise a cause or campaign, or

    (c) to mark or commemorate an event,

unless it is not reasonably practicable to give any advance notice of the procession.

(2) Subsection (1) does not apply where the procession is one commonly or customarily held in the police area (or areas) in which it is proposed to be held or is a funeral procession organised by a funeral director acting in the normal course of his business.

(3) The notice must specify the date when it is intended to hold the procession, the time when it is intended to start it, its proposed route, and the name and address of the person (or of one of the persons) proposing to organise it.

(4) Notice must be delivered to a police station –

    (a) in the police area in which it is proposed the procession will start, or

(b) where it is proposed the procession will start in Scotland and cross into England, in the first police area in England on the proposed route.

(5) If delivered not less than six clear days before the date when the procession is intended to be held, the notice may be delivered by post by the recorded delivery service; but section 7 of the Interpretation Act 1978 (under which a document sent by post is deemed to have been served when posted and to have been delivered in the ordinary course of post) does not apply.

(6) If not delivered in accordance with subsection (5), the notice must be delivered by hand not less than six clear days before the date when the procession is intended to be held or, if that is not reasonably practicable, as soon as delivery is reasonably practicable.

(7) Where a public procession is held, each of the persons organising it is guilty of an offence if –

(a) the requirements of this section as to notice have not been satisfied, or

(b) the date when it is held, the time when it starts, or its route, differs from the date, time or route specified in the notice.

(8) It is a defence for the accused to prove that he did not know of, and neither suspected nor had reason to suspect, the failure to satisfy the requirements or (as the case maybe) the difference of date, time or route.

(9) To the extent that an alleged offence turns on a difference of date, time or route, it is a defence for the accused to prove that the difference arose from circumstances beyond his control or from something done with the agreement of a police officer or by his direction.

(10) A person guilty of an offence under subsection (7) is liable on summary conviction to a fine not exceeding level 3 on the standard scale.

12   Imposing conditions on public processions

(1) If the senior police officer, having regard to the time or place at which and the circumstances in which any public procession is being held or is intended to be held and to its route or proposed route, reasonably believes that –

(a) it may result in serious public disorder, serious damage to property or serious disruption to the life of the community, or

(b) the purpose of the persons organising it is the intimidation of others with a view to compelling them not to do an act they have a right to do, or to do an act they have a right not to do,

he may give directions imposing on the persons organising or taking part in the procession such conditions as appear to him necessary to prevent such disorder, damage, disruption or intimidation, including conditions as to the route of the procession or prohibiting it from entering any public place specified in the directions.

(2) In subsection (1) 'the senior police officer' means –

(a) in relation to a procession being held, or to a procession intended to be held in a case where persons are assembling with a view to taking part in it, the most senior in rank of the police officers present at the scene, and

(b) in relation to a procession intended to be held in a case where paragraph (a) does not apply, the chief officer of police.

(3) A direction given by a chief officer of police by virtue of subsection (2)(b) shall be given in writing.

(4) A person who organises a public procession and knowingly fails to comply with a condition imposed under this section is guilty of an offence, but it is a defence for him to prove that the failure arose from circumstances beyond his control.

(5) A person who takes part in a public procession and knowingly fails to comply with a condition

imposed under this section is guilty of an offence, but it is a defence for him to prove that the failure arose from circumstances beyond his control.

(6) A person who incites another to commit an offence under subsection (5) is guilty of an offence.

(8) A person guilty of an offence under subsection (4) is liable on summary conviction to imprisonment for a term not exceeding three months or a fine not exceeding level 4 on the standard scale or both.

(9) A person guilty of an offence under subsection (5) is liable on summary conviction to a fine not exceeding level 3 on the standard scale.

(10) A person guilty of an offence under subsection (6) is liable on summary conviction to imprisonment for a term not exceeding three months or a fine not exceeding level 4 on the standard scale or both, notwithstanding section 45(3) of the Magistrates' Courts Act 1980 (inciter liable to same penalty as incited).

[See Appendix, Criminal Justice Act 2003, Schedule 26, para 37(1), (2).]

13 Prohibiting public processions

(1) If at any time the chief officer of police reasonably believes that, because of particular circumstances existing in any district or part of a district, the powers under section 12 will not be sufficient to prevent the holding of public processions in that district or part from resulting in serious public disorder, he shall apply to the council of the district for an order prohibiting for such period not exceeding three months as may be specified in the application the holding of all public processions (or of any class of public procession so specified) in the district or part concerned.

(2) On receiving such an application, a council may with the consent of the Secretary of State make an order either in the terms of the application or with such modifications as may be approved by the Secretary of State.

(3) Subsection (1) does not apply in the City of London or the metropolitan police district.

(4) If at any time the Commissioner of Police for the City of London or the Commissioner of Police of the Metropolis reasonably believes that, because of particular circumstances existing in his police area or part of it, the powers under section 12 will not be sufficient to prevent the holding of public processions in that area or part from resulting in serious public disorder, he may with the consent of the Secretary of State make an order prohibiting for such period not exceeding three months as may be specified in the order the holding of all public processions (or of any class of public procession so specified) in the area or part concerned.

(5) An order made under this section may be revoked or varied by a subsequent order made in the same way, that is, in accordance with subsections (1) and (2) or subsection (4), as the case may be.

(6) Any order under this section shall, if not made in writing, be recorded in writing as soon as practicable after being made.

(7) A person who organises a public procession the holding of which he knows is prohibited by virtue of an order under this section is guilty of an offence.

(8) A person who takes part in a public procession the holding of which he knows is prohibited by virtue of an order under this section is guilty of an offence.

(9) A person who incites another to commit an offence under subsection (8) is guilty of an offence.

(11) A person guilty of an offence under subsection (7) is liable on summary conviction to imprisonment for a term not exceeding three months or a fine not exceeding level 4 on the standard scale or both.

(12) A person guilty of an offence under subsection (8) is liable on summary conviction to a fine not exceeding level 3 on the standard scale.

(13) A person guilty of an offence under subsection (9) is liable on summary conviction to imprisonment for a term not exceeding three months or a fine not exceeding level 4 on the standard scale or both, notwithstanding section 45(3) of the Magistrates' Courts Act 1980.

[See Appendix, Criminal Justice Act 2003, Schedule 26, para 37(1), (3).]

14   Imposing conditions on public assemblies

(1) If the senior police officer, having regard to the time or place at which and the circumstances in which any public assembly is being held or is intended to be held, reasonably believes that –

    (a)   it may result in serious public disorder, serious damage to property or serious disruption to the life of the community, or

    (b)   the purpose of the persons organising it is the intimidation of others with a view to compelling them not to do an act they have a right to do, or to do an act they have a right not to do,

he may give directions imposing on the persons organising or taking part in the assembly such conditions as to the place at which the assembly may be (or continue to be) held, its maximum duration, or the maximum number of persons who may constitute it, as appear to him necessary to prevent such disorder, damage, disruption or intimidation.

(2) In subsection (1) 'the senior police officer' means –

    (a)   in relation to an assembly being held, the most senior in rank of the police officers present at the scene, and

    (b)   in relation to an assembly intended to be held, the chief officer of police.

(3) A direction given by a chief officer of police by virtue of subsection (2)(b) shall be given in writing.

(4) A person who organises a public assembly and knowingly fails to comply with a condition imposed under this section is guilty of an offence, but it is a defence for him to prove that the failure arose from circumstances beyond his control.

(5) A person who takes part in a public assembly and knowingly fails to comply with a condition imposed under this section is guilty of an offence, but it is a defence for him to prove that the failure arose from circumstances beyond his control.

(6) A person who incites another to commit an offence under subsection (5) is guilty of an offence.

(8) A person guilty of an offence under subsection (4) is liable on summary conviction to imprisonment for a term not exceeding 3 months or a fine not exceeding level 4 on the standard scale or both.

(9) A person guilty of an offence under subsection (5) is liable on summary conviction to a fine not exceeding level 3 on the standard scale.

(10) A person guilty of an offence under subsection (6) is liable on summary conviction to imprisonment for a term not exceeding three months or a fine not exceeding level 4 on the standard scale or both, notwithstanding section 45(3) of the Magistrates' Courts Act 1980.

[See Appendix, Criminal Justice Act 2003, Schedule 26, para 13(1), (4).]

14A Prohibiting trespassory assemblies

(1) If at any time the chief officer of police reasonably believes that an assembly is intended to be held in any district at a place on land to which the public has no right of access or only a limited right of access and that the assembly –

(a) is likely to be held without the permission of the occupier of the land or to conduct itself in such a way as to exceed the limits of any permission of his or the limits of the public's right of access, and

(b) may result –

(i) in serious disruption to the life of the community, or

(ii) where the land, or a building or monument on it, is of historical, architectural, archaeological or scientific importance, in significant damage to the land, building or monument,

he may apply to the council of the district for an order prohibiting for a specified period the holding of all trespassory assemblies in the district or a part of it, as specified.

(2) On receiving such an application, a council may –

(a) in England and Wales, with the consent of the Secretary of State make an order either in the terms of the application or with such modifications as may be approved by the Secretary of State; ...

(3) Subsection (1) does not apply in the City of London or the metropolitan police district.

(4) If at any time the Commissioner of Police for the City of London or the Commissioner of Police of the Metropolis reasonably believes that an assembly is intended to be held at a place on land to which the public has no right of access or only a limited right of access in his police area and that the assembly –

(a) is likely to be held without the permission of the occupier of the land or to conduct itself in such a way as to exceed the limits of any permission of his or the limits of the public's right of access, and

(b) may result –

(i) in serious disruption to the life of the community, or

(ii) where the land, or a building or monument on it, is of historical, architectural, archaeological or scientific importance, in significant damage to the land, building or monument,

he may with the consent of the Secretary of State make an order prohibiting for a specified period the holding of all trespassory assemblies in the area or a part of it, as specified.

(5) An order prohibiting the holding of trespassory assemblies operates to prohibit any assembly which –

(a) is held on land to which the public has no right of access or only a limited right of access, and

(b) takes place in the prohibited circumstances, that is to say, without the permission of the occupier of the land or so as to exceed the limits of any permission of his or the limits of the public's right of access.

(6) No order under this section shall prohibit the holding of assemblies for a period exceeding 4 days or in an area exceeding an area represented by a circle with a radius of 5 miles from a specified centre.

(7) An order made under this section may be revoked or varied by a subsequent order made in the same way, that is, in accordance with subsection (1) and (2) or subsection (4), as the case may be.

(8) Any order under this section shall, if not made in writing, be recorded in writing as soon as practicable after being made.

(9) In this section and sections 14B and 14C –

'assembly' means an assembly of 20 or more persons;

'land' means land in the open air;

'limited', in relation to a right of access by the public to land, means that their use of it is restricted to use for a particular purpose (as in the case of a highway or road) or is subject to other restrictions;

'occupier' means –

(a) in England and Wales, the person entitled to possession of the land by virtue of an estate or interest held by him; ...

and in subsections (1) and (4) includes the person reasonably believed by the authority applying for or making the order to be the occupier;

'public' includes a section of the public; and

'specified' means specified in an order under this section. ...

(11) In relation to Wales, the references in subsection (1) above to a district and to the council of the district shall be construed, as respects applications on and after 1 April 1996, as references to a county or county borough and to the council for that county or county borough.

14B Offences in connection with trespassory assemblies and arrest therefor

(1) A person who organises an assembly the holding of which he knows is prohibited by an order under section 14A is guilty of an offence.

(2) A person who takes part in an assembly which he knows is prohibited by an order under section 14A is guilty of an offence.

(3) In England and Wales, a person who incites another to commit an offence under subsection (2) is guilty of an offence.

(5) A person guilty of an offence under subsection (1) is liable on summary conviction to imprisonment for a term not exceeding 3 months or a fine not exceeding level 4 on the standard scale or both.

(6) A person guilty of an offence under subsection (2) is liable on summary conviction to a fine not exceeding level 3 on the standard scale.

(7) A person guilty of an offence under subsection (3) is liable on summary conviction to imprisonment for a term not exceeding 3 months or a fine not exceeding level 4 on the standard scale or both, notwithstanding section 45(3) of the Magistrates' Courts Act 1980.

[See Appendix, Criminal Justice Act 2003, Schedule 26, para 37(1), (5).]

14C Stopping persons from proceeding to trespassory assemblies

(1) If a constable in uniform reasonably believes that a person is on his way to an assembly within the area to which an order under section 14A applies which the constable reasonably believes is likely to be an assembly which is prohibited by that order, he may, subject to subsection (2) below –

(a) stop that person, and

(b) direct him not to proceed in the direction of the assembly.

(2) The power conferred by subsection (1) may only be exercised within the area to which the order applies.

(3) A person who fails to comply with a direction under subsection (1) which he knows has been given to him is guilty of an offence.

(5) A person guilty of an offence under subsection (3) is liable on summary conviction to a fine not exceeding level 3 on the standard scale.

16   Interpretation

In this Part – ...

'public assembly' means an assembly of 2 or more persons in a public place which is wholly or partly open to the air, 'public place' means –

(a) any highway, … and

(b) any place to which at the material time the public or any section of the public has access, on payment or otherwise, as of right or by virtue of express or implied permission;

'public procession' means a procession in a public place.

PART III

RACIAL HATRED

17   Meaning of 'racial hatred'

In this Part 'racial hatred' means hatred against a group of persons defined by reference to colour, race, nationality (including citizenship) or ethnic or national origins.

18   Use of words or behaviour or display of written material

A person who uses threatening, abusive or insulting words or behaviour, or displays any written material which is threatening, abusive or insulting, is guilty of an offence if –

(a) he intends thereby to stir up racial hatred, or

(b) having regard to all the circumstances racial hatred is likely to be stirred up thereby.

(2) An offence under this section may be committed in a public or a private place, except that no offence is committed where the words or behaviour are used, or the written material is displayed, by a person inside a dwelling and are not heard or seen except by other persons in that or another dwelling.

(4) In proceedings for an offence under this section it is a defence for the accused to prove that he was inside a dwelling and had no reason to believe that the words or behaviour used, or the written material displayed, would be heard or seen by a person outside that or any other dwelling.

(5) A person who is not shown to have intended to stir up racial hatred is not guilty of an offence under this section if he did not intend his words or behaviour, or the written material, to be, and was not aware that it might be, threatening, abusive or insulting.

(6) This section does not apply to words or behaviour used, or written material displayed, solely for the purpose of being included in a programme service.

19   Publishing or distributing written material

(1) A person who publishes or distributes written material which is threatening, abusive or insulting is guilty of an offence if –

(a) he intends thereby to stir up racial hatred, or

(b) having regard to all the circumstances racial hatred is likely to be stirred up thereby.

(2) In proceedings for an offence under this section it is a defence for an accused who is not shown to have intended to stir up racial hatred to prove that he was not aware of the content of the material and did not suspect, and had no reason to suspect, that it was threatening, abusive or insulting.

(3) References in this Part to the publication or distribution of written material are to its publication or distribution to the public or a section of the public.

20   Public performance of play

(1) If a public performance of a play is given which involves the use of threatening, abusive or insulting words or behaviour, any person who presents or directs the performance is guilty of an offence if –

(a) he intends thereby to stir up racial hatred, or

(b) having regard to all the circumstances (and, in particular, taking the performance as a whole) racial hatred is likely to be stirred up thereby.

(2) If a person presenting or directing the performance is not shown to have intended to stir up racial hatred, it is a defence for him to prove –

(a) that he did not know and had no reason to suspect that the performance would involve the use of the offending words or behaviour, or

(b) that he did not know and had no reason to suspect that the offending words or behaviour were threatening, abusive or insulting, or

(c) that he did not know and had no reason to suspect that the circumstances in which the performance would be given would be such that racial hatred would be likely to be stirred up.

(3) This section does not apply to a performance given solely or primarily for one or more of the following purposes –

(a) rehearsal,

(b) making a recording of the performance, or

(c) enabling the performance to be included in a programme service;

but if it is proved that the performance was attended by persons other than those directly connected with the giving of the performance or the doing in relation to it of the things mentioned in paragraph (b) or (c), the performance shall, unless the contrary is shown, be taken not to have been given solely or primarily for the purposes mentioned above.

(4) For the purposes of this section –

(a) a person shall not be treated as presenting a performance of a play by reason only of his taking part in it as a performer,

(b) a person taking part as a performer in a performance directed by another shall be treated as a person who directed the performance if without reasonable excuse he performs otherwise than in accordance with that person's direction, and

(c) a person shall be taken to have directed a performance of a play given under his direction notwithstanding that he was not present during the performance;

and a person shall not be treated as aiding or abetting the commission of an offence under this section by reason only of his taking part in a performance as a performer.

(5) In this section 'play' and 'public performance' have the same meaning as in the Theatres Act 1968.

(6) The following provisions of the Theatres Act 1968 apply in relation to an offence under this section as they apply to an offence under section 2 of that Act –

section 9 (script as evidence of what was performed),

section 10 (power to make copies of script),

section 15 (power of entry and inspection).

21 Distributing, showing or playing a recording

(1) A person who distributes, or shows or plays, a recording of visual images or sounds which are threatening, abusive or insulting is guilty of an offence if –

(a) he intends thereby to stir up racial hatred, or

(b) having regard to all the circumstances racial hatred is likely to be stirred up thereby.

(2) In this Part 'recording' means any record from which visual images or sounds may, by any means, be reproduced; and references to the distribution, showing or playing of a recording are to its distribution, showing or playing to the public or a section of the public.

(3) In proceedings for an offence under this section it is a defence for an accused who is not

shown to have intended to stir up racial hatred to prove that he was aware of the content of the recording and did not suspect, and had no reason to suspect, that it was threatening, abusive or insulting.

(4) This section does not apply to the showing or playing of a recording solely for the purpose of enabling the recording to be included in a programme service.

22   Broadcasting or including programme in cable programme service

(1) If a programme involving threatening, abusive or insulting visual images or sounds is included in a programme service, each of the persons mentioned in subsection (2) is guilty of an offence if –

    (a) he intends thereby to stir up racial hatred, or

    (b) having regard to all the circumstances racial hatred is likely to be stirred up thereby.

(2) The persons are –

    (a) the person providing the programme service,

    (b) any person by whom the programme is produced or directed, and

    (c) any person by whom offending words or behaviour are used.

(3) If the person providing the service, or a person by whom the programme was produced or directed, is not shown to have intended to stir up racial hatred, it is a defence for him to prove that –

    (a) he did not know and had no reason to suspect that the programme would involve the offending material, and

    (b) having regard to the circumstances in which the programme was included in a programme service, it was not reasonably practicable for him to secure the removal of the material.

(4) It is a defence for a person by whom the programme was produced or directed who is shown to have intended to stir up racial hatred to prove that he did not know and had no reason to suspect –

    (a) that the programme would be included in a programme service, or

    (b) that the circumstances in which the programme would be so included would be such that racial hatred would be likely to be stirred up.

(5) It is a defence for a person by whom offending words or behaviour were used and who is not shown to have intended to stir up racial hatred to prove that he did not know and had no reason to suspect –

    (a) that a programme involving the use of the offending material would be included in a programme service, or

    (b) that the circumstances in which a programme involving the use of the offending material would be so included, or in which a programme so included would involve the use of the offending material, would be such that racial hatred would be likely to be stirred up.

(6) A person who is not shown to have intended to stir up racial hatred is not guilty of an offence under this section if he did not know, and had no reason to suspect, that the offending material was threatening, abusive or insulting.

23   Possession of racially inflammatory material

(1) A person who has in his possession written material which is threatening, abusive or insulting, or a recording of visual images or sounds which are threatening, abusive or insulting, with a view to –

(a) in the case of written material, its being displayed, published, distributed, or included in a programme service, whether by himself or another, or

(b) in the case of a recording, its being distributed, shown, played, or included in a programme service, whether by himself or another,

is guilty of an offence if he intends racial hatred to be stirred up thereby or, having regard to all the circumstances, racial hatred is likely to be stirred up thereby.

(2) For this purpose regard shall be had to such display, publication, distribution, showing, playing, or inclusion in a programme service as he has, or it may reasonably be inferred that he has, in view.

(3) In proceedings for an offence under this section it is a defence for an accused who is not shown to have intended to stir up racial hatred to prove that he was not aware of the content of the written material or recording and did not suspect, and had no reason to suspect, that it was threatening, abusive or insulting.

[See Appendix, Racial and Religious Hatred Act 2006, s1.]

PART V

MISCELLANEOUS AND GENERAL

38   Contamination of or interference with goods with intention of causing public alarm or anxiety, etc

(1) It is an offence for a person, with the intention –

(a) of causing public alarm or anxiety, or

(b) of causing injury to members of the public consuming or using the goods, or

(c) of causing economic loss to any person by reason of the goods being shunned by members of the public, or

(d) of causing economic loss to any person by reason of steps taken to avoid any such alarm or anxiety, injury or loss,

to contaminate or interfere with goods, or make it appear that goods have been contaminated or interfered with, or to place goods which have been contaminated or interfered with, or which appear to have been contaminated or interfered with, in a place where goods of that description are consumed, used, sold or otherwise supplied.

(2) It is also an offence for a person, with any such intention as is mentioned in paragraph (a), (c) or (d) of subsection (1), to threaten that he or another will do, or to claim that he or another has done, any of the acts mentioned in that subsection.

(3) It is an offence for a person to be in possession of any of the following articles with a view to the commission of an offence under subsection (1) –

(a) materials to be used for contaminating or interfering with goods or making it appear that goods have been contaminated or interfered with, or

(b) goods which have been contaminated or interfered with, or which appear to have been contaminated or interfered with.

(4) A person guilty of an offence under this section is liable –

(a) on conviction on indictment to imprisonment for a term not exceeding 10 years or a fine or both, or

(b) on summary conviction to imprisonment for a term not exceeding six months or a fine not exceeding the statutory maximum or both.

(5) In this section 'goods' includes substances whether natural or manufactured and whether or not incorporated in or mixed with other goods.

(6) The reference in subsection (2) to a person claiming that certain acts have been committed does not include a person who in good faith reports or warns that such acts have been, or appear to have been, committed.

As amended by the Broadcasting Act 1990, ss164(1), (2)(b)(c), (3), (4), 203(3), Schedule 21; Criminal Justice and Public Order Act 1994, ss70, 71, 154; Public Order (Amendment) Act 1996, s1; Anti-terrorism, Crime and Security Act 2001, ss37, 125, Schedule 8, Pt 4; Anti-social Behaviour Act 2003, s57; Serious Organised Crime and Police Act 2005, ss111, 174(2), Schedule 7, Pt 1, para 26, Schedule 17, Pt 2.

CROSSBOWS ACT 1987
(1987 c 32)

1   Sale and letting on hire
A person who sells or lets on hire a crossbow to a person under the age of seventeen is guilty of an offence, unless he believes him to be seventeen years of age or older and has reasonable ground for the belief.

2   Purchase and hiring
A person under the age of seventeen who buys or hires a crossbow or a part of a crossbow is guilty of an offence.

3   Possession
A person under the age of seventeen who has with him –
      (a)   a crossbow which is capable of discharging a missile, or
      (b)   parts of a crossbow which together (and without any other parts) can be assembled to
           form a crossbow capable of discharging a missile,
is guilty of an offence, unless he is under the supervision of a person who is twenty-one years of age or older.

CRIMINAL JUSTICE ACT 1987
(1987 c 38)

12   Charges of and penalty for conspiracy to defraud
(1) If –
      (a)   a person agrees with any other person or persons that a course of conduct shall be
           pursued; and
      (b)   that course of conduct will necessarily amount to or involve the commission of any
           offence or offences by one or more of the parties to the agreement if the agreement is
           carried out in accordance with their intentions,
the fact that it will do so shall not preclude a charge of conspiracy to defraud being brought against any of them in respect of the agreement. ...

(3) A person guilty of conspiracy to defraud is liable on conviction on indictment to imprisonment for a term not exceeding 10 years or a fine or both.

MALICIOUS COMMUNICATIONS ACT 1988

(1988 c 27)

1   Offence of sending letters, etc with intent to cause distress or anxiety

(1) Any person who sends to another person –

    (a)   a letter, electronic communication or article of any description which conveys –

        (i)   a message which is indecent or grossly offensive;

        (ii)   a threat;

        (iii)   information which is false and known or believed to be false by the sender; or

        (iv)   under section 29(4) or (6) of the Violent Crime Reduction Act 2006

    (b)   any article or electronic communication which is, in whole or part, of an indecent or grossly offensive nature,

is guilty of an offence if his purpose, or one of his purposes, in sending it is that it should, so far as falling within paragraph (a) or (b) above, cause distress or anxiety to the recipient or to any other person to whom he intends that it is or its contents or nature should be communicated.

(2) A person is not guilty of an offence by virtue of subsection (1)(a)(ii) above if he shows –

    (a)   that the threat was used to reinforce a demand made by him on reasonable grounds; and

    (b)   that he believed, and had reasonable grounds for believing, that the use of the threat was a proper means of reinforcing the demand.

(2A) In this section 'electronic communication' includes –

    (a)   any oral or other communication by means of a telecommunication system (within the meaning of the Telecommunications Act 1984 (c 12)); and

    (b)   any communication (however sent) that is in electronic form.

(3) In this section references to sending include references to delivering or transmitting and to causing to be sent, delivered or transmitted and 'sender' shall be construed accordingly.

(4) A person guilty of an offence under this section shall be liable on summary conviction to imprisonment for a term not exceeding six months or to a fine not exceeding level 5 on the standard scale, or to both.

As amended by the Criminal Justice and Police Act 2001, s43.

CRIMINAL JUSTICE ACT 1988

(1988 c 33)

35   Scope of Part IV

(1) A case to which this Part of this Act applies may be referred to the Court of Appeal under section 36 below.

(2) Subject to Rules of Court, the jurisdiction of the Court of Appeal under section 36 below shall be exercised by the criminal division of the Court, and references to the Court of Appeal in this Part of this Act shall be construed as references to that division.

(3) This Part of this Act applies to any case –

    (a)   of a description specified in an order under this section; or

    (b)   in which sentence is passed on a person –

        (i)   for an offence triable only on indictment; or

        (ii)   for an offence of a description specified in an order under this section.

(4) The Secretary of State may by order made by statutory instrument provide that this Part of this Act shall apply to any case of a description specified in the order or to any case.

(5) A statutory instrument containing an order under this section shall be subject to annulment in pursuance of a resolution of either House of Parliament.

(6) In this Part of this Act 'sentence' has the same meaning as in the Criminal Appeal Act 1968, except that it does not include an interim hospital order under Part III of the Mental Health Act 1983, and 'sentencing' shall be construed accordingly. ...

36   Reviews of sentencing

(1) If it appears to the Attorney General –

    (a)   that the sentencing of a person in a proceeding in the Crown Court has been unduly lenient; and

    (b)   that the case is one to which this Part of this Act applies,

he may, with the leave of the Court of Appeal, refer the case to them for them to review the sentencing of that person; and on such a reference the Court of Appeal may –

    (i)   quash any sentence passed on him in the proceeding; and

    (ii)   in place of it pass such sentence as they think appropriate for the case and as the court below had power to pass when dealing with him.

(2) Without prejudice to the generality of subsection (1) above, the condition specified in paragraph (a) of that subsection may be satisfied if it appears to the Attorney General that the judge –

    (a)   erred in law as to his powers of sentencing; or

    (b)   failed to impose a sentence required by –

        (i)   section 51A(2) of the Firearms Act 1968;

        (ii)   section 110(2) or 111(2) of the Powers of Criminal Courts (Sentencing) Act 2000;

        (iii)   any of sections 225 to 228 of the Criminal Justice Act 2003; or

        (iv)   under section 29(4) or (6) of the Violent Crime Reduction Act 2006.

(3) For the purposes of this Part of this Act any two or more sentences are to be treated as passed in the same proceeding if they would be so treated for the purposes of section 11 of the Criminal Appeal Act 1968.

(3A) Where a reference under this section relates to an order under subsection (2) of section 269 of the Criminal Justice Act 2003 (determination of minimum term in relation to mandatory life sentence), the Court of Appeal shall not, in deciding what order under that section is appropriate for the case, make any allowance for the fact that the person to whom it relates is being sentenced for a second time.

(4) No judge shall sit as a member of the Court of Appeal on the hearing of, or shall determine any application in proceedings incidental or preliminary to, a reference under this section of a sentence passed by himself.

(5) Where the Court of Appeal have concluded their review of a case referred to them under this section the Attorney General or the person to whose sentencing the reference relates may refer a point of law involved in any sentence passed on that person in the proceeding to the House of Lords for their opinion, and the House shall consider the point and give their opinion on it accordingly, and either remit the case to the Court of Appeal to be dealt with or deal with it themselves; and section 35(1) of the Criminal Appeal Act 1968 (composition of House for appeals) shall apply also in relation to any proceedings of the House under this section.

(6) A reference under subsection (5) above shall be made only with the leave of the Court of Appeal or the House of Lords; and leave shall not be granted unless it is certified by the Court of Appeal that the point of law is of general public importance and it appears to the Court of

Appeal or the House of Lords (as the case may be) that the point is one which ought to be considered by that House.

(7) For the purpose of dealing with a case under this section the House of Lords may exercise any powers of the Court of Appeal.

(8) The supplementary provisions contained in Schedule 3 to this Act shall have effect. ...

39   Common assault and battery to be summary offences

Common assault and battery shall be summary offences and a person guilty of either of them shall be liable to a fine not exceeding level 5 on the standard scale, to imprisonment for a term not exceeding six months, or to both.

134   Torture

(1) A public official or person acting in an official capacity, whatever his nationality, commits the offence of torture if in the United Kingdom or elsewhere he intentionally inflicts severe pain or suffering on another in the performance or purported performance of his official duties.

(2) A person not falling within subsection (1) above commits the offence of torture, whatever his nationality, if –

    (a)   in the United Kingdom or elsewhere he intentionally inflicts severe pain or suffering on another at the instigation or with the consent or acquiescence –

        (i)   of a public official; or

        (ii) of a person acting in an official capacity; and

    (b)   the official or other person is performing or purporting to perform his official duties when he instigates the commission of the offence or consents to or acquiesces in it.

(3) It is immaterial whether the pain or suffering is physical or mental and whether it is caused by an act or an omission.

(4) It shall be a defence for a person charged with an offence under this section in respect of any conduct of his to prove that he had lawful authority, justification or excuse for that conduct.

(5) For the purposes of this section 'lawful authority, justification or excuse' means –

    (a)   in relation to pain or suffering inflicted in the United Kingdom, lawful authority, justification or excuse under the law of the part of the United Kingdom where it was inflicted;

    (b)   in relation to pain or suffering inflicted outside the United Kingdom –

        (i)   if it was inflicted by a United Kingdom official acting under the law of the United Kingdom or by a person acting in an official capacity under that law, lawful authority, justification or excuse under that law;

        (ii) if it was inflicted by a United Kingdom official acting under the law of any part of the United Kingdom or by a person acting in an official capacity under such law, lawful authority, justification or excuse under the law of the part of the United Kingdom under whose law he was acting; and

        (iii) in any other case, lawful authority, justification or excuse under the law of the place where it was inflicted.

(6) A person who commits the offence of torture shall be liable on conviction on indictment to imprisonment for life.

139   Offence of having article with blade or point in public place

(1) Subject to subsections (4) and (5) below, any person who has an article to which this section applies with him in a public place shall be guilty of an offence.

(2) Subject to subsection (3) below, this section applies to any article which has a blade or is sharply pointed except a folding penknife.

(3) This section applies to a folding pocketknife if the cutting edge of its blade exceeds three inches.

(4) It shall be a defence for a person charged with an offence under this section to prove that he had good reason or lawful authority for having the article with him in a public place.

(5) Without prejudice to the generality of subsection (4) above, it shall be a defence for a person charged with an offence under this section to prove that he had the article with him –

    (a) for use at work;

    (b) for religious reasons; or

    (c) as part of any national costume.

(6) A person guilty of an offence under subsection (1) above shall be liable –

    (a) on summary conviction, to imprisonment for a term not exceeding six months, or a fine not exceeding the statutory maximum, or both;

    (b) on conviction on indictment, to imprisonment for a term not exceeding four years, or a fine, or both.

(7) In this section 'public place' includes any place to which at the material time the public have or are permitted access, whether on payment or otherwise.

(8) This section shall not have effect in relation to anything done before it comes into force.

139A   Offence of having article with blade or point (or offensive weapon) on school premises

(1) Any person who has an article to which section 139 of this Act applies with him on school premises shall be guilty of an offence.

(2) Any person who has an offensive weapon within the meaning of section 1 of the Prevention of Crime Act 1953 with him on school premises shall be guilty of an offence.

(3) It shall be a defence for a person charged with an offence under subsection (1) or (2) above to prove that he had good reason or lawful authority for having the article or weapon with him on the premises in question.

(4) Without prejudice to the generality of subsection (3) above, it shall be a defence for a person charged with an offence under subsection (1) or (2) above to prove that he had the article or weapon in question with him –

    (a) for use at work,

    (b) for educational purposes,

    (c) for religious reasons, or

    (d) as part of any national costume.

(5) A person shall be guilty of an offence –

    (a) under subsection (1) above shall be liable –

        (i) on summary conviction to imprisonment for a term not exceeding six months, or a fine not exceeding the statutory maximum, or both;

        (ii) on conviction on indictment, to imprisonment for a term not exceeding four years, or a fine, or both;

    (b) under subsection (2) above shall be liable –

        (i) on summary conviction, to imprisonment for a term not exceeding six months, or a fine not exceeding the statutory maximum, or both;

        (ii) on conviction on indictment, to imprisonment for a term not exceeding four years, or a fine, or both.

(6) In this section and section 139B, 'school premises' means land used for the purposes of a school excluding any land occupied solely as a dwelling by a person employed at the school; and 'school' has the meaning given by section 4 of the Education Act 1996. ...

139B   Power of entry to search for articles with a blade or point and offensive weapons

(1) A constable may enter school premises and search those premises and any person on those premises for –

  (a) any article to which section 139 of this Act applies, or

  (b) any offensive weapon within the meaning of section 1 of the Prevention of Crime Act 1953,

if he has reasonable grounds for suspecting that an offence under section 139A of this Act is being, or has been, committed.

(2) If in the course of a search under this section a constable discovers an article or weapon which he has reasonable grounds for suspecting to be an article or weapon of a kind described in subsection (1) above, he may seize and retain it.

(3) The constable may use reasonable force, if necessary, in the exercise of the power of entry conferred by this section. …

141 Offensive weapons

(1) Any person who manufactures, sells or hires or offers for sale or hire, exposes of has in his possession for the purpose of sale or hire, or lends or gives to any other person, a weapon to which this section applies shall be guilty of an offence and liable on summary conviction to imprisonment for a term not exceeding six months or to a fine not exceeding level 5 on the standard scale or both.

(2) The Secretary of State may by order made by statutory instrument direct that this section shall apply to any description of weapon specified in the order except –

  (a) any weapon subject to the Firearms Act 1968; and

  (b) crossbows. …

(3) A statutory instrument containing an order under this section shall not be made unless a draft of the instrument has been laid before Parliament and has been approved by a resolution of each House of Parliament.

(4) The importation of a weapon to which this section applies is hereby prohibited.

(5) It shall be a defence for any person charged in respect of any conduct of his relating to a weapon to which this section applies –

  (a) with an offence under subsection (1) above; or

  (b) with an offence under section 50(2) or (3) of the Customs and Excise Management Act 1979 (improper importation),

to prove that his conduct was only for the purposes of functions carried out on behalf of the Crown or of a visiting force. …

(8) It shall be a defence for any person charged in respect of any conduct of his relating to a weapon to which this section applies –

  (a) with an offence under subsection (1) above; or

  (b) with an offence under section 50(2) or (3) of the Customs and Excise Management Act 1979,

to prove that the conduct in question was only for the purposes of making the weapon available to a museum or gallery to which this subsection applies.

(9) If a person acting on behalf of a museum or gallery to which subsection (8) above applies is charged with hiring or lending a weapon to which this section applies, it shall be a defence for him to prove that he had reasonable grounds for believing that the person to whom he lent or hired it would use it only for cultural, artistic or educational purposes.

(10) Subsection (8) above applies to a museum or gallery only if it does not distribute profits.

(11) In this section 'museum or gallery' includes any institution which has as its purpose, or one

of its purposes, the preservation, display and interpretation of material of historical, artistic or scientific interest and gives the public access to it. ...

141A   Sale of knives and certain articles with blade or point to persons under sixteen
(1) Any person who sells to a person under the age of sixteen years an article to which this section applies shall be guilty of an offence and liable on summary conviction to imprisonment for a term not exceeding six months, or a fine not exceeding level 5 on the standard scale, or both.
(2) Subject to subsection (3) below, this section applies to –
  (a) any knife, knife blade or razor blade,
  (b) any axe, and
  (c) any other article which has a blade or which is sharply pointed and which is made or adapted for use for causing injury to the person.
(3) This section does not apply to any article described in –
  (a) section 1 of the Restriction of Offensive Weapons Act 1959,
  (b) an order made under section 141(2) of this Act, or
  (c) an order made by the Secretary of State under this section.
(4) It shall be a defence for a person charged with an offence under subsection (1) above to prove that he took all reasonable precautions and exercised all due diligence to avoid the commission of the offence. ...

As amended by the Criminal Justice Act 1993, ss29(1), 30, 31 and 32; Criminal Justice and Public Order Act 1994, s168(1), Schedule 9, para 34; Offensive Weapons Act 1996, ss3(1), 4(1), 6(1); Education Act 1996, s582(1), Schedule 37, Pt I, para 69; Crime (Sentences) Act 1997, s55, Schedule 4, para 13; Powers of Criminal Courts (Sentencing) Act 2000, s165(1), Schedule 9, para 102; Criminal Justice Act 2003, ss272(1), 304, 331, Schedule 32, Pt 1, paras 45, 46, Schedule 36, Pt 6, para 96(a); Violent Crime Reduction Act 2006, ss42(1), 48, 49, 65, Schedule 1,para 3(1), (2), Schedule 5.

FIREARMS (AMENDMENT) ACT 1988
(1988 c 45)

5   Restriction on sale of ammunition for smooth-bore guns
(1) This section applies to ammunition to which section 1 of the [Firearms Act 1968] does not apply and which is capable of being used in a shot gun or in a smooth-bore gun to which that section applies.
(2) It is an offence for a person to sell any such ammunition to another person in the United Kingdom who is neither a registered firearms dealer nor a person who sells such ammunition by way of trade or business unless that other person –
  (a) produces a certificate authorising him to possess a gun of a kind mentioned in subsection (1) above; or
  (b) shows that he is by virtue of that Act or this Act entitled to have possession of such a gun without holding a certificate; or
  (c) produces a certificate authorising another person to possess such a gun, together with that person's written authority to purchase the ammunition on his behalf.
(3) An offence under this section shall be punishable on summary conviction with imprisonment for a term not exceeding six months or a fine not exceeding level 5 on the standard scale or both.

6   Shortening of barrels
(1) Subject to subsection (2) below, it is an offence to shorten to a length less than 24 inches the

barrel of any smooth-bore gun to which section 1 of the principal Act applies other than one which has a barrel with a bore exceeding two inches in diameter; and that offence shall be punishable –

    (a) on summary conviction, with imprisonment for a term not exceeding six months or a fine not exceeding the statutory maximum or both;

    (b) on indictment, with imprisonment for a term not exceeding five years or a fine or both.

(2) It is not an offence under this section for a registered firearms dealer to shorten the barrel of a gun for the sole purpose of replacing a defective part of the barrel so as to produce a barrel not less than 24 inches in length.

7   Conversion not to affect classification

(1) Any weapon which –

    (a) has at any time (whether before or after the passing of the Firearms (Amendment) Act 1997) been a weapon of a kind described in section 5(1) or (1A) of the principal Act (including any amendments to section 5(1) made under section 1(4) of this Act); and

    (b) is not a self-loading or pump-action smooth-bore gun which has at any such time been such a weapon by reason only of having had a barrel less than 24 inches in length,

shall be treated as a prohibited weapon notwithstanding anything done for the purpose of converting it into a weapon of a different kind.

(2) Any weapon which –

    (a) has at any time since the coming into force of section 2 above been a weapon to which section 1 of the principal Act applies; or

    (b) would at any previous time have been such a weapon if those sections had then been in force,

shall, if it has, or at any time has had, a rifled barrel less than 24 inches in length, be treated as a weapon to which section 1 of the principal Act applies notwithstanding anything done for the purpose of converting it into a shot gun or an air weapon.

(3) For the purposes of subsection (2) above there shall be disregarded the shortening of a barrel by a registered firearms dealer for the sole purpose of replacing part of it so as to produce a barrel not less than 24 inches in length.

8   De-activated weapons

For the purposes of the principal Act and this Act it shall be presumed, unless the contrary is shown, that a firearm has been rendered incapable of discharging any shot, bullet or other missile, and has consequently ceased to be a firearm within the meaning of those Acts, if –

    (a) it bears a mark which has been approved by the Secretary of State for denoting that fact and which has been made either by one or the two companies mentioned in section 58(1) of the principal Act or by such other person as may be approved by the Secretary of State for the purposes of this section; and

    (b) that company or person has certified in writing that work has been carried out on the firearm in a manner approved by the Secretary of State for rendering it incapable of discharging any shot, bullet or other missile.

25   Interpretation of supplementary provisions

(1) In this Act 'the principal Act' means the Firearms Act 1968 and any expression which is also used in that Act has the same meaning as in that Act. ...

As amended by the Firearms (Amendment) Act 1997, s52, Schedule 2, paras 15, 16.

ROAD TRAFFIC ACT 1988
(1988 c 52)

1   Causing death by dangerous driving
A person who causes the death of another person by driving a mechanically propelled vehicle dangerously on a road or other public place is guilty of an offence.

2   Dangerous driving
A person who drives a mechanically propelled vehicle dangerously on a road or other public place is guilty of an offence.

2A   Meaning of dangerous driving
(1) For the purposes of sections 1 and 2 above a person is to be regarded as driving dangerously if (and, subject to subsection (2) below, only if) –
      (a) the way he drives falls far below what would be expected of a competent and careful driver, and
      (b) it would be obvious to a competent and careful driver that driving in that way would be dangerous.

(2) A person is also to be regarded as driving dangerously for the purposes of sections 1 and 2 above if it would be obvious to a competent and careful driver that driving the vehicle in its current state would be dangerous.

(3) In subsections (1) and (2) above 'dangerous' refers to danger either of injury to any person or of serious damage to property; and in determining for the purposes of those subsections what would be expected of, or obvious to, a competent and careful driver in a particular case, regard shall be had not only to the circumstances of which he could be expected to be aware but also to any circumstances shown to have been within the knowledge of the accused.

(4) In determining for the purposes of subsection (2) above the state of a vehicle, regard may be had to anything attached to or carried on or in it and to the manner in which it is attached or carried.

[See Appendix, Road Safety Act 2006, s20(1).]

3   Careless, and inconsiderate, driving
If a person drives a mechanically propelled vehicle on a road or other public place without due care and attention, or without reasonable consideration for other persons using the road or place, he is guilty of an offence.

[See Appendix, Road Safety Act 2006, ss21(1), 30.]

3A   Causing death by careless driving when under the influence of drink or drugs
(1) If a person causes the death of another person by driving a mechanically propelled vehicle on a road or other public place without due care and attention, or without reasonable consideration for other persons using the road or place, and –
      (a) he is, at the time when he is driving, unfit to drive through drink or drugs, or
      (b) he has consumed so much alcohol that the proportion of it in his breath, blood or urine at that time exceeds the prescribed limit, or
      (c) he is, within 18 hours after that time, required to provide a specimen in pursuance of section 7 of this Act, but without reasonable excuse fails to provide it,
he is guilty of an offence.

(2) For the purposes of this section a person shall be taken to be unfit to drive at any time when his ability to drive properly is impaired.

(3) Subsection (1)(b) and (c) above shall not apply in relation to a person driving a mechanically propelled vehicle other than a motor vehicle.

[See Appendix, Road Safety Act 2006, ss31(1)–(3).]

4   Driving, or being in charge, when under influence of drink or drugs

(1) A person who, when driving or attempting to drive a mechanically propelled vehicle on a road or other public place, is unfit to drive through drink or drugs is guilty of an offence.

(2) Without prejudice to subsection (1) above, a person who, when in charge of a mechanically propelled vehicle which is on a road or other public place, is unfit to drive through drink or drugs is guilty of an offence.

(3) For the purposes of subsection (2) above, a person shall be deemed not to have been in charge of a mechanically propelled vehicle if he proves that at the material time the circumstances were such that there was no likelihood of his driving it so long as he remained unfit to drive through drinks or drugs.

(4) The court may, in determining whether there was such a likelihood as is mentioned in subsection (3) above, disregard any injury to him and any damage to the vehicle.

(5) For the purposes of this section, a person shall be taken to be unfit to drive if his ability to drive properly is for the time being impaired.

5   Driving or being in charge of a motor vehicle with alcohol concentration above prescribed limit

(1) If a person –
  (a)   drives or attempts to drive a motor vehicle on a road or other public place, or
  (b)   is in charge of a motor vehicle on a road or other public place,
after consuming so much alcohol that the proportion of it in his breath, blood or urine exceeds the prescribed limit he is guilty of an offence,

(2) It is a defence for a person charged with an offence under subsection (1)(b) above to prove that at the time he is alleged to have committed the offence the circumstances were such that there was no likelihood of his driving the vehicle whilst the proportion of alcohol in his breath, blood or urine remained likely to exceed the prescribed limit.

(3) The court may, in determining whether there was such a likelihood as is mentioned of subsection (2) above, disregard any injury to him and any damage to the vehicle.

6   Power to administer preliminary tests

(1) If any of subsections (2) to (5) applies a constable may require a person to co-operate with any one or more preliminary tests administered to the person by that constable or another constable.

(2) This subsection applies if a constable reasonably suspects that the person –
  (a)   is driving, is attempting to drive or is in charge of a motor vehicle on a road or other public place, and
  (b)   has alcohol or a drug in his body or is under the influence of a drug.

(3) This subsection applies if a constable reasonably suspects that the person –
  (a)   has been driving, attempting to drive or in charge of a motor vehicle on a road or other public place while having alcohol or a drug in his body or while unfit to drive because of a drug, and
  (b)   still has alcohol or a drug in his body or is still under the influence of a drug.

(4) This subsection applies if a constable reasonably suspects that the person –

    (a) is or has been driving, attempting to drive or in charge of a motor vehicle on a road or other public place, and

    (b) has committed a traffic offence while the vehicle was in motion.

(5) This subsection applies if –

    (a) an accident occurs owing to the presence of a motor vehicle on a road or other public place, and

    (b) a constable reasonably believes that the person was driving, attempting to drive or in charge of the vehicle at the time of the accident.

(6) A person commits an offence if without reasonable excuse he fails to co-operate with a preliminary test in pursuance of a requirement imposed under this section.

(7) A constable may administer a preliminary test by virtue of any of subsections (2) to (4) only if he is in uniform.

(8) In this section –

    (a) a reference to a preliminary test is to any of the tests described in sections 6A to 6C, and

    (b) 'traffic offence' means an offence under –

        (i)   a provision of Part II of the Public Passenger Vehicles Act 1981 (c 14),

        (ii) a provision of the Road Traffic Regulation Act 1984 (c 27),

        (iii) a provision of the Road Traffic Offenders Act 1988 (c 53) other than a provision of Part III, or

        (iv) a provision of this Act other than a provision of Part V [Driving instruction].

6A   Preliminary breath test

(1) A preliminary breath test is a procedure whereby the person to whom the test is administered provides a specimen of breath to be used for the purpose of obtaining, by means of a device of a type approved by the Secretary of State, an indication whether the proportion of alcohol in the person's breath or blood is likely to exceed the prescribed limit.

(2) A preliminary breath test administered in reliance on section 6(2) to (4) may be administered only at or near the place where the requirement to co-operate with the test is imposed.

(3) A preliminary breath test administered in reliance on section 6(5) may be administered –

    (a) at or near the place where the requirement to co-operate with the test is imposed, or

    (b) if the constable who imposes the requirement thinks it expedient, at a police station specified by him.

6B   Preliminary impairment test

(1) A preliminary impairment test is a procedure whereby the constable administering the test –

    (a) observes the person to whom the test is administered in his performance of tasks specified by the constable, and

    (b) makes such other observations of the person's physical state as the constable thinks expedient.

(2) The Secretary of State shall issue (and may from time to time revise) a code of practice about –

    (a) the kind of task that may be specified for the purpose of a preliminary impairment test,

    (b) the kind of observation of physical state that may be made in the course of a preliminary impairment test,

    (c) the manner in which a preliminary impairment test should be administered, and

    (d) the inferences that may be drawn from observations made in the course of a preliminary impairment test.

(3) In issuing or revising the code of practice the Secretary of State shall aim to ensure that a preliminary impairment test is designed to indicate –

    (a)   whether a person is unfit to drive, and

    (b)   if he is, whether or not his unfitness is likely to be due to drink or drugs.

(4) A preliminary impairment test may be administered –

    (a)   at or near the place where the requirement to co-operate with the test is imposed, or

    (b)   if the constable who imposes the requirement thinks it expedient, at a police station specified by him.

(5) A constable administering a preliminary impairment test shall have regard to the code of practice under this section.

(6) A constable may administer a preliminary impairment test only if he is approved for that purpose by the chief officer of the police force to which he belongs.

(7) A code of practice under this section may include provision about –

    (a)   the giving of approval under subsection (6), and

    (b)   in particular, the kind of training that a constable should have undergone, or the kind of qualification that a constable should possess, before being approved under that subsection.

6C   Preliminary drug test

(1) A preliminary drug test is a procedure by which a specimen of sweat or saliva is –

    (a)   obtained, and

    (b)   used for the purpose of obtaining, by means of a device of a type approved by the Secretary of State, an indication whether the person to whom the test is administered has a drug in his body.

(2) A preliminary drug test may be administered –

    (a)   at or near the place where the requirement to co-operate with the test is imposed, or

    (b)   if the constable who imposes the requirement thinks it expedient, at a police station specified by him.

6D   Arrest

(1) A constable may arrest a person without warrant if as a result of a preliminary breath test the constable reasonably suspects that the proportion of alcohol in the person's breath or blood exceeds the prescribed limit.

(1A) The fact that specimens of breath have been provided under section 7 of this Act by the person concerned does not prevent subsection (1) above having effect if the constable who imposed on him the requirement to provide the specimens has reasonable cause to believe that the device used to analyse the specimens has not produced a reliable indication of the proportion of alcohol in the breath of the person.

(2) A constable may arrest a person without warrant if –

    (a)   the person fails to co-operate with a preliminary test in pursuance of a requirement imposed under section 6, and

    (b)   the constable reasonably suspects that the person has alcohol or a drug in his body or is under the influence of a drug.

(2A) A person arrested under this section may, instead of being taken to a police station, be detained at or near the place where the preliminary test was, or would have been, administered, with a view to imposing on him there a requirement under section 7 of this Act.

(3) A person may not be arrested under this section while at a hospital as a patient.

6E Power of entry

(1) A constable may enter any place (using reasonable force if necessary) for the purpose of –

    (a) imposing a requirement by virtue of section 6(5) following an accident in a case where the constable reasonably suspects that the accident involved injury of any person, or

    (b) arresting a person under section 6D following an accident in a case where the constable reasonably suspects that the accident involved injury of any person.

(2) This section –

    (a) does not extend to Scotland, and

    (b) is without prejudice to any rule of law or enactment about the right of a constable in Scotland to enter any place.

7 Provision of specimens for analysis

(1) In the course of an investigation into whether a person has committed an offence under section 3A, 4 or 5 of this Act a constable may, subject to the following provisions of this section and section 9 of this Act, require him –

    (a) to provide two specimens of breath for analysis by means of a device of a type approved by the Secretary of State, or

    (b) to provide a specimen of blood or urine for a laboratory test.

(2) A requirement under this section to provide specimens of breath can only be made –

    (a) at a police station,

    (b) at a hospital, or

    (c) at or near a place where a relevant breath test has been administered to the person concerned or would have been so administered but for his failure to co-operate with it.

(2A) For the purposes of this section 'a relevant breath test' is a procedure involving the provision by the person concerned of a specimen of breath to be used for the purpose of obtaining an indication whether the proportion of alcohol in his breath or blood is likely to exceed the prescribed limit.

(2B) A requirement under this section to provide specimens of breath may not be made at or near a place mentioned in subsection (2)(c) above unless the constable making it –

    (a) is in uniform, or

    (b) has imposed a requirement on the person concerned to co-operate with a relevant breath test in circumstances in which section 6(5) of this Act applies.

(2C) Where a constable has imposed a requirement on the person concerned to co-operate with a relevant breath test at any place, he is entitled to remain at or near that place in order to impose on him there a requirement under this section.

(2D) If a requirement under subsection (1)(a) above has been made at a place other than at a police station, such a requirement may subsequently be made at a police station if (but only if) –

    (a) a device or a reliable device of the type mentioned in subsection (1)(a) above was not available at that place or it was for any other reason not practicable to use such a device there, or

    (b) the constable who made the previous requirement has reasonable cause to believe that the device used there has not produced a reliable indication of the proportion of alcohol in the breath of the person concerned.

(3) A requirement under this section to provide a specimen of blood or urine can only be made at a police station or at a hospital; and it cannot be made at a police station unless –

(a) the constable making the requirement has reasonable cause to believe that for medical reasons a specimen of breath cannot be provided or should not be required, or

(b) specimens of breath have not been provided elsewhere and at the time the requirement is made a device or a reliable device of the type mentioned in subsection (1)(a) above is not available at the police station or it is then for any other reason not practicable to use such a device there, or

(bb) a device of the type mentioned in subsection (1)(a) above has been used (at the police station or elsewhere) but the constable who required the specimens of breath has reasonable cause to believe that the device has not produced a reliable indication of the proportion of alcohol in the breath of the person concerned, or

(bc) as a result of the administration of a preliminary drug test, the constable making the requirement has reasonable cause to believe that the person required to provide a specimen of blood or urine has a drug in his body, or

(c) the suspected offence is one under section 3A or 4 of this Act and the constable making the requirement has been advised by a medical practitioner that the condition of the person required to provide the specimen might be due to some drug;

but may then be made notwithstanding that the person required to provide the specimen has already provided or been required to provide two specimens of breath.

(4) If the provision of a specimen other than a specimen of breath may be required in pursuance of this section the question whether it is to be a specimen of blood or a specimen of urine and, in the case of a specimen of blood, the question who is to be asked to take it shall be decided (subject to subsection (4A)) by the constable making the requirement.

(4A) Where a constable decides for the purposes of subsection (4) to require the provision of a specimen of blood, there shall be no requirement to provide such a specimen if –

(a) the medical practitioner who is asked to take the specimen is of the opinion that, for medical reasons, it cannot or should not be taken; or

(b) the registered health care professional who is asked to take it is of that opinion and there is no contrary opinion from a medical practitioner;

and, where by virtue of this subsection there can be no requirement to provide a specimen of blood, the constable may require a specimen of urine instead.

(5) A specimen of urine shall be provided within one hour of the requirement for its provision being made and after the provision of a previous specimen of urine.

(6) A person who, without reasonable excuse, fails to provide a specimen when required to do so in pursuance of this section is guilty of an offence.

(7) A constable must, on requiring any person to provide a specimen in pursuance of this section, warn him that a failure to provide it may render him liable to prosecution.

7A Specimens of blood taken from persons incapable of consenting

(1) A constable may make a request to a medical practitioner for him to take a specimen of blood from a person ('the person concerned') irrespective of whether that person consents if –

(a) that person is a person from whom the constable would (in the absence of any incapacity of that person and of any objection under section 9) be entitled under section 7 to require the provision of a specimen of blood for a laboratory test;

(b) it appears to that constable that that person has been involved in an accident that constitutes or is comprised in the matter that is under investigation or the circumstances of that matter;

(c) it appears to that constable that that person is or may be incapable (whether or not he has purported to do so) of giving a valid consent to the taking of a specimen of blood; and

    (d) it appears to that constable that that person's incapacity is attributable to medical reasons.

(2) A request under this section –

    (a) shall not be made to a medical practitioner who for the time being has any responsibility (apart from the request) for the clinical care of the person concerned; and

    (b) shall not be made to a medical practitioner other than a police medical practitioner unless –

        (i) it is not reasonably practicable for the request to made to a police medical practitioner; or

        (ii) it is not reasonably practicable for such a medical practitioner (assuming him to be willing to do so) to take the specimen.

(3) It shall be lawful for a medical practitioner to whom a request is made under this section, if he thinks fit –

    (a) to take a specimen of blood from the person concerned irrespective of whether that person consents; and

    (b) to provide the sample to a constable.

(4) If a specimen is taken in pursuance of a request under this section, the specimen shall not be subjected to a laboratory test unless the person from whom it was taken –

    (a) has been informed that it was taken; and

    (b) has been required by a constable to give his permission for a laboratory test of the specimen; and

    (c) has given his permission.

    (5) A constable must, on requiring a person to give his permission for the purposes of this section for a laboratory test of a specimen, warn that person that a failure to give the permission may render him liable to prosecution.

(6) A person who, without reasonable excuse, fails to give his permission for a laboratory test of a specimen of blood taken from him under this section is guilty of an offence.

(7) In this section 'police medical practitioner' means a medical practitioner who is engaged under any agreement to provide medical services for purposes connected with the activities of a police force.

8   Choice of specimens of breath

(1) Subject to subsection (2) below, of any two specimens of breath provided by any person in pursuance of section 7 of this Act that with the lower proportion of alcohol in the breath shall be used and the other shall be disregarded.

(2) If the specimen with the lower proportion of alcohol contains no more than 50 microgrammes of alcohol in 100 millilitres of breath, the person who provided it may claim that it should be replaced by such specimen as may be required under section 7(4) of this Act and, if he then provides such a specimen, neither specimen of breath shall be used.

(2A) If the person who makes a claim under subsection (2) above was required to provide specimens of breath under section 7 of this Act at or near a place mentioned in subsection (2)(c) of that section, a constable may arrest him without warrant.

(3) The Secretary of State may by regulations substitute another proportion of alcohol in the breath for that specified in subsection (2) above.

9   Protection for hospital patients

(1) While a person is at a hospital as a patient he shall not be required to co-operate with a preliminary test or to provide a specimen under section 7 of this Act unless the medical

practitioner in immediate charge of his case has been notified of the proposal to make the requirement; and –

    (a) if the requirement is then made, it shall be for co-operation with a test administered, or for the provision of a specimen, at the hospital, but

    (b) if the medical practitioner objects on the ground specified in subsection (2) below, the requirement shall not be made.

(1A) While a person is at a hospital as a patient, no specimen of blood shall be taken from him under section 7A of this Act and he shall not be required to give his permission for a laboratory test of a specimen taken under that section unless the medical practitioner in immediate charge of his case –

    (a) has been notified of the proposal to take the specimen or to make the requirement; and

    (b) has not objected on the ground specified in subsection (2).

(2) The ground on which the medical practitioner may object is –

    (a) in a case falling within subsection (1), that the requirement or the provision of the specimen or (if one is required) the warning required by section 7(7) of this Act would be prejudicial to the proper care and treatment of the patient; and

    (b) in a case falling within subsection (1A), that the taking of the specimen, the requirement or the warning required by section 7A(5) of this Act would be so prejudicial.

10   Detention of persons affected by alcohol or a drug

(1) Subject to subsections (2) and (3) below, a person required under section 7 or 7A to provide a specimen of breath, blood or urine may afterwards be detained at a police station (or, if the specimen was provided otherwise than at a police station, arrested and taken to and detained at a police station) if a constable has reasonable grounds for believing that, were that person then driving or attempting to drive a mechanically propelled vehicle on a road, he would commit an offence under section 4 or 5 of this Act.

(2) Subsection (1) above does not apply to the person if it ought reasonably to appear to the constable that there is no likelihood of his driving or attempting to drive a mechanically propelled vehicle whilst his ability to drive properly is impaired or whilst the proportion of alcohol in his breath, blood or urine exceeds the prescribed limit.

(2A) A person who is at a hospital as a patient shall not be arrested and taken from there to a police station in pursuance of this section if it would be prejudicial to his proper care and treatment as a patient.

(3) A constable must consult a medical practitioner on any question arising under this section whether a person's ability to drive properly is or might be impaired through drugs and must act on the medical practitioner's advice.

11   Interpretation of sections 4 to 10

(1) The following provisions apply for the interpretation of sections 3A to 10 of this Act.

(2) In those sections –

    'drug' includes any intoxicant other than alcohol,

    'fail' includes refuse,

    'hospital' means an institution which provides medical or surgical treatment for in-patients or out-patients,

    'the prescribed limit' means, as the case may require –

    (a) 35 microgrammes of alcohol in 100 millilitres of breath,

    (b) 80 milligrammes of alcohol in 100 millilitres of blood, or

(c) 107 milligrammes of alcohol in 100 millilitres of urine,

or such other proportion as may be prescribed by regulations made by the Secretary of State.

'registered health care professional' means a person (other than a medical practitioner) who is –

(a) a registered nurse; or

(b) a registered member of a health care profession which is designated for the purposes of this paragraph by an order made by the Secretary of State.

(2A) A health care profession is any profession mentioned in section 60(2) of the Health Act 1999 (c 8) other than the profession of practising medicine and the profession of nursing.

(2B) An order under subsection (2) shall be made by statutory instrument; and any such statutory instrument shall be subject to annulment in pursuance of a resolution of either House of Parliament.

(3) A person does not co-operate with a preliminary test or provide a specimen of breath for analysis unless his co-operation or the specimen –

(a) is sufficient to enable the test or the analysis to be carried out, and

(b) is provided in such a way as to enable the objective of the test or analysis to be satisfactorily achieved.

(4) A person provides a specimen of blood if and only if –

(a) he consents to taking of such a specimen from him; and

(b) the specimen is taken from him by a medical practitioner or, if it is taken in a police station, either by a medical practitioner or by a registered health care professional.

As amended by the Road Traffic (Consequential Provisions) Act 1988, s4, Schedule 2, Part III, para 31; Road Traffic Act 1991, ss1, 2, 3, 4, 48, Schedule 4, paras 32, 43, 44; Criminal Procedure and Investigations Act 1996, s63(1); Police Reform Act 2002, ss55, 56(1), (2); Railways and Transport Safety Act 2003, s107, Schedule 7, paras 1–5, Schedule 8; Serious Organised Crime and Police Act 2005, ss111, 154, 174(2), Schedule 7, Pt 1, para 27(1), (2), Schedule 17, Pt 2.

OFFICIAL SECRETS ACT 1989
(1989 c 6)

1   Security and intelligence

(1) A person who is or has been –

(a) a member of the security and intelligence services; or

(b) a person notified that he is subject to the provisions of this subsection,

is guilty of an offence if without lawful authority he discloses any information, document or other article relating to security or intelligence which is or has been in his possession by virtue of his position as a member of any of those services or in the course of his work while the notification is or was in force.

(2) The reference in subsection (1) above to disclosing information relating to security or intelligence includes a reference to making any statement which purports to be a disclosure of such information or is intended to be taken by those to whom it is addressed as being such a disclosure.

(3) A person who is or has been a Crown servant or government contractor is guilty of an offence if without lawful authority he makes a damaging disclosure of any information, document or other article relating to security or intelligence which is or has been in his possession by virtue of his position as such but otherwise than as mentioned in subsection (1) above.

(4) For the purposes of subsection (3) above a disclosure is damaging if –

    (a) it causes damage to the work of, or of any part of, the security and intelligence services; or

    (b) it is of information or a document or other article which is such that its unauthorised disclosure would be likely to cause such damage or which falls within a class or description of information or articles the unauthorised disclosure of which would be likely to have that effect.

(5) It is a defence for a person charged with an offence under this section to prove that at the time of the alleged offence he did not know, and has no reasonable cause to believe, that the information, document or article in question related to security or intelligence or, in the case of an offence under subsection (3), that the disclosure would be damaging within the meaning of that subsection.

(6) Notification that a person is subject to subsection (1) above shall be effected by a notice in writing served on him by a Minister of the Crown; and such a notice may be served if, in the Minister's opinion, the work undertaken by the person in question is or includes work connected with the security and intelligence services and its nature is such that the interests of national security require that he should be subject to the provisions of that subsection.

(7) Subject to subsection (8) below, a notification for the purposes of subsection (1) above shall be in force for the period of five years beginning with the day on which it is served but may be renewed by further notices under subsection (6) above for periods of five years at a time.

(8) A notification for the purposes of subsection (1) above may at any time be revoked by a further notice in writing served by the Minister on the person concerned; and the Minister shall serve such a further notice as soon as, in his opinion, the work undertaken by that person ceases to be such as is mentioned in subsection (6) above.

(9) In this section 'security or intelligence' means the work of, or in support of, the security and intelligence services or any part of them, and references to information relating to security or intelligence include references to information held or transmitted by those services or by persons in support of, or of any part of, them.

2   Defence

(1) A person who is or has been a Crown servant or government contractor is guilty of an offence if without lawful authority he makes a damaging disclosure of any information, document or other article relating to defence which is or has been in his possession by virtue of his position as such.

(2) For the purposes of subsection (1) above a disclosure is damaging if –

    (a) it damages the capability of, or of any part of, the armed forces of the Crown to carry out their tasks or leads to loss of life or injury to members of those forces or serious damage to the equipment or installation of those forces; or

    (b) otherwise than as mentioned in paragraph (a) above, it endangers the interests of the United Kingdom abroad, seriously obstructs the promotion or protection by the United Kingdom of those interests or endangers the safety of British citizens abroad; or

    (c) it is of information or of a document or article which is such that its unauthorised disclosure would be likely to have any of those effects.

(3) It is a defence for a person charged with an offence under this section to prove that at the time of the alleged offence he did not know, and had no reasonable cause to believe, that the information, document or article in question related to defence or that its disclosure would be damaging within the meaning of subsection (1) above.

(4) In this section 'defence' means –

    (a) the size, shape, organisation, logistics, order of battle, deployment, operations, state of readiness and training of the armed forces of the Crown;

    (b) the weapons, stores or other equipment of those forces and the invention, development, production and operation of such equipment and research relating to it;

    (c) defence policy and strategy and military planning and intelligence;

    (d) plans and measures for the maintenance of essential supplies and services that are or would be needed in time of war.

3   International relations

(1) A person who is or has been a Crown servant or government contractor is guilty of an offence if without lawful authority he makes a damaging disclosure of –

    (a) any information, document or other article relating to international relations; or

    (b) any confidential information, document or other article which was obtained from a State other than the United Kingdom or an international organisation,

being information or a document or article which is or has been in his possession by virtue of his position as a Crown servant or government contractor.

(2) For the purposes of subsection (1) above a disclosure is damaging if –

    (a) it endangers the interests of the United Kingdom abroad, seriously obstructs the promotion or protection by the United Kingdom of those interests or endangers the safety of British citizens abroad; or

    (b) it is of information or of a document or article which is such that its unauthorised disclosure would be likely to have any of those effects.

(3) In the case of information or a document or article within subsection (1)(b) above –

    (a) the fact that it is confidential, or

    (b) its nature or contents,

may be sufficient to establish for the purposes of subsection (2)(b) above that the information, document or article is such that its unauthorised disclosure would be likely to have any of the effects there mentioned.

(4) It is a defence for a person charged with an offence under this section to prove that at the time of the alleged offence he did not know, and had no reasonable cause to believe, that the information, document or article in question was such as is mentioned in subsection (1) above or that its disclosure would be damaging within the meaning of that subsection.

(5) In this section 'international relations' means the relations between States, between international organisations or between one or more States and one or more such organisations and includes any matter relating to a State other than the United Kingdom or to an international organisation which is capable of affecting the relations of the United Kingdom with another State or with an international organisation.

(6) For the purposes of this section any information, document or article obtained from a State or organisation is confidential at any time while the terms on which it was obtained require it to be held in confidence or while the circumstances in which it was obtained make it reasonable for the State or organisation to expect that it would be so held.

4   Crime and special investigation powers

(1) A person who is or has been a Crown servant or government contractor is guilty of an offence if without lawful authority it discloses any information, document or other article to which this section applies and which is or has been in his possession by virtue of his position as such.

(2) This section applies to any information, document or other article –

   (a) the disclosure of which –
      (i) results in the commission of an offence; or
      (ii) facilitates an escape from legal custody or the doing of any other act prejudicial to the safekeeping of person in legal custody; or
      (iii) impedes the prevention or detection of offences or the apprehension or prosecution of suspected offenders; or
   (b) which is such that its unauthorised disclosure would be likely to have any of those effects.

(3) This section also applies to –
   (a) any information obtained by reason of the interception of any communication in obedience to a warrant issued under section 2 of the Interception of Communications Act 1985 or under the authority of an interception warrant under section 5 of the Regulation of Investigatory Powers Act 2000, any information relating to the obtaining of information by reason of any such interception and any document or other article which is or has been used or held for use in, or has been obtained by reason of, any such interception; and
   (b) any information obtained by reason of action authorised by a warrant issued under section 3 of the Security Service Act 1989 or under section 5 of the Intelligence Services Act 1994 or by an authorisation given under section 7 of that Act, any information relating to the obtaining of information by reason of any such action and any document or other article which is or has been used or held for use in, or has been obtained by reason of, any such action.

(4) It is a defence for a person charged with an offence under this section in respect of a disclosure falling within subsection (2)(a) above to prove that at the time of the alleged offence he did not know, and had no reasonable cause to believe, that the disclosure would have any of the effects there mentioned.

(5) It is a defence for a person charged with an offence under this section in respect of any other disclosure to prove that at the time of the alleged offence he did not know, and had no reasonable cause to believe, that the information, document or article in question was information or a document or article to which this section applies.

(6) In this section 'legal custody' includes detention in pursuance of any enactment or any instrument made under an enactment.

5   Information resulting from unauthorised disclosures or entrusted in confidence

(1) Subsection (2) below applies where –
   (a) any information, document or other article protected against disclosure by the foregoing provisions of this Act has come into a person's possession as a result of having been –
      (i) disclosed (whether to him or another) by a Crown servant or government contractor without lawful authority; or
      (ii) entrusted to him by a Crown servant or government contractor on terms requiring it to be held in confidence or in circumstances in which the Crown servant or government contractor could reasonably expect that it would be so held; or
      (iii) disclosed (whether to him or another) without lawful authority by a person to whom it was entrusted as mentioned in sub-paragraph (ii) above; and
   (b) the disclosure without lawful authority of the information, document or article by the person into whose possession it has come is not an offence under any of those provisions.

(2) Subject to subsections (3) and (4) below, the person into whose possession the information, document or article has come is guilty of an offence if he discloses it without lawful authority knowing, or having reasonable cause to believe, that it is protected against disclosure by the foregoing provisions of this Act and that it has come into his possession as mentioned in subsection (1) above.

(3) In the case of information or a document or article protected against disclosure by sections 1 to 3 above, a person does not commit an offence under subsection (2) above unless –

(a) the disclosure by him is damaging; or

(b) he makes it knowing, or having reasonable cause to believe, that it would be damaging; and the question whether a disclosure is damaging shall be determined for the purposes of this subsection as it would be in relation to a disclosure of that information, document or article by a Crown servant in contravention of section 1(3), 2(1) or 3(1) above.

(4) A person does not commit an offence under subsection (2) above in respect of information or a document or other article which has come into his possession as a result of having been disclosed –

(a) as mentioned in subsection (1)(a)(i) above by a government contractor; or

(b) as mentioned in subsection (1)(a)(iii) above,

unless that disclosure was by a British citizen or took place in the United Kingdom, in any of the Channel Islands or in the Isle of Man or a colony.

(5) For the purposes of this section information or a document or article is protected against disclosure by the foregoing provisions of this Act if –

(a) it relates to security or intelligence, defence or international relations within the meaning of section 1, 2 or 3 above or is such as is mentioned in section 3(1)(b) above; or

(b) it is information or a document or article to which section 4 above applies;

and information or a document or article is protected against disclosure by sections 1 to 3 above if it falls within paragraph (a) above.

(6) A person is guilty of an offence if without lawful authority he discloses any information, document or other article which he knows, or has reasonable cause to believe, to have come into his possession as a result of a contravention of section 1 of the Official Secrets Act 1911.

6   Information entrusted in confidence to other States or international organisations

(1) This section applies where –

(a) any information, document or other article which –

(i)   relates to security or intelligence, defence or international relations; and

(ii) has been communicated in confidence by or on behalf of the United Kingdom to another State or to an international organisation,

has come into a person's possession as a result of having been disclosed (whether to him or another) without the authority of that State or organisation or, in the case of an organisation, of a member of it; and

(b) the disclosure without lawful authority of the information, document or article by the person into whose possession it has come is not an offence under any of the foregoing provisions of this Act.

(2) Subject to subsection (3) below, the person into whose possession the information, document or article has come is guilty of an offence if he makes a damaging disclosure of it knowing, or having reasonable cause to believe, that it is such as is mentioned in subsection (1) above, that it has come into his possession as there mentioned and that its disclosure would be damaging.

(3) A person does not commit an offence under subsection (2) above if the information,

document or article is disclosed by him with lawful authority or has previously been made available to the public with the authority of the State or organisation concerned or, in the case of an organisation, of a member of it.

(4) For the purposes of this section 'security or intelligence', 'defence' and 'international relations' have the same meaning as in sections 1, 2 and 3 above and the question whether a disclosure is damaging shall be determined as it would be in relation to a disclosure of the information, document or article in question by a Crown servant in contravention of section 1(3), 2(1) and 3(1) above.

(5) For the purposes of this section information or a document or article is communicated in confidence if it is communicated on terms requiring it to be held in confidence or in circumstances in which the person communicating it could reasonably expect that it would be so held.

7   Authorised disclosures

(1) For the purposes of this Act a disclosure by –

> (a) a Crown servant; or
>
> (b) a person, not being a Crown servant or government contractor, in whose case a notification for the purposes of section 1(1) above is in force,

is made with lawful authority if, and only if, it is made in accordance with his official duty.

(2) For the purposes of this Act a disclosure by a government contractor is made with lawful authority if, and only if, it is made –

> (a) in accordance with an official authorisation; or
>
> (b) for the purposes of the functions by virtue of which he is a government contractor and without contravening an official restriction.

(3) For the purposes of this Act a disclosure made by any other person is made with lawful authority of, and only if, it is made –

> (a) to a Crown servant for the purposes of his functions as such; or
>
> (b) in accordance with an official authorisation.

(4) It is a defence for a person charged with an offence under any of the foregoing provisions of this Act to prove that at the time of the alleged offence he believed that he had lawful authority to make the disclosure in question and had no reasonable cause to believe otherwise.

(5) In this section 'official authorisation' and 'official restriction' mean, subject to subsection (6) below, an authorisation or restriction duly given or imposed by a Crown servant or government contractor or by or on behalf of a prescribed body or a body of a prescribed class.

(6) In relation to subsection 5 above 'official authorisation' includes an authorisation duly given by or on behalf of the State or organisation concerned or, in the case of an organisation, a member of it.

8   Safeguarding of information

(1) Where a Crown servant or government contractor, by virtue of his position as such, has in his possession or under his control any document or other article which it would be an offence under any of the foregoing provisions of this Act for him to disclose without lawful authority he is guilty of an offence if –

> (a) being a Crown servant, he retains the document or article contrary to his official duty; or
>
> (b) being a government contractor, he fails to comply with an official direction for the return or disposal of the document or article,

or if he fails to take such care to prevent the unauthorised disclosure of the document or article as a person in his position may reasonably be expected to take.

(2) It is a defence for a Crown servant charged with an offence under subsection (1)(a) above to prove that at the time of the alleged offence he believed that he was acting in accordance with his official duty and had no reasonable cause to believe otherwise.

(3) In subsections (1) and (2) above references to a Crown servant include any person, not being a Crown servant or government contractor, in whose case a notification for the purposes of section 1(1) above is in force.

(4) Where a person has in his possession or under his control any document or other article which it would be an offence under section 5 above for him to disclose without lawful authority, he is guilty of an offence if –

    (a) he fails to comply with an official direction for his return or disposal; or

    (b) where he obtained it from a Crown servant or government contractor on terms requiring it to be held in confidence or in circumstances in which that servant or contractor could reasonably expect that it would be so held, he fails to take such care to prevent its unauthorised disclosure as a person in his position may reasonably be expected to take.

(5) Where a person has in his possession or under his control any document or other article which it would be an offence under section 6 above for him to disclose without lawful authority, he is guilty of an offence if he fails to comply with an official direction for its return or disposal.

(6) A person is guilty of an offence if he discloses any official information, document or other article which can be used for the purpose of obtaining access to any information, document or other article protected against disclosure by the foregoing provisions of this Act and the circumstances in which it is disclosed are such that it would be reasonable to expect that it might be used for that purpose without authority.

(7) For the purposes of subsection (6) above a person discloses information or a document or article which is official if –

    (a) he had or has had it in his possession by virtue of his position as a Crown servant or government contractor; or

    (b) he knows or has reasonable cause to believe that a Crown servant or government contractor has or has had it in his possession by virtue of his position as such.

(8) Subsection (5) of section 5 above applies for the purposes of subsection (6) above as it applies for the purposes of that section.

(9) In this section 'official direction' means a direction duly given by a Crown servant or government contractor or by or on behalf of a prescribed body or a body of a prescribed class.

13   Other interpretation provisions

(1) In this Act –

    'disclose' and 'disclosure', in relation to a document or other article, include parting with possession of it; …

As amended by the Intelligence Services Act 1994, s11(2), Schedule 4, para 4; Regulation of Investigatory Powers Act 2000, s82(1), Schedule 4, para 5.

COMPUTER MISUSE ACT 1990
(1990 c 18)

[See Appendix, Police and Justice Act 2006, ss35–38, 52, Schedule 14, paras 17–24, 26, 29, Schedule 15, Pt 4.]

1   Unauthorised access to computer material

(1) A person is guilty of an offence if –

    (a) he causes a computer to perform any function with intent to secure access to any program or data held in any computer;

    (b) the access he intends to secure is unauthorised; and

    (c) he knows at the time when he causes the computer to perform the function that that is the case.

(2) The intent a person has to have to commit an offence under this section need not be directed at –

    (a) any particular program or data;

    (b) a program or data of any particular kind; or

    (c) a program or data held in any particular computer.

(3) A person guilty of an offence under this section shall be liable on summary conviction to imprisonment for a term not exceeding six months or to a fine not exceeding level 5 on the standard scale or to both.

2   Unauthorised access with intent to commit or facilitate commission of further offences

(1) A person is guilty of an offence under this section if he commits an offence under section 1 above ('the unauthorised access offence') with intent –

    (a) to commit an offence to which this section applies; or

    (b) to facilitate the commission of such an offence (whether by himself or by any other person);

and the offence he intends to commit or facilitate is referred to below in this section as the further offence.

(2) This section applies to offences –

    (a) for which the sentence is fixed by law; or

    (b) for which a person of twenty-one years of age or over (not previously convicted) may be sentenced to imprisonment for a term of five years (or, in England and Wales, might be so sentenced but for the restrictions imposed by section 33 of the Magistrates' Courts Act 1980).

(3) It is immaterial for the purposes of this section whether the further offence is to be committed on the same occasion as the unauthorised access offence or on any future occasion.

(4) A person may be guilty of an offence under this section even though the facts are such that the commission of the further offence is impossible.

(5) A person guilty of an offence under this section shall be liable –

    (a) on summary conviction, to imprisonment for a term not exceeding six months or to a fine not exceeding the statutory maximum or to both; and

    (b) on conviction on indictment, to imprisonment for a term not exceeding five years or to a fine or to both.

3   Unauthorised modification of computer material

(1) A person is guilty of an offence if –

(a) he does any act which causes an unauthorised modification of the contents of any computer; and

(b) at the time when he does the act he has the requisite intent and the requisite knowledge.

(2) For the purposes of subsection (1)(b) above the requisite intent is an intent to cause a modification of the contents of any computer and by so doing –

(a) to impair the operation of any computer;

(b) to prevent or hinder access to any program or data held in any computer; or

(c) to impair the operation of any such program or the reliability of any such data.

(3) The intent need not be directed at –

(a) any particular computer;

(b) any particular program or data or a program or data of any particular kind; or

(c) any particular modification or a modification of any particular kind.

(4) For the purposes of subsection (1)(b) above the requisite knowledge is knowledge that any modification he intends to cause is unauthorised.

(5) It is immaterial for the purposes of this section whether an unauthorised modification or any intended effect of it of a kind mentioned in subsection (2) above is, or is intended to be, permanent or merely temporary.

(6) For the purposes of the Criminal Damage Act 1971 a modification of the contents of a computer shall not be regarded as damaging any computer or computer storage medium unless its effect on that computer or computer storage medium impairs its physical condition.

(7) A person guilty of an offence under this section shall be liable –

(a) on summary conviction, to imprisonment for a term not exceeding six months or to a fine not exceeding the statutory maximum or to both; and

(b) on conviction on indictment, to imprisonment for a term not exceeding five years or to a fine or to both.

4   Territorial scope of offences under this Act

(1) Except as provided below in this section, it is immaterial for the purposes of any offence under section 1 or 3 above –

(a) whether any act or other event proof of which is required for conviction of the offence occurred in the home country concerned; or

(b) whether the accused was in the home country concerned at the time of any such act or event.

(2) Subject to subsection (3) below, in the case of such an offence at least one significant link with domestic jurisdiction must exist in the circumstances of the case for the offence to be committed.

(3) There is no need for any such link to exist for the commission of an offence under section 1 above to be established in proof of an allegation to that effect in proceedings for an offence under section 2 above.

(4) Subject to section 8 below, where –

(a) any such link does in fact exist in the case of an offence under section 1 above; and

(b) commission of that offence is alleged in proceedings for an offence under section 2 above;

section 2 above shall apply as if anything the accused intended to do or facilitate in any place outside the home country concerned which would be an offence to which section 2 applies if it took place in the home country concerned were the offence in question. ...

(6) References in this Act to the home country concerned are references –

(a) in application of this Act to England and Wales, to England and Wales;

(b) in application of this Act to Scotland, to Scotland; and

(c) in the application of this Act to Northern Ireland, to Northern Ireland.

5 Significant links with domestic jurisdiction

(1) The following provisions of this section apply for the interpretation of section 4 above.

(2) In relation to an offence under section 1, either of the following is a significant link with domestic jurisdiction –

(a) that the accused was in the home country concerned at the time when he did the act which caused the computer to perform the function; or

(b) that any computer containing any program or data to which the accused secured or intended to secure unauthorised access by doing that act was in the home country concerned at that time.

(3) In relation to an offence under section 3, either of the following is a significant link with domestic jurisdiction –

(a) that the accused was in the home country concerned at the time when he did the act which caused the unauthorised modification; or

(b) that the unauthorised modification took place in the home country concerned.

6 Territorial scope of inchoate offences related to offences under this Act

(1) On a charge of conspiracy to commit an offence under this Act the following questions are immaterial to the accused's guilt –

(a) the question where any person became a party to the conspiracy; and

(b) the question whether any act, omission or other event occurred in the home country concerned.

(2) On a charge of attempting to commit an offence under section 3 above the following questions are immaterial to the accused's guilt –

(a) the question where the attempt was made; and

(b) the question whether it had an effect in the home country concerned.

(3) On a charge of incitement to commit an offence under this Act the question where the incitement took place is immaterial to the accused's guilt. …

7 Territorial scope of inchoate offences related to offences under external law corresponding to offences under this Act

(4) Subject to section 8 below, if any act done by a person in England and Wales would amount to the offence of incitement to commit an offence under this Act but for the fact that what he had in view would not be an offence triable in England and Wales –

(a) what he had in view shall be treated as an offence under this Act for the purposes of any charge of incitement brought in respect of that act; and

(b) any such charge shall accordingly be triable in England and Wales.

8 Relevance of external law

(1) A person is guilty of an offence triable by virtue of section 4(4) above only if what he intended to do or facilitate would involve the commission of an offence under the law in force where the whole or any part of it was intended to take place.

(3) A person is guilty of an offence triable by virtue of section 1(1A) of the Criminal Attempts Act 1981 or by virtue of section 7(4) above only if what he had in view would involve the commission of an offence under the law in force where the whole or any part of it was intended to take place.

(4) Conduct punishable under the law in force in any place is an offence under that law for the purposes of this section, however it is described in that law.

(5) Subject to subsection (7) below, a condition specified in subsection (1) or (3) above shall be taken to be satisfied unless not later than rules of court may provide the defence serve on the prosecution a notice –

    (a) stating that, on the facts as alleged with respect to the relevant conduct, the condition is not in their opinion satisfied;

    (b) showing their grounds for that opinion; and

    (c) requiring the prosecution to show that it is satisfied.

(6) In subsection (5) above 'the relevant conduct' means –

    (a) where the condition in subsection (1) above is in question, what the accused intended to do or facilitate; and

    (c) where the condition in subsection (3) above is in question, what the accused had in view.

(7) The court, if it thinks fit, may permit the defence to require the prosecution to show that the condition is satisfied without the prior service of a notice under subsection (5) above. …

(9) In the Crown Court the question whether the condition is satisfied shall be decided by the judge alone.

9   British citizenship immaterial

(1) In any proceedings brought in England and Wales in respect of any offence to which this section applies it is immaterial to guilt whether or not the accused was a British citizen at the time of any act, omission or other event proof of which is required for conviction of the offence.

(2) This section applies to the following offences –

    (a) any offence under this Act;

    (c) any attempt to commit an offence under section 3 above; and

    (d) incitement to commit an offence under this Act.

10   Saving for certain law enforcement powers

Section 1(1) above has effect without prejudice to the operation –

    (a) in England and Wales of any enactment relating to powers of inspection, search or seizure; …

and nothing designed to indicate a withholding of consent to access to any program or data from persons as enforcement officers shall have effect to make access unauthorised for the purposes of the said section 1(1).

In this section 'enforcement officer' means a constable or other person charged with the duty of investigating offences; and withholding consent from a person 'as' an enforcement officer of any description includes the operation, by the person entitled to control access, of rules whereby enforcement officers of that description are, as such, disqualified from membership of a class of persons who are authorised to have access.

12   Conviction of an offence under s1 in proceedings for an offence under s2 or 3

(1) If on the trial on indictment of a person charged with –

    (a) an offence under section 2 above; or

    (b) an offence under section 3 above or any attempt to commit such an offence;

the jury find him not guilty of the offence charged, they may find him guilty of an offence under section 1 above if on the facts shown he could have been found guilty of that offence in proceedings for that offence brought before the expiry of any time limit under section 11 above applicable to such proceedings. …

(3) This section is without prejudice to section 6(3) of the Criminal Law Act 1967 (conviction of alternative indictable offence on trial on indictment). ...

14   Search warrants for offences under s1

(1) Where a circuit judge is satisfied by information on oath given by a constable that there are reasonable grounds for believing –

    (a) that an offence under section 1 above has been or is about to be committed in any premises; and

    (b) that evidence that such an offence has been or is about to be committed is in those premises;

he may issue a warrant authorising a constable to enter and search the premises, using such reasonable force as is necessary.

(2) The power conferred by subsection (1) above does not extend to authorising a search for material of the kinds mentioned in section 9(2) of the Police and Criminal Evidence Act 1984 (privileged, excluded and special procedure material). ...

(4) In executing a warrant issued under this section a constable may seize an article if he reasonably believes that it is evidence that an offence under section 1 above has been or is about to be committed.

(5) In this section 'premises' includes land, buildings, movable structures, vehicles, vessels, aircraft and hovercraft. ...

17   Interpretation

(1) The following provisions of this section apply for the interpretation of this Act.

(2) A person secures access to any program or data held in a computer if by causing a computer to perform any function he –

    (a) alters or erases the program or data;

    (b) copies or moves it to any storage medium other than that in which it is held or to a different location in the storage medium in which it is held;

    (c) uses it; or

    (d) has it output from the computer in which it is held (whether by having it displayed or in any other manner);

and references to access to a program or data (and to an intent to secure such access) shall be read accordingly.

(3) For the purposes of subsection (2)(c) above a person uses a program if the function he causes the computer to perform –

    (a) causes the program to be executed; or

    (b) is itself a function of the program.

(4) For the purposes of subsection (2)(d) above –

    (a) a program is output if the instructions of which it consists are output; and

    (b) the form in which any such instructions or any other data is output (and in particular whether or not it represents a form in which, in the case of instructions, they are capable of being executed or, in the case of data, it is capable of being processed by a computer) is immaterial.

(5) Access of any kind by any person to any program or data held in a computer is unauthorised if –

    (a) he is not himself entitled to control access of the kind in question to the program or data; and

(b) he does not have consent to access by him of the kind in question to the program or data from any person who is so entitled,

but this subsection is subject to section 10.

(6) References to any program or data held in a computer include references to any program or data held in any removable storage medium which is for the time being in the computer; and a computer is to be regarded as containing any program or data held in any such medium.

(7) A modification of the contents of any computer takes place if, by the operation of any function of the computer concerned or any other computer –

(a) any program or data held in the computer concerned is altered or erased; or

(b) any program or data is added to its contents;

and any act which contributes towards causing such a modification shall be regarded as causing it.

(8) Such a modification is unauthorised if –

(a) the person whose act causes it is not himself entitled to determine whether the modification should be made; and

(b) he does not have consent to the modification from any person who is so entitled.

(9) References to the home country concerned shall be read in accordance with section 4(6) above.

(10) References to a program include references to part of a program.

As amended by the Criminal Justice and Public Order Act 1994, s162(1), (2); Criminal Justice (Terrorism and Conspiracy) Act 1998, s9, Schedule 1, para 6(1), Schedule 2, Pt II.

WAR CRIMES ACT 1991

(1991 c 13)

1   Jurisdiction over certain war crimes

(1) Subject to the provisions of this section, proceedings for murder, manslaughter or culpable homicide may be brought against a person in the United Kingdom irrespective of his nationality at the time of the alleged offence if that offence –

(a) was committed during the period beginning with 1 September 1939 and ending with 5 June 1945 in a place which at the time was part of Germany or under German occupation; and

(b) constituted a violation of the laws and customs of war.

(2) No proceedings shall by virtue of this section be brought against any person unless he was on 8 March 1990, or has subsequently become, a British citizen or resident in the United Kingdom, the Isle of man or any of the Channel Islands.

(3) No proceedings shall by virtue of this section be brought in England and Wales or in Northern Ireland except by or with the consent of the Attorney General, or, as the case may be, the Attorney General for Northern Ireland.

As amended by the Criminal Procedure and Investigations Act 1996, ss46(1)(a), 79(4), 80, Schedule 4, paras 1–3, 19, Schedule 5(2).

FOOTBALL (OFFENCES) ACT 1991
(1991 c 19)

1   Designated football matches

(1) In this Act a 'designated football match' means an association football match designated, or of a description designated, for the purposes of this Act by order of the Secretary of State.

Any such order shall be made by statutory instrument which shall be subject to annulment in pursuance of a resolution of either House of Parliament.

(2) References in this Act to things done at a designated football match include anything done at the ground –

  (a) within the period beginning two hours before the start of the match or (if earlier) two hours before the time at which it is advertised to start and ending one hour after the end of the match; or

  (b) where the match is advertised to start at a particular time on a particular day but does not take place on that day, within the period beginning two hours before and ending one hour after the advertised starting time.

2   Throwing of missiles

It is an offence for a person at a designated football match to throw anything at or towards –

  (a) the playing area, or any area adjacent to the playing area to which spectators are not generally admitted, or

  (b) any area in which spectators or other persons are or may be present,

without lawful authority or lawful excuse (which shall be for him to prove).

3   Indecent or racialist chanting

(1) It is an offence to engage or take part in chanting of an indecent or racialist nature at a designated football match.

(2) For this purpose –

  (a) 'chanting' means the repeated uttering of any words or sounds (whether alone or in concert with one or more others); and

  (b) 'of a racialist nature' means consisting of or including matter which is threatening, abusive or insulting to a person by reason of his colour, race, nationality (including citizenship) or ethnic or national origins.

4   Going onto the playing area

It is an offence for a person at a designated football match to go onto the playing area, or any area adjacent to the playing area to which spectators are not generally admitted, without lawful authority or lawful excuse (which shall be for him to prove).

5   Supplementary provisions

(2) A person guilty of an offence under this Act is liable on summary conviction to a fine not exceeding level 3 on the standard scale.

As amended by the Football (Offences and Disorder) Act 1999, s9; Football (Disorder) Act 2000, s1(3), Schedule 3; Serious Organised Crime and Police Act 2005, s174(2), Schedule 17, Pt 2.

CRIMINAL PROCEDURE (INSANITY AND UNFITNESS TO PLEAD) ACT 1991

(1991 c 25)

1   Acquittals on grounds of insanity

(1) A jury shall not return a special verdict under section 2 of the Trial of Lunatics Act 1883 (acquittal on ground of insanity) except on the written or oral evidence of two or more registered medical practitioners at least one of whom is duly approved.

(2) Subsections (2) and (3) of section 54 of the Mental Health Act 1983 ('the 1983 Act') shall have effect with respect to proof of the accused's mental condition for the purposes of the said section 2 as they have effect with respect to proof of an offender's mental condition for the purposes of section 37(2)(a) of that Act.

SEXUAL OFFENCES (AMENDMENT) ACT 1992

(1992 c 34)

1   Anonymity of victims of certain offences

(1) Where all allegation has been made that an offence to which this Act applies has been committed against a person, no matter relating to that person shall during that person's lifetime be included in any publication if it is likely to lead members of the public to identify that person as the person against whom the offence is alleged to have been committed.

(2) Where a person is accused of an offence to which this Act applies, no matter likely to lead members of the public to identify a person as the person against whom the offence is alleged to have been committed ('the complainant') shall during the complainant's lifetime be included in any publication.

(3) This section –

    (a) does not apply in relation to a person by virtue of subsection (1) at any time after a person has been accused of the offence, and

    (b) in its application in relation to a person by virtue of subsection (2), has effect subject to any direction given under section 3.

(3A) The matters relating to a person in relation to which the restrictions imposed by subsection (1) or (2) apply (if their inclusion in any publication is likely to have the result mentioned in that subsection) include in particular –

    (a) the person's name,

    (b) the person's address,

    (c) the identity of any school or other educational establishment attended by the person,

    (d) the identity of any place of work, and

    (e) any still or moving picture of the person.

(4) Nothing in this section prohibits the inclusion in a publication of matter consisting only of a report of criminal proceedings other than proceedings at, or intended to lead to, or on an appeal arising out of, a trial at which the accused is charged with the offence.

2   Offences to which this Act applies

(1) This Act applies to the following offences against the law of England and Wales –

    (aa) rape;

(ab) burglary with intent to rape;

(a) any offence under any of the provisions of the Sexual Offences Act 1956 mentioned in subsection (2);

(b) any offence under section 128 of the Mental Health Act 1959 (intercourse with mentally handicapped person by hospital staff etc);

(c) any offence under section 1 of the Indecency with Children Act 1960 (indecent conduct towards young child);

(d) any offence under section 54 of the Criminal Law Act 1977 (incitement by man of his grand-daughter, daughter or sister under the age of 16 to commit incest with him);

(da) any offence under any of the provisions of Part 1 of the Sexual Offences Act 2003 except section 64, 65, 69 or 71;

(e) any attempt to commit any of the offences mentioned in paragraphs (aa) to (da);

(f) any conspiracy to commit any of those offences;

(g) any incitement of another to commit any of those offences;

(h) aiding, abetting, counselling or procuring the commission of any of the offences mentioned in paragraphs (aa) to (e) and (g).

(2) The provisions of the Act of 1956 are –

(a) section 2 (procurement of a woman by threats);

(b) section 3 (procurement of a woman by false pretences);

(c) section 4 (administering drugs to obtain intercourse with a woman);

(d) section 5 (intercourse with a girl under the age of 13);

(e) section 6 (intercourse with a girl between the ages of 13 and 16);

(f) section 7 (intercourse with a mentally handicapped person);

(g) section 9 (procurement of a mentally handicapped person);

(h) section 10 (incest by a man);

(i) section 11 (incest by a woman);

(j) section 12 (buggery);

(k) section 14 (indecent assault on a woman);

(l) section 15 (indecent assault on a man);

(m) section 16 (assault with intent to commit buggery);

(n) section 17 (abduction of woman by force). ...

(4) This Act applies to a service offence (whenever committed) if the corresponding civil offence is mentioned in subsection (1).

3   Power to displace s1

(1) If, before the commencement of a trial at which a person is charged with an offence to which this Act applies, he or another person against whom the complainant may be expected to give evidence at the trial, applies to the judge for a direction under this subsection and satisfies the judge –

(a) that the direction is required for the purpose of inducing persons who are likely to be needed as witnesses at the trial to come forward; and

(b) that the conduct of the applicant's defence at the trial is likely to be substantially prejudiced if the direction is not given,

the judge shall direct that section 1 shall not, by virtue of the accusation alleging the offence in question, apply in relation to the complainant.

(2) If at a trial the judge is satisfied –

(a) that the effect of section 1 is to impose a substantial and unreasonable restriction upon the reporting of proceedings at the trial, and

(b) that it is in the public interest to remove or relax the restriction,

he shall direct that that section shall not apply to such matter as is specified in the direction.

(3) A direction shall not be given under subsection (2) by reason only of the outcome of the trial.

(4) If a person who has been convicted of an offence and has given notice of appeal against the conviction, or notice of an application for leave so to appeal, applies to the appellate court for a direction under this subsection and satisfies the court –

    (a) that the direction is required for the purpose of obtaining evidence in support of the appeal; and

    (b) that the applicant is likely to suffer substantial injustice if the direction is not given,

the court shall direct that section 1 shall not, by virtue of an accusation which alleges an offence to which this Act applies and is specified in the direction, apply in relation to a complainant so specified.

(5) A direction given under any provision of this section does not affect the operation of section 1 at any time before the direction is given.

(6) In subsections (1) and (2), 'judge' means –

    (a) in the case of an offence which is to be tried summarily or for which the mode of trial has not been determined, any justice of the peace; and

    (b) in any other case, any judge of the Crown Court in England and Wales. ...

(7) If, after the commencement of a trial at which a person is charged with an offence to which this Act applies, a new trial of the person for that offence is ordered, the commencement of any previous trial shall be disregarded for the purposes of subsection (1).

4   Special rules for cases of incest or buggery

(1) In this section –

    'section 10 offence' means an offence under section 10 of the Sexual Offences Act 1956 (incest by a man) or an attempt to commit that offence;

    'section 11 offence' means an offence under section 11 of that Act (incest by a woman) or an attempt to commit that offence;

    'section 12 offence' means an offence under section 12 of that Act (buggery) or an attempt to commit that offence.

(2) Section 1 does not apply to a woman against whom a section 10 offence is alleged to have been committed if she is accused of having committed a section 11 offence against the man who is alleged to have committed the section 10 offence against her.

(3) Section 1 does not apply to a man against whom a section 11 offence is alleged to have been committed if he is accused of having committed a section 10 offence against the woman who is alleged to have committed the section 11 offence against him.

(4) Section 1 does not apply to a person against whom a section 12 offence is alleged to have been committed if that person is accused of having committed a section 12 offence against the person who is alleged to have committed the section 12 offence against him.

(5) Subsection (2) does not affect the operation of this Act in relation to anything done at any time before the woman is accused.

(6) Subsection (3) does not affect the operation of this Act in relation to anything done at any time before the man is accused.

(7) Subsection (4) does not affect the operation of this Act in relation to anything done at any time before the person mentioned first in that subsection is accused. ...

(9) For the purposes of this section, a service offence is a section 10 offence, a section 11 offence or a section 12 offence if the corresponding civil offence is a section 10 offence, a section 11 offence or a section 12 offence, as the case may be.

5   Offences

(1) If any matter is included in a publication in contravention of section 1, the following persons shall be guilty of an offence and liable on summary conviction to a fine not exceeding level 5 on the standard scale –

(a) where the publication is a newspaper or periodical, any proprietor, any editor and any publisher of the newspaper or periodical;

(b) where the publication is a relevant programme –

(i) any body corporate or Scottish partnership engaged in providing the programme service in which the programme is included; and

(ii) any person having functions in relation to the programme corresponding to those of an editor of a newspaper;

(c) in the case of any other publication, any person publishing it.

(2) Where a person is charged with an offence under this section in respect of the inclusion of any matter in a publication, it shall be a defence, subject to subsection (3), to prove that the publication in which the matter appeared was one in respect of which the person against whom the offence mentioned in section 1 is alleged to have been committed had given written consent to the appearance of matter of that description.

(3) Written consent is not a defence if it is proved that any person interfered unreasonably with the peace or comfort of the person giving the consent, with intent to obtain it, or that person was under the age of 16 at the time when it was given.

(4) Proceedings for an offence under this section shall not be instituted except by or with the consent of the Attorney General if the offence is alleged to have been committed in England and Wales ...

(5) Where a person is charged with an offence under this section it shall be a defence to prove that at the time of the alleged offence he was not aware, and neither suspected nor had reason to suspect, that the publication included the matter in question.

(5A) Where –

(a) a person is charged with an offence under this section; and

(b) the offence relates to the inclusion of any matter in a publication in contravention of section 1(1),

it shall be a defence to prove that at the time of the alleged offence he was not aware, and neither suspected nor had reason to suspect, that the allegation in question had been made.

(6) Where an offence under this section committed by a body corporate is proved to have been committed with the consent or connivance of, or to be attributable to any neglect on the part of –

(a) a director, manager, secretary or other similar officer of the body corporate, or

(b) a person purporting to act in any such capacity,

he as well as the body corporate shall be guilty of the offence and liable to be proceeded against and punished accordingly.

(7) In relation to a body corporate whose affairs are managed by its members 'director', in subsection (6), means a member of the body corporate. ...

6   Interpretation, etc

(1) In this Act –

'complainant' has the meaning given in section 1(2);

'corresponding civil offence', in relation to a service offence, means the civil offence (within the meaning of the Army Act 1955, the Air Force Act 1955 or the Naval Discipline Act 1957) the commission of which constitutes the service offence;

'picture' includes a likeness however produced;

'publication' includes any speech, writing, relevant programme or other communication in whatever form, which is addressed to the public at large or any section of the public (and for this purpose every relevant programme shall be taken to be so addressed), but does not include an indictment or other document prepared for use in particular legal proceedings;

'relevant programme' means a programme included in a programme service, within the meaning of the Broadcasting Act 1990; and

'service offence' means an offence against section 70 of the Army Act 1955, section 70 of the Air Force Act 1955 or section 42 of the Naval Discipline Act 1957.

(2) For the purposes of this Act –

(a) where it is alleged that an offence to which this Act applies has been committed, the fact that any person has consented to an act which, on any prosecution for that offence, would fall to be proved by the prosecution, does not prevent that person from being regarded as a person against whom the alleged offence was committed; and

(b) where a person is accused of an offence of incest or buggery, the other party to the act in question shall be taken to be a person against whom the offence was committed even though he consented to that act.

(2A) For the purpose of this Act, where it is alleged or there is an accusation –

(a) that an offence of conspiracy or incitement of another to commit an offence mentioned in section 2(1)(aa) to (d) … has been committed, or

(b) that an offence of aiding, abetting, counselling or procuring the commission of an offence of incitement of another to commit an offence mentioned in section 2(1)(aa) to (d) … has been committed,

the person against whom the substantive offence is alleged to have been intended to be committed shall be regarded as the person against whom the conspiracy or incitement is alleged to have been committed. In this subsection, 'the substantive offence' means the offence to which the alleged conspiracy or incitement related.

(3) For the purposes of this Act, a person is accused of an offence, other than a service offence, if –

(a) an information is laid … alleging that he has committed the offence,

(b) he appears before a court charged with the offence,

(c) a court before which he is appearing sends him to the Crown Court for trial on a new charge alleging the offence, or

(d) a bill of indictment charging him with the offence is preferred before a court in which he may lawfully be indicted for the offence,

and references in subsection (2A) and in section 3 to an accusation alleging an offence shall be construed accordingly.

(3A) For the purposes of this Act, a person is accused of a service offence if he is treated by section 75(4) of the Army Act 1955, section 75(4) of the Air Force Act 1955 or section 47A(4) of the Naval Discipline Act 1957 as charged with the offence, and references in section 3 to an accusation alleging an offence shall be construed accordingly.

(4) Nothing in this Act affects any prohibition or restriction imposed by virtue of any other enactment upon a publication or upon matter included in a relevant programme.

As amended by the Criminal Justice and Public Order Act 1994, 168(1), Schedule 9, para 52; Youth Justice and Criminal Evidence Act 1999, ss48, 67(3), Schedule 2, paras 6–12, Schedule 6; Armed Forces Act 2001, s34, Schedule 6, Pt 1, paras 1–3; Criminal Justice Act 2003, s41, Schedule 4, para 63; Sexual Offences Act 2003, s139, Schedule 6, para 31(1), (2); Courts Act 2003 (Consequential Provisions) Order 2005, art 2, Schedule, para 49.

TRADE UNION AND LABOUR RELATIONS (CONSOLIDATION)ACT 1992
(1992 c 52)

242 Restriction of offence of conspiracy: England and Wales
(1) Where in pursuance of any such agreement as is mentioned in section 1(1) of the Criminal Law Act 1977 (which provides for the offence of conspiracy) the acts in question in relation to an offence are to be done in contemplation or furtherance of a trade dispute, the offence shall be disregarded for the purposes of that subsection if it is a summary offence which is not punishable with imprisonment.
(2) This section extends to England and Wales only.

SEXUAL OFFENCES ACT 1993
(1993 c 30)

1   Abolition of presumption of sexual incapacity
The presumption of criminal law that a boy under the age of fourteen is incapable of sexual intercourse (whether natural or unnatural) is hereby abolished.

CRIMINAL JUSTICE ACT 1993
(1993 c 36)

1   Offences to which this Part applies
(1) This Part applies to two groups of offences –
    (a) any offence mentioned in subsection (2) (a 'Group A offence'); and
    (b) any offence mentioned in subsection (3) (a 'Group B offence').
(2) The Group A offences are –
    (a) an offence under any of the following provisions of the Theft Act 1968 –
        section 1 (theft);
        section 17 (false accounting);
        section 19 (false statements by company directors, etc);
        section 21 (blackmail);
        section 22 (handling stolen goods);
        section 24A (retaining credits from dishonest sources, etc);
   (bb) an offence under any of the following provisions of the Fraud Act 2006 –
        (i)   section 1 (fraud);
        (ii) section 6 (possession etc of articles for use in frauds);
        (iii) section 7 (making or supplying articles for use in frauds);
        (iv) section 9 (participating in fraudulent business carried on by sole trader etc);
        (v)   section 11 (obtaining services dishonestly).
    (c) an offence under any of the following provisions of the Forgery and Counterfeiting Act 1981 –
        section 1 (forgery);

section 2 (copying a false instrument);

section 3 (using a false instrument);

section 4 (using a copy of a false instrument);

section 5 (offences which relate to money orders, share certificates, passports, etc);

section 14 (offences of counterfeiting notes and coins);

section 15 (offences of passing etc counterfeit notes and coins);

section 16 (offences involving the custody or control of counterfeit notes and coins);

section 17 (offences involving the making or custody or control of counterfeiting materials and implements);

section 20 (prohibition of importation of counterfeit notes and coins);

section 21 (prohibition of exportation of counterfeit notes and coins);

(ca) an offence under section 25 of the Identity Cards Act 2006;

(d) the common law offence of cheating in relation to the public revenue.

(3) The Group B offences are –

(a) conspiracy to commit a Group A offence;

(b) conspiracy to defraud;

(c) attempting to commit a Group A offence;

(d) incitement to commit a Group A offence.

(4) The Secretary of State may by order amend subsection (2) or (3) by adding or removing any offence. ...

5   Conspiracy, attempt and incitement

(3) A person may be guilty of conspiracy to defraud if –

(a) a party to the agreement constituting the conspiracy, or a party's agent, did anything in England and Wales in relation to the agreement before its formation, or

(b) a party to it because a party in England and Wales (by joining it either in person or through an agent), or

(c) a party to it, or a party's agent, did or omitted anything in England and Wales in pursuance of it,

and the conspiracy would be triable in England and Wales but for the fraud which the parties to it had in view not being intended to take place in England and Wales.

(4) A person may be guilty of incitement to commit a Group A offence if the incitement –

(a) takes place in England and Wales; and

(b) would be triable in England and Wales but for what the person charged had in view not being an offence triable in England and Wales.

(5) Subsections (3) and (4) are subject to section 6.

6   Relevance of external law

(1) A person is guilty of an offence triable by virtue of section 5(3), only if the pursuit of the agreed course of conduct would at some stage involve –

(a) an act or omission by one or more of the parties, or

(b) the happening of some other event,

constituting an offence under the law in force where the act, omission or other event was intended to take place.

(2) A person is guilty of an offence triable by virtue of section 1A of the Criminal Attempts Act 1981, or by virtue of section 5(4), only if what he had in view would involve the commission of an offence under the law in force where the whole or any part of it was intended to take place.

(3) Conduct punishable under the law in force in any place is an offence under that law for the purposes of this section, however it is described in that law. ...

As amended by the Theft (Amendment) Act 1996, s3; Criminal Justice (Terrorism and Conspiracy) Act 1998, s9(1), (2), Schedule 1, Pt II, para 7, Schedule 2, Pt II; Criminal Justice Act 1993 (Extension of Group A Offences) Order 2000, art 2; Fraud Act 2006, s14(1), (3), Schedule 1, para 24(1)–(3), Schedule 3; Identity Cards Act 2006, s30(1).

CRIMINAL JUSTICE AND PUBLIC ORDER ACT 1994
(1994 c 33)

61   Power to remove trespassers on land

(1) If the senior police officer present at the scene reasonably believes that two or more persons are trespassing on land and are present there with the common purpose of residing there for any period, that reasonable steps have been taken by or on behalf of the occupier to ask them to leave and –

(a) that any of those persons has caused damage to the land or to property on the land or used threatening, abusive or insulting words or behaviour towards the occupier, a member of his family or an employee or agent of his, or

(b) that those persons have between them six or more vehicles on the land,

he may direct those persons, or any of them, to leave the land and to remove any vehicles or other property they have with them on the land.

(2) Where the persons in question are reasonably believed by the senior police officer to be persons who were not originally trespassers but have become trespassers on the land, the officer must reasonably believe that the other conditions specified in subsection (1) are satisfied after those persons became trespassers before he can exercise the power conferred by that subsection.

(3) A direction under subsection (1) above, if not communicated to the persons referred to in subsection (1) by the police officer giving the direction, may be communicated to them by any constable at the scene.

(4) If a person knowing that a direction under subsection (1) above has been given which applies to him –

(a) fails to leave the land as soon as reasonably practicable, or

(b) having left again enters the land as a trespasser within the period of three months beginning with the day on which the direction was given,

he commits an offence and is liable on summary conviction to imprisonment for a term not exceeding three months or a fine not exceeding level 4 on the standard scale, or both. ...

(6) In proceedings for an offence under this section it is a defence for the accused to show –

(a) that he was not trespassing on the land, or

(b) that he had a reasonable excuse for failing to leave the land as soon as reasonably practicable or, as the case may be, for again entering the land as a trespasser.

(7) In its application in England and Wales to common land this section has effect as if in the preceding subsections of it –

(a) references to trespassing or trespassers were references to acts and persons doing acts which constitute either a trespass as against the occupier or an infringement of the commoners' rights; and

(b) references to 'the occupier' included the commoners or any of them or, in the case of common land to which the public has access, the local authority as well as any commoner.

(8) Subsection (7) above does not –

(a) require action by more than one occupier; or

(b) constitute persons trespassers as against any commoner or the local authority if they are permitted to be there by the other occupier.

(9) In this section –

'common land' means common land as defined in section 22 of the Commons Registration Act 1965;

'commoner' means a person with rights of common as defined in section 22 of the Commons Registration Act 1965;

'land' does not include –

(a) buildings other than –

(i) agricultural buildings within the meaning of, in England and Wales, paragraphs 3 to 8 of Schedule 5 to the Local Government Finance Act 1988 or, in Scotland, section 7(2) of the Valuation and Rating (Scotland) Act 1956, or

(ii) scheduled monuments within the meaning of the Ancient Monuments and Archaeological Areas Act 1979;

(b) land forming part of –

(i) a highway unless it is a footpath, bridleway or byway open to all traffic within the meaning of Part III of the Wildlife and Countryside Act 1981, is a restricted byway within the meaning of Part II of the Countryside and Rights of Way Act 2000 or is a cycle track under the Highways Act 1980 or the Cycle Tracks Act 1984; ...

'the local authority', in relation to common land, means any local authority which has powers in relation to the land under section 9 of the Commons Registration Act 1965;

'occupier' (and in subsection (8) 'the other occupier') means –

(a) in England and Wales, the person entitled to possession of the land by virtue of an estate or interest held by him; ...

'property', in relation to damage to property on land, means –

(a) in England and Wales, property within the meaning of section 10(1) of the Criminal Damage Act 1971; ...

and 'damage' includes the deposit of any substance capable of polluting the land;

'trespass' means, in the application of this section –

(a) in England and Wales, subject to the extensions effected by subsection (7) above, trespass as against the occupier of the land;

'trespassing' and 'trespasser' shall be construed accordingly;

'vehicle' includes –

(a) any vehicle, whether or not it is in a fit state for use on roads, and includes any chassis or body, with or without wheels, appearing to have formed part of such a vehicle, and any load carried by, and anything attached to, such a vehicle; and

(b) a caravan as defined in section 29(1) of the Caravan Sites and Control of Development Act 1960;

and a person may be regarded for the purposes of this section as having a purpose of residing in a place notwithstanding that he has a home elsewhere.

[See Appendix, Criminal Justice Act 2003, Schedule 26, para 45(1), (4).]

62 Supplementary powers of seizure

(1) If a direction has been given under section 61 and a constable reasonably suspects that any person to whom the direction applies has, without reasonable excuse –

    (a) failed to remove any vehicle on the land which appears to the constable to belong to him or to be in his possession or under his control; or

    (b) entered the land as a trespasser with a vehicle within the period of three months beginning with the day on which the direction was given,

the constable may seize and remove that vehicle.

(2) In this section, 'trespasser' and 'vehicle' have the same meaning as in section 61.

62A Power to remove trespassers: alternative site available

(1) If the senior police officer present at a scene reasonably believes that the conditions in subsection (2) are satisfied in relation to a person and land, he may direct the person –

    (a) to leave the land;

    (b) to remove any vehicle and other property he has with him on the land.

(2) The conditions are –

    (a) that the person and one or more others ('the trespassers') are trespassing on the land;

    (b) that the trespassers have between them at least one vehicle on the land;

    (c) that the trespassers are present on the land with the common purpose of residing there for any period;

    (d) if it appears to the officer that the person has one or more caravans in his possession or under his control on the land, that there is a suitable pitch on a relevant caravan site for that caravan or each of those caravans;

    (e) that the occupier of the land or a person acting on his behalf has asked the police to remove the trespassers from the land.

(3) A direction under subsection (1) may be communicated to the person to whom it applies by any constable at the scene.

(4) Subsection (5) applies if –

    (a) a police officer proposes to give a direction under subsection (1) in relation to a person and land, and

    (b) it appears to him that the person has one or more caravans in his possession or under his control on the land.

(5) The officer must consult every local authority within whose area the land is situated as to whether there is a suitable pitch for the caravan or each of the caravans on a relevant caravan site which is situated in the local authority's area.

(6) In this section –

    'caravan' and 'caravan site' have the same meanings as in Part 1 of the Caravan Sites and Control of Development Act 1960;

    'relevant caravan site' means a caravan site which is –

    (a) situated in the area of a local authority within whose area the land is situated, and

    (b) managed by a relevant site manager;

    'relevant site manager' means –

    (a) a local authority within whose area the land is situated;

    (b) a registered social landlord;

    'registered social landlord' means a body registered as a social landlord under Chapter 1 of Part 1 of the Housing Act 1996.

(7) The Secretary of State may by order amend the definition of 'relevant site manager' in subsection (6) by adding a person or description of person.

(8) An order under subsection (7) must be made by statutory instrument and is subject to annulment in pursuance of a resolution of either House of Parliament.

62B Failure to comply with direction under section 62A: offences
(1) A person commits an offence if he knows that a direction under section 62A(1) has been given which applies to him and –
  (a) he fails to leave the relevant land as soon as reasonably practicable, or
  (b) he enters any land in the area of the relevant local authority as a trespasser before the end of the relevant period with the intention of residing there.
(2) The relevant period is the period of 3 months starting with the day on which the direction is given.
(3) A person guilty of an offence under this section is liable on summary conviction to imprisonment for a term not exceeding 3 months or a fine not exceeding level 4 on the standard scale or both.
(5) In proceedings for an offence under this section it is a defence for the accused to show –
  (a) that he was not trespassing on the land in respect of which he is alleged to have committed the offence, or
  (b) that he had a reasonable excuse –
    (i) for failing to leave the relevant land as soon as reasonably practicable, or
    (ii) for entering land in the area of the relevant local authority as a trespasser with the intention of residing there, or
  (c) that, at the time the direction was given, he was under the age of 18 years and was residing with his parent or guardian.

[See Appendix, Criminal Justice Act 2003, Schedule 26, para 45(1), (5).]

62C Failure to comply with direction under section 62A: seizure
(1) This section applies if a direction has been given under section 62A(1) and a constable reasonably suspects that a person to whom the direction applies has, without reasonable excuse –
  (a) failed to remove any vehicle on the relevant land which appears to the constable to belong to him or to be in his possession or under his control; or
  (b) entered any land in the area of the relevant local authority as a trespasser with a vehicle before the end of the relevant period with the intention of residing there.
(2) The relevant period is the period of 3 months starting with the day on which the direction is given.
(3) The constable may seize and remove the vehicle.

62D Common land: modifications
(1) In their application to common land sections 62A to 62C have effect with these modifications.
(2) References to trespassing and trespassers have effect as if they were references to acts, and persons doing acts, which constitute –
  (a) a trespass as against the occupier, or
  (b) an infringement of the commoners' rights.
(3) References to the occupier –
  (a) in the case of land to which the public has access, include the local authority and any commoner;
  (b) in any other case, include the commoners or any of them.

(4) Subsection (1) does not –
- (a) require action by more than one occupier, or
- (b) constitute persons trespassers as against any commoner or the local authority if they are permitted to be there by the other occupier.

(5) In this section 'common land', 'commoner' and 'the local authority' have the meanings given by section 61.

62E   Sections 62A to 62D: interpretation

(1) Subsections (2) to (8) apply for the interpretation of sections 62A to 62D and this section.

(2) 'Land' does not include buildings other than –
- (a) agricultural buildings within the meaning of paragraphs 3 to 8 of Schedule 5 to the Local Government Finance Act 1988, or
- (b) scheduled monuments within the meaning of the Ancient Monuments and Archaeological Areas Act 1979.

(3) 'Local authority' means –
- (a) in Greater London, a London borough or the Common Council of the City of London;
- (b) in England outside Greater London, a county council, a district council or the Council of the Isles of Scilly;
- (c) in Wales, a county council or a county borough council.

(4) 'Occupier', 'trespass', 'trespassing' and 'trespasser' have the meanings given by section 61 in relation to England and Wales.

(5) 'The relevant land' means the land in respect of which a direction under section 62A(1) is given.

(6) 'The relevant local authority' means –
- (a) if the relevant land is situated in the area of more than one local authority (but is not in the Isles of Scilly), the district council or county borough council within whose area the relevant land is situated;
- (b) if the relevant land is situated in the Isles of Scilly, the Council of the Isles of Scilly;
- (c) in any other case, the local authority within whose area the relevant land is situated.

(7) 'Vehicle' has the meaning given by section 61.

(8) A person may be regarded as having a purpose of residing in a place even if he has a home elsewhere.

63   Powers to remove persons attending or preparing for a rave

(1) This section applies to a gathering on land in the open air of 20 or more persons (whether or not trespassers) at which amplified music is played during the night (with or without intermissions) and is such as, by reason of its loudness and duration and the time at which it is played, is likely to cause serious distress to the inhabitants of the locality; and for this purpose
- (a) such a gathering continues during intermissions in the music and, where the gathering extends over several days, throughout the period during which amplified music is played at night (with or without intermissions); and
- (b) 'music' includes sounds wholly or predominantly characterised by the emission of a succession of repetitive beats.

(1A) This section also applies to a gathering if –
- (a) it is a gathering on land of 20 or more persons who are trespassing on the land; and
- (b) it would be a gathering of a kind mentioned in subsection (1) above if it took place on land in the open air.

(2) If, as respects any land, a police officer of at least the rank of superintendent reasonably believes that –

   (a) two or more persons are making preparations for the holding there of a gathering to which this section applies,

   (b) ten or more persons are waiting for such a gathering to begin there, or

   (c) ten or more persons are attending such a gathering which is in progress,

he may give a direction that those persons and any other persons who come to prepare or wait for or to attend the gathering are to leave the land and remove any vehicles or other property which they have with them on the land.

(3) A direction under subsection (2) above, if not communicated to the persons referred to in subsection (2) by the police officer giving the direction, may be communicated to them by any constable at the scene.

(4) Persons shall be treated as having had a direction under subsection (2) above communicated to them if reasonable steps have been taken to bring it to their attention.

(5) A direction under subsection (2) above does not apply to an exempt person.

(6) If a person knowing that a direction has been given which applies to him –

   (a) fails to leave the land as soon as reasonably practicable, or

   (b) having left again enters the land within the period of 7 days beginning with the day on which the direction was given,

he commits an offence and is liable on summary conviction to imprisonment for a term not exceeding three months or a fine not exceeding level 4 on the standard scale, or both.

(7) In proceedings for an offence under subsection (6) above it is a defence for the accused to show that he had a reasonable excuse for failing to leave the land as soon as reasonably practicable or, as the case may be, for again entering the land.

(7A) A person commits an offence if –

   (a) he knows that a direction under subsection (2) above has been given which applies to him, and

   (b) he makes preparations for or attends a gathering to which this section applies within the period of 24 hours starting when the direction was given.

(7B) A person guilty of an offence under subsection (7A) above is liable on summary conviction to imprisonment for a term not exceeding three months or a fine not exceeding level 4 on the standard scale, or both.

(9) This section does not apply –

   (a) in England and Wales, to a gathering in relation to a licensable activity within section 1(1)(c) of the Licensing Act 2003 (provision of certain forms of entertainment) carried on under and in accordance with an authorisation within the meaning of section 136 of that Act …

(10) In this section –

   'exempt person', in relation to land (or any gathering on land), means the occupier, any member of his family and any employee or agent of his and any person whose home is situated on the land;

   'land in the open air' includes a place partly open to the air;

   'occupier', 'trespasser' and 'vehicle' have the same meaning as in section 61.

[See Appendix, Criminal Justice Act 2003, Schedule 26, para 45(1), (6).]

64   Supplementary powers of entry and seizure

(1) If a police officer of at least the rank of superintendant reasonably believes that circumstances

exist in relation to any land which would justify the giving of a direction under section 63 in relation to a gathering to which that section applies he may authorise any constable to enter the land for any of the purposes specified in subsection (2) below:

(2) Those purposes are –

    (a) to ascertain whether such circumstances exist; and

    (b) to exercise any power conferred on a constable by section 63 or subsection (4) below.

(3) A constable who is so authorised to enter land for any purpose may enter the land without a warrant.

(4) If a direction has been given under section 63 and a constable reasonably suspects that any person to whom the direction applies has, without reasonable excuse –

    (a) failed to remove any vehicle or sound equipment on the land which appears to the constable to belong to him or to be in his possession or under his control; or

    (b) entered the land as a trespasser with a vehicle or sound equipment within the period of 7 days beginning with the day on which the direction was given,

the constable may seize and remove that vehicle or sound equipment.

(5) Subsection (4) above does not authorise the seizure of any vehicle or sound equipment of an exempt person. …

(6) In this section –

    'exempt person' has the same meaning as in section 63;

    'sound equipment' means equipment designed or adapted for amplifying music and any equipment suitable for use in connection with such equipment, and 'music' has the same meaning as in section 63; and

    'vehicle' has the same meaning as in section 61.

65   Raves: power to stop persons from proceeding

(1) If a constable in uniform reasonably believes that a person is on his way to a gathering to which section 63 applies in relation to which a direction under section 63(2) is in force, he may, subject to subsections (2) and (3) below –

    (a) stop that person, and

    (b) direct him not to proceed in the direction of the gathering.

(2) The power conferred by subsection (1) above may only be exercised at a place within 5 miles of the boundary of the site of the gathering.

(3) No direction may be given under subsection (1) above to an exempt person.

(4) If a person knowing that a direction under subsection (1) above has been given to him fails to comply with that direction, he commits an offence and is liable on summary conviction to a fine not exceeding level 3 on the standard scale.

(6) In this section 'exempt person' has the same meaning as in section 63.

66   Power of court to forfeit sound equipment

(1) Where a person is convicted of an offence under section 63 in relation to a gathering to which that section applies and the court is satisfied that any sound equipment which has been seized from him under section 64(4), or which was in his possession or under his control at the relevant time, has been used at the gathering the court may make an order for forfeiture under this subsection in respect of that property.

(2) The court may make an order under subsection (1) above whether or not it also deals with the offender in respect of the offence in any other way and without regard to any restrictions on forfeiture in any enactment.

(3) In considering whether to make an order under subsection (1) above in respect of any property a court shall have regard –

(a) to the value of the property; and

(b) to the likely financial and other effects on the offender of the making of the order (taken together with any other order that the court contemplates making).

(4) An order under subsection (1) above shall operate to deprive the offender of his rights, if any, in the property to which it relates, and the property shall (if not already in their possession) be taken into the possession of the police.

(5) Except in a case to which subsection (6) below applies, where any property has been forfeited under subsection (1) above, a magistrates' court may, on application by a claimant of the property, other than the offender from whom it was forfeited under subsection (1) above, make an order for delivery of the property to the applicant if it appears to the court that he is the owner of the property.

(6) In a case where forfeiture under subsection (1) above has been by order of a Scottish court, a claimant such as is mentioned in subsection (5) above may, in such manner as may be prescribed by act of adjournal, apply to that court for an order for the return of the property in question.

(7) No application shall be made under subsection (5), or by virtue of subsection (6), above by any claimant of the property after the expiration of 6 months from the date on which an order under subsection (1) above was made in respect of the property.

(8) No such application shall succeed unless the claimant satisfies the court either that he had not consented to the offender having possession of the property or that he did not know, and had no reason to suspect, that the property was likely to be used at a gathering to which section 63 applies.

(9) An order under subsection (5), or by virtue of subsection (6), above shall not affect the right of any person to take, within the period of 6 months from the date of an order under subsection (5), or as the case may be by virtue of subsection (6), above, proceedings for the recovery of the property from the person in possession of it in pursuance of the order, but on the expiration of that period the right shall cease.

(10) The Secretary of State may make regulations for the disposal of property, and for the application of the proceeds of sale of property, forfeited under subsection (1) above where no application by a claimant of the property under subsection (5), or by virtue of subsection (6), above has been made within the period specified in subsection (7) above or no such application has succeeded.

(11) The regulations may also provide for the investment of money and for the audit of accounts.

(12) The power to make regulations under subsection (10) above shall be exercisable by statutory instrument which shall be subject to annulment in pursuance of a resolution of either House of Parliament.

(13) In this section –

'relevant time', in relation to a person –

(a) convicted in England and Wales of an offence under section 63, means the time of his arrest for the offence or of the issue of a summons in respect of it; …

'sound equipment' has the same meaning as in section 64.

67   Retention and charges for seized property

(1) Any vehicles which have been seized and removed by a constable under section 62(1), 62C(3) or 64(4) may be retained in accordance with regulations made by the Secretary of State under subsection (3) below.

(2) Any sound equipment which has been seized and removed by a constable under section 64(4)

may be retained until the conclusion of proceedings against the person from whom it was seized for an offence under section 63.

(3) The Secretary of State may make regulations –

  (a) regulating the retention and safe keeping and the disposal and the destruction in prescribed circumstances of vehicles; and

  (b) prescribing charges in respect of the removal, retention, disposal and destruction of vehicles.

(4) Any authority shall be entitled to recover from a person from whom a vehicle has been seized such charges as may be prescribed in respect of the removal, retention, disposal and destruction of the vehicle by the authority.

(5) Regulations under subsection (3) above may make different provisions for different classes of vehicles or for different circumstances.

(6) Any charges under subsection (4) above shall be recoverable as a simple contract debt.

(7) Any authority having custody of vehicles under regulations under subsection (3) above shall be entitled to retain custody until any charges under subsection (4) are paid.

(8) The power to make regulations under subsection (3) above shall be exercisable by statutory instrument which shall be subject to annulment in pursuance of a resolution of either House of Parliament.

(9) In this section –

  'conclusion of proceedings' against a person means –

  (a) his being sentenced or otherwise dealt with for the offence or his acquittal;

  (b) the discontinuance of the proceedings; or

  (c) the decision not to prosecute him,

  whichever is the earlier;

  'sound equipment' has the same meaning as in section 64; and

  'vehicle' has the same meaning as in section 61.

68   Offence of aggravated trespass

(1) A person commits the offence of aggravated trespass if he trespasses on land and, in relation to any lawful activity which persons are engaging in or are about to engage in on that or adjoining land, does there anything which is intended by him to have the effect –

  (a) of intimidating those persons or any of them so as to deter them or any of them from engaging in the activity,

  (b) of obstructing that activity, or

  (c) of disrupting that activity. ...

(2) Activity on any occasion on the part of a person or persons on land is 'lawful' for the purposes of this section if he or they may engage in the activity on the land on that occasion without committing an offence or trespassing on the land.

(3) A person guilty of an offence under this section is liable on summary conviction to imprisonment for a term not exceeding three months or a fine not exceeding level 4 on the standard scale, or both.

(5) In this section 'land' does not include –

  (a) the highways and roads excluded from the application of section 61 by paragraph (b) of the definition of 'land' in subsection (9) of that section; or

  (b) a road within the meaning of the Roads (Northern Ireland) Order 1993.

[See Appendix, Criminal Justice Act 2003, Schedule 26, para 45(1), (7).]

69   Powers to remove persons committing or participating in aggravated trespass

(1) If the senior police officer present at the scene reasonably believes –

(a)   that a person is committing, has committed or intends to commit the offence of aggravated trespass on land; or

(b)   that two or more persons are trespassing on land and are present there with the common purpose of intimidating persons so as to deter them from engaging in a lawful activity or of obstructing or disrupting a lawful activity,

he may direct that person or (as the case may be) those persons (or any of them) to leave the land.

(2) A direction under subsection (1) above, if not communicated to the persons referred to in subsection (1) by the police officer giving the direction, may be communicated to them by any constable at the scene.

(3) If a person knowing that a direction under subsection (1) above has been given which applies to him –

(a)   fails to leave the land as soon as practicable, or

(b)   having left again enters the land as a trespasser within the period of three months beginning with the day on which the direction was given,

he commits an offence and is liable on summary conviction to imprisonment for a term not exceeding three months or a fine not exceeding level 4 on the standard scale, or both.

(4) In proceedings for an offence under subsection (3) it is a defence for the accused to show –

(a)   that he was not trespassing on the land, or

(b)   that he had a reasonable excuse for failing to leave the land as soon as practicable or, as the case may be, for again entering the land as a trespasser.

(6) In this section 'lawful activity' and 'land' have the same meaning as in section 68.

[See Appendix, Criminal Justice Act 2003, Schedule 26, para 45(1), (8).]

75   Interim possession orders: false or misleading statements

(1) A person commits an offence if, for the purpose of obtaining an interim possession order, he –

(a)   makes a statement which he knows to be false or misleading in a material particular; or

(b)   recklessly makes a statement which is false or misleading in a material particular.

(2) A person commits an offence if, for the purpose of resisting the making of an interim possession order, he –

(a)   makes a statement which he knows to be false or misleading in a material particular; or

(b)   recklessly makes a statement which is false or misleading in a material particular.

(3) A person guilty of an offence under this section shall be liable –

(a)   on conviction on indictment, to imprisonment for a term not exceeding two years or a fine or both;

(b)   on summary conviction, to imprisonment for a term not exceeding six months or a fine not exceeding the statutory maximum or both.

(4) In this section –

'interim possession order' means an interim possession order (so entitled) made under rules of court for the bringing of summary proceedings for possession of premises which are occupies by trespassers;

'premises' has the same meaning as in Part II of the Criminal Law Act 1977 (offences relating to entering and remaining on property); and 'statement', in relation to an interim possession order, means any statement, in writing or oral and whether as to fact or belief, made in or for the purposes of the proceedings.

76 Interim possession orders: trespassing during currency of order

(1) This section applies where an interim possession order has been made in respect of any premises and served in accordance with rules of court; and references to 'the order' and 'the premises' shall be construed accordingly.

(2) Subject to subsection (3), a person who is present on the premises as a trespasser at any time during the currency of the order commits an offence.

(3) No offence under subsection (2) is committed by a person if –

(a) he leaves the premises within 24 hours of the time of service of the order and does not return; or

(b) a copy of the order was not fixed to the premises in accordance with rules of court.

(4) A person who was in occupation of the premises at the time of service of the order but leaves them commits an offence if he re-enters the premises as a trespasser or attempts to do so after the expiry of the order but within the period of one year beginning with the day on which it was served.

(5) A person guilty of an offence under this section shall be liable on summary conviction to imprisonment for a term not exceeding six months or a fine not exceeding level 5 on the standard scale or both.

(6) A person who is in occupation of the premises at the time of service of the order shall be treated for the purposes of this section as being present as a trespasser.

(8) In this section –

'interim possession order' has the same meaning as in section 75 above and 'rules of court' is to be construed accordingly; and

'premises' has the same meaning as in that section, that is to say, the same meaning as in Part II of the Criminal Law Act 1977 (offences relating to entering and remaining on property).

77 Power of local authority to direct unauthorised campers to leave land

(1) If it appears to a local authority that persons are for the time being residing in a vehicle or vehicles within the authority's area –

(a) on any land forming part of a highway;

(b) on any other unoccupied land; or

(c) on any occupied land without the consent of the occupier,

the authority may give a direction that those persons and any others with them are to leave the land and remove the vehicle or vehicles and any other property they have with them on the land.

(2) Notice of a direction under subsection (1) must be served on the persons to whom the direction applies, but it shall be sufficient for this purpose for the direction to specify the land and (except where the direction applies to only one person) to be addressed to all occupants of the vehicles on the land, without naming them.

(3) If a person knowing that a direction under subsection (1) above has been given which applies to him –

(a) fails, as soon as practicable, to leave the land or remove from the land any vehicle or other property which is the subject of the direction, or

(b) having removed any such vehicle or property again enters the land with a vehicle within the period of three months beginning with the day on which the direction was given,

he commits an offence and is liable on summary conviction to a fine not exceeding level 3 on the standard scale.

(4) A direction under subsection (1) operates to require persons who re-enter the land within the said period with vehicles or other property to leave and remove the vehicles or other property as it operates in relation to the persons and vehicles or other property on the land when the direction was given.

(5) In proceedings for an offence under this section it is a defence for the accused to show that this failure to leave or to remove the vehicle or other property as soon as practicable or his re-entry with a vehicle was due to illness, mechanical breakdown or other immediate emergency.

(6) In this section –

'land' means land in the open air;

'local authority' means –

(a) in Greater London, a London borough or the Common Council of the City of London;

(b) in England outside Greater London, a county council, a district council or the Council of the Isles of Scilly;

(c) in Wales, a county council or a county borough council;

'occupier' means the person entitled to possession of the land by virtue of an estate or interest held by him;

'vehicle' includes –

(a) any vehicle, whether or not it is in a fit state for use on roads, and includes any body, with or without wheels, appearing to have formed part of such a vehicle, and any load carried by, and anything attached to, such a vehicle; and

(b) a caravan as defined in section 19(1) of the Caravan Sites and Control of Development Act 1960;

and a person may be regarded for the purposes of this section as residing on any land notwithstanding that he has a home elsewhere.

(7) Until 1 April 1996, in this section 'local authority' means, in Wales, a county council or a district council.

78   Orders for removal of persons and their vehicles unlawfully on land

(1) A magistrates' court may, on a complaint made by a local authority, if satisfied that persons and vehicles in which they are residing are present on land within that authority's area in contravention of a direction given under section 77, make an order requiring the removal of any vehicle or other property which is so present on the land and any person residing in it.

(2) An order under this section may authorise the local authority to take such steps as are reasonably necessary to ensure that the order is complied with and, in particular, may authorise the authority, by its officers and servants –

(a) to enter upon the land specified in the order; and

(b) to take, in relation to any vehicle or property to be removed in pursuance of the order, such steps for securing entry and rendering it suitable for removal as may be so specified.

(3) The local authority shall not enter upon any occupied land unless they have given to the owner and occupier at least 24 hours notice of their intention to do so, or unless after reasonable inquiries they are unable to ascertain their names and addresses.

(4) A person who wilfully obstructs any person in the exercise of any power conferred on him by an order under this section commits an offence and is liable on summary conviction to a fine not exceeding level 3 on the standard scale.

(5) Where a complaint is made under this section, a summons issued by the court requiring the

person or persons to whom it is directed to appear before the court to answer to the complaint may be directed –

    (a) to the occupant of a particular vehicle on the land in question; or

    (b) to all occupants of vehicles on the land in question, without naming him or them.

(6) Section 55(2) of the Magistrates' Courts Act 1980 (warrant for arrest of defendant failing to appear) does not apply to proceedings on a complaint made under this section.

(7) Section 77(6) of this Act applies also for the interpretation of this section.

79   Provisions as to directions under s77 and orders under s78

(1) The following provisions apply in relation to the service of notice of a direction under section 77 and of a summons under section 78, referred to in those provisions as a 'relevant document'.

(2) Where it is impracticable to serve a relevant document on a person named in it, the document shall be treated as duly served on him if a copy of it is fixed in a prominent place to the vehicle concerned; and where a relevant document is directed to the unnamed occupants of vehicles, it shall be treated as duly served on those occupants if a copy of it is fixed in a prominent place to every vehicle on the land in question at the time when service is thus effected.

(3) A local authority shall take such steps as may be reasonably practicable to secure that a copy of any relevant document is displayed on the land in question (otherwise than by being fixed to a vehicle) in a manner designed to ensure that it is likely to be seen by any person camping on the land.

(4) Notice of any relevant document shall be given by the local authority to the owner of the land in question and to any occupier of that land unless, after reasonable inquiries, the authority is unable to ascertain the name and address of the owner or occupier; and the owner of any such land and any occupier of such land shall be entitled to appear and to be heard in the proceedings.

(5) Section 77(6) applies also for the interpretation of this section.

166 Sale of tickets by unauthorised persons

(1) It is an offence for an unauthorised person to –

    (a) sell a ticket for a designated football match, or

    (b) otherwise to dispose of such a ticket to another person.

(2) For this purpose –

    (a) a person is 'unauthorised' unless he is authorised in writing to sell or otherwise dispose of tickets for the match by the organisers of the match;

    (aa) a reference to selling a ticket includes a reference to –

        (i) offering to sell a ticket;

        (ii) exposing a ticket for sale;

        (iii) making a ticket available for sale by another;

        (iv) advertising that a ticket is available for purchase; and

        (v) giving a ticket to a person who pays or agrees to pay for some other goods or services or offering to do so.

    (b) a 'ticket' means anything which purports to be a ticket; and

    (c) a 'designated football match' means a football match of a description, or a particular football match, for the time being designated for the purposes of this section by order made by the Secretary of State.

(2A) An order under subsection (2)(c) may designate descriptions of football matches wherever played or when played at descriptions of ground or in any area specified in the order.

(2B) The power of the Secretary of State to make an order under subsection (2)(c) shall be exercisable by statutory instrument which shall be subject to annulment in pursuance of a resolution of either House of Parliament.

(3) A person guilty of an offence under this section is liable on summary conviction to a fine not exceeding level 5 on the standard scale.

(5) Section 32 of the Police and Criminal Evidence Act 1984 (search of persons and premises (including vehicles) upon arrest) shall have effect, in its application in relation to an offence under this section, as if the power conferred on a constable to enter and search any vehicle extended to any vehicle which the constable has reasonable grounds for believing was being used for any purpose connected with the offence. ...

166A Supplementary provision relating to sale and disposal of tickets on internet

(1) Nothing in section 166 makes it an offence for a service provider established outside of the United Kingdom to do anything in the course of providing information society services.

(2) If –

- (a) a service provider established in the United Kingdom does anything in an EEA State other than the United Kingdom in the course of providing information society services, and
- (b) the action, if done in England and Wales, would constitute an offence falling within section 166(1),

the service provider shall be guilty in England and Wales of an offence under that section.

(3) A service provider is not capable of being guilty of an offence under section 166 in respect of anything done in the course of providing so much of an information society service as consists in –

- (a) the transmission in a communication network of information falling within subsection (4), or
- (b) the storage of information provided by a recipient of the service,

except where subsection (5) applies.

(4) Information falls within this subsection if –

- (a) it is provided by a recipient of the service; and
- (b) it is the subject of automatic, intermediate and temporary storage which is solely for the purpose of making the onward transmission of the information to other recipients of the service at their request more efficient.

(5) This subsection applies at any time in relation to information if –

- (a) the service provider knew when that information was provided that it contained material contravening section 166; or
- (b) that information is stored at that time (whether as mentioned in subsection (3)(b) or (4)) in consequence of the service provider's failure expeditiously to remove the information, or to disable access to it, upon obtaining actual knowledge that the information contained material contravening section 166.

(6) In this section –

'the Directive' means Directive 2000/31/EC of the European Parliament and of the Council of 8 June 2000 on certain legal aspects of information society services, in particular electronic commerce, in the Internal Market (Directive on electronic commerce);

'information society services'-

- (a) has the meaning set out in Article 2(a) of the Directive (which refers to Article 1(2) of Directive 98/34/EC of the European Parliament and of the Council of 22 June 1998 laying down a procedure for the provision of information in the field of technical standards and regulations, as amended by Directive 98/48/EC of 20 July 1998); and
- (b) is summarised in recital 17 of the Directive as covering 'any service normally provided

for remuneration, at a distance, by means of electronic equipment for the processing (including digital compression) and storage of data, and at the individual request of a recipient of a service';

'EEA State' means a state which is for the time being a member State, Norway, Iceland or Liechtenstein;

'recipient of the service' means any person who, for professional ends or otherwise, uses an information society service, in particular for the purposes of seeking information or making it accessible;

'service provider' means any person providing an information society service.

As amended by the Football (Offences and Disorder) Act 1999, s10; Football (Disorder) Act 2000, s1(2), (3), Schedule 2, para 20, Schedule 3; Anti-social Behaviour Act 2003, ss58–64, 92, Schedule 3; Licensing Act 2003, ss198, 199, Schedule 6, para 111, Schedule 7; Serious Organised Crime and Police Act 2005, ss111, 174(2), Schedule 7, Pt 1, para 31, Schedule 17, Pt 2; Violent Crime Reduction Act 2006, ss53(1)–(4), (6), 65, Schedule 5.

CRIMINAL APPEAL ACT 1995

(1995 c 35)

PART II

THE CRIMINAL CASES REVIEW COMMISSION

8   The Commission

(1) There shall be a body corporate to be known as the Criminal Cases Review Commission. ...

(3) The Commission shall consist of not fewer than eleven members.

(4) The members of the Commission shall be appointed by Her Majesty on the recommendation of the Prime Minister. ...

(7) Schedule 1 (further provisions with respect to the Commission) shall have effect

9   Cases dealt with on indictment in England and Wales

(1) Where a person has been convicted of an offence on indictment in England and Wales, the Commission –

  (a) may at any time refer the conviction to the Court of Appeal, and

  (b) (whether or not they refer the conviction) may at any time refer to the Court of Appeal any sentence (not being a sentence fixed by law) imposed on, or in subsequent proceedings relating to, the conviction.

(2) A reference under subsection (1) of a person's conviction shall be treated for all purposes as an appeal by the person under section 1 of the [Criminal Appeal Act 1968] against the conviction.

(3) A reference under subsection (1) of a sentence imposed on, or in subsequent proceedings relating to, a person's conviction on an indictment shall be treated for all purposes as an appeal by the person under section 9 of the 1968 Act [appeal against sentence following conviction on indictment] against –

  (a) the sentence, and

  (b) any other sentence (not being a sentence fixed by law) imposed on, or in subsequent proceedings relating to, the conviction or any other conviction on the indictment.

(4) On a reference under subsection (1) of a person's conviction on an indictment the

Commission may give notice to the Court of Appeal that any other conviction on the indictment which is specified in the notice is to be treated as referred to the Court of Appeal under subsection (1).

(5) Where a verdict of not guilty by reason of insanity has been returned in England and Wales in the case of a person, the Commission may at any time refer the verdict to the Court of Appeal; and a reference under this subsection shall be treated for all purposes as an appeal by the person under section 12 of the 1968 Act against the verdict.

(6) Where in England and Wales there have been findings that a person is under a disability and that he did the act or made the omission charged against him, the Commission may at any time refer either or both of those findings to the Court of Appeal; and a reference under this subsection shall be treated for all purposes as an appeal by the person under section 15 of the 1968 Act against the finding or findings referred.

11 Cases dealt with summarily in England and Wales

(1) Where a person has been convicted of an offence by a magistrates' court in England and Wales, the Commission –

    (a) may at any time refer the conviction to the Crown Court, and

    (b) (whether or not they refer the conviction) may at any time refer to the Crown Court any sentence imposed on, or in subsequent proceedings relating to, the conviction.

(2) A reference under subsection (1) of a person's conviction shall be treated for all purposes as an appeal by the person under section 108(1) of the Magistrates' Courts Act 1980 [right of appeal to the Crown Court] against the conviction (whether or not he pleaded guilty).

(3) A reference under subsection (1) of a sentence imposed on, or in subsequent proceedings relating to, a person's conviction shall be treated for all purposes as an appeal by the person under section 108(1) of the Magistrates' Courts Act 1980 against –

    (a) the sentence, and

    (b) any other sentence imposed on, or in subsequent proceedings relating to, the conviction or any related conviction.

(4) On a reference under subsection (1) of a person's conviction the Commission may give notice to the Crown Court that any related conviction which is specified in the notice is to be treated as referred to the Crown Court under subsection (1).

(5) For the purposes of this section convictions are related if they are convictions of the same person by the same court on the same day.

(6) On a reference under this section the Crown Court may not award any punishment more severe than that awarded by the court whose decision is referred.

(7) The Crown Court may grant bail to a person whose conviction or sentence has been referred under this section; and any time during which he is released on bail shall not count as part of any term of imprisonment or detention under his sentence.

13 Conditions for making of references

(1) A reference of a conviction, verdict, finding or sentence shall not be made under any of sections 9 to 12 unless –

    (a) the Commission consider that there is a real possibility that the conviction, verdict, finding or sentence would not be upheld were the reference to be made,

    (b) the Commission so consider –

        (i) in the case of a conviction, verdict or finding, because of an argument, or evidence, not raised in the proceedings which led to it or on any appeal or application for leave to appeal against it, or

(ii) in the case of a sentence, because of an argument on a point of law, or information, not so raised, and

(c) an appeal against the conviction, verdict, finding or sentence has been determined or leave to appal against it has been refused.

(2) Nothing in subsection (1)(b)(i) or (c) shall prevent the making of a reference if it appears to the Commission that there are exceptional circumstances which justify making it.

14   Further provisions about references

(1) A reference of a conviction, verdict, finding or sentence may be made under any of sections 9 to 12 either after an application has been made by or on behalf of the person to whom it relates or without an application having been so made.

(2) In so considering whether to make a reference of a conviction, verdict, finding or sentence under any of sections 9 to 12 the Commission shall have regard to –

(a) any application or representations made to the Commission by or on behalf of the person to whom it relates,

(b) any other representations made to the Commission in relation to it, and

(c) any other matters which appear to the Commission to be relevant.

(3) In considering whether to make a reference under section 9 or 10 the Commission may at any time refer any point on which they desire the assistance of the Court of Appeal to that Court for the Court's opinion on it; and on a reference under this subsection the Court of Appeal shall consider the point referred and furnish the Commission with the Court's opinion on the point.

(4) Where the Commission make a reference under any of sections 9 to 12 the Commission shall –

(a) give to the court to which the reference is made a statement of the Commission's reasons for making the reference, and

(b) send a copy of the statement to every person who appears to the Commission to be likely to be a party to any proceedings on the appeal arising from the reference.

(4A) Subject to subsection (4B), where a reference under section 9 or 10 is treated as an appeal against any conviction, verdict, finding or sentence, the appeal may not be on any ground which is not related to any reason given by the Commission for making the reference.

(4B) The Court of Appeal may give leave for an appeal mentioned in subsection (4A) to be on a ground relating to the conviction, verdict, finding or sentence which is not related to any reason given by the Commission for making the reference.

(5) Where a reference under section 11 or 12 is treated as an appeal against any conviction, verdict, finding or sentence, the appeal may be on any ground relating to the conviction, verdict, finding or sentence (whether or not the ground is related to any reason given by the Commission for making the reference).

(6) In every case in which –

(a) an application has been made to the Commission by or on behalf of any person for the reference under any of sections 9 to 12 of any conviction, verdict, finding or sentence, but

(b) the Commission decide not to make a reference of the conviction, verdict, finding or sentence,

the Commission shall give a statement of the reasons for their decision to the person who made the application.

15   Investigations for Court of Appeal

(1) Where a direction is given by the Court of Appeal under section 23A(1) of the 1968 Act ...

the Commission shall investigate the matter specified in the direction in such manner as the Commission think fit.

(2) Where, in investigating a matter specified in such a direction, it appears to the Commission that –

    (a) another matter (a 'related matter') which is relevant to the determination of the appeal or application for leave to appeal by the Court of Appeal ought, if possible, to be resolved before the appeal or application for leave to appeal is determined by that Court, and

    (b) an investigation of the related matter is likely to result in the Court's being able to resolve it,

the Commission may also investigate the related matter.

(3) The Commission shall –

    (a) keep the Court of Appeal informed as to the progress of the investigation of any matter specified in a direction under section 23A(1) of the 1968 Act … , and

    (b) if they decide to investigate any related matter, notify the Court of Appeal of their decision and keep the Court informed as to the progress of the investigation.

(4) The Commission shall report to the Court of Appeal on the investigation of any matter specified in a direction under section 23A(1) of the 1968 Act … when –

    (a) they complete the investigation of that matter and of any related matter investigated by them, or

    (b) they are directed to do so by the Court of Appeal,

whichever happens first.

(5) A report under subsection (4) shall include details of any inquiries made by or for the Commission in the investigation of the matter specified in the direction or any related matter investigated by them.

(6) Such a report shall be accompanied –

    (a) by any statements and opinions received by the Commission in the investigation of the matter specified in the direction or any related matter investigated by them, and

    (b) subject to subsection (7), by any reports so received.

(7) Such a report need not be accompanied by any reports submitted to the Commission under section 20(6) by an investigating officer.

16   Assistance in connection with prerogative of mercy

(1) Where the Secretary of State refers to the Commission any matter which arises in the consideration of whether to recommend the exercise of Her Majesty's prerogative of mercy in relation to a conviction and on which he desires their assistance, the Commission shall –

    (a) consider the matter referred, and

    (b) give to the Secretary of State a statement of their conclusions on it;

and the Secretary of State shall, in considering whether so to recommend, treat the Commission's statement as conclusive of the matter referred.

(2) Where in any case the Commission are of the opinion that the Secretary of State should consider whether to recommend the exercise of Her Majesty's prerogative of mercy in relation to the case they shall give him the reasons for their opinion.

19   Power to require appointment of investigating officers

(1) Where the Commission believe that inquiries should be made for assisting them in the exercise of any of their functions in relation to any case they may require the appointment of an investigating officer to carry out the inquiries.

(2) Where any offence to which the case relates was investigated by persons serving in a public body, a requirement under this section may be imposed –

(a) on the person who is the appropriate person in relation to the public body, or

(b) where the public body has ceased to exist, on any chief officer of police or on the person who is the appropriate person in relation to any public body which appears to the Commission to have functions which consist of or include functions similar to any of those of the public body which has ceased to exist.

(3) Where no offence to which the case relates was investigated by persons serving in a public body, a requirement under this section may be imposed on any chief officer of police. ...

20   Inquiries by investigating officers

(1) A person appointed as the investigating officer in relation to a case shall undertake such inquiries as the Commission may from time to time reasonably direct him to undertake in relation to the case. ...

(4) The Commission may take any steps which they consider appropriate for supervising the undertaking of inquiries by an investigating officer. ...

(6) When a person appointed as the investigating officer in relation to a case has completed the inquiries which he has been directed by the Commission to undertake in relation to the case, he shall –

(a) prepare a report of his findings,

(b) submit it to the Commission, and

(c) send a copy of it to the person by whom he was appointed.

(7) When a person appointed as the investigating officer in relation to a case submits to the Commission a report of his findings he shall also submit to them any statements, opinions and reports received by him in connection with the inquiries which he was directed to undertake in relation to the case.

22   Meaning of 'public body' etc

(1) In sections 17 [power to obtain documents, etc], 19 and 20 and this section 'public body' means –

(a) any police force.

(b) any government department, local authority or other body constituted for purposes of the public service, local government or the administration of justice, or

(c) any other body whose members are appointed by Her Majesty, any Minister or any government department or whose revenues consist wholly or mainly of money provided by Parliament or appropriated by Measure of the Northern Ireland Assembly.
   ...

SCHEDULE 1

THE COMMISSION: FURTHER PROVISIONS

1. Her Majesty shall, on the recommendation of the Prime Minister, appoint one of the members of the Commission to be the chairman of the Commission.

2. – (1) Subject to the following provisions of this paragraph, a person shall hold and vacate office as a member of the Commission, or as chairman of the Commission, in accordance with the terms of his appointment. ...

(5) No person may hold office as a member of the Commission for a continuous period which is longer than ten years. ...

(8) If the chairman of the Commission ceases to be a member of the Commission he shall also cease to be chairman.

As amended by the Criminal Justice Act 2003, ss315, 331, Schedule 36, Pt 6, para 97; Domestic Violence, Crime and Victims Act 2004, s58(1), Schedule 10, para 31.

POLICE ACT 1996
(1996 c 16)

89 Assaults on constables

(1) Any person who assaults a constable in the execution of his duty, or a person assisting a constable in the execution of his duty, shall be guilty of an offence and liable on summary conviction to imprisonment for a term not exceeding six months or to a fine not exceeding level 5 on the standard scale, or to both.

(2) Any person who resists or wilfully obstructs a constable in the execution of his duty, or a person assisting a constable in the execution of his duty, shall be guilty of an offence and liable on summary conviction to imprisonment for a term not exceeding one month or to a fine not exceeding level 3 on the standard scale, or to both.

(3) This section also applies to a constable who is a member of a police force maintained in Scotland or Northern Ireland when he is executing a warrant, or otherwise acting in England or Wales, by virtue of any enactment conferring powers on him in England and Wales.

(4) In this section references to a person assisting a constable in the execution of his duty include references to any person who is neither a constable nor in the company of a constable but who –

    (a) is a member of an international joint investigation team that is led by a member of a police force; and

    (b) is carrying out his functions as a member of that team.

(5) In this section 'international joint investigation team' means any investigation team formed in accordance with –

    (a) any framework decision on joint investigation teams adopted under article 34 of the Treaty on European Union;

    (b) the Convention on Mutual Assistance in Criminal Matters between the Member States of the European Union, and the Protocol to that Convention, established in accordance with that Article of that Treaty; or

    (c) any international agreement to which the United Kingdom is a party and which is specified for the purposes of this section in an order made by the Secretary of State.
       ...

[See Appendix, Criminal Justice Act 2003, Schedule 26, para 47.]

90 Impersonation, etc

(1) Any person who with intent to deceive impersonates a member of a police force or special constable, or makes any statement or does any act calculated falsely to suggest that he is such a member or constable, shall be guilty of an offence and liable on summary conviction to

imprisonment for a term not exceeding six months or to a fine not exceeding level 5 on the standard scale, or to both.

(2) Any person who, not being a constable, wears any article of police uniform in circumstances where it gives him an appearance so nearly resembling that of a member of a police force as to be calculated to deceive shall be guilty of an offence and liable on summary conviction to a fine not exceeding level 3 on the standard scale.

(3) Any person who, not being a member of a police force or special constable, has in his possession any article of police uniform shall, unless he proves that he obtained possession of that article lawfully and has possession of it for a lawful purpose, be guilty of an offence and liable on summary conviction to a fine not exceeding level 1 on the standard scale.

(4) In this section –

> (a) 'article of police uniform' means any article of uniform or any distinctive badge or mark or document of identification usually issued to members of police forces or special constables, or anything having the appearance of such an article, badge, mark or document,
>
> (aa) 'member of the police force' include a member of the British Transport Police Force, and
>
> (ab) 'member of a police force' includes a member of the staff of the National Policing Improvement Agency who is a constable, and
>
> (b) 'special constable' means a special constable appointed for a police area.

91   Causing disaffection

(1) Any person who causes, or attempts to cause, or does any act calculated to cause, disaffection amongst the members of any police force, or induces or attempts to induce, or does any act calculated to induce, any member of a police force to withhold his services, shall be guilty of an offence and liable –

> (a) on summary conviction, to imprisonment for a term not exceeding six months or to a fine not exceeding the statutory maximum, or to both;
>
> (b) on conviction on indictment, to imprisonment for a term not exceeding two years or to a fine, or to both.

(2) This section applies in the case of –

> (a) special constables appointed for a police area,
>
> (aa) members of the staff of the National Policing Improvement Agency who are constables,
>
> (b) members of the Civil Nuclear Constabulary, and
>
> (c) members of the British Transport Police Force,

as it applies in the case of members of a police force.

(3) Liability under subsection(1) for any behaviour is in addition to any civil liability for that behaviour.

As amended by the Anti-terrorism, Crime and Security Act 2001, s101, Schedule 7, paras 20, 25, 26; Police Reform Act 2002, s104(1); Energy Act 2004, s68(3); Serious Organised Crime and Police Act 2005, ss59, 174(2), Schedule 4, paras 68, 81, Schedule 17, Pt 2; Police and Justice Act 2006, ss1(3), 52, Schedule 1, Pt 7, paras 61, 70, 71, Schedule 14, para 30.

LAW REFORM (YEAR AND A DAY RULE) ACT 1996
(1996) c 19)

1   Abolition of 'year and a day' rule

The rule known as the 'year and a day rule' (that is, the rule that, for the purposes of offences involving death and of suicide, an act or omission is conclusively presumed not to have caused a person's death if more than a year and a day elapsed before he died) is abolished for all purposes.

2   Restriction on institution of proceedings for a fatal offence

(1) Proceedings to which this section applies may only be instituted by or with the consent of the Attorney General.

(2) This section applies to proceedings against a person for a fatal offence if –

    (a) the injury alleged to have caused the death was sustained more than three years before the death occurred, or

    (b) the person has previously been convicted of an offence committed in circumstances alleged to be connected with the death.

(3) In subsection (2) 'fatal offence' means –

    (a) murder, manslaughter, infanticide or any other offence of which one of the elements is causing a person's death,

    (b) the offence of aiding, abetting, counselling or procuring a person's suicide; or

    (c) an offence under section 5 of the Domestic Violence, Crime and Victims Act 2004 (causing or allowing the death of a child or vulnerable adult).

(4) No provision that proceedings may be instituted only by or with the consent of the Director of Public Prosecutions shall apply to proceedings to which this section applies. …

As amended by the Domestic Violence, Crime and Victims Act 2004, s58, Schedule 10, para 33, Schedule 11.

CRIMINAL PROCEDURE AND INVESTIGATIONS ACT 1996
(1996 c 25)

54   Acquittals tainted by intimidation, etc

(1) This section applies where –

    (a) a person has been acquitted of an offence, and

    (b) a person has been convicted of an administration of justice offence involving interference with or intimidation of a juror or a witness (or potential witness) in any proceedings which led to the acquittal.

(2) Where it appears to the court before which the person was convicted that –

    (a) there is a real possibility that, but for the interference or intimidation, the acquitted person would not have been acquitted, and

    (b) subsection (5) does not apply,

the court shall certify that it so appears.

(3) Where a court certifies under subsection (2) an application may be made to the High Court for an order quashing the acquittal, and the Court shall make the order if (but shall not do so unless) the four conditions in section 55 are satisfied.

(4) Where an order is made under subsection (3) proceedings may be taken against the acquitted person for the offence of which he was acquitted.

(5) This subsection applies if, because of lapse of time or for any other reason, it would be contrary to the interests of justice to take proceedings against the acquitted person for the offence of which he was acquitted.

(6) For the purposes of this section the following offences are administration of justice offences –

    (a) the offence of perverting the course of justice;

    (b) the offence under section 51(1) of the Criminal Justice and Public Order Act 1994 (intimidation, etc. of witnesses, jurors and others);

    (c) an offence of aiding, abetting, counselling, procuring, suborning or inciting another person to commit an offence under section 1 of the Perjury Act 1911.

(7) This section applies in relation to acquittals in respect of offences alleged to be committed on or after the appointed day.

(8) The reference in subsection (7) to the appointed day is to such day as is appointed for the purposes of this section by the Secretary of State by order.

55   Conditions for making order

(1) The first condition is that it appears to the High Court likely that, but for the interference or intimidation, the acquitted person would not have been acquitted.

(2) The second condition is that it does not appear to the Court that, because of lapse of time or for any other reason, it would be contrary to the interests of justice to take proceedings against the acquitted person for the offence of which he was acquitted.

(3) The third condition is that it appears to the Court that the acquitted person has been given a reasonable opportunity to make written representations to the Court.

(4) The fourth condition is that it appears to the Court that the conviction for the administration of justice offence will stand.

(5) In applying subsection (4) the Court shall –

    (a) take into account all the information before it, but

    (b) ignore the possibility of new factors coming to light.

(6) Accordingly, the fourth condition has the effect that the Court shall not make an order under section 54(3) if (for instance) it appears to the Court that any time allowed for giving notice of appeal has not expired or that an appeal is pending.

56   Time limits for proceedings

(1) Where –

    (a) an order is made under section 54(3) quashing an acquittal,

    (b) by virtue of section 54(4) it is proposed to take proceedings against the acquitted person for the offence of which he was acquitted, and

    (c) apart from this subsection, the effect of an enactment would be that the proceedings must be commenced before a specified period calculated by reference to the commission of the offence,

in relation to the proceedings the enactment shall have effect as if the period were instead one calculated by reference to the time the order is made under section 54(3).

(2) Subsection (1)(c) applies however the enactment is expressed so that (for instance) it applies in the case of –

    (b) section 127(1) of the Magistrates' Courts Act 1980 (magistrates' court not to try information unless it is laid within 6 months from time when offence committed);

    (c) an enactment that imposes a time limit only in certain circumstances (as where proceedings are not instituted by or with the consent of the Director of Public Prosecutions).

As amended by the Sexual Offences Act 2003, s140, Schedule 7.

SEXUAL OFFENCES (CONSPIRACY AND INCITEMENT) ACT 1996
(1996 c 29)

2 Incitement to commit certain sexual acts outside the United Kingdom
(1) This section applies where –
  (a) any act done by a person in England and Wales would amount to the offence of incitement to commit a listed sexual offence but for the fact that what he had in view would not be an offence triable in England and Wales,
  (b) the whole or part of what he had in view was intended to take place in a country or territory outside the United Kingdom, and
  (c) what he had in view would involve the commission of an offence under the law in force in that country or territory.
(2) Where this section applies –
  (a) what he had in view is to be treated as that listed sexual offence for the purposes of any charge of incitement brought in respect of that act, and
  (b) any such charge is accordingly triable in England and Wales.
(3) Any act of incitement by means of a message (however communicated) is to be treated as done in England and Wales if the message is sent or received in England and Wales.

3 Sections 1 and 2: supplementary
(1) Conduct punishable under the law in force in any country or territory is an offence under that law for the purposes of section 2, however it is described in that law.
(2) Subject to subsection(3), a condition in section 2(1)(c) is to be taken to be satisfied unless, not later than rules of court may provide, the defence serve on the prosecution a notice –
  (a) stating that, on the facts as alleged with respect to what the accused had in view, the condition is not in their opinion satisfied,
  (b) showing their grounds for that opinion, and
  (c) requiring the prosecution to show that it is satisfied.
(4) The court, if it thinks fit, may permit the defence to require the prosecution to show that the condition is satisfied without the prior service of a notice under subsection(2).
(5) In the Crown Court the question whether the condition is satisfied is to be decided by the judge alone.
(6) In any proceedings in respect of any offence triable by virtue of section 2, it is immaterial to guilt whether or not the accused was a British citizen at the time of any act or other event proof of which is required for conviction of the offence.
(8) References to an offence of incitement to commit a listed sexual offence include an offence triable in England and Wales as such an incitement by virtue of section 2(without prejudice to subsection(2) of that section).
(9) Subsection (8) applies to references in any enactment, instrument or document (except those in section 2 of this Act and in Part I of the Criminal Law Act 1977).

5   Interpretation
In this Act 'listed sexual offence' has the meaning given by the Schedule.

7   Short title, commencement and extent ...
(2) This Act is to come into force on such day as the Secretary of State may by order made by statutory instrument appoint, and different days may be appointed for different purposes and for different areas.
(3) Nothing in section 2 or 6 applies to any act or other event occurring before the coming into force of that section.

SCHEDULE

LISTED SEXUAL OFFENCES

1 – (1) In relation to England and Wales, the following are listed sexual offences:
   (b) an offence under any of sections 1 to 12, 14 and 15 to 26 of the Sexual Offences Act 2003.
(2) Sub-paragraph (1)(b) does not apply where the victim of the offence has attained the age of sixteen years. ...

As amended by the Criminal Justice (Terrorism and Conspiracy) Act 1998, s9, Schedule 1, Pt II, para 9(1), (2), (4), Schedule 2, Pt II; Sexual Offences Act 2003, ss139, 140, Schedule 6, para 35, Schedule 7.

FIREARMS (AMENDMENT) ACT 1997
(1997 c 5)

PART I

PROHIBITION OF WEAPONS AND AMMUNITION AND CONTROL OF SMALL-CALIBRE PISTOLS

1   Extension of s5 of the 1968 Act to prohibit certain small firearms, etc ...
(7) The general prohibition by section 5 of the [Firearms Act 1968] of firearms falling within subsection (1)(aba) of that section is subject to the special exemptions in sections 2 to 8 below.
(8) In sections 2 to 8 below any reference to a firearm certificate shall include a reference to a visitor's firearm permit. ...

2   Slaughtering instruments ...

3   Firearms used for humane killing of animals ...

4   Shot pistols used for shooting vermin ...

5   Races at athletic meetings ...

6   Trophies of war ...

7   Firearms of historic interest ...

8   Weapons and ammunition used for treating animals ...

PART III

REGULATION OF FIREARMS AND AMMUNITION

32   Transfers of firearms, etc to be in person

(1) This section applies where, in Great Britain –

>   (a) a firearm or ammunition to which section 1 of the 1968 Act applies is sold, let on hire, lent or given by any person, or

>   (b) a shot gun is sold, let on hire or given, or lent for a period of more than 72 hours by any person,

to another person who is neither a registered firearms dealer nor a person who is entitled to purchase or acquire the firearm or ammunition without holding a firearm or shot gun certificate or a visitor's firearm or shot gun permit.

(2) Where a transfer to which this section applies takes place –

>   (a) the transferee must produce to the transferor the certificate or permit entitling him to purchase or acquire the firearm or ammunition being transferred;

>   (b) the transferor must comply with any instructions contained in the certificate or permit produced by the transferee;

>   (c) the transferor must hand the firearm or ammunition to the transferee, and the transferee must receive it, in person.

(3) A failure by the transferor or transferee to comply with subsection (2) above shall be an offence.

36   Penalty for offences under ss32 to 35

An offence under section 32, 33 [notification of transfers involving firearms], 34 [notification of de-activation, destruction or loss of firearms, etc] or 35 [notification of events taking place outside Great Britain involving firearms, etc] above shall –

>   (a) if committed in relation to a transfer or other event involving a firearm or ammunition to which section 1 of the 1968 Act applies be punishable –

>   (i) on summary conviction with imprisonment for a term not exceeding six months or a fine not exceeding the statutory maximum or both;

>   (ii) on conviction on indictment with imprisonment for a term not exceeding five years or a fine or both;

>   (b) if committed in relation to a transfer or other event involving a shot gun be punishable on summary conviction with imprisonment for a term not exceeding six months or a fine not exceeding level 5 on the standard scale or both.

39   Register of holders of shot gun and firearm certificates

(1) There shall be established a central register of all persons who have applied for a firearm or shot gun certificate or to whom a firearm or shot gun certificate has been granted or whose certificate has been renewed.

(2) The register shall –

>   (a) record a suitable identifying number for each person to whom a certificate is issued; and

>   (b) be kept by means of a computer which provides access on-line to all police forces.

48   Firearms powered by compressed carbon dioxide

Any reference to an air rifle, air pistol or air gun –

    (a)   in the Firearms Acts 1968 to 1997; or

    (b)   in the Firearms (Dangerous Air Weapons) Rules 1969 …,

shall include a reference to a rifle, pistol or gun powered by compressed carbon dioxide.

PART IV

FINAL PROVISIONS

50   Interpretation and supplementary provisions …

(2) Any expression used in this Act which is also used in the 1968 Act or the [Firearms (Amendment) Act 1988] has the same meaning as in that Act.

(3) Any reference in the 1968 Act to a person who is by virtue of that Act entitled to possess, purchase or acquire any weapon or ammunition without holding a certificate shall include a reference to a person who is so entitled by virtue of any provision of this Act. …

(6) The provisions of this Act shall be treated as contained in the 1968 Act for the purposes of the Firearms Act 1982 (imitation firearms readily convertible into firearms to which section 1 of the 1968 Act applies).

KNIVES ACT 1997

(1997 c 21)

1   Unlawful marketing of knives

(1) A person is guilty of an offence if he markets a knife in a way which –

    (a)   indicates, or suggests, that it is suitable for combat; or

    (b)   is otherwise likely to stimulate or encourage violent behaviour involving the use of the knife as a weapon.

(2) 'Suitable for combat' and 'violent behaviour' are defined in section 10.

(3) For the purposes of this Act, an indication or suggestion that a knife is suitable for combat may, in particular, be given or made by a name or description –

    (a)   applied to the knife;

    (b)   on the knife or on any packaging in which it is contained; or

    (c)   included in any advertisement which, expressly or by implication, relates to the knife.

(4) For the purposes of this Act, a person markets a knife if –

    (a)   he sells or hires it;

    (b)   he offers, or exposes, it for sale or hire; or

    (c)   he has it in his possession for the purpose of sale or hire.

(5) A person who is guilty of an offence under this section is liable –

    (a)   on summary conviction to imprisonment for a term not exceeding six months or to a fine not exceeding the statutory maximum, or to both;

    (b)   on conviction on indictment to imprisonment for a term not exceeding two years or to a fine, or to both.

2   Publications

(1) A person is guilty of an offence if he publishes any written, pictorial or other material in connection with the marketing of any knife and that material –

- (a) indicates, or suggests, that the knife is suitable for combat; or
- (b) is otherwise likely to stimulate or encourage violent behaviour involving the use of the knife as a weapon.

(2) A person who is guilty of an offence under this section is liable –

- (a) on summary conviction to imprisonment for a term not exceeding six months or to a fine not exceeding the statutory maximum, or to both;
- (b) on conviction on indictment to imprisonment for a term not exceeding two years or to a fine, or to both.

3   Exempt trades

(1) It is a defence for a person charged with an offence under section 1 to prove that –

- (a) the knife was marketed –
    - (i)   for use by the armed forces of any country;
    - (ii) as an antique or curio; or
    - (iii) as falling within such other category (if any) as may be prescribed;
- (b) it was reasonable for the knife to be marketed in that way; and
- (c) there were no reasonable grounds for suspecting that a person into whose possession the knife might come in consequence of the way in which it was marketed would use it for an unlawful purpose.

(2) It is a defence for a person charged with an offence under section 2 to prove that –

- (a) the material was published in connection with marketing a knife –
    - (i)   for use by the armed forces of any country;
    - (ii) as an antique or curio; or
    - (iii) as falling within such other category (if any) as may be prescribed;
- (b) it was reasonable for the knife to be marketed in that way; and
- (c) there were no reasonable grounds for suspecting that a person into whose possession the knife might come in consequence of the publishing of the material would use it for an unlawful purpose.

(3) In this section 'prescribed' means prescribed by regulations made by the Secretary of State.

4   Other defences

(1) It is a defence for a person charged with an offence under section 1 to prove that he did not know or suspect, and had no reasonable grounds for suspecting, that the way in which the knife was marketed –

- (a) amounted to an indication or suggestion that the knife was suitable for combat; or
- (b) was likely to stimulate or encourage violent behaviour involving the use of the knife as a weapon.

(2) It is a defence for a person charged with an offence under section 2 to prove that he did not know or suspect, and had no reasonable grounds for suspecting, that the material –

- (a) amounted to an indication or suggestion that the knife was suitable for combat; or
- (b) was likely to stimulate or encourage violent behaviour involving the use of the knife as a weapon.

(3) It is a defence for a person charged with an offence under section 1 or 2 to prove that he took all reasonable precautions and exercised all due diligence to avoid committing the offence.

9   Offences by bodies corporate

(1) If an offence under this Act committed by a body corporate is proved –

    (a) to have been committed with the consent or connivance of an officer, or

    (b) to be attributable to any neglect on his part, he as well as the body corporate is guilty of the offence and liable to be proceeded against and punished accordingly.

(2) In subsection (1) 'officer', in relation to a body corporate, means a director, manager, secretary or other similar officer of the body, or a person purporting to act in any such capacity.

(3) If the affairs of a body corporate are managed by its members, subsection (1) applies in relation to the acts and defaults of a member in connection with his functions of management as if he were a director of the body corporate. …

10   Interpretation

In this Act –

    'the court' means –

    (a) in relation to England and Wales or Northern Ireland, the Crown Court or a magistrate's court;

    (b) in relation to Scotland, the sheriff;

    'knife' means an instrument which has a blade or is sharply pointed;

    'marketing' and related expressions are to be read with section 1(4);

    'publication' includes a publication in electronic form and, in the case of a publication which is, or may be, produced from electronic data, any medium on which the data are stored;

    'suitable for combat' means suitable for use as a weapon for inflicting injury on a person or causing a person to fear injury;

    'violent behaviour' means an unlawful act inflicting injury on a person or causing a person to fear injury.

PROTECTION FROM HARASSMENT ACT 1997
(1997 c 40)

1   Prohibition of harassment

(1) A person must not pursue a course of conduct –

    (a) which amounts to harassment of another, and

    (b) which he knows or ought to know amounts to harassment of the other.

(1A) A person must not pursue a course of conduct –

    (a) which involves harassment of two or more persons, and

    (b) which he knows or ought to know involves harassment of those persons, and

    (c) by which he intends to persuade any person (whether or not one of those mentioned above) –

        (i)   not to do something that he is entitled or required to do, or

        (ii) to do something that he is not under any obligation to do.

(2) For the purposes of this section, the person whose course of conduct is in question ought to know that it amounts to or involves harassment of another if a reasonable person in possession of the same information would think the course of conduct amounted to or involved harassment of the other.

(3) Subsection (1) or (1A) does not apply to a course of conduct if the person who pursued it shows –

  (a) that it was pursued for the purpose of preventing or detecting crime,
  (b) that it was pursued under any enactment or rule of law or to comply with any condition or requirement imposed by any person under any enactment, or
  (c) that in the particular circumstances the pursuit of the course of conduct was reasonable.

2 Offence of harassment

(1) A person who pursues a course of conduct in breach of section 1(1) or (1A) is guilty of an offence.

(2) A person guilty of an offence under this section is liable on summary conviction to imprisonment for a term not exceeding six months, or a fine not exceeding level 5 on the standard scale, or both.

3 Civil remedy

(1) An actual or apprehended breach of section 1(1) may be the subject of a claim in civil proceedings by the person who is or may be the victim of the course of conduct in question.

(2) On such a claim, damages may be awarded for (among other things) any anxiety caused by the harassment and any financial loss resulting from the harassment.

(3) Where –

  (a) in such proceedings the High Court or a county court grants an injunction for the purpose of restraining the defendant from pursuing any conduct which amounts to harassment, and
  (b) the plaintiff considers that the defendant has done anything which he is prohibited from doing by the injunction,

the plaintiff may apply for the issue of a warrant for the arrest of the defendant.

(4) An application under subsection (3) may be made –

  (a) where the injunction was granted by the High Court, to a judge of that court, and
  (b) where the injunction was granted by a county court, to a judge or district judge of that or any other county court.

(5) The judge or district judge to whom an application under subsection (3) is made may only issue a warrant if –

  (a) the application is substantiated on oath, and
  (b) the judge or district judge has reasonable grounds for believing that the defendant has done anything which he is prohibited from doing by the injunction.

(6) Where –

  (a) the High Court or a county court grants an injunction for the purpose mentioned in subsection (3)(a), and
  (b) without reasonable excuse the defendant does anything which he is prohibited from doing by the injunction,

he is guilty of an offence.

(7) Where a person is convicted of an offence under subsection (6) in respect of any conduct, that conduct is not punishable as a contempt of court.

(8) A person cannot be convicted of an offence under subsection (6) in respect of any conduct which has been punished as a contempt of court.

(9) A person guilty of an offence under subsection (6) is liable –

  (a) on conviction on indictment, to imprisonment for a term not exceeding five years, or a fine, or both, or

(b) on summary conviction, to imprisonment for a term not exceeding six months, or a fine not exceeding the statutory maximum, or both.

3A   Injunctions to protect persons from harassment within section 1(1A)

(1) This section applies where there is an actual or apprehended breach of section 1(1A) by any person ('the relevant person').

(2) In such a case –

(a) any person who is or may be a victim of the course of conduct in question, or

(b) any person who is or may be a person falling within section 1(1A)(c),

may apply to the High Court or a county court for an injunction restraining the relevant person from pursuing any conduct which amounts to harassment in relation to any person or persons mentioned or described in the injunction.

(3) Section 3(3) to (9) apply in relation to an injunction granted under subsection (2) above as they apply in relation to an injunction granted as mentioned in section 3(3)(a).

4   Putting people in fear of violence

(1) A person whose course of conduct causes another to fear, on at least two occasions, that violence will be used against him is guilty of an offence if he knows or ought to know that his course of conduct will cause the other so to fear on each of those occasions.

(2) For the purposes of this section, the person whose course of conduct is in question ought to know that it will cause another to fear that violence will be used against him on any occasion if a reasonable person in possession of the same information would think the course of conduct would cause the other so to fear on that occasion.

(3) It is a defence for a person charged with an offence under this section to show that –

(a) his course of conduct was pursued for the purpose of preventing or detecting crime,

(b) his course of conduct was pursued under any enactment or rule of law or to comply with any condition or requirement imposed by any person under any enactment, or

(c) the pursuit of his course of conduct was reasonable for the protection of himself or another or for the protection of his or another's property.

(4) A person guilty of an offence under this section is liable –

(a) on conviction on indictment, to imprisonment for a term not exceeding five years, or a fine, or both, or

(b) on summary conviction, to imprisonment for a term not exceeding six months, or a fine not exceeding the statutory maximum, or both.

(5) If on the trial on indictment of a person charged with an offence under this section the jury find him not guilty of the offence charged, they may find him guilty of an offence under section 2.

(6) The Crown Court has the same powers and duties in relation to a person who is by virtue of subsection (5) convicted before it of an offence under section 2 as a magistrates' court would have on convicting him of the offence.

5   Restraining orders on conviction

(1) A court sentencing or otherwise dealing with a person ('the defendant') convicted of an offence may (as well as sentencing him or dealing with him in any other way) make an order under this section.

(2) The order may, for the purpose of protecting the victim or victims of the offence, or any other person mentioned in the order, from conduct which –

(a) amounts to harassment, or

(b) will cause a fear of violence, prohibit the defendant from doing anything described in the order.

(3) The order may have effect for a specified period or until further order.

(3A) In proceedings under this section both the prosecution and the defence may lead, as further evidence, any evidence that would be admissible in proceedings for an injunction under section 3.

(4) The prosecutor, the defendant or any other person mentioned in the order may apply to the court which made the order for it to be varied or discharged by a further order.

(4A) Any person mentioned in the order is entitled to be heard on the hearing of an application under subsection (4).

(5) If without reasonable excuse the defendant does anything which he is prohibited from doing by an order under this section, he is guilty of an offence.

(6) A person guilty of an offence under this section is liable –

  (a) on conviction on indictment, to imprisonment for a term not exceeding five years, or a fine, or both, or

  (b) on summary conviction, to imprisonment for a term not exceeding six months, or a fine not exceeding the statutory maximum, or both.

(7) A court dealing with a person for an offence under this section may vary or discharge the order in question by a further order.

5A Restraining orders on acquittal

(1) A court before which a person ('the defendant') is acquitted of an offence may, if it considers it necessary to do so to protect a person from harassment by the defendant, make an order prohibiting the defendant from doing anything described in the order.

(2) Subsections (3) to (7) of section 5 apply to an order under this section as they apply to an order under that one.

(3) Where the Court of Appeal allow an appeal against conviction they may remit the case to the Crown Court to consider whether to proceed under this section.

(4) Where –

  (a) the Crown Court allows an appeal against conviction, or

  (b) a case is remitted to the Crown Court under subsection (3),

the reference in subsection (1) to a court before which a person is acquitted of an offence is to be read as referring to that court.

(5) A person made subject to an order under this section has the same right of appeal against the order as if –

  (a) he had been convicted of the offence in question before the court which made the order, and

  (b) the order had been made under section 5.

7 Interpretation of this group of sections

(1) This section applies for the interpretation of sections 1 to 5A.

(2) References to harassing a person include alarming the person or causing the person distress.

(3) A 'course of conduct' must involve –

  (a) in the case of conduct in relation to a single person (see section 1(1)), conduct on at least two occasions in relation to that person, or

  (b) in the case of conduct in relation to two or more persons (see section 1(1A)), conduct on at least one occasion in relation to each of those persons.

(3A) A person's conduct on any occasion shall be taken, if aided, abetted, counselled or procured by another –

    (a) to be conduct on that occasion of the other (as well as conduct of the person whose conduct it is); and

    (b) to be conduct in religion to which the other's knowledge and purpose, and what he ought to have known, are the same as they were in relation to what was contemplated or reasonably foreseeable at the time of the aiding, abetting, counselling or procuring.

(4) 'Conduct' includes speech.

(5) References to a person, in the context of harassment of a person, are references to a person who is an individual.

12   National security, etc

(1) If the Secretary of State certifies that in his opinion anything done by a specified person on a specified occasion related to –

    (a) national security,

    (b) the economic well-being of the United Kingdom, or

    (c) the prevention or detection of serious crime,

and was done on behalf of the Crown, the certificate is conclusive evidence that this Act does not apply to any conduct of that person on that occasion.

(2) In subsection (1), 'specified' means specified in the certificate in question.

(3) A document purporting to be a certificate under subsection (1) is to be received in evidence and, unless the contrary is proved, be treated as being such a certificate.

NB. The amending provisions of the Domestic Violence, Crime and Victims Act 2004 shown below were not in force on 1 June 2007.

As amended by the Criminal Justice and Police Act 2001, s44; Police Reform Act 2002, s107(2), Schedule 8; Domestic Violence, Crime and Victims Act 2004, ss12, 58, Schedule 10, paras 43, 44, Schedule 11; Serious Organised Crime and Police Act 2005, s125.

CRIME AND DISORDER ACT 1998

(1998 c 37)

PART II

CRIMINAL LAW

28   Meaning of 'racially or religiosly aggravated'

(1) An offence is racially or religiously aggravated for the purposes of sections 29 to 32 below if –

    (a) at the time of committing the offence, or immediately before or after doing so, the offender demonstrates towards the victim of the offence hostility based on the victim's membership (or presumed membership) of a racial or religious group; or

    (b) the offence is motivated (wholly or partly) by hostility towards members of a racial group based on their membership of that group.

(2) In subsection (1)(a) above –

    'membership', in relation to a racial or religious group, includes association with members of that group;

    'presumed' means presumed by the offender.

(3) It is immaterial for the purposes of paragraph (a) or (b) of subsection (1) above whether or not the offender's hostility is also based, to any extent, on any other factor not mentioned in that paragraph.

(4) In this section 'racial group' means a group of persons defined by reference to race, colour, nationality (including citizenship) or ethnic or national origins.

(5) In this section 'religious group' means a group of persons defined by reference to religious belief or lack of religious belief.

29   Racially-or religiously aggravated assaults

(1) A person is guilty of an offence under this section if he commits –

(a)   an offence under section 20 of the Offences Against the Person Act 1861 (malicious wounding or grievous bodily harm);

(b)   an offence under section 47 of that Act (actual bodily harm); or

(c)   common assault,

which is racially or religiously aggravated for the purposes of this section.

(2) A person guilty of an offence falling within subsection (1)(a) or (b) above shall be liable –

(a)   on summary conviction, to imprisonment for a term not exceeding six months or to a fine not exceeding the statutory maximum, or to both;

(b)   on conviction on indictment, to imprisonment for a term not exceeding seven years or to a fine, or to both.

(3) A person guilty of an offence falling within subsection (1)(c) above shall be liable –

(a)   on summary conviction, to imprisonment for a term not exceeding six months or to a fine not exceeding the statutory maximum, or to both;

(b)   on conviction on indictment, to imprisonment for a term not exceeding two years or to a fine, or to both.

30   Racially or religiously aggravated criminal damage

(1) A person is guilty of an offence under this section if he commits an offence under section 1(1) of the Criminal Damage Act 1971 (destroying or damaging property belonging to another) which is racially or religiously aggravated for the purposes of this section.

(2) A person guilty of an offence under this section shall be liable –

(a)   on summary conviction, to imprisonment for a term not exceeding six months or to a fine not exceeding the statutory maximum, or to both;

(b)   on conviction on indictment, to imprisonment for a term not exceeding fourteen years or to a fine, or to both.

(3) For the purposes of this section, section 28(1)(a) above shall have effect as if the person to whom the property belongs or is treated as belonging for the purposes of that Act were the victim of the offence.

31   Racially or religiously aggravated public order offences

(1) A person is guilty of an offence under this section if he commits –

(a)   an offence under section 4 of the Public Order Act 1986 (fear or provocation of violence);

(b)   an offence under section 4A of that Act (intentional harassment, alarm or distress); or

(c)   an offence under section 5 of that Act (harassment, alarm or distress),

which is racially or religiously aggravated for the purposes of this section.

(4) A person guilty of an offence falling within subsection (1)(a) or (b) above shall be liable –

(a)   on summary conviction, to imprisonment for a term not exceeding six months or to a fine not exceeding the statutory maximum, or to both;

(b) on conviction on indictment, to imprisonment for a term not exceeding two years or to a fine, or to both.

(5) A person guilty of an offence falling within subsection (1)(c) above shall be liable on summary conviction to a fine not exceeding level 4 on the standard scale.

(6) If, on the trial on indictment of a person charged with an offence falling within subsection (1)(a) or (b) above, the jury find him not guilty of the offence charged, they may find him guilty of the basic offence mentioned in that provision.

(7) For the purposes of subsection (1)(c) above, section 28(1)(a) above shall have effect as if the person likely to be caused harassment, alarm or distress were the victim of the offence.

32   Racially or religiously aggravated harassment, etc

(1) A person is guilty of an offence under this section if he commits –
- (a) an offence under section 2 of the Protection from Harassment Act 1997 (offence of harassment); or
- (b) an offence under section 4 of that Act (putting people in fear of violence),

which is racially or religiously aggravated for the purposes of this section.

(3) A person guilty of an offence falling within subsection (1)(a) above shall be liable –
- (a) on summary conviction, to imprisonment for a term not exceeding six months or to a fine not exceeding the statutory maximum, or to both;
- (b) on conviction on indictment, to imprisonment for a term not exceeding two years or to a fine, or to both.

(4) A person guilty of an offence falling within subsection (1)(b) above shall be liable –
- (a) on summary conviction, to imprisonment for a term not exceeding six months or to a fine not exceeding the statutory maximum, or to both;
- (b) on conviction on indictment, to imprisonment for a term not exceeding seven years or to a fine, or to both.

(5) If, on the trial on indictment of a person charged with an offence falling within subsection (1)(a) above, the jury find him not guilty of the offence charged, they may find him guilty of the basic offence mentioned in that provision.

(6) If, on the trial on indictment of a person charged with an offence falling within subsection (1)(b) above, the jury find him not guilty of the offence charged, they may find him guilty of an offence falling within subsection (1)(a) above.

34   Abolition of rebuttable presumption that a child is doli incapax

The rebuttable presumption of criminal law that a child aged 10 or over is incapable of committing an offence is hereby abolished.

NB. The amending provisions of the Domestic Violence, Crime and Victims Act 2004 shown below were not in force on 1 June 2007.

As amended by the Anti-terrorism, Crime and Security Act 2001, s39; Police Reform Act 2002, s107(2), Schedule 8; Domestic Violence, Crime and Victims Act 2004, s58, Schedule 10, para 48, Schedule 11; Serious Organised Crime and Police Act 2005, ss111, 174(2), Schedule 7, Pt 1, para 34, Schedule 17, Pt 2.

CRIMINAL CASES REVIEW (INSANITY) ACT 1999
(1999 c 25)

1   Reference of former verdict of guilty but insane
(1) Where a verdict was returned in England and Wales or Northern Ireland to the effect that a person was guilty of the act or omission charged against him but was insane at the time, the Criminal Cases Review Commission may at any time refer the verdict to the Court of Appeal if subsection (2) below applies.
(2) This subsection applies if the Commission consider that there is a real possibility that the verdict would not be upheld were the reference to be made and either –
  (a) the Commission so consider because of an argument, or evidence, not raised in the proceedings which led to the verdict, or
  (b) it appears to the Commission that there are exceptional circumstances which justify the making of the reference.
(3) Section 14 of the Criminal Appeal Act 1995 (supplementary provision about the reference of a verdict) shall apply in relation to a reference under subsection (1) above as it applies in relation to references under section 9 or 10 of that Act.

2   Reference treated as appeal: England and Wales
(1) A reference under section 1(1) above of a verdict returned in England and Wales in the case of a person shall be treated for all purposes as an appeal by the person under section 12 of the Criminal Appeal Act 1968.
(2) In their application to such a reference by virtue of subsection (1) above, sections 13 and 14 of that Act shall have effect –
  (a) as if references to the verdict of not guilty by reason of insanity were to the verdict referred under section 1(1) above, and
  (b) as if, in section 14(1)(b), for the words from the beginning to 'that he' there were substituted 'the accused was under a disability and'.

POWERS OF CRIMINAL COURTS (SENTENCING) ACT 2000
(2000 c 6)

PART V

CUSTODIAL SENTENCES ETC ...

CHAPTER III

REQUIRED CUSTODIAL SENTENCES FOR CERTAIN OFFENCES

110   Minimum of seven years for third class A drug trafficking offence
(1) This section applies where –
  (a) a person is convicted of a class A drug trafficking offence committed after 30th September 1997;

(b) at the time when that offence was committed, he was 18 or over and had been convicted in any part of the United Kingdom of two other class A drug trafficking offences; and

(c) one of those other offences was committed after he had been convicted of the other.

(2) The court shall impose an appropriate custodial sentence for a term of at least seven years except where the court is of the opinion that there are particular circumstances which –

(a) relate to any of the offences or to the offender; and

(b) would make it unjust to do so in all the circumstances.

(4) Where –

(a) a person is charged with a class A drug trafficking offence (which, apart from this subsection, would be triable either way), and

(b) the circumstances are such that, if he were convicted of the offence, he could be sentenced for it under subsection (2) above,

the offence shall be triable only on indictment.

(5) In this section 'class A drug trafficking offence' means a drug trafficking offence committed in respect of a class A drug; and for this purpose –

'class A drug' has the same meaning as in the Misuse of Drugs Act 1971;

'drug trafficking offence' means an offence which is specified in –

(a) paragraph 1 of Schedule 2 to the Proceeds of Crime Act 2002 (drug trafficking offences), or

(b) so far as it relates to that paragraph, paragraph 10 of that Schedule.

(6) In this section 'an appropriate custodial sentence' means –

(a) in relation to a person who is 21 or over when convicted of the offence mentioned in subsection (1)(a) above, a sentence of imprisonment;

(b) in relation to a person who is under 21 at that time, a sentence of detention in a young offender institution.

111 Minimum of three years for third domestic burglary

(1) This section applies where –

(a) a person is convicted of a domestic burglary committed after 30th November 1999;

(b) at the time when that burglary was committed, he was 18 or over and had been convicted in England and Wales of two other domestic burglaries; and

(c) one of those other burglaries was committed after he had been convicted of the other, and both of them were committed after 30th November 1999.

(2) The court shall impose an appropriate custodial sentence for a term of at least three years except where the court is of the opinion that there are particular circumstances which –

(a) relate to any of the offences or to the offender; and

(b) would make it unjust to do so in all the circumstances.

(4) Where –

(a) a person is charged with a domestic burglary which, apart from this subsection, would be triable either way, and

(b) the circumstances are such that, if he were convicted of the burglary, he could be sentenced for it under subsection (2) above,

the burglary shall be triable only on indictment.

(5) In this section 'domestic burglary' means a burglary committed in respect of a building or part of a building which is a dwelling.

(6) In this section 'an appropriate custodial sentence' means –

(a) in relation to a person who is 21 or over when convicted of the offence mentioned in subsection (1)(a) above, a sentence of imprisonment;

(b) in relation to a person who is under 21 at that time, a sentence of detention in a young offender institution.

112 Appeals where previous convictions set aside

(1) This section applies where –

(a) a sentence has been imposed on any person under subsection (2) of section 109, 110 or 111 above; and

(b) any previous conviction of his without which that section would not have applied has been subsequently set aside on appeal.

(2) Notwithstanding anything in section 18 of the Criminal Appeal Act 1968, notice of appeal against the sentence may be given at any time within 28 days from the date on which the previous conviction was set aside.

115 Determination of day when offence committed

Where an offence is found to have been committed over a period of two or more days, or at some time during a period of two or more days, it shall be taken for the purposes of sections 109, 110 and 111 above to have been committed on the last of those days.

As amended by the Proceeds of Crime Act 2002, s456, Schedule 11, para 37(1), (2); Criminal Justice Act 2003, ss304, 332, Schedule 32, Pt 1, paras 90, 114, 115, Schedule 37, Pt 7.

CRIMINAL JUSTICE AND POLICE ACT 2001
(2001 c 16)

1   Offences leading to penalties on the spot

(1) For the purposes of this Chapter 'penalty offence' means an offence committed under any of the provisions mentioned in the first column of the following Table and described, in general terms, in the second column:

Offence creating provision	*Description of offence*
Section 12 of the Licensing 1872 (c 94)	Being drunk in a highway, other Act public place or licensed premises
Section 80 of the Explosives Act 1875 (c 17)	Throwing fireworks in a thoroughfare
Section 55 of the British Transport Commission Act 1949 (c xxix)	Trespassing on a railway
Section 56 of the British Transport Commission Act 1949 (c xxix)	Throwing stones, etc at trains or other things on railways
Section 91 of the Criminal Justice Act 1967 (c 80)	Disorderly behaviour while drunk in a public place
Section 5(2) of the Criminal Law Act 1967 (c 58)	Wasting police time or giving false report
Section 1 of the Theft Act 1968 (c 60)	Theft
Section 1(1) of the Criminal Damage Act 1991 (c 48)	Destroyoying or damaging property

Section 5 of the Public Order Act 1986 (c 64)	Behaviour likely to cause harassment, alarm or distress
Section 87 of the Environmental Protection Act 1990 (c 43)	Depositing and leaving litter
Section 12 of this Act	Consumption of alcohol in designated public place
Section 127(2) of the Communications Act 2003	Using public electronic communications network in order to cause annoyance, inconvenience or needless anxiety
Section 11 of the Fireworks Act 2003 (c 22)	Contravention of a prohibition or failure to comply with a requirement imposed by or under fireworks regulations or making false statements.
Section 49 of the Fire and Rescue Services Act 2004 (c 21)	Knowingly giving a false alarm of fire
Section 141 of the Licensing Act 2003 (c 17)	Sale of alcohol to a person who is drunk
Section 1146(1) and (3) of the Licensing Act 2003 (c 17)	Sale of alcohol to children
Section 149 of the Licensing Act 2003 (c 17)	Purchase of alcohol by or on behalf of children
Section 149(4) of the Licensing Act 2003 (c 17)	Buying or attempting to buy alcohol for consumption on licensed premises, etc by child
Section 150 of the Licensing Act 2003 (c 17)	Consumption of alcohol by children or allowing such consumption
Section 151 of the Licensing Act 2003 (c 17)	Delivering alcohol to children or allowing such delivery

(2) The Secretary of State may by order amend an entry in the Table or add or remove an entry. ...

2   Penalty notices

(1) A constable who has reason to believe that a person aged 10 or over has committed a penalty offence may give him a penalty notice in respect of the offence.

(2) Unless the notice is given in a police station, the constable giving it must be in uniform.

(3) At a police station, a penalty notice may be given only by an authorised constable.

(4) In this Chapter 'penalty notice" means a notice offering the opportunity, by paying a penalty in accordance with this Chapter, to discharge any liability to be convicted of the offence to which the notice relates.

(5) 'Authorised constable' means a constable authorised, on behalf of the chief officer of police for the area in which the police station is situated, to give penalty notices.

(6) The Secretary of State may by order –
    (a)   amend subsection (1) by substituting for the age for the time being specified in that subsection a different age which is not lower than 10, and
    (b)   if that different age is lower than 16, make provision as follows –
        (i)   where a person whose age is lower than 16 is given a penalty notice, for a parent or guardian of that person to be notified of the giving of the notice, and
        (ii) for that parent or guardian to be liable to pay the penalty under the notice.

(7) The provision which may be made by virtue of subsection (6)(b) includes provision amending, or applying (with or without modifications), this Chapter or any other enactment (whenever passed or made).

(8) The power conferred by subsection (6) is exercisable by statutory instrument.

(9) No order shall be made under subsection (6) unless a draft of the order has been laid before and approved by a resolution of each House of Parliament.

3 Amount of penalty and form of penalty notice

(1) The penalty payable in respect of a penalty offence is such amount as the Secretary of State may specify by order.

(1A) The Secretary of State may specify different amounts for persons of different ages.

(2) But the Secretary of State may not specify an amount which is more than a quarter of the amount of the maximum fine for which a person is liable on summary conviction of the offence plus half of the relevant surcharge.

(2A) The 'relevant surcharge', in relation to a person of a given age, is the amount payable by way of surcharge under section 161A of the Criminal Justice Act 2003 by a person of that age who is fined the maximum amount for the offence. …

4 Effect of penalty notice

(1) This section applies if a penalty notice is given to a person ("A") under section 2.

(2) If A asks to be tried for the alleged offence, proceedings may be brought against him.

(3) Such a request must be made by a notice given by A –

    (a) in the manner specified in the penalty notice; and

    (b) before the end of the period of suspended enforcement (as to which see section 5).

(4) A request which is made in accordance with subsection (3) is referred to in this Chapter as a 'request to be tried'.

(5) If, by the end of the suspended enforcement period –

    (a) the penalty has not been paid in accordance with this Chapter, and

    (b) A has not made a request to be tried,

a sum equal to one and a half times the amount of the penalty may be registered under section 8 for enforcement against A as a fine.

5 General restriction on proceedings

(1) Proceedings for the offence to which a penalty notice relates may not be brought until the end of the period of 21 days beginning with the date on which the notice was given ('the suspended enforcement period').

(2) If the penalty is paid before the end of the suspended enforcement period, no proceedings may be brought for the offence.

(3) Subsection (1) does not apply if the person to whom the penalty notice was given has made a request to be tried.

39 Intimidation of witnesses

(1) A person commits an offence if –

    (a) he does an act which intimidates, and is intended to intimidate, another person ('the victim');

    (b) he does the act –

        (i) knowing or believing that the victim is or may be a witness in any relevant proceedings; and

      (ii) intending, by his act, to cause the course of justice to be obstructed, perverted or interfered with;

   and

    (c) the act is done after the commencement of those proceedings.

(2) For the purposes of subsection (1) it is immaterial –

    (a) whether or not the act that is done is done in the presence of the victim;

    (b) whether that act is done to the victim himself or to another person; and

    (c) whether or not the intention to cause the course of justice to be obstructed, perverted or interfered with is the predominating intention of the person doing the act in question.

(3) If, in proceedings against a person for an offence under this section, it is proved –

    (a) that he did any act that intimidated, and was intended to intimidate, another person, and

    (b) that he did that act knowing or believing that that other person was or might be a witness in any relevant proceedings that had already commenced,

he shall be presumed, unless the contrary is shown, to have done the act with the intention of causing the course of justice to be obstructed, perverted or interfered with.

(4) A person guilty of an offence under this section shall be liable –

    (a) on conviction on indictment, to imprisonment for a term not exceeding five years or to a fine, or to both;

    (b) on summary conviction, to imprisonment for a term not exceeding six months or to a fine not exceeding the statutory maximum, or to both.

(5) References in this section to a witness, in relation to any proceedings, include references to a person who provides, or is able to provide, any information or any document or other thing which might be used as evidence in those proceedings or which (whether or not admissible as evidence in those proceedings) –

    (a) might tend to confirm evidence which will be or might be admitted in those proceedings;

    (b) might be referred to in evidence given in those proceedings by another witness; or

    (c) might be used as the basis for any cross examination in the course of those proceedings.

(6) References in this section to doing an act include references to issuing any threat (whether against a person or his finances or property or otherwise), or making any other statement.

(7) This section is in addition to, and not in derogation of, any offence subsisting at common law.

40   Harming witnesses, etc

(1) A person commits an offence if, in circumstances falling within subsection (2) –

    (a) he does an act which harms, and is intended to harm, another person; or

    (b) intending to cause another person to fear harm, he threatens to do an act which would harm that other person.

(2) The circumstances fall within this subsection if –

    (a) the person doing or threatening to do the act does so knowing or believing that some person (whether or not the person harmed or threatened or the person against whom harm is threatened) has been a witness in relevant proceedings; and

    (b) he does or threatens to do that act because of that knowledge or belief.

(3) If, in proceedings against a person for an offence under this section, it is proved that, within the relevant period –

    (a) he did an act which harmed, and was intended to harm, another person, or

(b) intending to cause another person to fear harm, he threatened to do an act which would harm that other person,

and that he did the act, or (as the case may be) threatened to do the act, with the knowledge or belief required by paragraph (a) of subsection (2), he shall be presumed, unless the contrary is shown, to have done the act, or (as the case may be) threatened to do the act, because of that knowledge or belief.

(4) For the purposes of this section it is immaterial –

(a) whether or not the act that is done or threatened, or the threat that is made, is or would be done or is made in the presence of the person who is or would be harmed or of the person who is threatened;

(b) whether or not the motive mentioned in subsection (2)(b) is the predominating motive for the act or threat; and

(c) whether the harm that is done or threatened is physical or financial or is harm to a person or to his property.

(5) A person guilty of an offence under this section shall be liable –

(a) on conviction on indictment, to imprisonment for a term not exceeding five years or to a fine, or to both;

(b) on summary conviction, to imprisonment for a term not exceeding six months or to a fine not exceeding the statutory maximum, or to both.

(6) In this section 'the relevant period', in relation to an act done, or threat made, with the knowledge or belief that a person has been a witness in any relevant proceedings, means the period that begins with the commencement of those proceedings and ends one year after they are finally concluded.

(7) References in this section to a witness, in relation to any proceedings, include references to a person who has provided any information or any document or other thing which was or might have been used as evidence in those proceedings or which (whether or not it was admissible as evidence in those proceedings) –

(a) tended to confirm or might have tended to confirm any evidence which was or could have been given in those proceedings;

(b) was or might have been referred to in evidence given in those proceedings by another witness; or

(c) was or might have been used as the basis for any cross examination in the course of those proceedings.

(8) This section is in addition to, and not in derogation of, any offence subsisting at common law.

41   Relevant proceedings

(1) A reference in section 39 or 40 to relevant proceedings is a reference to any proceedings in or before the Court of Appeal, the High Court, the Crown Court or any county court or magistrates' court which –

(a) are not proceedings for an offence; and

(b) were commenced after the coming into force of that section.

(2) For the purposes of any reference in section 39 or 40 or this section to the commencement of any proceedings relevant proceedings are commenced (subject to subsection (5)) at the earliest time at which one of the following occurs –

(a) an information is laid or application, claim form, complaint, petition, summons or other process made or issued for the purpose of commencing the proceedings;

(b) any other step is taken by means of which the subject matter of the proceedings is brought for the first time (whether as part of the proceedings or in anticipation of them) before the court.

(3) For the purposes of any reference in section 39 or 40 to the time when any proceedings are finally concluded, relevant proceedings are finally concluded (subject to subsection (4)) –

    (a) if proceedings for an appeal against, or an application for a review of, those proceedings or of any decision taken in those proceedings are brought or is made, at the time when proceedings on that appeal or application are finally concluded;

    (b) if the proceedings are withdrawn or discontinued, at the time when they are withdrawn or discontinued; and

    (c) in any other case, when the court in or before which the proceedings are brought finally disposes of all the matters arising in those proceedings.

(4) Relevant proceedings shall not be taken to be finally concluded by virtue of subsection (3)(a) where –

    (a) the matters to which the appeal or application relate are such that the proceedings in respect of which it is brought or made continue or resume after the making of any determination on that appeal or application; or

    (b) a determination made on that appeal or application requires those proceedings to continue or to be resumed.

(5) Where, after having appeared to be finally concluded, any relevant proceedings continue by reason of –

    (a) the giving of permission to bring an appeal after a fixed time for appealing has expired,

    (b) the lifting of any stay in the proceedings,

    (c) the setting aside, without an appeal, of any judgment or order, or

    (d) the revival of any discontinued proceedings,

42   Police directions stopping the harassment, etc of a person in his home

(1) Subject to the following provisions of this section, a constable who is at the scene may give a direction under this section to any person if –

    (a) that person is present outside or in the vicinity of any premises that are used by any individual ('the resident') as his dwelling;

    (b) that constable believes, on reasonable grounds, that that person is present there for the purpose (by his presence or otherwise) of representing to the resident or another individual (whether or not one who uses the premises as his dwelling), or of persuading the resident or such another individual –

        (i) that he should not do something that he is entitled or required to do; or

        (ii) that he should do something that he is not under any obligation to do;

   and

    (c) that constable also believes, on reasonable grounds, that the presence of that person (either alone or together with that of any other persons who are also present) –

        (i) amounts to, or is likely to result in, the harassment of the resident; or

        (ii) is likely to cause alarm or distress to the resident.

(2) A direction under this section is a direction requiring the person to whom it is given to do all such things as the constable giving it may specify as the things he considers necessary to prevent one or both of the following –

    (a) the harassment of the resident; or

    (b) the causing of any alarm or distress to the resident.

(3) A direction under this section may be given orally; and where a constable is entitled to give a direction under this section to each of several persons outside, or in the vicinity of, any premises,

he may give that direction to those persons by notifying them of his requirements either individually or all together.

(4) The requirements that may be imposed by a direction under this section include –

(a) a requirement to leave the vicinity of the premises in question, and

(b) a requirement to leave that vicinity and not to return to it within such period as the constable may specify, not being longer than 3 months;

and (in either case) the requirement to leave the vicinity may be to do so immediately or after a specified period of time.

(5) A direction under this section may make exceptions to any requirement imposed by the direction, and may make any such exception subject to such conditions as the constable giving the direction thinks fit; and those conditions may include –

(a) conditions as to the distance from the premises in question at which, or otherwise as to the location where, persons who do not leave their vicinity must remain; and

(b) conditions as to the number or identity of the persons who are authorised by the exception to remain in the vicinity of those premises.

(6) The power of a constable to give a direction under this section shall not include –

(a) any power to give a direction at any time when there is a more senior-ranking police officer at the scene; or

(b) any power to direct a person to refrain from conduct that is lawful under section 220 of the Trade Union and Labour Relations (Consolidation) Act 1992 (c 52) (right peacefully to picket a work place);

but it shall include power to vary or withdraw a direction previously given under this section.

(7) Any person who knowingly fails to comply with a requirement in a direction given to him under this section (other than a requirement under subsection (4)(b)) shall be guilty of an offence and liable, on summary conviction, to imprisonment for a term not exceeding three months or to a fine not exceeding level 4 on the standard scale, or to both.

(7A) Any person to whom a constable has given a direction including a requirement under subsection (4)(b) commits an offence if he –

(a) returns to the vicinity of the premises in question within the period specified in the direction beginning with the date on which the direction is given; and

(b) does so for the purpose described in subsection (1)(b).

(7B) A person guilty of an offence under subsection (7A) shall be liable, on summary conviction, to imprisonment for a term not exceeding 51 weeks or to a fine not exceeding level 4 on the standard scale, or to both.

(7C) In relation to an offence committed before the commencement of section 281(5) of the Criminal Justice Act 2003 (alteration of penalties for summary offences), the reference in subsection (7B) to 51 weeks is to be read as a reference to 6 months.

(9) In this section 'dwelling' has the same meaning as in Part 1 of the Public Order Act 1986 (c 64).

[See Appendix, Criminal Justice Act 2003, Schedule 26, para 56(1), (3).]

42A   Offence of harassment, etc of a person in his home

(1) A person commits an offence if –

(a) that person is present outside or in the vicinity of any premises that are used by any individual ('the resident') as his dwelling;

(b) that person is present there for the purpose (by his presence or otherwise) of representing to the resident or another individual (whether or not one who uses the premises as his dwelling), or of persuading the resident or such another individual –

          (i)   that he should not do something that he is entitled or required to do; or

          (ii) that he should do something that he is not under any obligation to do;

  (c) that person –

          (i)   intends his presence to amount to the harassment of, or to cause alarm or distress to, the resident; or

          (ii) knows or ought to know that his presence is likely to result in the harassment of, or to cause alarm or distress to, the resident; and

  (d) the presence of that person –

          (i)   amounts to the harassment of, or causes alarm or distress to, any person falling within subsection (2); or

          (ii) is likely to result in the harassment of, or to cause alarm or distress to, any such person.

(2) A person falls within this subsection if he is –

  (a) the resident,

  (b) a person in the resident's dwelling, or

  (c) a person in another dwelling in the vicinity of the resident's dwelling.

(3) The references in subsection (1)(c) and (d) to a person's presence are references to his presence either alone or together with that of any other persons who are also present.

(4) For the purposes of this section a person (A) ought to know that his presence is likely to result in the harassment of, or to cause alarm or distress to, a resident if a reasonable person in possession of the same information would think that A's presence was likely to have that effect.

(5) A person guilty of an offence under this section shall be liable, on summary conviction, to imprisonment for a term not exceeding 51 weeks or to a fine not exceeding level 4 on the standard scale, or to both.

(6) In relation to an offence committed before the commencement of section 281(5) of the Criminal Justice Act 2003 (alteration of penalties for summary offences), the reference in subsection (5) to 51 weeks is to be read as a reference to 6 months.

(7) In this section 'dwelling' has the same meaning as in Part 1 of the Public Order Act 1986.

NB. The amending provision of the Domestic Violence, Crime and Victims Act 2004 shown below was not in force on 1 June 2007.

As amended by the Criminal Justice and Police Act 2001 (Amendment) Order 2002, art 2; Anti-social Behaviour Act 2003, s87; Fireworks Act 2003, s15, Schedule; Licensing Act 2003, ss198, 199, Schedule 6, paras 119, 120, Schedule 7; Communications Act 2003, s406(1), (7), Schedule 17, para 169, Schedule 19(1); Fire and Rescue Services Act 2004, ss53(1), 54, Schedule 1, para 97; Criminal Justice and Police Act 2001 (Amendment) and Police Reform Act 2002 (Modification) Order 2004, arts 2, 3; Penalties for Disorderly Behaviour (Amendment of Minimum Age) Order 2004, art 2; Domestic Violence, Crime and Victims Act 2004, s15; Serious Organised Crime and Police Act 2005, ss111, 126(1), 127, 174(2), Schedule 7, Pt 1, para 35(a), Schedule 17, Pt 2.

POLICE REFORM ACT 2002

(2002 c 30)

59   Vehicles used in manner causing alarm, distress or annoyance

(1) Where a constable in uniform has reasonable grounds for believing that a motor vehicle is being used on any occasion in a manner which –

(a) contravenes section 3 or 34 of the Road Traffic Act 1988 (c 52) (careless and inconsiderate driving and prohibition of off-road driving), and

(b) is causing, or is likely to cause, alarm, distress or annoyance to members of the public,

he shall have the powers set out in subsection (3).

(2) A constable in uniform shall also have the powers set out in subsection (3) where he has reasonable grounds for believing that a motor vehicle has been used on any occasion in a manner falling within subsection (1).

(3) Those powers are –

(a) power, if the motor vehicle is moving, to order the person driving it to stop the vehicle;

(b) power to seize and remove the motor vehicle;

(c) power, for the purposes of exercising a power falling within paragraph (a) or (b), to enter any premises on which he has reasonable grounds for believing the motor vehicle to be;

(d) power to use reasonable force, if necessary, in the exercise of any power conferred by any of paragraphs to (a) to (c).

(4) A constable shall not seize a motor vehicle in the exercise of the powers conferred on him by this section unless –

(a) he has warned the person appearing to him to be the person whose use falls within subsection (1) that he will seize it, if that use continues or is repeated; and

(b) it appears to him that the use has continued or been repeated after the the warning.

(5) Subsection (4) does not require a warning to be given by a constable on any occasion on which he would otherwise have the power to seize a motor vehicle under this section if –

(a) the circumstances make it impracticable for him to give the warning;

(b) the constable has already on that occasion given a warning under that subsection in respect of any use of that motor vehicle or of another motor vehicle by that person or any other person;

(c) the constable has reasonable grounds for believing that such a warning has been given on that occasion otherwise than by him; or

(d) the constable has reasonable grounds for believing that the person whose use of that motor vehicle on that occasion would justify the seizure is a person to whom a warning under that subsection has been given (whether or not by that constable or in respect the same vehicle or the same or a similar use) on a previous occasion in the previous twelve months.

(6) A person who fails to comply with an order under subsection (3)(a) is guilty of an offence and shall be liable, on summary conviction, to a fine not exceeding level 3 on the standard scale.

(7) Subsection (3)(c) does not authorise entry into a private dwelling house.

(8) The powers conferred on a constable by this section shall be exercisable only at a time when regulations under section 60 [Retention, etc, of vehicles seized under section 59] are in force.

(9) In this section –

'driving' has the same meaning as in the Road Traffic Act 1988 (c 52);

'motor vehicle' means any mechanically propelled vehicle, whether or not it is intended or adapted for use on roads; and

'private dwelling house' does not include any garage or other structure occupied with the dwelling house, or any land appurtenant to the dwelling house.

SEXUAL OFFENCES ACT 2003
(2003 c 42)

PART 1

SEXUAL OFFENCES

1 Rape

(1) A person (A) commits an offence if –
- (a) he intentionally penetrates the vagina, anus or mouth of another person (B) with his penis,
- (b) B does not consent to the penetration, and
- (c) A does not reasonably believe that B consents.

(2) Whether a belief is reasonable is to be determined having regard to all the circumstances, including any steps A has taken to ascertain whether B consents.

(3) Sections 75 and 76 apply to an offence under this section.

(4) A person guilty of an offence under this section is liable, on conviction on indictment, to imprisonment for life.

2 Assault by penetration

(1) A person (A) commits an offence if –
- (a) he intentionally penetrates the vagina or anus of another person (B) with a part of his body or anything else,
- (b) the penetration is sexual,
- (c) B does not consent to the penetration, and
- (d) A does not reasonably believe that B consents.

(2) Whether a belief is reasonable is to be determined having regard to all the circumstances, including any steps A has taken to ascertain whether B consents.

(3) Sections 75 and 76 apply to an offence under this section.

(4) A person guilty of an offence under this section is liable, on conviction on indictment, to imprisonment for life.

3 Sexual assault

(1) A person (A) commits an offence if –
- (a) he intentionally touches another person (B),
- (b) the touching is sexual,
- (c) B does not consent to the touching, and
- (d) A does not reasonably believe that B consents.

(2) Whether a belief is reasonable is to be determined having regard to all the circumstances, including any steps A has taken to ascertain whether B consents.

(3) Sections 75 and 76 apply to an offence under this section.

(4) A person guilty of an offence under this section is liable –
- (a) on summary conviction, to imprisonment for a term not exceeding 6 months or a fine not exceeding the statutory maximum or both;
- (b) on conviction on indictment, to imprisonment for a term not exceeding 10 years.

4 Causing a person to engage in sexual activity without consent

(1) A person (A) commits an offence if –

(a) he intentionally causes another person (B) to engage in an activity,
(b) the activity is sexual,
(c) B does not consent to engaging in the activity, and
(d) A does not reasonably believe that B consents.

(2) Whether a belief is reasonable is to be determined having regard to all the circumstances, including any steps A has taken to ascertain whether B consents.

(3) Sections 75 and 76 apply to an offence under this section.

(4) A person guilty of an offence under this section, if the activity caused involved –

(a) penetration of B's anus or vagina,
(b) penetration of B's mouth with a person's penis,
(c) penetration of a person's anus or vagina with a part of B's body or by B with anything else, or
(d) penetration of a person's mouth with B's penis,

is liable, on conviction on indictment, to imprisonment for life.

(5) Unless subsection (4) applies, a person guilty of an offence under this section is liable –

(a) on summary conviction, to imprisonment for a term not exceeding 6 months or to a fine not exceeding the statutory maximum or both;
(b) on conviction on indictment, to imprisonment for a term not exceeding 10 years.

5   Rape of a child under 13

(1) A person commits an offence if –

(a) he intentionally penetrates the vagina, anus or mouth of another person with his penis, and
(b) the other person is under 13.

(2) A person guilty of an offence under this section is liable, on conviction on indictment, to imprisonment for life.

6   Assault of a child under 13 by penetration

(1) A person commits an offence if –

(a) he intentionally penetrates the vagina or anus of another person with a part of his body or anything else,
(b) the penetration is sexual, and
(c) the other person is under 13.

(2) A person guilty of an offence under this section is liable, on conviction on indictment, to imprisonment for life.

7   Sexual assault of a child under 13

(1) A person commits an offence if –

(a) he intentionally touches another person,
(b) the touching is sexual, and
(c) the other person is under 13.

(2) A person guilty of an offence under this section is liable –

(a) on summary conviction, to imprisonment for a term not exceeding 6 months or a fine not exceeding the statutory maximum or both;
(b) on conviction on indictment, to imprisonment for a term not exceeding 14 years.

8   Causing or inciting a child under 13 to engage in sexual activity

(1) A person commits an offence if –

(a) he intentionally causes or incites another person (B) to engage in an activity,

    (b) the activity is sexual, and

    (c) B is under 13.

(2) A person guilty of an offence under this section, if the activity caused or incited involved –

    (a) penetration of B's anus or vagina,

    (b) penetration of B's mouth with a person's penis,

    (c) penetration of a person's anus or vagina with a part of B's body or by B with anything else, or

    (d) penetration of a person's mouth with B's penis,

is liable, on conviction on indictment, to imprisonment for life.

(3) Unless subsection (2) applies, a person guilty of an offence under this section is liable –

    (a) on summary conviction, to imprisonment for a term not exceeding 6 months or to a fine not exceeding the statutory maximum or both;

    (b) on conviction on indictment, to imprisonment for a term not exceeding 14 years.

9   Sexual activity with a child

(1) A person aged 18 or over (A) commits an offence if –

    (a) he intentionally touches another person (B),

    (b) the touching is sexual, and

    (c) either –

        (i) B is under 16 and A does not reasonably believe that B is 16 or over, or

        (ii) B is under 13.

(2) A person guilty of an offence under this section, if the touching involved –

    (a) penetration of B's anus or vagina with a part of A's body or anything else,

    (b) penetration of B's mouth with A's penis,

    (c) penetration of A's anus or vagina with a part of B's body, or

    (d) penetration of A's mouth with B's penis,

is liable, on conviction on indictment, to imprisonment for a term not exceeding 14 years.

(3) Unless subsection (2) applies, a person guilty of an offence under this section is liable –

    (a) on summary conviction, to imprisonment for a term not exceeding 6 months or to a fine not exceeding the statutory maximum or both;

    (b) on conviction on indictment, to imprisonment for a term not exceeding 14 years.

10   Causing or inciting a child to engage in sexual activity

(1) A person aged 18 or over (A) commits an offence if –

    (a) he intentionally causes or incites another person (B) to engage in an activity,

    (b) the activity is sexual, and

    (c) either –

        (i) B is under 16 and A does not reasonably believe that B is 16 or over, or

        (ii) B is under 13.

(2) A person guilty of an offence under this section, if the activity caused or incited involved –

    (a) penetration of B's anus or vagina,

    (b) penetration of B's mouth with a person's penis,

    (c) penetration of a person's anus or vagina with a part of B's body or by B with anything else, or

    (d) penetration of a person's mouth with B's penis,

is liable, on conviction on indictment, to imprisonment for a term not exceeding 14 years.

(3) Unless subsection (2) applies, a person guilty of an offence under this section is liable –

(a) on summary conviction, to imprisonment for a term not exceeding 6 months or to a fine not exceeding the statutory maximum or both;

(b) on conviction on indictment, to imprisonment for a term not exceeding 14 years.

11   Engaging in sexual activity in the presence of a child

(1) A person aged 18 or over (A) commits an offence if –

    (a) he intentionally engages in an activity,

    (b) the activity is sexual,

    (c) for the purpose of obtaining sexual gratification, he engages in it –

       (i) when another person (B) is present or is in a place from which A can be observed, and

       (ii) knowing or believing that B is aware, or intending that B should be aware, that he is engaging in it, and

    (d) either –

       (i) B is under 16 and A does not reasonably believe that B is 16 or over, or

       (ii) B is under 13.

(2) A person guilty of an offence under this section is liable –

    (a) on summary conviction, to imprisonment for a term not exceeding 6 months or a fine not exceeding the statutory maximum or both;

    (b) on conviction on indictment, to imprisonment for a term not exceeding 10 years.

12   Causing a child to watch a sexual act

(1) A person aged 18 or over (A) commits an offence if –

    (a) for the purpose of obtaining sexual gratification, he intentionally causes another person (B) to watch a third person engaging in an activity, or to look at an image of any person engaging in an activity,

    (b) the activity is sexual, and

    (c) either –

       (i) B is under 16 and A does not reasonably believe that B is 16 or over, or

       (ii) B is under 13.

(2) A person guilty of an offence under this section is liable –

    (a) on summary conviction, to imprisonment for a term not exceeding 6 months or a fine not exceeding the statutory maximum or both;

    (b) on conviction on indictment, to imprisonment for a term not exceeding 10 years.

13   Child sex offences committed by children or young persons

(1) A person under 18 commits an offence if he does anything which would be an offence under any of sections 9 to 12 if he were aged 18.

(2) A person guilty of an offence under this section is liable –

    (a) on summary conviction, to imprisonment for a term not exceeding 6 months or a fine not exceeding the statutory maximum or both;

    (b) on conviction on indictment, to imprisonment for a term not exceeding 5 years.

14   Arranging or facilitating commission of a child sex offence

(1) A person commits an offence if –

    (a) he intentionally arranges or facilitates something that he intends to do, intends another person to do, or believes that another person will do, in any part of the world, and

    (b) doing it will involve the commission of an offence under any of sections 9 to 13.

(2) A person does not commit an offence under this section if –

(a) he arranges or facilitates something that he believes another person will do, but that he does not intend to do or intend another person to do, and

(b) any offence within subsection (1)(b) would be an offence against a child for whose protection he acts.

(3) For the purposes of subsection (2), a person acts for the protection of a child if he acts for the purpose of –

(a) protecting the child from sexually transmitted infection,

(b) protecting the physical safety of the child,

(c) preventing the child from becoming pregnant, or

(d) promoting the child's emotional well-being by the giving of advice,

and not for the purpose of obtaining sexual gratification or for the purpose of causing or encouraging the activity constituting the offence within subsection (1)(b) or the child's participation in it.

(4) A person guilty of an offence under this section is liable –

(a) on summary conviction, to imprisonment for a term not exceeding 6 months or a fine not exceeding the statutory maximum or both;

(b) on conviction on indictment, to imprisonment for a term not exceeding 14 years.

15 Meeting a child following sexual grooming, etc

(1) A person aged 18 or over (A) commits an offence if –

(a) having met or communicated with another person (B) on at least two earlier occasions, he –

    (i) intentionally meets B, or

    (ii) travels with the intention of meeting B in any part of the world,

(b) at the time, he intends to do anything to or in respect of B, during or after the meeting and in any part of the world, which if done will involve the commission by A of a relevant offence,

(c) B is under 16, and

(d) A does not reasonably believe that B is 16 or over.

(2) In subsection (1) –

(a) the reference to A having met or communicated with B is a reference to A having met B in any part of the world or having communicated with B by any means from, to or in any part of the world;

(b) 'relevant offence' means –

    (i) an offence under this Part,

    (ii) an offence within any of paragraphs 61 to 92 of Schedule 3 [Northern Ireland], or

    (iii) anything done outside England and Wales and Northern Ireland which is not an offence within sub-paragraph (i) or (ii) but would be an offence within sub-paragraph (i) if done in England and Wales. ...

(4) A person guilty of an offence under this section is liable –

(a) on summary conviction, to imprisonment for a term not exceeding 6 months or a fine not exceeding the statutory maximum or both;

(b) on conviction on indictment, to imprisonment for a term not exceeding 10 years.

16 Abuse of position of trust: sexual activity with a child

(1) A person aged 18 or over (A) commits an offence if –

(a) he intentionally touches another person (B),

    (b) the touching is sexual,
    (c) A is in a position of trust in relation to B,
    (d) where subsection (2) applies, A knows or could reasonably be expected to know of the circumstances by virtue of which he is in a position of trust in relation to B, and
    (e) either –
        (i) B is under 18 and A does not reasonably believe that B is 18 or over, or
        (ii) B is under 13.
(2) This subsection applies where A –
    (a) is in a position of trust in relation to B by virtue of circumstances within section 21(2), (3), (4) or (5), and
    (b) is not in such a position of trust by virtue of other circumstances.
(3) Where in proceedings for an offence under this section it is proved that the other person was under 18, the defendant is to be taken not to have reasonably believed that that person was 18 or over unless sufficient evidence is adduced to raise an issue as to whether he reasonably believed it.
(4) Where in proceedings for an offence under this section –
    (a) it is proved that the defendant was in a position of trust in relation to the other person by virtue of circumstances within section 21(2), (3), (4) or (5), and
    (b) it is not proved that he was in such a position of trust by virtue of other circumstances,
it is to be taken that the defendant knew or could reasonably have been expected to know of the circumstances by virtue of which he was in such a position of trust unless sufficient evidence is adduced to raise an issue as to whether he knew or could reasonably have been expected to know of those circumstances.
(5) A person guilty of an offence under this section is liable –
    (a) on summary conviction, to imprisonment for a term not exceeding 6 months or a fine not exceeding the statutory maximum or both;
    (b) on conviction on indictment, to imprisonment for a term not exceeding 5 years.

17   Abuse of position of trust: causing or inciting a child to engage in sexual activity

(1) A person aged 18 or over (A) commits an offence if –
    (a) he intentionally causes or incites another person (B) to engage in an activity,
    (b) the activity is sexual,
    (c) A is in a position of trust in relation to B,
    (d) where subsection (2) applies, A knows or could reasonably be expected to know of the circumstances by virtue of which he is in a position of trust in relation to B, and
    (e) either –
        (i) B is under 18 and A does not reasonably believe that B is 18 or over, or
        (ii) B is under 13.
(2) This subsection applies where A –
    (a) is in a position of trust in relation to B by virtue of circumstances within section 21(2), (3), (4) or (5), and
    (b) is not in such a position of trust by virtue of other circumstances.
(3) Where in proceedings for an offence under this section it is proved that the other person was under 18, the defendant is to be taken not to have reasonably believed that that person was 18 or over unless sufficient evidence is adduced to raise an issue as to whether he reasonably believed it.
(4) Where in proceedings for an offence under this section –
    (a) it is proved that the defendant was in a position of trust in relation to the other person by virtue of circumstances within section 21(2), (3), (4) or (5), and

(b) it is not proved that he was in such a position of trust by virtue of other circumstances, it is to be taken that the defendant knew or could reasonably have been expected to know of the circumstances by virtue of which he was in such a position of trust unless sufficient evidence is adduced to raise an issue as to whether he knew or could reasonably have been expected to know of those circumstances.

(5) A person guilty of an offence under this section is liable –

    (a) on summary conviction, to imprisonment for a term not exceeding 6 months or a fine not exceeding the statutory maximum or both;

    (b) on conviction on indictment, to imprisonment for a term not exceeding 5 years.

18 Abuse of position of trust: sexual activity in the presence of a child

(1) A person aged 18 or over (A) commits an offence if –

    (a) he intentionally engages in an activity,

    (b) the activity is sexual,

    (c) for the purpose of obtaining sexual gratification, he engages in it –

        (i)   when another person (B) is present or is in a place from which A can be observed, and

        (ii) knowing or believing that B is aware, or intending that B should be aware, that he is engaging in it,

    (d) A is in a position of trust in relation to B,

    (e) where subsection (2) applies, A knows or could reasonably be expected to know of the circumstances by virtue of which he is in a position of trust in relation to B, and

    (f) either –

        (i)   B is under 18 and A does not reasonably believe that B is 18 or over, or

        (ii) B is under 13.

(2) This subsection applies where A –

    (a) is in a position of trust in relation to B by virtue of circumstances within section 21(2), (3), (4) or (5), and

    (b) is not in such a position of trust by virtue of other circumstances.

(3) Where in proceedings for an offence under this section it is proved that the other person was under 18, the defendant is to be taken not to have reasonably believed that that person was 18 or over unless sufficient evidence is adduced to raise an issue as to whether he reasonably believed it.

(4) Where in proceedings for an offence under this section –

    (a) it is proved that the defendant was in a position of trust in relation to the other person by virtue of circumstances within section 21(2), (3), (4) or (5), and

    (b) it is not proved that he was in such a position of trust by virtue of other circumstances, it is to be taken that the defendant knew or could reasonably have been expected to know of the circumstances by virtue of which he was in such a position of trust unless sufficient evidence is adduced to raise an issue as to whether he knew or could reasonably have been expected to know of those circumstances.

(5) A person guilty of an offence under this section is liable –

    (a) on summary conviction, to imprisonment for a term not exceeding 6 months or a fine not exceeding the statutory maximum or both;

    (b) on conviction on indictment, to imprisonment for a term not exceeding 5 years.

19 Abuse of position of trust: causing a child to watch a sexual act

(1) A person aged 18 or over (A) commits an offence if –

    (a) for the purpose of obtaining sexual gratification, he intentionally causes another person (B) to watch a third person engaging in an activity, or to look at an image of any person engaging in an activity,

    (b) the activity is sexual,

    (c) A is in a position of trust in relation to B,

    (d) where subsection (2) applies, A knows or could reasonably be expected to know of the circumstances by virtue of which he is in a position of trust in relation to B, and

    (e) either –

        (i) B is under 18 and A does not reasonably believe that B is 18 or over, or

        (ii) B is under 13.

(2) This subsection applies where A –

    (a) is in a position of trust in relation to B by virtue of circumstances within section 21(2), (3), (4) or (5), and

    (b) is not in such a position of trust by virtue of other circumstances.

(3) Where in proceedings for an offence under this section it is proved that the other person was under 18, the defendant is to be taken not to have reasonably believed that that person was 18 or over unless sufficient evidence is adduced to raise an issue as to whether he reasonably believed it.

(4) Where in proceedings for an offence under this section –

    (a) it is proved that the defendant was in a position of trust in relation to the other person by virtue of circumstances within section 21(2), (3), (4) or (5), and

    (b) it is not proved that he was in such a position of trust by virtue of other circumstances,

it is to be taken that the defendant knew or could reasonably have been expected to know of the circumstances by virtue of which he was in such a position of trust unless sufficient evidence is adduced to raise an issue as to whether he knew or could reasonably have been expected to know of those circumstances.

(5) A person guilty of an offence under this section is liable –

    (a) on summary conviction, to imprisonment for a term not exceeding 6 months or a fine not exceeding the statutory maximum or both;

    (b) on conviction on indictment, to imprisonment for a term not exceeding 5 years.

21   Positions of trust

(1) For the purposes of sections 16 to 19, a person (A) is in a position of trust in relation to another person (B) if –

    (a) any of the following subsections applies, or

    (b) any condition specified in an order made by the Secretary of State is met.

(2) This subsection applies if A looks after persons under 18 who are detained in an institution by virtue of a court order or under an enactment, and B is so detained in that institution.

(3) This subsection applies if A looks after persons under 18 who are resident in a home or other place in which –

    (a) accommodation and maintenance are provided by an authority under section 23(2) of the Children Act 1989 (c 41)…, or

    (b) accommodation is provided by a voluntary organisation under section 59(1) of that Act …,

and B is resident, and is so provided with accommodation and maintenance or accommodation, in that place.

(4) This subsection applies if A looks after persons under 18 who are accommodated and cared for in one of the following institutions –

(a) a hospital,

(b) an independent clinic,

(c) a care home, residential care home or private hospital,

(d) a community home, voluntary home or children's home,

(e) a home provided under section 82(5) of the Children Act 1989, or

(f) a residential family centre,

and B is accommodated and cared for in that institution.

(5) This subsection applies if A looks after persons under 18 who are receiving education at an educational institution and B is receiving, and A is not receiving, education at that institution.

...

(7) This subsection applies if A is engaged in the provision of services under, or pursuant to anything done under –

(a) sections 8 to 10 of the Employment and Training Act 1973 (c 50), or

(b) section 114 of the Learning and Skills Act 2000 (c 21),

and, in that capacity, looks after B on an individual basis.

(8) This subsection applies if A regularly has unsupervised contact with B (whether face to face or by any other means) –

(a) in the exercise of functions of a local authority under section 20 or 21 of the Children Act 1989 (c 41) ...

(9) This subsection applies if A, as a person who is to report to the court under section 7 of the Children Act 1989 ... on matters relating to the welfare of B, regularly has unsupervised contact with B (whether face to face or by any other means).

(10) This subsection applies if A is a personal adviser appointed for B under –

(a) section 23B(2) of, or paragraph 19C of Schedule 2 to, the Children Act 1989 ...

and, in that capacity, looks after B on an individual basis.

(11) This subsection applies if –

(a) B is subject to a care order, a supervision order or an education supervision order, and

(b) in the exercise of functions conferred by virtue of the order on an authorised person or the authority designated by the order, A looks after B on an individual basis.

(12) This subsection applies if A –

(a) is an officer of the Service or Welsh family proceedings officer (within the meaning given by section 35 of the Children Act 2004) appointed for B under section 41(1) of the Children Act 1989,

(b) is appointed a children's guardian of B under rule 6 or rule 18 of the Adoption Rules 1984 (SI 1984/265), or

(c) is appointed to be the guardian ad litem of B under rule 9.5 of the Family Proceedings Rules 1991 (SI 1991/1247) ...,

and, in that capacity, regularly has unsupervised contact with B (whether face to face or by any other means).

(13) This subsection applies if –

(a) B is subject to requirements imposed by or under an enactment on his release from detention for a criminal offence, or is subject to requirements imposed by a court order made in criminal proceedings, and

(b) A looks after B on an individual basis in pursuance of the requirements.

22   Positions of trust: interpretation

(1) The following provisions apply for the purposes of section 21.

(2) Subject to subsection (3), a person looks after persons under 18 if he is regularly involved in caring for, training, supervising or being in sole charge of such persons.

(3) A person (A) looks after another person (B) on an individual basis if –

    (a) A is regularly involved in caring for, training or supervising B, and

    (b) in the course of his involvement, A regularly has unsupervised contact with B (whether face to face or by any other means).

(4) A person receives education at an educational institution if –

    (a) he is registered or otherwise enrolled as a pupil or student at the institution, or

    (b) he receives education at the institution under arrangements with another educational institution at which he is so registered or otherwise enrolled.

(5) In section 21 –

'authority' –

    (a) in relation to England and Wales, means a local authority; …

'care home' means an establishment which is a care home for the purposes of the Care Standards Act 2000 (c 14);

'care order' has –

    (a) in relation to England and Wales, the same meaning as in the Children Act 1989 (c 41) …;

'children's home' has –

    (a) in relation to England and Wales, the meaning given by section 1 of the Care Standards Act 2000 …;

'community home' has the meaning given by section 53 of the Children Act 1989;

'education supervision order' has –

    (a) in relation to England and Wales, the meaning given by section 36 of the Children Act 1989 …;

'hospital' –

    (a) in relation to England and Wales, means a hospital within the meaning given by section 275(1) of the National Health Service Act 2006 or section 206(1) of the National Health Service Act 2006, or any other establishment which is a hospital within the meaning given by section 2(3) of the Care Standards Act 2000 (c 14) …;

'independent clinic' has –

    (a) in relation to England and Wales, the meaning given by section 2 of the Care Standards Act 2000 …; …

'residential care home' means an establishment which is a residential care home for the purposes of the 2003 Order; …

'supervision order' has –

    (a) in relation to England and Wales, the meaning given by section 31(11) of the Children Act 1989 (c 41) …;

'voluntary home' has –

    (a) in relation to England and Wales, the meaning given by section 60(3) of the Children Act 1989 …

23 Sections 16 to 19: exception for spouses or civil partners

(1) Conduct by a person (A) which would otherwise be an offence under any of sections 16 to 19 against another person (B) is not an offence under that section if at the time –

    (a) B is 16 or over, and

    (b) A and B are lawfully married or civil partners of each other.

(2) In proceedings for such an offence it is for the defendant to prove that A and B were at the time lawfully married or civil partners of each other.

24   Sections 16 to 19: sexual relationships which pre-date position of trust

(1) Conduct by a person (A) which would otherwise be an offence under any of sections 16 to 19 against another person (B) is not an offence under that section if, immediately before the position of trust arose, a sexual relationship existed between A and B.

(2) Subsection (1) does not apply if at that time sexual intercourse between A and B would have been unlawful.

(3) In proceedings for an offence under any of sections 16 to 19 it is for the defendant to prove that such a relationship existed at that time.

25   Sexual activity with a child family member

(1) A person (A) commits an offence if –
  (a) he intentionally touches another person (B),
  (b) the touching is sexual,
  (c) the relation of A to B is within section 27,
  (d) A knows or could reasonably be expected to know that his relation to B is of a description falling within that section, and
  (e) either –
      (i) B is under 18 and A does not reasonably believe that B is 18 or over, or
      (ii) B is under 13.

(2) Where in proceedings for an offence under this section it is proved that the other person was under 18, the defendant is to be taken not to have reasonably believed that that person was 18 or over unless sufficient evidence is adduced to raise an issue as to whether he reasonably believed it.

(3) Where in proceedings for an offence under this section it is proved that the relation of the defendant to the other person was of a description falling within section 27, it is to be taken that the defendant knew or could reasonably have been expected to know that his relation to the other person was of that description unless sufficient evidence is adduced to raise an issue as to whether he knew or could reasonably have been expected to know that it was.

(4) A person guilty of an offence under this section, if aged 18 or over at the time of the offence, is liable –
  (a) where subsection (6) applies, on conviction on indictment to imprisonment for a term not exceeding 14 years;
  (b) in any other case –
      (i) on summary conviction, to imprisonment for a term not exceeding 6 months or a fine not exceeding the statutory maximum or both;
      (ii) on conviction on indictment, to imprisonment for a term not exceeding 14 years.

(5) Unless subsection (4) applies, a person guilty of an offence under this section is liable –
  (a) on summary conviction, to imprisonment for a term not exceeding 6 months or a fine not exceeding the statutory maximum or both;
  (b) on conviction on indictment, to imprisonment for a term not exceeding 5 years.

(6) This subsection applies where the touching involved –
  (a) penetration of B's anus or vagina with a part of A's body or anything else,
  (b) penetration of B's mouth with A's penis,
  (c) penetration of A's anus or vagina with a part of B's body, or
  (d) penetration of A's mouth with B's penis.

26 Inciting a child family member to engage in sexual activity

(1) A person (A) commits an offence if –

(a) he intentionally incites another person (B) to touch, or allow himself to be touched by, A,

(b) the touching is sexual,

(c) the relation of A to B is within section 27,

(d) A knows or could reasonably be expected to know that his relation to B is of a description falling within that section, and

(e) either –

(i) B is under 18 and A does not reasonably believe that B is 18 or over, or

(ii) B is under 13.

(2) Where in proceedings for an offence under this section it is proved that the other person was under 18, the defendant is to be taken not to have reasonably believed that that person was 18 or over unless sufficient evidence is adduced to raise an issue as to whether he reasonably believed it.

(3) Where in proceedings for an offence under this section it is proved that the relation of the defendant to the other person was of a description falling within section 27, it is to be taken that the defendant knew or could reasonably have been expected to know that his relation to the other person was of that description unless sufficient evidence is adduced to raise an issue as to whether he knew or could reasonably have been expected to know that it was.

(4) A person guilty of an offence under this section, if he was aged 18 or over at the time of the offence, is liable –

(a) where subsection (6) applies, on conviction on indictment to imprisonment for a term not exceeding 14 years;

(b) in any other case –

(i) on summary conviction, to imprisonment for a term not exceeding 6 months or a fine not exceeding the statutory maximum or both;

(ii) on conviction on indictment, to imprisonment for a term not exceeding 14 years.

(5) Unless subsection (4) applies, a person guilty of an offence under this section is liable –

(a) on summary conviction, to imprisonment for a term not exceeding 6 months or a fine not exceeding the statutory maximum or both;

(b) on conviction on indictment, to imprisonment for a term not exceeding 5 years.

(6) This subsection applies where the touching to which the incitement related involved –

(a) penetration of B's anus or vagina with a part of A's body or anything else,

(b) penetration of B's mouth with A's penis,

(c) penetration of A's anus or vagina with a part of B's body, or

(d) penetration of A's mouth with B's penis.

27 Family relationships

(1) The relation of one person (A) to another (B) is within this section if –

(a) it is within any of subsections (2) to (4), or

(b) it would be within one of those subsections but for section 67 of the Adoption and Children Act 2002 (c 38) (status conferred by adoption).

(2) The relation of A to B is within this subsection if –

(a) one of them is the other's parent, grandparent, brother, sister, half-brother, half-sister, aunt or uncle, or

(b) A is or has been B's foster parent.

(3) The relation of A to B is within this subsection if A and B live or have lived in the same

household, or A is or has been regularly involved in caring for, training, supervising or being in sole charge of B, and –

    (a) one of them is or has been the other's step-parent,

    (b) A and B are cousins,

    (c) one of them is or has been the other's stepbrother or stepsister, or

    (d) the parent or present or former foster parent of one of them is or has been the other's foster parent.

(4) The relation of A to B is within this subsection if –

    (a) A and B live in the same household, and

    (b) A is regularly involved in caring for, training, supervising or being in sole charge of B.

(5) For the purposes of this section –

    (a) 'aunt' means the sister or half-sister of a person's parent, and 'uncle' has a corresponding meaning;

    (b) 'cousin' means the child of an aunt or uncle;

    (c) a person is a child's foster parent if –

        (i) he is a person with whom the child has been placed under section 23(2)(a) or 59(1)(a) of the Children Act 1989 (c 41) (fostering for local authority or voluntary organisation), or

        (ii) he fosters the child privately, within the meaning given by section 66(1)(b) of that Act;

    (d) a person is another's partner (whether they are of different sexes or the same sex) if they live together as partners in an enduring family relationship;

    (e) 'step-parent' includes a parent's partner and 'stepbrother' and 'stepsister' include the child of a parent's partner.

28   Sections 25 and 26: exception for spouses and civil partners

(1) Conduct by a person (A) which would otherwise be an offence under section 25 or 26 against another person (B) is not an offence under that section if at the time –

    (a) B is 16 or over, and

    (b) A and B are lawfully married or civil partners of each other.

(2) In proceedings for such an offence it is for the defendant to prove that A and B were at the time lawfully married or civil partners of each other.

29   Sections 25 and 26: sexual relationships which pre-date family relationships

(1) Conduct by a person (A) which would otherwise be an offence under section 25 or 26 against another person (B) is not an offence under that section if –

    (a) the relation of A to B is not within subsection (2) of section 27,

    (b) t would not be within that subsection if section 67 of the Adoption and Children Act 2002 (c 38) did not apply, and

    (c) immediately before the relation of A to B first became such as to fall within section 27, a sexual relationship existed between A and B.

(2) Subsection (1) does not apply if at the time referred to in subsection (1)(c) sexual intercourse between A and B would have been unlawful.

(3) In proceedings for an offence under section 25 or 26 it is for the defendant to prove the matters mentioned in subsection (1)(a) to (c).

47   Paying for sexual services of a child

(1) A person (A) commits an offence if –

    (a) he intentionally obtains for himself the sexual services of another person (B),

(b) before obtaining those services, he has made or promised payment for those services to B or a third person, or knows that another person has made or promised such a payment, and

(c) either –

(i) B is under 18, and A does not reasonably believe that B is 18 or over, or

(ii) B is under 13.

(2) In this section, 'payment' means any financial advantage, including the discharge of an obligation to pay or the provision of goods or services (including sexual services) gratuitously or at a discount.

(3) A person guilty of an offence under this section against a person under 13, where subsection (6) applies, is liable on conviction on indictment to imprisonment for life.

(4) Unless subsection (3) applies, a person guilty of an offence under this section against a person under 16 is liable –

(a) where subsection (6) applies, on conviction on indictment, to imprisonment for a term not exceeding 14 years;

(b) in any other case –

(i) on summary conviction, to imprisonment for a term not exceeding 6 months or a fine not exceeding the statutory maximum or both;

(ii) on conviction on indictment, to imprisonment for a term not exceeding 14 years.

(5) Unless subsection (3) or (4) applies, a person guilty of an offence under this section is liable –

(a) on summary conviction, to imprisonment for a term not exceeding 6 months or a fine not exceeding the statutory maximum or both;

(b) on conviction on indictment, to imprisonment for a term not exceeding 7 years.

(6) This subsection applies where the offence involved –

(a) penetration of B's anus or vagina with a part of A's body or anything else,

(b) penetration of B's mouth with A's penis,

(c) penetration of A's anus or vagina with a part of B's body or by B with anything else, or

(d) penetration of A's mouth with B's penis. ...

48   Causing or inciting child prostitution or pornography

(1) A person (A) commits an offence if –

(a) he intentionally causes or incites another person (B) to become a prostitute, or to be involved in pornography, in any part of the world, and

(b) either –

(i) B is under 18, and A does not reasonably believe that B is 18 or over, or

(ii) B is under 13.

(2) A person guilty of an offence under this section is liable –

(a) on summary conviction, to imprisonment for a term not exceeding 6 months or a fine not exceeding the statutory maximum or both;

(b) on conviction on indictment, to imprisonment for a term not exceeding 14 years.

49   Controlling a child prostitute or a child involved in pornography

(1) A person (A) commits an offence if –

(a) he intentionally controls any of the activities of another person (B) relating to B's prostitution or involvement in pornography in any part of the world, and

(b) either –

(i) B is under 18, and A does not reasonably believe that B is 18 or over, or

(ii) B is under 13.

(2) A person guilty of an offence under this section is liable –

    (a) on summary conviction, to imprisonment for a term not exceeding 6 months or a fine not exceeding the statutory maximum or both;

    (b) on conviction on indictment, to imprisonment for a term not exceeding 14 years.

50 Arranging or facilitating child prostitution or pornography

(1) A person (A) commits an offence if –

    (a) he intentionally arranges or facilitates the prostitution or involvement in pornography in any part of the world of another person (B), and

    (b) either –

        (i) B is under 18, and A does not reasonably believe that B is 18 or over, or

        (ii) B is under 13.

(2) A person guilty of an offence under this section is liable –

    (a) on summary conviction, to imprisonment for a term not exceeding 6 months or a fine not exceeding the statutory maximum or both;

    (b) on conviction on indictment, to imprisonment for a term not exceeding 14 years.

51 Sections 48 to 50: interpretation

(1) For the purposes of sections 48 to 50, a person is involved in pornography if an indecent image of that person is recorded; and similar expressions, and 'pornography', are to be interpreted accordingly.

(2) In those sections 'prostitute' means a person (A) who, on at least one occasion and whether or not compelled to do so, offers or provides sexual services to another person in return for payment or a promise of payment to A or a third person; and 'prostitution' is to be interpreted accordingly.

(3) In subsection (2), 'payment' means any financial advantage, including the discharge of an obligation to pay or the provision of goods or services (including sexual services) gratuitously or at a discount.

52 Causing or inciting prostitution for gain

(1) A person commits an offence if –

    (a) he intentionally causes or incites another person to become a prostitute in any part of the world, and

    (b) he does so for or in the expectation of gain for himself or a third person.

(2) A person guilty of an offence under this section is liable –

    (a) on summary conviction, to imprisonment for a term not exceeding 6 months or a fine not exceeding the statutory maximum or both;

    (b) on conviction on indictment, to imprisonment for a term not exceeding 7 years.

53 Controlling prostitution for gain

(1) A person commits an offence if –

    (a) he intentionally controls any of the activities of another person relating to that person's prostitution in any part of the world, and

    (b) he does so for or in the expectation of gain for himself or a third person.

(2) A person guilty of an offence under this section is liable –

    (a) on summary conviction, to imprisonment for a term not exceeding 6 months or a fine not exceeding the statutory maximum or both;

    (b) on conviction on indictment, to imprisonment for a term not exceeding 7 years.

54 Sections 52 and 53: interpretation

(1) In sections 52 and 53, 'gain' means –

    (a) any financial advantage, including the discharge of an obligation to pay or the provision of goods or services (including sexual services) gratuitously or at a discount; or

    (b) the goodwill of any person which is or appears likely, in time, to bring financial advantage.

(2) In those sections 'prostitute' and 'prostitution' have the meaning given by section 51(2).

61 Administering a substance with intent

(1) A person commits an offence if he intentionally administers a substance to, or causes a substance to be taken by, another person (B) –

    (a) knowing that B does not consent, and

    (b) with the intention of stupefying or overpowering B, so as to enable any person to engage in a sexual activity that involves B.

(2) A person guilty of an offence under this section is liable –

    (a) on summary conviction, to imprisonment for a term not exceeding 6 months or a fine not exceeding the statutory maximum or both;

    (b) on conviction on indictment, to imprisonment for a term not exceeding 10 years.

62 Committing an offence with intent to commit a sexual offence

(1) A person commits an offence under this section if he commits any offence with the intention of committing a relevant sexual offence.

(2) In this section, 'relevant sexual offence' means any offence under this Part (including an offence of aiding, abetting, counselling or procuring such an offence).

(3) A person guilty of an offence under this section is liable on conviction on indictment, where the offence is committed by kidnapping or false imprisonment, to imprisonment for life.

(4) Unless subsection (3) applies, a person guilty of an offence under this section is liable –

    (a) on summary conviction, to imprisonment for a term not exceeding 6 months or a fine not exceeding the statutory maximum or both;

    (b) on conviction on indictment, to imprisonment for a term not exceeding 10 years.

63 Trespass with intent to commit a sexual offence

(1) A person commits an offence if –

    (a) he is a trespasser on any premises,

    (b) he intends to commit a relevant sexual offence on the premises, and

    (c) he knows that, or is reckless as to whether, he is a trespasser.

(2) In this section –

    'premises' includes a structure or part of a structure;

    'relevant sexual offence' has the same meaning as in section 62;

    'structure' includes a tent, vehicle or vessel or other temporary or movable structure.

(3) A person guilty of an offence under this section is liable –

    (a) on summary conviction, to imprisonment for a term not exceeding 6 months or a fine not exceeding the statutory maximum or both;

    (b) on conviction on indictment, to imprisonment for a term not exceeding 10 years.

73 Exceptions to aiding, abetting and counselling

(1) A person is not guilty of aiding, abetting or counselling the commission against a child of an offence to which this section applies if he acts for the purpose of –

(a) protecting the child from sexually transmitted infection,

(b) protecting the physical safety of the child,

(c) preventing the child from becoming pregnant, or

(d) promoting the child's emotional well-being by the giving of advice,

and not for the purpose of obtaining sexual gratification or for the purpose of causing or encouraging the activity constituting the offence or the child's participation in it.

(2) This section applies to –

(a) an offence under any of sections 5 to 7 (offences against children under 13);

(b) an offence under section 9 (sexual activity with a child);

(c) an offence under section 13 which would be an offence under section 9 if the offender were aged 18;

(d) an offence under any of sections 16, 25, 30, 34 and 38 (sexual activity) against a person under 16.

(3) This section does not affect any other enactment or any rule of law restricting the circumstances in which a person is guilty of aiding, abetting or counselling an offence under this Part.

74 'Consent'

For the purposes of this Part, a person consents if he agrees by choice, and has the freedom and capacity to make that choice.

75 Evidential presumptions about consent

(1) If in proceedings for an offence to which this section applies it is proved –

(a) that the defendant did the relevant act,

(b) that any of the circumstances specified in subsection (2) existed, and

(c) that the defendant knew that those circumstances existed,

the complainant is to be taken not to have consented to the relevant act unless sufficient evidence is adduced to raise an issue as to whether he consented, and the defendant is to be taken not to have reasonably believed that the complainant consented unless sufficient evidence is adduced to raise an issue as to whether he reasonably believed it.

(2) The circumstances are that –

(a) any person was, at the time of the relevant act or immediately before it began, using violence against the complainant or causing the complainant to fear that immediate violence would be used against him;

(b) any person was, at the time of the relevant act or immediately before it began, causing the complainant to fear that violence was being used, or that immediate violence would be used, against another person;

(c) the complainant was, and the defendant was not, unlawfully detained at the time of the relevant act;

(d) the complainant was asleep or otherwise unconscious at the time of the relevant act;

(e) because of the complainant's physical disability, the complainant would not have been able at the time of the relevant act to communicate to the defendant whether the complainant consented;

(f) any person had administered to or caused to be taken by the complainant, without the complainant's consent, a substance which, having regard to when it was administered or taken, was capable of causing or enabling the complainant to be stupefied or overpowered at the time of the relevant act.

(3) In subsection (2)(a) and (b), the reference to the time immediately before the relevant act

began is, in the case of an act which is one of a continuous series of sexual activities, a reference to the time immediately before the first sexual activity began.

76   Conclusive presumptions about consent

(1) If in proceedings for an offence to which this section applies it is proved that the defendant did the relevant act and that any of the circumstances specified in subsection (2) existed, it is to be conclusively presumed –

    (a) that the complainant did not consent to the relevant act, and

    (b) that the defendant did not believe that the complainant consented to the relevant act.

(2) The circumstances are that –

    (a) the defendant intentionally deceived the complainant as to the nature or purpose of the relevant act;

    (b) the defendant intentionally induced the complainant to consent to the relevant act by impersonating a person known personally to the complainant.

77   Sections 75 and 76: relevant acts

In relation to an offence to which sections 75 and 76 apply, references in those sections to the relevant act and to the complainant are to be read as follows –

Offence	*Relevant Act*
An offence under section 1 (rape).	The defendant intentionally penetrating, with his penis, the vagina, anus or mouth of another person ('the complainant').
An offence under section 2 (assault by penetration).	The defendant intentionally penetrating, with a part of his body or anything else, the vagina or anus of another person ('the complainant'), where the penetration is sexual.
An offence under section 3 (sexual assault).	The defendant intentionally touching another person ('the complainant'), where the touching is sexual.
An offence under section 4 (causing a person to engage in sexual activity without consent).	The defendant intentionally causing another person ('the complainant') to engage in an activity, where the activity is sexual.

78   'Sexual'

For the purposes of this Part (except section 71), penetration, touching or any other activity is sexual if a reasonable person would consider that –

    (a) whatever its circumstances or any person's purpose in relation to it, it is because of its nature sexual, or

    (b) because of its nature it may be sexual and because of its circumstances or the purpose of any person in relation to it (or both) it is sexual.

79   Part 1: general interpretation

(1) The following apply for the purposes of this Part.

(2) Penetration is a continuing act from entry to withdrawal.

(3) References to a part of the body include references to a part surgically constructed (in particular, through gender reassignment surgery).

(4) 'Image' means a moving or still image and includes an image produced by any means and, where the context permits, a three-dimensional image.

(5) References to an image of a person include references to an image of an imaginary person.

(6) 'Mental disorder' has the meaning given by section 1 of the Mental Health Act 1983 (c 20).

(7) References to observation (however expressed) are to observation whether direct or by looking at an image.

(8) Touching includes touching –

    (a) with any part of the body,

    (b) with anything else,

    (c) through anything,

and in particular includes touching amounting to penetration.

(9) 'Vagina' includes vulva.

(10) In relation to an animal, references to the vagina or anus include references to any similar part.

As amended by the Children Act 2004, s40, Schedule 3, para 18; Civil Partnership Act 2004, s261(1), Schedule 27, paras 173, 17; National Health Service (Consequential Provisions) Act 2006, s2, Schedule 1, paras 237, 238.

CRIMINAL JUSTICE ACT 2003

(2003 c 44)

PART 7

TRIALS ON INDICTMENT WITHOUT A JURY

43   Applications by prosecution for certain fraud cases to be conducted without a jury

(1) This section applies where –

    (a) one or more defendants are to be tried on indictment for one or more offences, and

    (b) notice has been given under section 51B of the Crime and Disorder Act 1998 (c 37) (notices in serious or complex fraud cases) in respect of that offence or those offences.

(2) The prosecution may apply to a judge of the Crown Court for the trial to be conducted without a jury.

(3) If an application under subsection (2) is made and the judge is satisfied that the condition in subsection (5) is fulfilled, he may make an order that the trial is to be conducted without a jury; but if he is not so satisfied he must refuse the application.

(4) The judge may not make such an order without the approval of the Lord Chief Justice or a judge nominated by him.

(5) The condition is that the complexity of the trial or the length of the trial (or both) is likely to make the trial so burdensome to the members of a jury hearing the trial that the interests of justice require that serious consideration should be given to the question of whether the trial should be conducted without a jury.

(6) In deciding whether or not he is satisfied that that condition is fulfilled, the judge must have regard to any steps which might reasonably be taken to reduce the complexity or length of the trial.

(7) But a step is not to be regarded as reasonable if it would significantly disadvantage the prosecution.

44 Application by prosecution for trial to be conducted without a jury where danger of jury tampering

(1) This section applies where one or more defendants are to be tried on indictment for one or more offences.

(2) The prosecution may apply to a judge of the Crown Court for the trial to be conducted without a jury.

(3) If an application under subsection (2) is made and the judge is satisfied that both of the following two conditions are fulfilled, he must make an order that the trial is to be conducted without a jury; but if he is not so satisfied he must refuse the application.

(4) The first condition is that there is evidence of a real and present danger that jury tampering would take place.

(5) The second condition is that, notwithstanding any steps (including the provision of police protection) which might reasonably be taken to prevent jury tampering, the likelihood that it would take place would be so substantial as to make it necessary in the interests of justice for the trial to be conducted without a jury.

(6) The following are examples of cases where there may be evidence of a real and present danger that jury tampering would take place –

    (a) a case where the trial is a retrial and the jury in the previous trial was discharged because jury tampering had taken place,

    (b) a case where jury tampering has taken place in previous criminal proceedings involving the defendant or any of the defendants,

    (c) a case where there has been intimidation, or attempted intimidation, of any person who is likely to be a witness in the trial.

46 Discharge of jury because of jury tampering

(1) This section applies where –

    (a) a judge is minded during a trial on indictment to discharge the jury, and

    (b) he is so minded because jury tampering appears to have taken place.

(2) Before taking any steps to discharge the jury, the judge must –

    (a) inform the parties that he is minded to discharge the jury,

    (b) inform the parties of the grounds on which he is so minded, and

    (c) allow the parties an opportunity to make representations.

(3) Where the judge, after considering any such representations, discharges the jury, he may make an order that the trial is to continue without a jury if, but only if, he is satisfied –

    (a) that jury tampering has taken place, and

    (b) that to continue the trial without a jury would be fair to the defendant or defendants; but this is subject to subsection (4).

(4) If the judge considers that it is necessary in the interests of justice for the trial to be terminated, he must terminate the trial.

(5) Where the judge terminates the trial under subsection (4), he may make an order that any new trial which is to take place must be conducted without a jury if he is satisfied in respect of the new trial that both of the conditions set out in section 44 are likely to be fulfilled.

(6) Subsection (5) is without prejudice to any other power that the judge may have on terminating the trial.

(7) Subject to subsection (5), nothing in this section affects the application of section 43 or 44 in relation to any new trial which takes place following the termination of the trial.

47   Appeals

(1) An appeal shall lie to the Court of Appeal from an order under section 46(3) or (5).

(2) Such an appeal may be brought only with the leave of the judge or the Court of Appeal.

(3) An order from which an appeal under this section lies is not to take effect –

> (a) before the expiration of the period for bringing an appeal under this section, or
>
> (b) if such an appeal is brought, before the appeal is finally disposed of or abandoned.

(4) On the termination of the hearing of an appeal under this section, the Court of Appeal may confirm or revoke the order. ...

48   Further provision about trials without a jury

(1) The effect of an order under section 43, 44 or 46(5) is that the trial to which the order relates is to be conducted without a jury.

(2) The effect of an order under section 46(3) is that the trial to which the order relates is to be continued without a jury.

(3) Where a trial is conducted or continued without a jury, the court is to have all the powers, authorities and jurisdiction which the court would have had if the trial had been conducted or continued with a jury (including power to determine any question and to make any finding which would be required to be determined or made by a jury).

(4) Except where the context otherwise requires, any reference in an enactment to a jury, the verdict of a jury or the finding of a jury is to be read, in relation to a trial conducted or continued without a jury, as a reference to the court, the verdict of the court or the finding of the court.

(5) Where a trial is conducted or continued without a jury and the court convicts a defendant –

> (a) the court must give a judgment which states the reasons for the conviction at, or as soon as reasonably practicable after, the time of the conviction, and
>
> (b) the reference in section 18(2) of the Criminal Appeal Act 1968 (c 19) (notice of appeal or of application for leave to appeal to be given within 28 days from date of conviction etc) to the date of the conviction is to be read as a reference to the date of the judgment mentioned in paragraph (a).

(6) Nothing in this Part affects the requirement under section 4A of Criminal Procedure (Insanity) Act 1964 that any question, finding or verdict mentioned in that section be determined, made or returned by a jury.

49   Rules of court

(1) Rules of court may make such provision as appears to the authority making them to be necessary or expedient for the purposes of this Part. ...

PART 9

PROSECUTION APPEALS

57   Introduction

(1) In relation to a trial on indictment, the prosecution is to have the rights of appeal for which provision is made by this Part.

(2) But the prosecution is to have no right of appeal under this Part in respect of –

    (a) a ruling that a jury be discharged, or

    (b) a ruling from which an appeal lies to the Court of Appeal by virtue of any other enactment.

(3) An appeal under this Part is to lie to the Court of Appeal.

(4) Such an appeal may be brought only with the leave of the judge or the Court of Appeal.

58   General right of appeal in respect of rulings

(1) This section applies where a judge makes a ruling in relation to a trial on indictment at an applicable time and the ruling relates to one or more offences included in the indictment.

(2) The prosecution may appeal in respect of the ruling in accordance with this section.

(3) The ruling is to have no effect whilst the prosecution is able to take any steps under subsection (4).

(4) The prosecution may not appeal in respect of the ruling unless –

    (a) following the making of the ruling, it –

        (i) informs the court that it intends to appeal, or

        (ii) requests an adjournment to consider whether to appeal, and

    (b) if such an adjournment is granted, it informs the court following the adjournment that it intends to appeal.

(5) If the prosecution requests an adjournment under subsection (4)(a)(ii), the judge may grant such an adjournment.

(6) Where the ruling relates to two or more offences –

    (a) any one or more of those offences may be the subject of the appeal, and

    (b) if the prosecution informs the court in accordance with subsection (4) that it intends to appeal, it must at the same time inform the court of the offence or offences which are the subject of the appeal.

(7) Where –

    (a) the ruling is a ruling that there is no case to answer, and

    (b) the prosecution, at the same time that it informs the court in accordance with subsection (4) that it intends to appeal, nominates one or more other rulings which have been made by a judge in relation to the trial on indictment at an applicable time and which relate to the offence or offences which are the subject of the appeal,

that other ruling, or those other rulings, are also to be treated as the subject of the appeal.

(8) The prosecution may not inform the court in accordance with subsection (4) that it intends to appeal, unless, at or before that time, it informs the court that it agrees that, in respect of the offence or each offence which is the subject of the appeal, the defendant in relation to that offence should be acquitted of that offence if either of the conditions mentioned in subsection (9) is fulfilled.

(9) Those conditions are –

    (a) that leave to appeal to the Court of Appeal is not obtained, and

    (b) that the appeal is abandoned before it is determined by the Court of Appeal.

(10) If the prosecution informs the court in accordance with subsection (4) that it intends to appeal, the ruling mentioned in subsection (1) is to continue to have no effect in relation to the offence or offences which are the subject of the appeal whilst the appeal is pursued.

(11) If and to the extent that a ruling has no effect in accordance with this section –

    (a) any consequences of the ruling are also to have no effect,

    (b) the judge may not take any steps in consequence of the ruling, and

    (c) if he does so, any such steps are also to have no effect.

(12) Where the prosecution has informed the court of its agreement under subsection (8) and

either of the conditions mentioned in subsection (9) is fulfilled, the judge or the Court of Appeal must order that the defendant in relation to the offence or each offence concerned be acquitted of that offence.

(13) In this section 'applicable time', in relation to a trial on indictment, means any time (whether before or after the commencement of the trial) before the time when the judge starts his summing-up to the jury.

(14) The reference in subsection (13) to the time when the judge starts his summing-up to the jury includes the time when the judge would start his summing-up to the jury but for the making of an order under Part 7.

59   Expedited and non-expedited appeals

(1) Where the prosecution informs the court in accordance with section 58(4) that it intends to appeal, the judge must decide whether or not the appeal should be expedited.

(2) If the judge decides that the appeal should be expedited, he may order an adjournment.

(3) If the judge decides that the appeal should not be expedited, he may –

    (a) order an adjournment, or

    (b) discharge the jury (if one has been sworn).

(4) If he decides that the appeal should be expedited, he or the Court of Appeal may subsequently reverse that decision and, if it is reversed, the judge may act as mentioned in subsection (3)(a) or (b).

60   Continuation of proceedings for offences not affected by ruling

(1) This section applies where the prosecution informs the court in accordance with section 58(4) that it intends to appeal.

(2) Proceedings may be continued in respect of any offence which is not the subject of the appeal.

61   Determination of appeal by Court of Appeal

(1) On an appeal under section 58, the Court of Appeal may confirm, reverse or vary any ruling to which the appeal relates.

(2) Subsections (3) to (5) apply where the appeal relates to a single ruling.

(3) Where the Court of Appeal confirms the ruling, it must, in respect of the offence or each offence which is the subject of the appeal, order that the defendant in relation to that offence be acquitted of that offence.

(4) Where the Court of Appeal reverses or varies the ruling, it must, in respect of the offence or each offence which is the subject of the appeal, do any of the following –

    (a) order that proceedings for that offence may be resumed in the Crown Court,

    (b) order that a fresh trial may take place in the Crown Court for that offence,

    (c) order that the defendant in relation to that offence be acquitted of that offence.

(5) But the Court of Appeal may not make an order under subsection (4)(a) or (b) in respect of an offence unless it considers it necessary in the interests of justice to do so.

(6) Subsections (7) and (8) apply where the appeal relates to a ruling that there is no case to answer and one or more other rulings.

(7) Where the Court of Appeal confirms the ruling that there is no case to answer, it must, in respect of the offence or each offence which is the subject of the appeal, order that the defendant in relation to that offence be acquitted of that offence.

(8) Where the Court of Appeal reverses or varies the ruling that there is no case to answer, it must in respect of the offence or each offence which is the subject of the appeal, make any of the orders mentioned in subsection (4)(a) to (c) (but subject to subsection (5)).

62   Right of appeal in respect of evidentiary rulings

(1) The prosecution may, in accordance with this section and section 63, appeal in respect of –

(a) a single qualifying evidentiary ruling, or

(b) two or more qualifying evidentiary rulings.

(2) A 'qualifying evidentiary ruling' is an evidentiary ruling of a judge in relation to a trial on indictment which is made at any time (whether before or after the commencement of the trial) before the opening of the case for the defence.

(3) The prosecution may not appeal in respect of a single qualifying evidentiary ruling unless the ruling relates to one or more qualifying offences (whether or not it relates to any other offence).

(4) The prosecution may not appeal in respect of two or more qualifying evidentiary rulings unless each ruling relates to one or more qualifying offences (whether or not it relates to any other offence).

(5) If the prosecution intends to appeal under this section, it must before the opening of the case for the defence inform the court –

(a) of its intention to do so, and

(b) of the ruling or rulings to which the appeal relates.

(6) In respect of the ruling, or each ruling, to which the appeal relates –

(a) the qualifying offence, or at least one of the qualifying offences, to which the ruling relates must be the subject of the appeal, and

(b) any other offence to which the ruling relates may, but need not, be the subject of the appeal.

(7) The prosecution must, at the same time that it informs the court in accordance with subsection (5), inform the court of the offence or offences which are the subject of the appeal.

(8) For the purposes of this section, the case for the defence opens when, after the conclusion of the prosecution evidence, the earliest of the following events occurs –

(a) evidence begins to be adduced by or on behalf of a defendant,

(b) it is indicated to the court that no evidence will be adduced by or on behalf of a defendant,

(c) a defendant's case is opened, as permitted by section 2 of the Criminal Procedure Act 1865 (c 18).

(9) In this section –

'evidentiary ruling' means a ruling which relates to the admissibility or exclusion of any prosecution evidence,

'qualifying offence' means an offence described in Part 1 of Schedule 4.

(10) The Secretary of State may by order amend that Part by doing any one or more of the following –

(a) adding a description of offence,

(b) removing a description of offence for the time being included,

(c) modifying a description of offence for the time being included.

(11) Nothing in this section affects the right of the prosecution to appeal in respect of an evidentiary ruling under section 58.

63   Condition that evidentiary ruling significantly weakens prosecution case

(1) Leave to appeal may not be given in relation to an appeal under section 62 unless the judge or, as the case may be, the Court of Appeal is satisfied that the relevant condition is fulfilled.

(2) In relation to an appeal in respect of a single qualifying evidentiary ruling, the relevant condition is that the ruling significantly weakens the prosecution's case in relation to the offence or offences which are the subject of the appeal.

(3) In relation to an appeal in respect of two or more qualifying evidentiary rulings, the relevant condition is that the rulings taken together significantly weaken the prosecution's case in relation to the offence or offences which are the subject of the appeal.

64   Expedited and non-expedited appeals

(1) Where the prosecution informs the court in accordance with section 62(5), the judge must decide whether or not the appeal should be expedited.

(2) If the judge decides that the appeal should be expedited, he may order an adjournment.

(3) If the judge decides that the appeal should not be expedited, he may –

    (a)   order an adjournment, or

    (b)   discharge the jury (if one has been sworn).

(4) If he decides that the appeal should be expedited, he or the Court of Appeal may subsequently reverse that decision and, if it is reversed, the judge may act as mentioned in subsection (3)(a) or (b).

65   Continuation of proceedings for offences not affected by ruling

(1) This section applies where the prosecution informs the court in accordance with section 62(5).

(2) Proceedings may be continued in respect of any offence which is not the subject of the appeal.

66   Determination of appeal by Court of Appeal

(1) On an appeal under section 62, the Court of Appeal may confirm, reverse or vary any ruling to which the appeal relates.

(2) In addition, the Court of Appeal must, in respect of the offence or each offence which is the subject of the appeal, do any of the following –

    (a)   order that proceedings for that offence be resumed in the Crown Court,

    (b)   order that a fresh trial may take place in the Crown Court for that offence,

    (c)   order that the defendant in relation to that offence be acquitted of that offence.

(3) But no order may be made under subsection (2)(c) in respect of an offence unless the prosecution has indicated that it does not intend to continue with the prosecution of that offence.

67   Reversal of rulings

The Court of Appeal may not reverse a ruling on an appeal under this Part unless it is satisfied –

    (a)   that the ruling was wrong in law,

    (b)   that the ruling involved an error of law or principle, or

    (c)   that the ruling was a ruling that it was not reasonable for the judge to have made.

73   Rules of court

(1) Rules of court may make such provision as appears to the authority making them to be necessary or expedient for the purposes of this Part.

(2) Without limiting subsection (1), rules of court may in particular make provision –

    (a)   for time limits which are to apply in connection with any provisions of this Part,

    (b)   as to procedures to be applied in connection with this Part,

    (c)   enabling a single judge of the Court of Appeal to give leave to appeal under this Part or to exercise the power of the Court of Appeal under section 58(12).

(3) Nothing in this section is to be taken as affecting the generality of any enactment conferring powers to make rules of court.

74   Interpretation of Part 9

(1) In this Part – …

'qualifying evidentiary ruling' is to be construed in accordance with section 62(2), …

'the relevant condition' is to be construed in accordance with section 63(2) and (3), …

'ruling' includes a decision, determination, direction, finding, notice, order, refusal, rejection or requirement,

'the 1968 Act' means the Criminal Appeal Act 1968 (c 19).

(2) Any reference in this Part (other than section 73(2)(c)) to a judge is a reference to a judge of the Crown Court.

(3) There is to be no right of appeal under this Part in respect of a ruling in relation to which the prosecution has previously informed the court of its intention to appeal under either section 58(4) or 62(5).

(4) Where a ruling relates to two or more offences but not all of those offences are the subject of an appeal under this Part, nothing in this Part is to be regarded as affecting the ruling so far as it relates to any offence which is not the subject of the appeal.

(5) Where two or more defendants are charged jointly with the same offence, the provisions of this Part are to apply as if the offence, so far as relating to each defendant, were a separate offence (so that, for example, any reference in this Part to a ruling which relates to one or more offences includes a ruling which relates to one or more of those separate offences).

(6) Subject to rules of court made under section 53(1) of the Supreme Court Act 1981 (c 54) (power by rules to distribute business of Court of Appeal between its civil and criminal divisions) –

  (a) the jurisdiction of the Court of Appeal under this Part is to be exercised by the criminal division of that court, and

  (b) references in this Part to the Court of Appeal are to be construed as references to that division.

(7) In its application to a trial on indictment in respect of which an order under section 17(2) of the Domestic Violence, Crime and Victims Act 2004 has been made, this Part is to have effect with such modifications as the Secretary of State may by order specify.

PART 10

RETRIAL FOR SERIOUS OFFENCES

75   Cases that may be retried

(1) This Part applies where a person has been acquitted of a qualifying offence in proceedings –

  (a) on indictment in England and Wales,

  (b) on appeal against a conviction, verdict or finding in proceedings on indictment in England and Wales, or

  (c) on appeal from a decision on such an appeal.

(2) A person acquitted of an offence in proceedings mentioned in subsection (1) is treated for the purposes of that subsection as also acquitted of any qualifying offence of which he could have been convicted in the proceedings because of the first-mentioned offence being charged in the indictment, except an offence –

  (a) of which he has been convicted,

  (b) of which he has been found not guilty by reason of insanity, or

  (c) in respect of which, in proceedings where he has been found to be under a disability (as defined by section 4 of the Criminal Procedure (Insanity) Act 1964 (c 84)), a finding has been made that he did the act or made the omission charged against him.

(3) References in subsections (1) and (2) to a qualifying offence do not include references to an offence which, at the time of the acquittal, was the subject of an order under section 77(1) or (3).

(4) This Part also applies where a person has been acquitted, in proceedings elsewhere than in the United Kingdom, of an offence under the law of the place where the proceedings were held, if the commission of the offence as alleged would have amounted to or included the commission (in the United Kingdom or elsewhere) of a qualifying offence.

(5) Conduct punishable under the law in force elsewhere than in the United Kingdom is an offence under that law for the purposes of subsection (4), however it is described in that law.

(6) This Part applies whether the acquittal was before or after the passing of this Act.

(7) References in this Part to acquittal are to acquittal in circumstances within subsection (1) or (4).

(8) In this Part 'qualifying offence' means an offence listed in Part 1 of Schedule 5.

76   Application to Court of Appeal

(1) A prosecutor may apply to the Court of Appeal for an order –
- (a)   quashing a person's acquittal in proceedings within section 75(1), and
- (b)   ordering him to be retried for the qualifying offence.

(2) A prosecutor may apply to the Court of Appeal, in the case of a person acquitted elsewhere than in the United Kingdom, for –
- (a)   a determination whether the acquittal is a bar to the person being tried in England and Wales for the qualifying offence, and
- (b)   if it is, an order that the acquittal is not to be a bar.

(3) A prosecutor may make an application under subsection (1) or (2) only with the written consent of the Director of Public Prosecutions.

(4) The Director of Public Prosecutions may give his consent only if satisfied that –
- (a)   there is evidence as respects which the requirements of section 78 appear to be met,
- (b)   it is in the public interest for the application to proceed, and
- (c)   any trial pursuant to an order on the application would not be inconsistent with obligations of the United Kingdom under Article 31 or 34 of the Treaty on European Union relating to the principle of ne bis in idem.

(5) Not more than one application may be made under subsection (1) or (2) in relation to an acquittal.

77   Determination by Court of Appeal

(1) On an application under section 76(1), the Court of Appeal –
- (a)   if satisfied that the requirements of sections 78 and 79 are met, must make the order applied for;
- (b)   otherwise, must dismiss the application.

(2) Subsections (3) and (4) apply to an application under section 76(2).

(3) Where the Court of Appeal determines that the acquittal is a bar to the person being tried for the qualifying offence, the court –
- (a)   if satisfied that the requirements of sections 78 and 79 are met, must make the order applied for;
- (b)   otherwise, must make a declaration to the effect that the acquittal is a bar to the person being tried for the offence.

(4) Where the Court of Appeal determines that the acquittal is not a bar to the person being tried for the qualifying offence, it must make a declaration to that effect.

78   New and compelling evidence

(1) The requirements of this section are met if there is new and compelling evidence against the acquitted person in relation to the qualifying offence.

(2) Evidence is new if it was not adduced in the proceedings in which the person was acquitted (nor, if those were appeal proceedings, in earlier proceedings to which the appeal related).

(3) Evidence is compelling if –

(a) it is reliable,

(b) it is substantial, and

(c) in the context of the outstanding issues, it appears highly probative of the case against the acquitted person.

(4) The outstanding issues are the issues in dispute in the proceedings in which the person was acquitted and, if those were appeal proceedings, any other issues remaining in dispute from earlier proceedings to which the appeal related.

(5) For the purposes of this section, it is irrelevant whether any evidence would have been admissible in earlier proceedings against the acquitted person.

79   Interests of justice

(1) The requirements of this section are met if in all the circumstances it is in the interests of justice for the court to make the order under section 77.

(2) That question is to be determined having regard in particular to –

(a) whether existing circumstances make a fair trial unlikely;

(b) for the purposes of that question and otherwise, the length of time since the qualifying offence was allegedly committed;

(c) whether it is likely that the new evidence would have been adduced in the earlier proceedings against the acquitted person but for a failure by an officer or by a prosecutor to act with due diligence or expedition;

(d) whether, since those proceedings or, if later, since the commencement of this Part, any officer or prosecutor has failed to act with due diligence or expedition.

(3) In subsection (2) references to an officer or prosecutor include references to a person charged with corresponding duties under the law in force elsewhere than in England and Wales.

(4) Where the earlier prosecution was conducted by a person other than a prosecutor, subsection (2)(c) applies in relation to that person as well as in relation to a prosecutor.

80   Procedure and evidence

(1) A prosecutor who wishes to make an application under section 76(1) or (2) must give notice of the application to the Court of Appeal.

(2) Within two days beginning with the day on which any such notice is given, notice of the application must be served by the prosecutor on the person to whom the application relates, charging him with the offence to which it relates or, if he has been charged with it in accordance with section 87(4), stating that he has been so charged.

(3) Subsection (2) applies whether the person to whom the application relates is in the United Kingdom or elsewhere, but the Court of Appeal may, on application by the prosecutor, extend the time for service under that subsection if it considers it necessary to do so because of that person's absence from the United Kingdom.

(4) The Court of Appeal must consider the application at a hearing.

(5) The person to whom the application relates –

(a) is entitled to be present at the hearing, although he may be in custody, unless he is in custody elsewhere than in England and Wales or Northern Ireland, and

(b) is entitled to be represented at the hearing, whether he is present or not.

(6) For the purposes of the application, the Court of Appeal may, if it thinks it necessary or expedient in the interests of justice –

(a) order the production of any document, exhibit or other thing, the production of which appears to the court to be necessary for the determination of the application, and

(b) order any witness who would be a compellable witness in proceedings pursuant to an order or declaration made on the application to attend for examination and be examined before the court.

(7) The Court of Appeal may at one hearing consider more than one application (whether or not relating to the same person), but only if the offences concerned could be tried on the same indictment.

84 Retrial

(1) Where a person –

(a) is tried pursuant to an order under section 77(1), or

(b) is tried on indictment pursuant to an order under section 77(3),

the trial must be on an indictment preferred by direction of the Court of Appeal.

(2) After the end of 2 months after the date of the order, the person may not be arraigned on an indictment preferred in pursuance of such a direction unless the Court of Appeal gives leave.

(3) The Court of Appeal must not give leave unless satisfied that –

(a) the prosecutor has acted with due expedition, and

(b) there is a good and sufficient cause for trial despite the lapse of time since the order under section 77.

(4) Where the person may not be arraigned without leave, he may apply to the Court of Appeal to set aside the order and –

(a) for any direction required for restoring an earlier judgment and verdict of acquittal of the qualifying offence, or

(b) in the case of a person acquitted elsewhere than in the United Kingdom, for a declaration to the effect that the acquittal is a bar to his being tried for the qualifying offence.

(5) An indictment under subsection (1) may relate to more than one offence, or more than one person, and may relate to an offence which, or a person who, is not the subject of an order or declaration under section 77. ...

85 Authorisation of investigations

(1) This section applies to the investigation of the commission of a qualifying offence by a person –

(a) acquitted in proceedings within section 75(1) of the qualifying offence, or

(b) acquitted elsewhere than in the United Kingdom of an offence the commission of which as alleged would have amounted to or included the commission (in the United Kingdom or elsewhere) of the qualifying offence.

(2) Subject to section 86, an officer may not do anything within subsection (3) for the purposes of such an investigation unless the Director of Public Prosecutions –

(a) has certified that in his opinion the acquittal would not be a bar to the trial of the acquitted person in England and Wales for the qualifying offence, or

(b) has given his written consent to the investigation (whether before or after the start of the investigation).

(3) The officer may not, either with or without the consent of the acquitted person –

    (a) arrest or question him,

    (b) search him or premises owned or occupied by him,

    (c) search a vehicle owned by him or anything in or on such a vehicle,

    (d) seize anything in his possession, or

    (e) take his fingerprints or take a sample from him.

(4) The Director of Public Prosecutions may only give his consent on a written application, and such an application may be made only by an officer who –

    (a) if he is an officer of the metropolitan police force or the City of London police force, is of the rank of commander or above, or

    (b) in any other case, is of the rank of assistant chief constable or above.

(5) An officer may make an application under subsection (4) only if –

    (a) he is satisfied that new evidence has been obtained which would be relevant to an application under section 76(1) or (2) in respect of the qualifying offence to which the investigation relates, or

    (b) he has reasonable grounds for believing that such new evidence is likely to be obtained as a result of the investigation.

(6) The Director of Public Prosecutions may not give his consent unless satisfied that –

    (a) there is, or there is likely as a result of the investigation to be, sufficient new evidence to warrant the conduct of the investigation, and

    (b) it is in the public interest for the investigation to proceed.

(7) In giving his consent, the Director of Public Prosecutions may recommend that the investigation be conducted otherwise than by officers of a specified police force or specified team of officers of Revenue and Customs.

86   Urgent investigative steps

(1) Section 85 does not prevent an officer from taking any action for the purposes of an investigation if –

    (a) the action is necessary as a matter of urgency to prevent the investigation being substantially and irrevocably prejudiced,

    (b) the requirements of subsection (2) are met, and

    (c) either –

        (i) the action is authorised under subsection (3), or

        (ii) the requirements of subsection (5) are met.

(2) The requirements of this subsection are met if –

    (a) there has been no undue delay in applying for consent under section 85(2),

    (b) that consent has not been refused, and

    (c) aking into account the urgency of the situation, it is not reasonably practicable to obtain that consent before taking the action.

(3) An officer of the rank of superintendent or above may authorise the action if –

    (a) he is satisfied that new evidence has been obtained which would be relevant to an application under section 76(1) or (2) in respect of the qualifying offence to which the investigation relates, or

    (b) he has reasonable grounds for believing that such new evidence is likely to be obtained as a result of the investigation.

(4) An authorisation under subsection (3) must –

    (a) if reasonably practicable, be given in writing;

    (b) otherwise, be recorded in writing by the officer giving it as soon as is reasonably practicable.

(5) The requirements of this subsection are met if –

    (a) there has been no undue delay in applying for authorisation under subsection (3),

    (b) that authorisation has not been refused, and

    (c) taking into account the urgency of the situation, it is not reasonably practicable to obtain that authorisation before taking the action.

(6) Where the requirements of subsection (5) are met, the action is nevertheless to be treated as having been unlawful unless, as soon as reasonably practicable after the action is taken, an officer of the rank of superintendent or above certifies in writing that he is satisfied that, when the action was taken –

    (a) new evidence had been obtained which would be relevant to an application under section 76(1) or (2) in respect of the qualifying offence to which the investigation relates, or

    (b) the officer who took the action had reasonable grounds for believing that such new evidence was likely to be obtained as a result of the investigation.

87   Arrest and charge

(1) Where section 85 applies to the investigation of the commission of an offence by any person and no certification has been given under subsection (2) of that section –

    (a) a justice of the peace may issue a warrant to arrest that person for that offence only if satisfied by written information that new evidence has been obtained which would be relevant to an application under section 76(1) or (2) in respect of the commission by that person of that offence, and

    (b) that person may not be arrested for that offence except under a warrant so issued.

(2) Subsection (1) does not affect section 89(3)(b) or 91(3), or any other power to arrest a person, or to issue a warrant for the arrest of a person, otherwise than for an offence. …

93   Rules of court

(1) Rules of court may make such provision as appears to the authority making them to be necessary or expedient for the purposes of this Part.

(2) Without limiting subsection (1), rules of court may in particular make provision as to procedures to be applied in connection with sections 76 to 82, 84 and 88 to 90.

(3) Nothing in this section is to be taken as affecting the generality of any enactment conferring power to make rules of court.

95   Interpretation of Part 10

(1) In this Part –

    'the 1984 Act' means the Police and Criminal Evidence Act 1984 (c 60),

    'acquittal' and related expressions are to be read in accordance with section 75(7), …

    'new evidence' is to be read in accordance with section 78(2),

    'officer', except in section 83, means an officer of a police force or an officer of Revenue and Customs, …

    'prosecutor' means an individual or body charged with duties to conduct criminal prosecutions,

    'qualifying offence' has the meaning given by section 75(8).

(2) Subject to rules of court made under section 53(1) of the Supreme Court Act 1981 (c 54) (power by rules to distribute business of Court of Appeal between its civil and criminal divisions) –

    (a) the jurisdiction of the Court of Appeal under this Part is to be exercised by the criminal division of that court, and

(b) references in this Part to the Court of Appeal are to be construed as references to that division. …

97 Application of Criminal Appeal Acts to proceedings under Part 10

Subject to the provisions of this Part, the Secretary of State may make an order containing provision, in relation to proceedings before the Court of Appeal under this Part, which corresponds to any provision, in relation to appeals or other proceedings before that court, which is contained in the Criminal Appeal Act 1968 (c 19) … (subject to any specified modifications).

PART 12

SENTENCING

CHAPTER 1

GENERAL PROVISIONS ABOUT SENTENCING

142 Purposes of sentencing

(1) Any court dealing with an offender in respect of his offence must have regard to the following purposes of sentencing –
  (a) the punishment of offenders,
  (b) the reduction of crime (including its reduction by deterrence),
  (c) the reform and rehabilitation of offenders,
  (d) the protection of the public, and
  (e) the making of reparation by offenders to persons affected by their offences.
(2) Subsection (1) does not apply –
  (a) in relation to an offender who is aged under 18 at the time of conviction,
  (b) to an offence the sentence for which is fixed by law,
  (c) to an offence the sentence for which falls to be imposed under section 51A(2) of the Firearms Act 1968 (c 27) (minimum sentence for certain firearms offences), under subsection (2) of section 110 or 111 of the Sentencing Act (required custodial sentences), under section 29(4) or (6) of the Violent Crime Reduction Act 2006 (minimum sentences in certain cases of using someone to mind a weapon) or under any of sections 225 to 228 of this Act (dangerous offenders), or
  (d) in relation to the making under Part 3 of the Mental Health Act 1983 (c 20) of a hospital order (with or without a restriction order), an interim hospital order, a hospital direction or a limitation direction.
(3) In this Chapter 'sentence', in relation to an offence, includes any order made by a court when dealing with the offender in respect of his offence; and 'sentencing' is to be construed accordingly.

143 Determining the seriousness of an offence

(1) In considering the seriousness of any offence, the court must consider the offender's culpability in committing the offence and any harm which the offence caused, was intended to cause or might forseeably have caused.
(2) In considering the seriousness of an offence ('the current offence') committed by an offender who has one or more previous convictions, the court must treat each previous conviction as an aggravating factor if (in the case of that conviction) the court considers that it can reasonably be so treated having regard, in particular, to –

(a) the nature of the offence to which the conviction relates and its relevance to the current offence, and

(b) the time that has elapsed since the conviction.

(3) In considering the seriousness of any offence committed while the offender was on bail, the court must treat the fact that it was committed in those circumstances as an aggravating factor.

(4) Any reference in subsection (2) to a previous conviction is to be read as a reference to –

(a) a previous conviction by a court in the United Kingdom, or

(b) a previous finding of guilt in service disciplinary proceedings.

(5) Subsections (2) and (4) do not prevent the court from treating a previous conviction by a court outside the United Kingdom as an aggravating factor in any case where the court considers it appropriate to do so.

144 Reduction in sentences for guilty pleas

(1) In determining what sentence to pass on an offender who has pleaded guilty to an offence in proceedings before that or another court, a court must take into account –

(a) the stage in the proceedings for the offence at which the offender indicated his intention to plead guilty, and

(b) the circumstances in which this indication was given.

(2) In the case of an offence the sentence for which falls to be imposed under subsection (2) of section 110 or 111 of the Sentencing Act, nothing in that subsection prevents the court, after taking into account any matter referred to in subsection (1) of this section, from imposing any sentence which is not less than 80 per cent of that specified in that subsection.

145 Increase in sentences for racial or religious aggravation

(1) This section applies where a court is considering the seriousness of an offence other than one under sections 29 to 32 of the Crime and Disorder Act 1998 (c 37) (racially or religiously aggravated assaults, criminal damage, public order offences and harassment etc).

(2) If the offence was racially or religiously aggravated, the court –

(a) must treat that fact as an aggravating factor, and

(b) must state in open court that the offence was so aggravated.

(3) Section 28 of the Crime and Disorder Act 1998 (meaning of 'racially or religiously aggravated') applies for the purposes of this section as it applies for the purposes of sections 29 to 32 of that Act.

146 Increase in sentences for aggravation related to disability or sexual orientation

(1) This section applies where the court is considering the seriousness of an offence committed in any of the circumstances mentioned in subsection (2).

(2) Those circumstances are –

(a) that, at the time of committing the offence, or immediately before or after doing so, the offender demonstrated towards the victim of the offence hostility based on –

(i) the sexual orientation (or presumed sexual orientation) of the victim, or

(ii) a disability (or presumed disability) of the victim, or

(b) that the offence is motivated (wholly or partly) –

(i) by hostility towards persons who are of a particular sexual orientation, or

(ii) by hostility towards persons who have a disability or a particular disability.

(3) The court –

(a) must treat the fact that the offence was committed in any of those circumstances as an aggravating factor, and

(b) must state in open court that the offence was committed in such circumstances.

(4) It is immaterial for the purposes of paragraph (a) or (b) of subsection (2) whether or not the offender's hostility is also based, to any extent, on any other factor not mentioned in that paragraph.

(5) In this section 'disability' means any physical or mental impairment.

154 General limit on magistrates' court's power to impose imprisonment

(1) A magistrates' court does not have power to impose imprisonment for more than 12 months in respect of any one offence.

(2) Unless expressly excluded, subsection (1) applies even if the offence in question is one for which a person would otherwise be liable on summary conviction to imprisonment for more than 12 months.

(3) Subsection (1) is without prejudice to section 133 of the Magistrates' Courts Act 1980 (c 43) (consecutive terms of imprisonment).

(4) Any power of a magistrates' court to impose a term of imprisonment for non-payment of a fine, or for want of sufficient distress to satisfy a fine, is not limited by virtue of subsection (1).

(5) In subsection (4) 'fine' includes a pecuniary penalty but does not include a pecuniary forfeiture or pecuniary compensation.

(6) In this section 'impose imprisonment' means pass a sentence of imprisonment or fix a term of imprisonment for failure to pay any sum of money, or for want of sufficient distress to satisfy any sum of money, or for failure to do or abstain from doing anything required to be done or left undone.

(7) Section 132 of the Magistrates' Courts Act 1980 contains provisions about the minimum term of imprisonment which may be imposed by a magistrates' court.

161A Court's duty to order payment of surcharge

(1) A court when dealing with a person for one or more offences must also (subject to subsections (2) and (3)) order him to pay a surcharge.

(2) Subsection (1) does not apply in such cases as may be prescribed by an order made by the Secretary of State.

(3) Where a court dealing with an offender considers –
  (a) that it would be appropriate to make a compensation order, but
  (b) that he has insufficient means to pay both the surcharge and appropriate compensation,
the court must reduce the surcharge accordingly (if necessary to nil).

(4) For the purposes of this section a court does not 'deal with' a person if it –
  (a) discharges him absolutely, or
  (b) makes an order under the Mental Health Act 1983 in respect of him.

161B Amount of surcharge

(1) The surcharge payable under section 161A is such amount as the Secretary of State may specify by order.

(2) An order under this section may provide for the amount to depend on –
  (a) the offence or offences committed,
  (b) how the offender is otherwise dealt with (including, where the offender is fined, the amount of the fine),
  (c) the age of the offender.
This is not to be read as limiting section 330(3) (power to make different provision for different purposes etc).

162　Powers to order statement as to offender's financial circumstances

(1) Where an individual has been convicted of an offence, the court may, before sentencing him, make a financial circumstances order with respect to him.

(2) Where a magistrates' court has been notified in accordance with section 12(4) of the Magistrates' Courts Act 1980 (c 43) that an individual desires to plead guilty without appearing before the court, the court may make a financial circumstances order with respect to him.

(3) In this section 'a financial circumstances order' means, in relation to any individual, an order requiring him to give to the court, within such period as may be specified in the order, such a statement of his financial circumstances as the court may require.

(4) An individual who without reasonable excuse fails to comply with a financial circumstances order is liable on summary conviction to a fine not exceeding level 3 on the standard scale.

(5) If an individual, in furnishing any statement in pursuance of a financial circumstances order –

>　(a)　makes a statement which he knows to be false in a material particular,
>
>　(b)　recklessly furnishes a statement which is false in a material particular, or
>
>　(c)　knowingly fails to disclose any material fact,

he is liable on summary conviction to a fine not exceeding level 4 on the standard scale.

(6) Proceedings in respect of an offence under subsection (5) may, notwithstanding anything in section 127(1) of the Magistrates' Courts Act 1980 (c 43) (limitation of time), be commenced at any time within two years from the date of the commission of the offence or within six months from its first discovery by the prosecutor, whichever period expires the earlier.

163　General power of Crown Court to fine offender convicted on indictment

Where a person is convicted on indictment of any offence, other than an offence for which the sentence is fixed by law or falls to be imposed under section 110(2) or 111(2) of the Sentencing Act or under any of sections 225 to 228 of this Act, the court, if not precluded from sentencing an offender by its exercise of some other power, may impose a fine instead of or in addition to dealing with him in any other way in which the court has power to deal with him, subject however to any enactment requiring the offender to be dealt with in a particular way.

164　Fixing of fines

(1) Before fixing the amount of any fine to be imposed on an offender who is an individual, a court must inquire into his financial circumstances.

(2) The amount of any fine fixed by a court must be such as, in the opinion of the court, reflects the seriousness of the offence.

(3) In fixing the amount of any fine to be imposed on an offender (whether an individual or other person), a court must take into account the circumstances of the case including, among other things, the financial circumstances of the offender so far as they are known, or appear, to the court.

(4) Subsection (3) applies whether taking into account the financial circumstances of the offender has the effect of increasing or reducing the amount of the fine.

(4A) In applying subsection (3), a court must not reduce the amount of a fine on account of any surcharge it orders the offender to pay under section 161A, except to the extent that he has insufficient means to pay both.

(5) Where –

>　(a)　an offender has been convicted in his absence in pursuance of section 11 or 12 of the Magistrates' Courts Act 1980 (c 43) (non-appearance of accused), or
>
>　(b)　an offender –

> (i) has failed to furnish a statement of his financial circumstances in response to a request which is an official request for the purposes of section 20A of the Criminal Justice Act 1991 (c.53) (offence of making false statement as to financial circumstances),
>
> (ii) has failed to comply with an order under section 162(1), or
>
> (iii) has otherwise failed to co-operate with the court in its inquiry into his financial circumstances,

and the court considers that it has insufficient information to make a proper determination of the financial circumstances of the offender, it may make such determination as it thinks fit.

165   Remission of fines

(1) This section applies where a court has, in fixing the amount of a fine, determined the offender's financial circumstances under section 164(5).

(2) If, on subsequently inquiring into the offender's financial circumstances, the court is satisfied that had it had the results of that inquiry when sentencing the offender it would –

> (a) have fixed a smaller amount, or
>
> (b) not have fined him,

it may remit the whole or part of the fine.

(3) Where under this section the court remits the whole or part of a fine after a term of imprisonment has been fixed under section 139 of the Sentencing Act (powers of Crown Court in relation to fines) or section 82(5) of the Magistrates' Courts Act 1980 (magistrates' powers in relation to default) it must reduce the term by the corresponding proportion.

(4) In calculating any reduction required by subsection (3), any fraction of a day is to be ignored.

167   The Sentencing Guidelines Council

(1) There shall be a Sentencing Guidelines Council (in this Chapter referred to as the Council) consisting of –

> (a) the Lord Chief Justice, who is to be chairman of the Council,
>
> (b) seven members (in this section and section 168 referred to as 'judicial members') appointed by the Lord Chief Justice after consultation with the Secretary of State and the Lord Chancellor, and
>
> (c) four members (in this section and section 168 referred to as 'non-judicial members') appointed by the Secretary of State after consultation with the Lord Chancellor and the Lord Chief Justice.

(2) A person is eligible to be appointed as a judicial member if he is –

> (a) a Lord Justice of Appeal,
>
> (b) a judge of the High Court,
>
> (c) a Circuit judge,
>
> (d) a District Judge (Magistrates' Courts), or
>
> (e) a lay justice.

(3) The judicial members must include a Circuit judge, a District Judge (Magistrates' Courts) and a lay justice.

(4) A person is eligible for appointment as a non-judicial member if he appears to the Secretary of State to have experience in one or more of the following areas –

> (a) policing,
>
> (b) criminal prosecution,
>
> (c) criminal defence, and
>
> (d) the promotion of the welfare of victims of crime.

(5) The persons eligible for appointment as a non-judicial member by virtue of experience of criminal prosecution include the Director of Public Prosecutions.

(6) The non-judicial members must include at least one person appearing to the Secretary of State to have experience in each area.

(7) The Lord Chief Justice must appoint one of the judicial members or non-judicial members to be deputy chairman of the Council.

(8) In relation to any meeting of the Council from which the Lord Chief Justice is to be absent, he may nominate any person eligible for appointment as a judicial member to act as a member on his behalf at the meeting.

(9) The Secretary of State may appoint a person appearing to him to have experience of sentencing policy and the administration of sentences to attend and speak at any meeting of the Council. ...

(10) In this section and section 168 'lay justice' means a justice of the peace who is not a District Judge (Magistrates' Courts).

168 Sentencing Guidelines Council: supplementary provisions

(1) In relation to the Council, the Lord Chancellor may by order make provision –

  (a) as to the term of office, resignation and re-appointment of judicial members and non-judicial members,

  (b) enabling the Lord Chancellor to remove a judicial member from office, with the concurrence of the Lord Chief Justice, on the grounds of incapacity or misbehaviour, and

  (c) enabling the Secretary of State to remove a non-judicial member from office on the grounds of incapacity or misbehaviour.

(1A) The following provisions apply to an order under subsection (1) –

  (a) if the order includes provision falling within subsection (1)(a), the Lord Chancellor must consult the Lord Chief Justice about that provision before making the order;

  (b) if the order includes provision falling within subsection (1)(b), the order may not be made unless the Lord Chief Justice agrees to the inclusion of that provision.

(1B) The Lord Chief Justice may, with the concurrence of the Lord Chancellor, by order make provision as to the proceedings of the Council.

(3) The validity of anything done by the Council is not affected by any vacancy among its members, by any defect in the appointment of a member or by any failure to comply with section 167(3), (6) or (7).

(4) The Lord Chancellor may pay –

  (a) to any judicial member who is appointed by virtue of being a lay justice, such remuneration or expenses as he may determine, and

  (b) to any other judicial member or the Lord Chief Justice, such expenses as he may determine.

(5) The Secretary of State may pay to any non-judicial member such remuneration or expenses as he may determine. ...

169 The Sentencing Advisory Panel

(1) There shall continue to be a Sentencing Advisory Panel (in this Chapter referred to as 'the Panel') constituted by the Lord Chancellor after consultation with the Secretary of State and the Lord Chief Justice.

(2) The Lord Chancellor must, after consultation with the Secretary of State and the Lord Chief Justice, appoint one of the members of the Panel to be its chairman.

(3) The Lord Chancellor may pay to any member of the Panel such remuneration or expenses as he may determine.

170 Guidelines relating to sentencing and allocation
(1) In this Chapter –
- (a) 'sentencing guidelines' means guidelines relating to the sentencing of offenders, which may be general in nature or limited to a particular category of offence or offender, and
- (b) 'allocation guidelines' means guidelines relating to decisions by a magistrates' court under section 19 of the Magistrates' Courts Act 1980 (c 43) as to whether an offence is more suitable for summary trial or trial on indictment.

(2) The Secretary of State may at any time propose to the Council –
- (a) that sentencing guidelines be framed or revised by the Council –
    - (i) in respect of offences or offenders of a particular category, or
    - (ii) in respect of a particular matter affecting sentencing, or
- (b) that allocation guidelines be framed or revised by the Council.

(3) The Council may from time to time consider whether to frame sentencing guidelines or allocation guidelines and, if it receives –
- (a) a proposal under section 171(2) from the Panel, or
- (b) a proposal under subsection (2) from the Secretary of State,

must consider whether to do so.

(4) Where sentencing guidelines or allocation guidelines have been issued by the Council as definitive guidelines, the Council must from time to time (and, in particular, if it receives a proposal under section 171(2) from the Panel or under subsection (2) from the Secretary of State) consider whether to revise them.

(5) Where the Council decides to frame or revise sentencing guidelines, the matters to which the Council must have regard include –
- (a) the need to promote consistency in sentencing,
- (b) the sentences imposed by courts in England and Wales for offences to which the guidelines relate,
- (c) the cost of different sentences and their relative effectiveness in preventing re-offending,
- (d) the need to promote public confidence in the criminal justice system, and
- (e) the views communicated to the Council, in accordance with section 171(3)(b), by the Panel.

(6) Where the Council decides to frame or revise allocation guidelines, the matters to which the Council must have regard include –
- (a) the need to promote consistency in decisions under section 19 of the Magistrates' Courts Act 1980 (c 43), and
- (b) the views communicated to the Council, in accordance with section 171(3)(b), by the Panel.

(7) Sentencing guidelines in respect of an offence or category of offences must include criteria for determining the seriousness of the offence or offences, including (where appropriate) criteria for determining the weight to be given to any previous convictions of offenders.

(8) Where the Council has prepared or revised any sentencing guidelines or allocation guidelines, it must –
- (a) publish them as draft guidelines, and
- (b) consult about the draft guidelines –
    - (i) the Secretary of State,

(ii) such persons as the Lord Chancellor, after consultation with the Secretary of State, may direct, and

(iii) such other persons as the Council considers appropriate.

(9) The Council may, after making any amendment of the draft guidelines which it considers appropriate, issue the guidelines as definitive guidelines.

171 Functions of Sentencing Advisory Panel in relation to guidelines

(1) Where the Council decides to frame or revise any sentencing guidelines or allocation guidelines, otherwise than in response to a proposal from the Panel under subsection (2), the Council must notify the Panel.

(2) The Panel may at any time propose to the Council –

(a) that sentencing guidelines be framed or revised by the Council –

(i) in respect of offences or offenders of a particular category, or

(ii) in respect of a particular matter affecting sentencing, or

(b) that allocation guidelines be framed or revised by the Council.

(3) Where the Panel receives a notification under subsection (1) or makes a proposal under subsection (2), the Panel must –

(a) obtain and consider the views on the matters in issue of such persons or bodies as may be determined, after consultation with the Secretary of State and the Lord Chancellor, by the Council, and

(b) formulate its own views on those matters and communicate them to the Council.

(4) Paragraph (a) of subsection (3) does not apply where the Council notifies the Panel of the Council's view that the urgency of the case makes it impracticable for the Panel to comply with that paragraph.

172 Duty of court to have regard to sentencing guidelines

(1) Every court must –

(a) in sentencing an offender, have regard to any guidelines which are relevant to the offender's case, and

(b) in exercising any other function relating to the sentencing of offenders, have regard to any guidelines which are relevant to the exercise of the function.

(2) In subsection (1) 'guidelines' means sentencing guidelines issued by the Council under section 170(9) as definitive guidelines, as revised by subsequent guidelines so issued.

174 Duty to give reasons for, and explain effect of, sentence

(1) Subject to subsections (3) and (4), any court passing sentence on an offender –

(a) must state in open court, in ordinary language and in general terms, its reasons for deciding on the sentence passed, and

(b) must explain to the offender in ordinary language –

(i) the effect of the sentence,

(ii) where the offender is required to comply with any order of the court forming part of the sentence, the effects of non-compliance with the order,

(iii) any power of the court, on the application of the offender or any other person, to vary or review any order of the court forming part of the sentence, and

(iv) where the sentence consists of or includes a fine, the effects of failure to pay the fine.

(2) In complying with subsection (1)(a), the court must –

(a) where guidelines indicate that a sentence of a particular kind, or within a particular range, would normally be appropriate for the offence and the sentence is of a different kind, or is outside that range, state the court's reasons for deciding on a sentence of a different kind or outside that range,

(b) where the sentence is a custodial sentence and the duty in subsection (2) of section 152 is not excluded by subsection (1)(a) or (b) or (3) of that section, state that it is of the opinion referred to in section 152(2) and why it is of that opinion,

(c) where the sentence is a community sentence and the case does not fall within section 151(2), state that it is of the opinion that section 148(1) applies and why it is of that opinion,

(d) where as a result of taking into account any matter referred to in section 144(1), the court imposes a punishment on the offender which is less severe than the punishment it would otherwise have imposed, state that fact, and

(e) in any case, mention any aggravating or mitigating factors which the court has regarded as being of particular importance.

(3) Subsection (1)(a) does not apply –

(a) to an offence the sentence for which is fixed by law (provision relating to sentencing for such an offence being made by section 270), or

(b) to an offence the sentence for which falls to be imposed under section 51A(2) of the Firearms Act 1968 (c 27), under subsection (2) of section 110 or 111 of the Sentencing Act or under section 29(4) or (6) of the Violent Crime Reduction Act 2006 (required custodial sentences).

(4) The Secretary of State may by order –

(a) prescribe cases in which subsection (1)(a) or (b) does not apply, and

(b) prescribe cases in which the statement referred to in subsection (1)(a) or the explanation referred to in subsection (1)(b) may be made in the absence of the offender, or may be provided in written form.

(5) Where a magistrates' court passes a custodial sentence, it must cause any reason stated by virtue of subsection (2)(b) to be specified in the warrant of commitment and entered on the register.

(6) In this section –

'guidelines' has the same meaning as in section 172;

'the register' has the meaning given by section 163 of the Sentencing Act.

176 Interpretation of Chapter 1

In this Chapter –

'allocation guidelines' has the meaning given by section 170(1)(b);

'the Council' means the Sentencing Guidelines Council;

'the Panel' means the Sentencing Advisory Panel;

'sentence' and 'sentencing' are to be read in accordance with section 142(3);

'sentencing guidelines' has the meaning given by section 170(1)(a);

'youth community order' has the meaning given by section 147(2).

CHAPTER 3

PRISON SENTENCES OF LESS THAN 12 MONTHS

181 Prison sentences of less than 12 months

(1) Any power of a court to impose a sentence of imprisonment for a term of less than 12 months

on an offender may be exercised only in accordance with the following provisions of this section unless the court makes an intermittent custody order (as defined by section 183).

(2) The term of the sentence –

    (a) must be expressed in weeks,

    (b) must be at least 28 weeks,

    (c) must not be more than 51 weeks in respect of any one offence, and

    (d) must not exceed the maximum term permitted for the offence.

(3) The court, when passing sentence, must –

    (a) specify a period (in this Chapter referred to as 'the custodial period') at the end of which the offender is to be released on a licence, and

    (b) by order require the licence to be granted subject to conditions requiring the offender's compliance during the remainder of the term (in this Chapter referred to as 'the licence period') or any part of it with one or more requirements falling within section 182(1) and specified in the order.

(4) In this Part 'custody plus order' means an order under subsection (3)(b).

(5) The custodial period –

    (a) must be at least 2 weeks, and

    (b) in respect of any one offence, must not be more than 13 weeks.

(6) In determining the term of the sentence and the length of the custodial period, the court must ensure that the licence period is at least 26 weeks in length.

(7) Where a court imposes two or more terms of imprisonment in accordance with this section to be served consecutively –

    (a) the aggregate length of the terms of imprisonment must not be more than 65 weeks, and

    (b) the aggregate length of the custodial periods must not be more than 26 weeks.

(8) A custody plus order which specifies two or more requirements may, in relation to any requirement, refer to compliance within such part of the licence period as is specified in the order.

(9) Subsection (3)(b) does not apply where the sentence is a suspended sentence.

182 Licence conditions

(1) The requirements falling within this subsection are –

    (a) an unpaid work requirement (as defined by section 199),

    (b) an activity requirement (as defined by section 201),

    (c) a programme requirement (as defined by section 202),

    (d) a prohibited activity requirement (as defined by section 203),

    (e) a curfew requirement (as defined by section 204),

    (f) an exclusion requirement (as defined by section 205),

    (g) a supervision requirement (as defined by section 213), and

    (h) in a case where the offender is aged under 25, an attendance centre requirement (as defined by section 214).

(2) The power under section 181(3)(b) to determine the conditions of the licence has effect subject to section 218 and to the following provisions of Chapter 4 relating to particular requirements –

    (a) section 199(3) (unpaid work requirement),

    (b) section 201(3) and (4) (activity requirement),

    (c) section 202(4) and (5) (programme requirement), and

    (d) section 203(2) (prohibited activity requirement).

(3) Where the court makes a custody plus order requiring a licence to contain a curfew requirement or an exclusion requirement, the court must also require the licence to contain an electronic monitoring requirement (as defined by section 215) unless –

    (a) the court is prevented from doing so by section 215(2) or 218(4), or

    (b) in the particular circumstances of the case, it considers it inappropriate to do so.

(4) Where the court makes a custody plus order requiring a licence to contain an unpaid work requirement, an activity requirement, a programme requirement, a prohibited activity requirement, a supervision requirement or an attendance centre requirement, the court may also require the licence to contain an electronic monitoring requirement unless the court is prevented from doing so by section 215(2) or 218(4).

(5) Before making a custody plus order requiring a licence to contain two or more different requirements falling within subsection (1), the court must consider whether, in the circumstances of the case, the requirements are compatible with each other.

183 Intermittent custody

(1) A court may, when passing a sentence of imprisonment for a term complying with subsection (4) –

    (a) specify the number of days that the offender must serve in prison under the sentence before being released on licence for the remainder of the term, and

    (b) by order –

        (i) specify periods during which the offender is to be released temporarily on licence before he has served that number of days in prison, and

        (ii) require any licence to be granted subject to conditions requiring the offender's compliance during the licence periods with one or more requirements falling within section 182(1) and specified in the order.

(2) In this Part 'intermittent custody order' means an order under subsection (1)(b).

(3) In this Chapter –

'licence period', in relation to a term of imprisonment to which an intermittent custody order relates, means any period during which the offender is released on licence by virtue of subsection (1)(a) or (b)(i);

'the number of custodial days', in relation to a term of imprisonment to which an intermittent custody order relates, means the number of days specified under subsection (1)(a).

(4) The term of the sentence –

    (a) must be expressed in weeks,

    (b) must be at least 28 weeks,

    (c) must not be more than 51 weeks in respect of any one offence, and

    (d) must not exceed the maximum term permitted for the offence.

(5) The number of custodial days –

    (a) must be at least 14, and

    (b) in respect of any one offence, must not be more than 90.

(6) A court may not exercise its powers under subsection (1) unless the offender has expressed his willingness to serve the custodial part of the proposed sentence intermittently, during the parts of the sentence that are not to be licence periods.

(7) Where a court exercises its powers under subsection (1) in respect of two or more terms of imprisonment that are to be served consecutively –

    (a) the aggregate length of the terms of imprisonment must not be more than 65 weeks, and

(b) the aggregate of the numbers of custodial days must not be more than 180.

(8) The Secretary of State may by order require a court, in specifying licence periods under subsection (1)(b)(i), to specify only –

(a) periods of a prescribed duration,

(b) periods beginning or ending at prescribed times, or

(c) periods including, or not including, specified parts of the week.

(9) An intermittent custody order which specifies two or more requirements may, in relation to any requirement, refer to compliance within such licence period or periods, or part of a licence period, as is specified in the order.

184 Restrictions on power to make intermittent custody order

(1) A court may not make an intermittent custody order unless it has been notified by the Secretary of State that arrangements for implementing such orders are available in the area proposed to be specified in the intermittent custody order and the notice has not been withdrawn.

(2) The court may not make an intermittent custody order in respect of any offender unless –

(a) it has consulted an officer of a local probation board,

(b) it has received from the Secretary of State notification that suitable prison accommodation is available for the offender during the custodial periods, and

(c) it appears to the court that the offender will have suitable accommodation available to him during the licence periods.

(3) In this section 'custodial period', in relation to a sentence to which an intermittent custody order relates, means any part of the sentence that is not a licence period.

185 Intermittent custody: licence conditions

(1) Section 183(1)(b) has effect subject to section 218 and to the following provisions of Chapter 4 limiting the power to require the licence to contain particular requirements –

(a) section 199(3) (unpaid work requirement),

(b) section 201(3) and (4) (activity requirement),

(c) section 202(4) and (5) (programme requirement), and

(d) section 203(2) (prohibited activity requirement).

(2) Subsections (3) to (5) of section 182 have effect in relation to an intermittent custody order as they have effect in relation to a custody plus order.

189 Suspended sentences of imprisonment

(1) A court which passes a sentence of imprisonment for a term of at least 28 weeks but not more than 51 weeks in accordance with section 181 may –

(a) order the offender to comply during a period specified for the purposes of this paragraph in the order (in this Chapter referred to as 'the supervision period') with one or more requirements falling within section 190(1) and specified in the order, and

(b) order that the sentence of imprisonment is not to take effect unless either –

(i) during the supervision period the offender fails to comply with a requirement imposed under paragraph (a), or

(ii) during a period specified in the order for the purposes of this sub-paragraph (in this Chapter referred to as 'the operational period') the offender commits in the United Kingdom another offence (whether or not punishable with imprisonment),

and (in either case) a court having power to do so subsequently orders under paragraph 8 of Schedule 12 that the original sentence is to take effect.

(2) Where two or more sentences imposed on the same occasion are to be served consecutively,

the power conferred by subsection (1) is not exercisable in relation to any of them unless the aggregate of the terms of the sentences does not exceed 65 weeks.

(3) The supervision period and the operational period must each be a period of not less than six months and not more than two years beginning with the date of the order.

(4) The supervision period must not end later than the operational period.

(5) A court which passes a suspended sentence on any person for an offence may not impose a community sentence in his case in respect of that offence or any other offence of which he is convicted by or before the court or for which he is dealt with by the court.

(6) Subject to any provision to the contrary contained in the Criminal Justice Act 1967 (c 80), the Sentencing Act or any other enactment passed or instrument made under any enactment after 31st December 1967, a suspended sentence which has not taken effect under paragraph 8 of Schedule 12 is to be treated as a sentence of imprisonment for the purposes of all enactments and instruments made under enactments.

(7) In this Part –

    (a) 'suspended sentence order' means an order under subsection (1),

    (b) 'suspended sentence' means a sentence to which a suspended sentence order relates, and

    (c) 'community requirement', in relation to a suspended sentence order, means a requirement imposed under subsection (1)(a).

190 Imposition of requirements by suspended sentence order

(1) The requirements falling within this subsection are –

    (a) an unpaid work requirement (as defined by section 199),

    (b) an activity requirement (as defined by section 201),

    (c) a programme requirement (as defined by section 202),

    (d) a prohibited activity requirement (as defined by section 203),

    (e) a curfew requirement (as defined by section 204),

    (f) an exclusion requirement (as defined by section 205),

    (g) a residence requirement (as defined by section 206),

    (h) a mental health treatment requirement (as defined by section 207),

    (i) a drug rehabilitation requirement (as defined by section 209),

    (j) an alcohol treatment requirement (as defined by section 212),

    (k) a supervision requirement (as defined by section 213), and

    (l) in a case where the offender is aged under 25, an attendance centre requirement (as defined by section 214).

(2) Section 189(1)(a) has effect subject to section 218 and to the following provisions of Chapter 4 relating to particular requirements –

    (a) section 199(3) (unpaid work requirement),

    (b) section 201(3) and (4) (activity requirement),

    (c) section 202(4) and (5) (programme requirement),

    (d) section 203(2) (prohibited activity requirement),

    (e) section 207(3) (mental health treatment requirement),

    (f) section 209(2) (drug rehabilitation requirement), and

    (g) section 212(2) and (3) (alcohol treatment requirement).

(3) Where the court makes a suspended sentence order imposing a curfew requirement or an exclusion requirement, it must also impose an electronic monitoring requirement (as defined by section 215) unless –

    (a) the court is prevented from doing so by section 215(2) or 218(4), or

    (b) in the particular circumstances of the case, it considers it inappropriate to do so.

(4) Where the court makes a suspended sentence order imposing an unpaid work requirement, an activity requirement, a programme requirement, a prohibited activity quirement, a residence requirement, a mental health treatment requirement, a drug rehabilitation requirement, an alcohol treatment requirement, a supervision requirement or an attendance centre requirement, the court may also impose an electronic monitoring requirement unless the court is prevented from doing so by section 215(2) or 218(4).

(5) Before making a suspended sentence order imposing two or more different requirements falling within subsection (1), the court must consider whether, in the circumstances of the case, the requirements are compatible with each other.

191 Power to provide for review of suspended sentence order

(1) A suspended sentence order may –
- (a) provide for the order to be reviewed periodically at specified intervals,
- (b) provide for each review to be made, subject to section 192(4), at a hearing held for the purpose by the court responsible for the order (a 'review hearing'),
- (c) require the offender to attend each review hearing, and
- (d) provide for the responsible officer to make to the court responsible for the order, before each review, a report on the offender's progress in complying with the community requirements of the order.

(2) Subsection (1) does not apply in the case of an order imposing a drug rehabilitation requirement (provision for such a requirement to be subject to review being made by section 210).

(3) In this section references to the court responsible for a suspended sentence order are references –
- (a) where a court is specified in the order in accordance with subsection (4), to that court;
- (b) in any other case, to the court by which the order is made.

(4) Where the area specified in a suspended sentence order made by a magistrates' court is not the area for which the court acts, the court may, if it thinks fit, include in the order provision specifying for the purpose of subsection (3) a magistrates' court which acts for the area specified in the order.

(5) Where a suspended sentence order has been made on an appeal brought from the Crown Court or from the criminal division of the Court of Appeal, it is to be taken for the purposes of subsection (3)(b) to have been made by the Crown Court.

192 Periodic reviews of suspended sentence order

(1) At a review hearing (within the meaning of subsection (1) of section 191) the court may, after considering the responsible officer's report referred to in that subsection, amend the community requirements of the suspended sentence order, or any provision of the order which relates to those requirements.

(2) The court –
- (a) may not amend the community requirements of the order so as to impose a requirement of a different kind unless the offender expresses his willingness to comply with that requirement,
- (b) may not amend a mental health treatment requirement, a drug rehabilitation requirement or an alcohol treatment requirement unless the offender expresses his willingness to comply with the requirement as amended,
- (c) may amend the supervision period only if the period as amended complies with section 189(3) and (4),
- (d) may not amend the operational period of the suspended sentence, and

    (e) except with the consent of the offender, may not amend the order while an appeal against the order is pending.

(3) For the purposes of subsection (2)(a) –

    (a) a community requirement falling within any paragraph of section 190(1) is of the same kind as any other community requirement falling within that paragraph, and

    (b) an electronic monitoring requirement is a community requirement of the same kind as any requirement falling within section 190(1) to which it relates.

(4) If before a review hearing is held at any review the court, after considering the responsible officer's report, is of the opinion that the offender's progress in complying with the community requirements of the order is satisfactory, it may order that no review hearing is to be held at that review; and if before a review hearing is held at any review, or at a review hearing, the court, after considering that report, is of that opinion, it may amend the suspended sentence order so as to provide for each subsequent review to be held without a hearing.

(5) If at a review held without a hearing the court, after considering the responsible officer's report, is of the opinion that the offender's progress under the order is no longer satisfactory, the court may require the offender to attend a hearing of the court at a specified time and place.

(6) If at a review hearing the court is of the opinion that the offender has without reasonable excuse failed to comply with any of the community requirements of the order, the court may adjourn the hearing for the purpose of dealing with the case under paragraph 8 of Schedule 12.

(7) At a review hearing the court may amend the suspended sentence order so as to vary the intervals specified under section 191(1).

(8) In this section any reference to the court, in relation to a review without a hearing, is to be read –

    (a) in the case of the Crown Court, as a reference to a judge of the court, and

    (b) in the case of a magistrates' court, as a reference to a justice of the peace acting for the commission area for which the court acts.

195 Interpretation of Chapter 3

In this Chapter –

    'custodial period', in relation to a term of imprisonment imposed in accordance with section 181, has the meaning given by subsection (3)(a) of that section;

    'licence period' –

    (a) in relation to a term of imprisonment imposed in accordance with section 181, has the meaning given by subsection (3)(b) of that section, and

    (b) in relation to a term of imprisonment to which an intermittent custody order relates, has the meaning given by section 183(3);

    'the number of custodial days', in relation to a term of imprisonment to which an intermittent custody order relates, has the meaning given by section 183(3);

    'operational period' and 'supervision period', in relation to a suspended sentence, are to be read in accordance with section 189(1);

    'sentence of imprisonment' does not include a committal for contempt of court or any kindred offence.

CHAPTER 5

DANGEROUS OFFENDERS

224 Meaning of 'specified offence', etc

(1) An offence is a 'specified offence' for the purposes of this Chapter if it is a specified violent offence or a specified sexual offence.

(2) An offence is a 'serious offence' for the purposes of this Chapter if and only if –

  (a) it is a specified offence, and

  (b) it is, apart from section 225, punishable in the case of a person aged 18 or over by –

    (i) imprisonment for life, or

    (ii) imprisonment for a determinate period of ten years or more.

(3) In this Chapter –

  'relevant offence' has the meaning given by section 229(4);

  'serious harm' means death or serious personal injury, whether physical or psychological;

  'specified violent offence' means an offence specified in Part 1 of Schedule 15;

  'specified sexual offence' means an offence specified in Part 2 of that Schedule.

225 Life sentence or imprisonment for public protection for serious offences

(1) This section applies where –

  (a) a person aged 18 or over is convicted of a serious offence committed after the commencement of this section, and

  (b) the court is of the opinion that there is a significant risk to members of the public of serious harm occasioned by the commission by him of further specified offences.

(2) If –

  (a) the offence is one in respect of which the offender would apart from this section be liable to imprisonment for life, and

  (b) the court considers that the seriousness of the offence, or of the offence and one or more offences associated with it, is such as to justify the imposition of a sentence of imprisonment for life,

the court must impose a sentence of imprisonment for life.

(3) In a case not falling within subsection (2), the court must impose a sentence of imprisonment for public protection.

(4) A sentence of imprisonment for public protection is a sentence of imprisonment for an indeterminate period, subject to the provisions of Chapter 2 of Part 2 of the Crime (Sentences) Act 1997 (c 43) as to the release of prisoners and duration of licences.

(5) An offence the sentence for which is imposed under this section is not to be regarded as an offence the sentence for which is fixed by law.

226 Detention for life or detention for public protection for serious offences committed by those under 18

(1) This section applies where –

  (a) a person aged under 18 is convicted of a serious offence committed after the commencement of this section, and

  (b) the court is of the opinion that there is a significant risk to members of the public of serious harm occasioned by the commission by him of further specified offences.

(2) If –

  (a) the offence is one in respect of which the offender would apart from this section be liable to a sentence of detention for life under section 91 of the Sentencing Act, and

(b) the court considers that the seriousness of the offence, or of the offence and one or more offences associated with it, is such as to justify the imposition of a sentence of detention for life,

the court must impose a sentence of detention for life under that section.

(3) If, in a case not falling within subsection (2), the court considers that an extended sentence under section 228 would not be adequate for the purpose of protecting the public from serious harm occasioned by the commission by the offender of further specified offences, the court must impose a sentence of detention for public protection.

(4) A sentence of detention for public protection is a sentence of detention for an indeterminate period, subject to the provisions of Chapter 2 of Part 2 of the Crime (Sentences) Act 1997 (c 43) as to the release of prisoners and duration of licences.

(5) An offence the sentence for which is imposed under this section is not to be regarded as an offence the sentence for which is fixed by law.

227 Extended sentence for certain violent or sexual offences: persons 18 or over

(1) This section applies where –
- (a) a person aged 18 or over is convicted of a specified offence, other than a serious offence, committed after the commencement of this section, and
- (b) the court considers that there is a significant risk to members of the public of serious harm occasioned by the commission by the offender of further specified offences.

(2) The court must impose on the offender an extended sentence of imprisonment, that is to say, a sentence of imprisonment the term of which is equal to the aggregate of –
- (a) the appropriate custodial term, and
- (b) a further period ('the extension period') for which the offender is to be subject to a licence and which is of such length as the court considers necessary for the purpose of protecting members of the public from serious harm occasioned by the commission by him of further specified offences.

(3) In subsection (2) 'the appropriate custodial term' means a term of imprisonment (not exceeding the maximum term permitted for the offence) which –
- (a) is the term that would (apart from this section) be imposed in compliance with section 153(2), or
- (b) where the term that would be so imposed is a term of less than 12 months, is a term of 12 months.

(4) The extension period must not exceed –
- (a) five years in the case of a specified violent offence, and
- (b) eight years in the case of a specified sexual offence.

(5) The term of an extended sentence of imprisonment passed under this section in respect of an offence must not exceed the maximum term permitted for the offence.

228 Extended sentence for certain violent or sexual offences: persons under 18

(1) This section applies where –
- (a) a person aged under 18 is convicted of a specified offence committed after the commencement of this section, and
- (b) the court considers –
  - (i) that there is a significant risk to members of the public of serious harm occasioned by the commission by the offender of further specified offences, and
  - (ii) where the specified offence is a serious offence, that the case is not one in which the court is required by section 226(2) to impose a sentence of detention for life

under section 91 of the Sentencing Act or by section 226(3) to impose a sentence of detention for public protection.

(2) The court must impose on the offender an extended sentence of detention, that is to say, a sentence of detention the term of which is equal to the aggregate of –

(a) the appropriate custodial term, and

(b) a further period ('the extension period') for which the offender is to be subject to a licence and which is of such length as the court considers necessary for the purpose of protecting members of the public from serious harm occasioned by the commission by him of further specified offences.

(3) In subsection (2) 'the appropriate custodial term' means such term as the court considers appropriate, which –

(a) must be at least 12 months, and

(b) must not exceed the maximum term of imprisonment permitted for the offence.

(4) The extension period must not exceed –

(a) five years in the case of a specified violent offence, and

(b) eight years in the case of a specified sexual offence.

(5) The term of an extended sentence of detention passed under this section in respect of an offence must not exceed the maximum term of imprisonment permitted for the offence.

(6) Any reference in this section to the maximum term of imprisonment permitted for an offence is a reference to the maximum term of imprisonment that is, apart from section 225, permitted for the offence in the case of a person aged 18 or over.

229 The assessment of dangerousness

(1) This section applies where –

(a) a person has been convicted of a specified offence, and

(b) it falls to a court to assess under any of sections 225 to 228 whether there is a significant risk to members of the public of serious harm occasioned by the commission by him of further such offences.

(2) If at the time when that offence was committed the offender had not been convicted in any part of the United Kingdom of any relevant offence or was aged under 18, the court in making the assessment referred to in subsection (1)(b) –

(a) must take into account all such information as is available to it about the nature and circumstances of the offence,

(b) may take into account any information which is before it about any pattern of behaviour of which the offence forms part, and

(c) may take into account any information about the offender which is before it.

(3) If at the time when that offence was committed the offender was aged 18 or over and had been convicted in any part of the United Kingdom of one or more relevant offences, the court must assume that there is such a risk as is mentioned in subsection (1)(b) unless, after taking into account –

(a) all such information as is available to it about the nature and circumstances of each of the offences,

(b) where appropriate, any information which is before it about any pattern of behaviour of which any of the offences forms part, and

(c) any information about the offender which is before it,

the court considers that it would be unreasonable to conclude that there is such a risk.

(4) In this Chapter 'relevant offence' means –

(a) a specified offence, …

231 Appeals where previous convictions set aside

(1) This section applies where –

    (a) a sentence has been imposed on any person under section 225 or 227, and

    (b) any previous conviction of his without which the court would not have been required to make the assumption mentioned in section 229(3) has been subsequently set aside on appeal.

(2) Notwithstanding anything in section 18 of the Criminal Appeal Act 1968 (c 19), notice of appeal against the sentence may be given at any time within 28 days from the date on which the previous conviction was set aside.

235 Detention under sections 226 and 228

A person sentenced to be detained under section 226 or 228 is liable to be detained in such place, and under such conditions, as may be determined by the Secretary of State or by such other person as may be authorised by him for the purpose.

CHAPTER 7

EFFECT OF LIFE SENTENCE

269 Determination of minimum term in relation to mandatory life sentence

(1) This section applies where after the commencement of this section a court passes a life sentence in circumstances where the sentence is fixed by law.

(2) The court must, unless it makes an order under subsection (4), order that the provisions of section 28(5) to (8) of the Crime (Sentences) Act 1997 (referred to in this Chapter as 'the early release provisions') are to apply to the offender as soon as he has served the part of his sentence which is specified in the order.

(3) The part of his sentence is to be such as the court considers appropriate taking into account –

    (a) the seriousness of the offence, or of the combination of the offence and any one or more offences associated with it, and

    (b) the effect of any direction which it would have given under section 240 (crediting periods of remand in custody) if it had sentenced him to a term of imprisonment.

(4) If the offender was 21 or over when he committed the offence and the court is of the opinion that, because of the seriousness of the offence, or of the combination of the offence and one or more offences associated with it, no order should be made under subsection (2), the court must order that the early release provisions are not to apply to the offender.

(5) In considering under subsection (3) or (4) the seriousness of an offence (or of the combination of an offence and one or more offences associated with it), the court must have regard to –

    (a) the general principles set out in Schedule 21, and

    (b) any guidelines relating to offences in general which are relevant to the case and are not incompatible with the provisions of Schedule 21.

(6) The Secretary of State may by order amend Schedule 21.

(7) Before making an order under subsection (6), the Secretary of State shall consult the Sentencing Guidelines Council.

270 Duty to give reasons

(1) Any court making an order under subsection (2) or (4) of section 269 must state in open court, in ordinary language, its reasons for deciding on the order made.

(2) In stating its reasons the court must, in particular –

  (a) state which of the starting points in Schedule 21 it has chosen and its reasons for doing so, and

  (b) state its reasons for any departure from that starting point.

SCHEDULE 4

QUALIFYING OFFENCES FOR PURPOSES OF SECTION 62

PART 1

LIST OF OFFENCES

Offences Against the Person
Murder
1. Murder.

Attempted murder
2. An offence under section 1 of the Criminal Attempts Act 1981 (c 47) of attempting to commit murder.

Soliciting murder
3. An offence under section 4 of the Offences against the Person Act 1861 (c 100).

Manslaughter
4. Manslaughter.

Wounding or causing grievous bodily harm with intent
5. An offence under section 18 of the Offences against the Person Act 1861 (c 100).

Kidnapping
6. Kidnapping.

Sexual Offences
Rape
7. An offence under section 1 of the Sexual Offences Act 1956 (c 69) or section 1 of the Sexual Offences Act 2003 (c 42).

Attempted rape
8. An offence under section 1 of the Criminal Attempts Act 1981 (c 47) of attempting to commit an offence under section 1 of the Sexual Offences Act 1956 or section 1 of the Sexual Offences Act 2003.

Intercourse with a girl under thirteen
9. An offence under section 5 of the Sexual Offences Act 1956.

Incest by a man with a girl under thirteen
10. An offence under section 10 of the Sexual Offences Act 1956 alleged to have been committed with a girl under thirteen.

Assault by penetration
11. An offence under section 2 of the Sexual Offences Act 2003.

Causing a person to engage in sexual activity without consent
12. An offence under section 4 of the Sexual Offences Act 2003 where it is alleged that the activity caused involved penetration within subsection (4)(a) to (d) of that section.

Rape of a child under thirteen
13. An offence under section 5 of the Sexual Offences Act 2003.

Attempted rape of a child under thirteen
14. An offence under section 1 of the Criminal Attempts Act 1981 of attempting to commit an offence under section 5 of the Sexual Offences Act 2003.

Assault of a child under thirteen by penetration
15. An offence under section 6 of the Sexual Offences Act 2003.

Causing a child under thirteen to engage in sexual activity
16. An offence under section 8 of the Sexual Offences Act 2003 (c 42) where it is alleged that an activity involving penetration within subsection (2)(a) to (d) of that section was caused.

Sexual activity with a person with a mental disorder impeding choice
17. An offence under section 30 of the Sexual Offences Act 2003 where it is alleged that the touching involved penetration within subsection (3)(a) to (d) of that section.

Causing or inciting a person with a mental disorder impeding choice to engage in sexual activity
18. An offence under section 31 of the Sexual Offences Act 2003 where it is alleged that an activity involving penetration within subsection (3)(a) to (d) of that section was caused.

Drugs Offences
Unlawful importation of Class A drug
19. An offence under section 50(2) of the Customs and Excise Management Act 1979 (c 2) alleged to have been committed in respect of a Class A drug (as defined by section 2 of the Misuse of Drugs Act 1971 (c 38)).

Unlawful exportation of Class A drug
20. An offence under section 68(2) of the Customs and Excise Management Act 1979 alleged to have been committed in respect of a Class A drug (as defined by section 2 of the Misuse of Drugs Act 1971).

Fraudulent evasion in respect of Class A drug
21. An offence under section 170(1) or (2) of the Customs and Excise Management Act 1979 alleged to have been committed in respect of a Class A drug (as defined by section 2 of the Misuse of Drugs Act 1971).

Producing or being concerned in production of Class A drug
22. An offence under section 4(2) of the Misuse of Drugs Act 1971 alleged to have been committed in relation to a Class A drug (as defined by section 2 of that Act).

Supplying or offering to supply Class A drug
23. An offence under section 4(3) of the Misuse of Drugs Act 1971 alleged to have been committed in relation to a Class A drug (as defined by section 2 of that Act).

Theft Offences
Robbery
24. An offence under section 8(1) of the Theft Act 1968 (c 60) where it is alleged that, at some time during the commission of the offence, the defendant had in his possession a firearm or imitation firearm (as defined by section 57 of the Firearms Act 1968 (c 27)).

Criminal Damage Offences
Arson endangering life
25. An offence under section 1(2) of the Criminal Damage Act 1971 (c 48) alleged to have been committed by destroying or damaging property by fire.

Causing explosion likely to endanger life or property
26. An offence under section 2 of the Explosive Substances Act 1883 (c 3).

Intent or conspiracy to cause explosion likely to endanger life or property
27. An offence under section 3(1)(a) of the Explosive Substances Act 1883.

War Crimes and Terrorism
Genocide, crimes against humanity and war crimes
28. An offence under section 51 or 52 of the International Criminal Court Act 2001 (c 17).

Grave breaches of the Geneva Conventions
29. An offence under section 1 of the Geneva Conventions Act 1957 (c 52).

Directing terrorist organisation
30. An offence under section 56 of the Terrorism Act 2000 (c 11).

Hostage-taking
31. An offence under section 1 of the Taking of Hostages Act 1982 (c 28).

Hijacking and Other Offences Relating to Aviation, Maritime and Rail Security
Hijacking of aircraft
32. An offence under section 1 of the Aviation Security Act 1982 (c 36).

Destroying, damaging or endangering the safety of an aircraft
33. An offence under section 2 of the Aviation Security Act 1982.

Hijacking of ships
34. An offence under section 9 of the Aviation and Maritime Security Act 1990 (c 31).

Seizing or exercising control of fixed platforms
35. An offence under section 10 of the Aviation and Maritime Security Act 1990.

Destroying ships or fixed platforms or endangering their safety
36. An offence under section 11 of the Aviation and Maritime Security Act 1990.

Hijacking of Channel Tunnel trains
37. An offence under article 4 of the Channel Tunnel (Security) Order 1994 (SI 1994/570).

Seizing or exercising control of the Channel Tunnel system
38. An offence under article 5 of the Channel Tunnel (Security) Order 1994 (SI 1994/570).

Conspiracy
Conspiracy
39. An offence under section 1 of the Criminal Law Act 1977 (c 45) of conspiracy to commit an offence listed in this Part of this Schedule.

PART 2

SUPPLEMENTARY

40. A reference in Part 1 of this Schedule to an offence includes a reference to an offence of aiding, abetting, counselling or procuring the commission of the offence.

41. A reference in Part 1 of this Schedule to an enactment includes a reference to the enactment as enacted and as amended from time to time.

SCHEDULE 5

QUALIFYING OFFENCES FOR PURPOSES OF PART 10

PART 1

LIST OF OFFENCES FOR ENGLAND AND WALES

Offences Against the Person
Murder
1. Murder.

Attempted murder
2. An offence under section 1 of the Criminal Attempts Act 1981 (c 47) of attempting to commit murder.

Soliciting murder
3. An offence under section 4 of the Offences against the Person Act 1861 (c 100).

Manslaughter
4. Manslaughter.

Kidnapping
5. Kidnapping.

Sexual Offences
Rape
6. An offence under section 1 of the Sexual Offences Act 1956 (c 69) or section 1 of the Sexual Offences Act 2003 (c 42).

Attempted rape
7. An offence under section 1 of the Criminal Attempts Act 1981 of attempting to commit an

offence under section 1 of the Sexual Offences Act 1956 or section 1 of the Sexual Offences Act 2003.

Intercourse with a girl under thirteen
8. An offence under section 5 of the Sexual Offences Act 1956.

Incest by a man with a girl under thirteen
9. An offence under section 10 of the Sexual Offences Act 1956 alleged to have been committed with a girl under thirteen.

Assault by penetration
10. An offence under section 2 of the Sexual Offences Act 2003 (c 42).

Causing a person to engage in sexual activity without consent
11. An offence under section 4 of the Sexual Offences Act 2003 where it is alleged that the activity caused involved penetration within subsection (4)(a) to (d) of that section.

Rape of a child under thirteen
12. An offence under section 5 of the Sexual Offences Act 2003.

Attempted rape of a child under thirteen
13. An offence under section 1 of the Criminal Attempts Act 1981 (c 47) of attempting to commit an offence under section 5 of the Sexual Offences Act 2003.

Assault of a child under thirteen by penetration
14. An offence under section 6 of the Sexual Offences Act 2003.

Causing a child under thirteen to engage in sexual activity
15. An offence under section 8 of the Sexual Offences Act 2003 where it is alleged that an activity involving penetration within subsection (2)(a) to (d) of that section was caused.

Sexual activity with a person with a mental disorder impeding choice
16. An offence under section 30 of the Sexual Offences Act 2003 where it is alleged that the touching involved penetration within subsection (3)(a) to (d) of that section.

Causing a person with a mental disorder impeding choice to engage in sexual activity
17. An offence under section 31 of the Sexual Offences Act 2003 where it is alleged that an activity involving penetration within subsection (3)(a) to (d) of that section was caused.

Drugs Offences
Unlawful importation of Class A drug
1. An offence under section 50(2) of the Customs and Excise Management Act 1979 (c 2) alleged to have been committed in respect of a Class A drug (as defined by section 2 of the Misuse of Drugs Act 1971 (c 38)).

Unlawful exportation of Class A drug
19. An offence under section 68(2) of the Customs and Excise Management Act 1979 alleged to have been committed in respect of a Class A drug (as defined by section 2 of the Misuse of Drugs Act 1971).

Fraudulent evasion in respect of Class A drug
20. An offence under section 170(1) or (2) of the Customs and Excise Management Act 1979

(c 2) alleged to have been committed in respect of a Class A drug (as defined by section 2 of the Misuse of Drugs Act 1971 (c 38)).

Producing or being concerned in production of Class A drug
21. An offence under section 4(2) of the Misuse of Drugs Act 1971 alleged to have been committed in relation to a Class A drug (as defined by section 2 of that Act).

Criminal Damage Offences
Arson endangering life
22. An offence under section 1(2) of the Criminal Damage Act 1971 (c 48) alleged to have been committed by destroying or damaging property by fire.

Causing explosion likely to endanger life or property
23. An offence under section 2 of the Explosive Substances Act 1883 (c 3).

Intent or conspiracy to cause explosion likely to endanger life or property
24. An offence under section 3(1)(a) of the Explosive Substances Act 1883.

War Crimes and Terrorism
Genocide, crimes against humanity and war crimes
25. An offence under section 51 or 52 of the International Criminal Court Act 2001 (c 17).

Grave breaches of the Geneva Conventions
26. An offence under section 1 of the Geneva Conventions Act 1957 (c 52).

Directing terrorist organisation
27. An offence under section 56 of the Terrorism Act 2000 (c 11).

Hostage-taking
28. An offence under section 1 of the Taking of Hostages Act 1982 (c 28).

Conspiracy
Conspiracy
29. An offence under section 1 of the Criminal Law Act 1977 (c 45) of conspiracy to commit an offence listed in this Part of this Schedule.

SCHEDULE 15

SPECIFIED OFFENCES FOR PURPOSES OF CHAPTER 5 OF PART 12

PART 1

SPECIFIED VIOLENT OFFENCES

1. Manslaughter.

2. Kidnapping.

3. False imprisonment.

4. An offence under section 4 of the Offences against the Person Act 1861 (c 100) (soliciting murder).

5. An offence under section 16 of that Act (threats to kill).

6. An offence under section 18 of that Act (wounding with intent to cause grievous bodily harm).

7. An offence under section 20 of that Act (malicious wounding).

8. An offence under section 21 of that Act (attempting to choke, suffocate or strangle in order to commit or assist in committing an indictable offence).

9. An offence under section 22 of that Act (using chloroform etc. to commit or assist in the committing of any indictable offence).

10. An offence under section 23 of that Act (maliciously administering poison etc. so as to endanger life or inflict grievous bodily harm).

11. An offence under section 27 of that Act (abandoning children).

12. An offence under section 28 of that Act (causing bodily injury by explosives).

13. An offence under section 29 of that Act (using explosives etc. with intent to do grievous bodily harm).

14. An offence under section 30 of that Act (placing explosives with intent to do bodily injury).

15. An offence under section 31 of that Act (setting spring guns etc. with intent to do grievous bodily harm).

16. An offence under section 32 of that Act (endangering the safety of railway passengers).

17. An offence under section 35 of that Act (injuring persons by furious driving).

18. An offence under section 37 of that Act (assaulting officer preserving wreck).

19. An offence under section 38 of that Act (assault with intent to resist arrest).

20. An offence under section 47 of that Act (assault occasioning actual bodily harm).

21. An offence under section 2 of the Explosive Substances Act 1883 (c 3) (causing explosion likely to endanger life or property).

22. An offence under section 3 of that Act (attempt to cause explosion, or making or keeping explosive with intent to endanger life or property).

23. An offence under section 1 of the Infant Life (Preservation) Act 1929 (c 34) (child destruction).

24. An offence under section 1 of the Children and Young Persons Act 1933 (c 12) (cruelty to children).

25. An offence under section 1 of the Infanticide Act 1938 (c 36) (infanticide).

26. An offence under section 16 of the Firearms Act 1968 (c 27) (possession of firearm with intent to endanger life).

27. An offence under section 16A of that Act (possession of firearm with intent to cause fear of violence).

28. An offence under section 17(1) of that Act (use of firearm to resist arrest).

29. An offence under section 17(2) of that Act (possession of firearm at time of committing or being arrested for offence specified in Schedule 1 to that Act).

30. An offence under section 18 of that Act (carrying a firearm with criminal intent).

31. An offence under section 8 of the Theft Act 1968 (c 60) (robbery or assault with intent to rob).

32. An offence under section 9 of that Act of burglary with intent to –
    (a) inflict grievous bodily harm on a person, or
    (b) do unlawful damage to a building or anything in it.

33. An offence under section 10 of that Act (aggravated burglary).

34. An offence under section 12A of that Act (aggravated vehicle-taking) involving an accident which caused the death of any person.

35. An offence of arson under section 1 of the Criminal Damage Act 1971 (c 48).

36. An offence under section 1(2) of that Act (destroying or damaging property) other than an offence of arson.

37. An offence under section 1 of the Taking of Hostages Act 1982 (c 28) (hostage-taking).

38. An offence under section 1 of the Aviation Security Act 1982 (c 36) (hijacking).

39. An offence under section 2 of that Act (destroying, damaging or endangering safety of aircraft).

40. An offence under section 3 of that Act (other acts endangering or likely to endanger safety of aircraft).

41. An offence under section 4 of that Act (offences in relation to certain dangerous articles).

42. An offence under section 127 of the Mental Health Act 1983 (c 20) (ill-treatment of patients).

43. An offence under section 1 of the Prohibition of Female Circumcision Act 1985 (c 38) (prohibition of female circumcision).

44. An offence under section 1 of the Public Order Act 1986 (c 64) (riot).

45. An offence under section 2 of that Act (violent disorder).

46. An offence under section 3 of that Act (affray).

47. An offence under section 134 of the Criminal Justice Act 1988 (c 33) (torture).

48. An offence under section 1 of the Road Traffic Act 1988 (c 52) (causing death by dangerous driving).

49. An offence under section 3A of that Act (causing death by careless driving when under influence of drink or drugs).

50. An offence under section 1 of the Aviation and Maritime Security Act 1990 (c 31) (endangering safety at aerodromes).

51. An offence under section 9 of that Act (hijacking of ships).

52. An offence under section 10 of that Act (seizing or exercising control of fixed platforms).

53. An offence under section 11 of that Act (destroying fixed platforms or endangering their safety).

54. An offence under section 12 of that Act (other acts endangering or likely to endanger safe navigation).

55. An offence under section 13 of that Act (offences involving threats).

56. An offence under Part II of the Channel Tunnel (Security) Order 1994 (SI 1994/570) (offences relating to Channel Tunnel trains and the tunnel system).

57. An offence under section 4 of the Protection from Harassment Act 1997 (c 40) (putting people in fear of violence).

58. An offence under section 29 of the Crime and Disorder Act 1998 (c 37) (racially or religiously aggravated assaults).

59. An offence falling within section 31(1)(a) or (b) of that Act (racially or religiously aggravated offences under section 4 or 4A of the Public Order Act 1986 (c 64)).

60. An offence under section 51 or 52 of the International Criminal Court Act 2001 (c 17) (genocide, crimes against humanity, war crimes and related offences), other than one involving murder.

61. An offence under section 1 of the Female Genital Mutilation Act 2003 (c 31) (female genital mutilation).

62. An offence under section 2 of that Act (assisting a girl to mutilate her own genitalia).

63. An offence under section 3 of that Act (assisting a non-UK person to mutilate overseas a girl's genitalia).

63A. An offence under section 5 of the Domestic Violence, Crime and Victims Act 2004 (causing or allowing the death of a child or vulnerable adult).

64. An offence of –
    (a) aiding, abetting, counselling, procuring or inciting the commission of an offence specified in this Part of this Schedule,
    (b) conspiring to commit an offence so specified, or
    (c) attempting to commit an offence so specified.

65. An attempt to commit murder or a conspiracy to commit murder.

PART 2

SPECIFIED SEXUAL OFFENCES

66. An offence under section 1 of the Sexual Offences Act 1956 (c 69) (rape).

67. An offence under section 2 of that Act (procurement of woman by threats).

68. An offence under section 3 of that Act (procurement of woman by false pretences).

69. An offence under section 4 of that Act (administering drugs to obtain or facilitate intercourse).

70. An offence under section 5 of that Act (intercourse with girl under thirteen).

71. An offence under section 6 of that Act (intercourse with girl under 16).

72. An offence under section 7 of that Act (intercourse with a defective).

73. An offence under section 9 of that Act (procurement of a defective).

74. An offence under section 10 of that Act (incest by a man).

75. An offence under section 11 of that Act (incest by a woman).

76. An offence under section 14 of that Act (indecent assault on a woman).

77. An offence under section 15 of that Act (indecent assault on a man).

78. An offence under section 16 of that Act (assault with intent to commit buggery).

79. An offence under section 17 of that Act (abduction of woman by force or for the sake of her property).

80. An offence under section 19 of that Act (abduction of unmarried girl under eighteen from parent or guardian).

81. An offence under section 20 of that Act (abduction of unmarried girl under sixteen from parent or guardian).

82. An offence under section 21 of that Act (abduction of defective from parent or guardian).

83. An offence under section 22 of that Act (causing prostitution of women).

84. An offence under section 23 of that Act (procuration of girl under twenty-one).

85. An offence under section 24 of that Act (detention of woman in brothel).

86. An offence under section 25 of that Act (permitting girl under thirteen to use premises for intercourse).

87. An offence under section 26 of that Act (permitting girl under sixteen to use premises for intercourse).

88. An offence under section 27 of that Act (permitting defective to use premises for intercourse).

89. An offence under section 28 of that Act (causing or encouraging the prostitution of, intercourse with or indecent assault on girl under sixteen).

90. An offence under section 29 of that Act (causing or encouraging prostitution of defective).

91. An offence under section 32 of that Act (soliciting by men).

92. An offence under section 33 of that Act (keeping a brothel).

93. An offence under section 128 of the Mental Health Act 1959 (c 72) (sexual intercourse with patients).

94. An offence under section 1 of the Indecency with Children Act 1960 (c 33) (indecent conduct towards young child).

95. An offence under section 4 of the Sexual Offences Act 1967 (c 60) (procuring others to commit homosexual acts).

96. An offence under section 5 of that Act (living on earnings of male prostitution).

97. An offence under section 9 of the Theft Act 1968 (c 60) of burglary with intent to commit rape.

98. An offence under section 54 of the Criminal Law Act 1977 (c 45) (inciting girl under sixteen to have incestuous sexual intercourse).

99. An offence under section 1 of the Protection of Children Act 1978 (c 37) (indecent photographs of children).

100. An offence under section 170 of the Customs and Excise Management Act 1979 (c 2) (penalty for fraudulent evasion of duty etc.) in relation to goods prohibited to be imported under section 42 of the Customs Consolidation Act 1876 (c 36) (indecent or obscene articles).

101. An offence under section 160 of the Criminal Justice Act 1988 (c 33) (possession of indecent photograph of a child).

102. An offence under section 1 of the Sexual Offences Act 2003 (c 42) (rape).

103. An offence under section 2 of that Act (assault by penetration).

104. An offence under section 3 of that Act (sexual assault).

105. An offence under section 4 of that Act (causing a person to engage in sexual activity without consent).

106. An offence under section 5 of that Act (rape of a child under 13).

107. An offence under section 6 of that Act (assault of a child under 13 by penetration).

108. An offence under section 7 of that Act (sexual assault of a child under 13).

109. An offence under section 8 of that Act (causing or inciting a child under 13 to engage in sexual activity).

110. An offence under section 9 of that Act (sexual activity with a child).

111. An offence under section 10 of that Act (causing or inciting a child to engage in sexual activity).

112. An offence under section 11 of that Act (engaging in sexual activity in the presence of a child).

113. An offence under section 12 of that Act (causing a child to watch a sexual act).

114. An offence under section 13 of that Act (child sex offences committed by children or young persons).

115. An offence under section 14 of that Act (arranging or facilitating commission of a child sex offence).

116. An offence under section 15 of that Act (meeting a child following sexual grooming etc).

117. An offence under section 16 of that Act (abuse of position of trust: sexual activity with a child).

118. An offence under section 17 of that Act (abuse of position of trust: causing or inciting a child to engage in sexual activity).

119. An offence under section 18 of that Act (abuse of position of trust: sexual activity in the presence of a child).

120. An offence under section 19 of that Act (abuse of position of trust: causing a child to watch a sexual act).

121. An offence under section 25 of that Act (sexual activity with a child family member).

122. An offence under section 26 of that Act (inciting a child family member to engage in sexual activity).

123. An offence under section 30 of that Act (sexual activity with a person with a mental disorder impeding choice).

124. An offence under section 31 of that Act (causing or inciting a person with a mental disorder impeding choice to engage in sexual activity).

125. An offence under section 32 of that Act (engaging in sexual activity in the presence of a person with a mental disorder impeding choice).

126. An offence under section 33 of that Act (causing a person with a mental disorder impeding choice to watch a sexual act).

127. An offence under section 34 of that Act (inducement, threat or deception to procure sexual activity with a person with a mental disorder).

128. An offence under section 35 of that Act (causing a person with a mental disorder to engage in or agree to engage in sexual activity by inducement, threat or deception).

129. An offence under section 36 of that Act (engaging in sexual activity in the presence, procured by inducement, threat or deception, of a person with a mental disorder).

130. An offence under section 37 of that Act (causing a person with a mental disorder to watch a sexual act by inducement, threat or deception).

131. An offence under section 38 of that Act (care workers: sexual activity with a person with a mental disorder).

132. An offence under section 39 of that Act (care workers: causing or inciting sexual activity).

133. An offence under section 40 of that Act (care workers: sexual activity in the presence of a person with a mental disorder).

134. An offence under section 41 of that Act (care workers: causing a person with a mental disorder to watch a sexual act).

135. An offence under section 47 of that Act (paying for sexual services of a child).

136. An offence under section 48 of that Act (causing or inciting child prostitution or pornography).

137. An offence under section 49 of that Act (controlling a child prostitute or a child involved in pornography).

138. An offence under section 50 of that Act (arranging or facilitating child prostitution or pornography).

139. An offence under section 52 of that Act (causing or inciting prostitution for gain).

140. An offence under section 53 of that Act (controlling prostitution for gain).

141. An offence under section 57 of that Act (trafficking into the UK for sexual exploitation).

142. An offence under section 58 of that Act (trafficking within the UK for sexual exploitation).

143. An offence under section 59 of that Act (trafficking out of the UK for sexual exploitation).

144. An offence under section 61 of that Act (administering a substance with intent).

145. An offence under section 62 of that Act (committing an offence with intent to commit a sexual offence).

146. An offence under section 63 of that Act (trespass with intent to commit a sexual offence).

147. An offence under section 64 of that Act (sex with an adult relative: penetration).

148 . An offence under section 65 of that Act (sex with an adult relative: consenting to penetration).

149. An offence under section 66 of that Act (exposure).

150. An offence under section 67 of that Act (voyeurism).

151. An offence under section 69 of that Act (intercourse with an animal).

152. An offence under section 70 of that Act (sexual penetration of a corpse).

153. An offence of –
   (a) aiding, abetting, counselling, procuring or inciting the commission of an offence specified in this Part of this Schedule,
   (b) conspiring to commit an offence so specified, or
   (c) attempting to commit an offence so specified.

SCHEDULE 21

DETERMINATION OF MINIMUM TERM IN RELATION TO MANDATORY LIFE SENTENCE

1. In this Schedule –
   'child' means a person under 18 years;
   'mandatory life sentence' means a life sentence passed in circumstances where the sentence is fixed by law;
   'minimum term', in relation to a mandatory life sentence, means the part of the sentence to be specified in an order under section 269(2);
   'whole life order' means an order under subsection (4) of section 269.

2. Section 28 of the Crime and Disorder Act 1998 (c 37) (meaning of 'racially or religiously aggravated') applies for the purposes of this Schedule as it applies for the purposes of sections 29 to 32 of that Act.

3. For the purposes of this Schedule an offence is aggravated by sexual orientation if it is committed in circumstances falling within subsection (2)(a)(i) or (b)(i) of section 146.

4. – (1) If –
   (a) the court considers that the seriousness of the offence (or the combination of the offence and one or more offences associated with it) is exceptionally high, and
   (b) the offender was aged 21 or over when he committed the offence,
the appropriate starting point is a whole life order.
(2) Cases that would normally fall within sub-paragraph (1)(a) include –
   (a) the murder of two or more persons, where each murder involves any of the following –
      (i) a substantial degree of premeditation or planning,
      (ii) the abduction of the victim, or
      (iii) sexual or sadistic conduct,
   (b) the murder of a child if involving the abduction of the child or sexual or sadistic motivation,
   (c) a murder done for the purpose of advancing a political, religious or ideological cause, or
   (d) a murder by an offender previously convicted of murder.

5. – (1) If –
   (a) the case does not fall within paragraph 4(1) but the court considers that the seriousness

of the offence (or the combination of the offence and one or more offences associated with it) is particularly high, and

    (b) the offender was aged 18 or over when he committed the offence,

the appropriate starting point, in determining the minimum term, is 30 years.

(2) Cases that (if not falling within paragraph 4(1)) would normally fall within sub-paragraph (1)(a) include –

    (a) the murder of a police officer or prison officer in the course of his duty,

    (b) a murder involving the use of a firearm or explosive,

    (c) a murder done for gain (such as a murder done in the course or furtherance of robbery or burglary, done for payment or done in the expectation of gain as a result of the death),

    (d) a murder intended to obstruct or interfere with the course of justice,

    (e) a murder involving sexual or sadistic conduct,

    (f) the murder of two or more persons,

    (g) a murder that is racially or religiously aggravated or aggravated by sexual orientation, or

    (h) a murder falling within paragraph 4(2) committed by an offender who was aged under 21 when he committed the offence.

6. If the offender was aged 18 or over when he committed the offence and the case does not fall within paragraph 4(1) or 5(1), the appropriate starting point, in determining the minimum term, is 15 years.

7. If the offender was aged under 18 when he committed the offence, the appropriate starting point, in determining the minimum term, is 12 years.

8. Having chosen a starting point, the court should take into account any aggravating or mitigating factors, to the extent that it has not allowed for them in its choice of starting point.

9. Detailed consideration of aggravating or mitigating factors may result in a minimum term of any length (whatever the starting point), or in the making of a whole life order.

10. Aggravating factors (additional to those mentioned in paragraph 4(2) and 5(2)) that may be relevant to the offence of murder include –

    (a) a significant degree of planning or premeditation,

    (b) the fact that the victim was particularly vulnerable because of age or disability,

    (c) mental or physical suffering inflicted on the victim before death,

    (d) the abuse of a position of trust,

    (e) the use of duress or threats against another person to facilitate the commission of the offence,

    (f) the fact that the victim was providing a public service or performing a public duty, and

    (g) concealment, destruction or dismemberment of the body.

11. Mitigating factors that may be relevant to the offence of murder include –

    (a) an intention to cause serious bodily harm rather than to kill,

    (b) lack of premeditation,

    (c) the fact that the offender suffered from any mental disorder or mental disability which (although not falling within section 2(1) of the Homicide Act 1957 (c 11)), lowered his degree of culpability,

(d) the fact that the offender was provoked (for example, by prolonged stress) in a way not amounting to a defence of provocation,

(e) the fact that the offender acted to any extent in self-defence,

(f) a belief by the offender that the murder was an act of mercy, and

(g) the age of the offender.

12. Nothing in this Schedule restricts the application of –

(a) section 143(2) (previous convictions),

(b) section 143(3) (bail), or

(c) section 144 (guilty plea).

NB. Sections 43, 62–66 and 181 and Schedule 4, above, were not in force on 1 June 2007.

As amended by the Domestic Violence, Crime and Victims Act 2004, ss14(1), (2), 30, 58(1), Schedule 10, paras 60, 62, 65; Commissioners for Revenue and Customs Act 2005, s50(2), (7); Constitutional Reform Act 2005, s15(1), Schedule 4, Pt 1, paras 356, 357(1), (2), 358(1)–(3); Violent Crime Reduction Act 2006, ss49, 65, Schedule 1, para 9(1), (2), (6), Schedule 5.

DOMESTIC VIOLENCE, CRIME AND VICTIMS ACT 2004

(2004 c 28)

5　The offence

(1) A person ('D') is guilty of an offence if –

(a) a child or vulnerable adult ('V') dies as a result of the unlawful act of a person who –

(i) was a member of the same household as V, and

(ii) had frequent contact with him,

(b) D was such a person at the time of that act,

(c) at that time there was a significant risk of serious physical harm being caused to V by the unlawful act of such a person, and

(d) either D was the person whose act caused V's death or –

(i) D was, or ought to have been, aware of the risk mentioned in paragraph (c),

(ii) D failed to take such steps as he could reasonably have been expected to take to protect V from the risk, and

(iii) the act occurred in circumstances of the kind that D foresaw or ought to have foreseen.

(2) The prosecution does not have to prove whether it is the first alternative in subsection (1)(d) or the second (sub-paragraphs (i) to (iii)) that applies.

(3) If D was not the mother or father of V –

(a) D may not be charged with an offence under this section if he was under the age of 16 at the time of the act that caused V's death;

(b) for the purposes of subsection (1)(d)(ii) D could not have been expected to take any such step as is referred to there before attaining that age.

(4) For the purposes of this section –

(a) a person is to be regarded as a 'member' of a particular household, even if he does not live in that household, if he visits it so often and for such periods of time that it is reasonable to regard him as a member of it;

(b) where V lived in different households at different times, 'the same household as V' refers to the household in which V was living at the time of the act that caused V's death.

(5) For the purposes of this section an 'unlawful' act is one that –

    (a) constitutes an offence, or

    (b) would constitute an offence but for being the act of –

        (i) a person under the age of ten, or

        (ii) a person entitled to rely on a defence of insanity.

Paragraph (b) does not apply to an act of D.

(6) In this section –

    'act' includes a course of conduct and also includes omission;

    'child' means a person under the age of 16;

    'serious' harm means harm that amounts to grievous bodily harm for the purposes of the Offences against the Person Act 1861 (c 100);

    'vulnerable adult' means a person aged 16 or over whose ability to protect himself from violence, abuse or neglect is significantly impaired through physical or mental disability or illness, through old age or otherwise.

(7) A person guilty of an offence under this section is liable on conviction on indictment to imprisonment for a term not exceeding 14 years or to a fine, or to both.

PART 2

CRIMINAL JUSTICE

17   Application by prosecution for certain counts to be tried without a jury

(1) The prosecution may apply to a judge of the Crown Court for a trial on indictment to take place on the basis that the trial of some, but not all, of the counts included in the indictment may be conducted without a jury.

(2) If such an application is made and the judge is satisfied that the following three conditions are fulfilled, he may make an order for the trial to take place on the basis that the trial of some, but not all, of the counts included in the indictment may be conducted without a jury.

(3) The first condition is that the number of counts included in the indictment is likely to mean that a trial by jury involving all of those counts would be impracticable.

(4) The second condition is that, if an order under subsection (2) were made, each count or group of counts which would accordingly be tried with a jury can be regarded as a sample of counts which could accordingly be tried without a jury.

(5) The third condition is that it is in the interests of justice for an order under subsection (2) to be made.

(6) In deciding whether or not to make an order under subsection (2), the judge must have regard to any steps which might reasonably be taken to facilitate a trial by jury.

(7) But a step is not to be regarded as reasonable if it could lead to the possibility of a defendant in the trial receiving a lesser sentence than would be the case if that step were not taken.

(8) An order under subsection (2) must specify the counts which may be tried without a jury.

(9) For the purposes of this section and sections 18 to 20, a count may not be regarded as a sample of other counts unless the defendant in respect of each count is the same person.

19   Effect of order under section 17(2)

(1) The effect of an order under section 17(2) is that where, in the course of the proceedings to

which the order relates, a defendant is found guilty by a jury on a count which can be regarded as a sample of other counts to be tried in those proceedings, those other counts may be tried without a jury in those proceedings.

(2) Where the trial of a count is conducted without a jury because of an order under section 17(2), the court is to have all the powers, authorities and jurisdiction which the court would have had if the trial of that count had been conducted with a jury (including power to determine any question and to make any finding which would be required to be determined or made by a jury).

(3) Except where the context otherwise requires, any reference in an enactment to a jury, the verdict of a jury or the finding of a jury is to be read, in relation to the trial of a count conducted without a jury because of an order under section 17(2), as a reference to the court, the verdict of the court or the finding of the court.

(4) Where the trial of a count is conducted without a jury because of an order under section 17(2) and the court convicts the defendant of that count –

(a) the court must give a judgment which states the reasons for the conviction at, or as soon as reasonably practicable after, the time of the conviction, and

(b) the reference in section 18(2) of the Criminal Appeal Act 1968 (c 19) (notice of appeal or of application for leave to appeal to be given within 28 days from date of conviction etc) to the date of the conviction is to be read as a reference to the date of the judgment mentioned in paragraph (a).

(5) Where, in the case of proceedings in respect of which an order under section 17(2) has been made, a jury convicts a defendant of a count, time does not begin to run under section 18(2) of the Criminal Appeal Act 1968 in relation to an appeal against that conviction until the date on which the proceedings end.

(6) In determining for the purposes of subsection (5) the date on which proceedings end, any part of those proceedings which takes place after the time when matters relating to sentencing begin to be dealt with is to be disregarded.

(7) Nothing in this section or section 17, 18 or 20 affects the requirement under section 4A of the Criminal Procedure (Insanity) Act 1964 (c 84) that any question, finding or verdict mentioned in that section be determined, made or returned by a jury.

20   Rules of court
(1) Rules of court may make such provision as appears to the authority making them to be necessary or expedient for the purposes of sections 17 to 19. …

PART 3

VICTIMS ETC

CHAPTER 1

THE VICTIMS' CODE

32   Code of practice for victims
(1) The Secretary of State must issue a code of practice as to the services to be provided to a victim of criminal conduct by persons appearing to him to have functions relating to –

(a) victims of criminal conduct, or

(b) any aspect of the criminal justice system.

(2) The code may restrict the application of its provisions to –
- (a) specified descriptions of victims;
- (b) victims of specified offences or descriptions of conduct;
- (c) specified persons or descriptions of persons appearing to the Secretary of State to have functions of the kind mentioned in subsection (1).

(3) The code may include provision requiring or permitting the services which are to be provided to a victim to be provided to one or more others –
- (a) instead of the victim (for example where the victim has died);
- (b) as well as the victim.

(4) The code may make different provision for different purposes, including different provision for –
- (a) different descriptions of victims;
- (b) persons who have different functions or descriptions of functions;
- (c) different areas.

(5) The code may not require anything to be done by –
- (a) a person acting in a judicial capacity;
- (b) a person acting in the discharge of a function of a member of the Crown Prosecution Service which involves the exercise of a discretion.

(6) In determining whether a person is a victim of criminal conduct for the purposes of this section, it is immaterial that no person has been charged with or convicted of an offence in respect of the conduct.

(7) In this section –

'criminal conduct' means conduct constituting an offence;

'specified' means specified in the code.

CHAPTER 2

REPRESENTATIONS AND INFORMATION

35   Victims' rights to make representations and receive information

(1) This section applies if –
- (a) a court convicts a person ('the offender') of a sexual or violent offence, and
- (b) a relevant sentence is imposed on him in respect of the offence.

(2) But section 39 applies (instead of this section) if a hospital direction and a limitation direction are given in relation to the offender.

(3) The local probation board for the area in which the sentence is imposed must take all reasonable steps to ascertain whether a person who appears to the board to be the victim of the offence or to act for the victim of the offence wishes –
- (a) to make representations about the matters specified in subsection (4);
- (b) to receive the information specified in subsection (5).

(4) The matters are –
- (a) whether the offender should be subject to any licence conditions or supervision requirements in the event of his release;
- (b) if so, what licence conditions or supervision requirements.

(5) The information is information about any licence conditions or supervision requirements to which the offender is to be subject in the event of his release.

(6) If a person whose wishes have been ascertained under subsection (3) makes representations to the local probation board mentioned in that subsection or the relevant local probation board

about a matter specified in subsection (4), the relevant local probation board must forward those representations to the persons responsible for determining the matter.

(7) If a local probation board has ascertained under subsection (3) that a person wishes to receive the information specified in subsection (5), the relevant local probation board must take all reasonable steps –

  (a) to inform the person whether or not the offender is to be subject to any licence conditions or supervision requirements in the event of his release,

  (b) if he is, to provide the person with details of any licence conditions or supervision requirements which relate to contact with the victim or his family, and

  (c) to provide the person with such other information as the relevant local probation board considers appropriate in all the circumstances of the case.

(8) The relevant local probation board is –

  (a) in a case where the offender is to be supervised on release by an officer of a local probation board, that local probation board;

  (b) in any other case, the local probation board for the area in which the prison or other place in which the offender is detained is situated.

42 Victims' rights: preliminary

(1) This section applies if –

  (a) a person ('the offender') is convicted of a sexual or violent offence,

  (b) a relevant sentence is imposed on him in respect of the offence, and

  (c) while the offender is serving the sentence, the Secretary of State gives a transfer direction and a restriction direction in respect of him.

(2) The local probation board for the area in which the hospital specified in the transfer direction is situated must take all reasonable steps to ascertain whether a person who appears to the board to be the victim of the offence or to act for the victim of the offence wishes –

  (a) to make representations about the matters specified in subsection (3);

  (b) to receive the information specified in subsection (4).

(3) The matters are –

  (a) whether the offender should be subject to any conditions in the event of his discharge from hospital;

  (b) if so, what conditions.

(4) The information is information about any conditions to which the offender is to be subject in the event of his discharge from hospital.

43 Representations

(1) This section applies if section 42 applies.

(2) If –

  (a) a person makes representations about a matter specified in section 42(3) to the local probation board mentioned in section 42(2) or the relevant local probation board, and

  (b) it appears to the relevant local probation board that the person is the victim of the offence or acts for the victim of the offence,

the relevant local probation board must forward the representations to the persons responsible for determining the matter.

(3) The duty in subsection (2) applies only while the restriction direction given in respect of the offender is in force.

(4) The Secretary of State must inform the relevant local probation board if he is considering –

    (a) whether to give a direction in respect of the offender under section 42(1) of the Mental Health Act 1983 (c 20) (directions lifting restrictions),

    (b) whether to discharge the offender under section 42(2) of that Act, either absolutely or subject to conditions, or

    (c) if the offender has been discharged subject to conditions, whether to vary the conditions.

(5) A Mental Health Review Tribunal must inform the relevant local probation board if –

    (a) an application is made to the tribunal by the offender under section 69, 70 or 75 of the Mental Health Act 1983 (applications concerning restricted patients), or

    (b) the Secretary of State refers the offender's case to the tribunal under section 71 of that Act (references concerning restricted patients).

(6) Subsection (7) applies if –

    (a) the relevant local probation board receives information under subsection (4) or (5), and

    (b) a person who appears to the relevant local probation board to be the victim of the offence or to act for the victim of the offence –

        (i) when his wishes were ascertained under section 42(2), expressed a wish to make representations about a matter specified in section 42(3), or

        (ii) has made representations about such a matter to the relevant local probation board or the local probation board mentioned in section 42(2).

(7) The relevant local probation board must provide the information to the person.

(8) The relevant local probation board is –

    (a) if the offender is to be discharged subject to a condition that he reside in a particular area, the local probation board for the area;

    (b) in any other case, the local probation board for the area in which the hospital in which the offender is detained is situated.

44   Information

(1) This section applies if section 42 applies.

(2) Subsection (3) applies if a person who appears to the relevant local probation board to be the victim of the offence or to act for the victim of the offence –

    (a) when his wishes were ascertained under section 42(2), expressed a wish to receive the information specified in section 42(4), or

    (b) has subsequently informed the relevant local probation board that he wishes to receive that information.

(3) The relevant local probation board must take all reasonable steps –

    (a) to inform that person whether or not the offender is to be subject to any conditions in the event of his discharge;

    (b) if he is, to provide that person with details of any conditions which relate to contact with the victim or his family;

    (c) if the restriction direction in respect of the offender is to cease to have effect, to notify that person of the date on which it is to cease to have effect;

    (d) to provide that person with such other information as the board considers appropriate in all the circumstances of the case.

(4) The Secretary of State must inform the relevant local probation board –

    (a) whether the offender is to be discharged;

    (b) if he is, whether he is to be discharged absolutely or subject to conditions;

    (c) if he is to be discharged subject to conditions, what the conditions are to be;

    (d) if he has been discharged subject to conditions –

    (i) of any variation of the conditions by the Secretary of State;

    (ii) of any recall to hospital under section 42(3) of the Mental Health Act 1983 (c 20);

  (e) if the restriction direction is to cease to have effect by virtue of action to be taken by the Secretary of State, of the date on which the restriction direction is to cease to have effect.

(5) Subsections (6) and (7) apply (instead of subsection (4)) if –

  (a) an application is made to a Mental Health Review Tribunal by the offender under section 69, 70 or 75 of the Mental Health Act 1983 (applications concerning restricted patients), or

  (b) the Secretary of State refers the offender's case to a Mental Health Review Tribunal under section 71 of that Act (references concerning restricted patients).

(6) The tribunal must inform the relevant local probation board –

  (a) of the matters specified in subsection (4)(a) to (c);

  (b) if the offender has been discharged subject to conditions, of any variation of the conditions by the tribunal;

  (c) if the restriction direction is to cease to have effect by virtue of action to be taken by the tribunal, of the date on which the restriction direction is to cease to have effect.

(7) The Secretary of State must inform the relevant local probation board of the matters specified in subsection (4)(d) and (e).

(8) The duties in subsections (3) to (7) apply only while the restriction direction is in force.

(9) The relevant local probation board has the meaning given in section 43(8).

45   Interpretation: sections 35 to 44

(1) In sections 35 to 44 –

'court' does not include a court-martial or the Courts-Martial Appeal Court;

'hospital direction' has the meaning given in section 45A(3)(a) of the Mental Health Act 1983 (c 20);

'hospital order' has the meaning given in section 37(4) of that Act;

'licence condition' means a condition in a licence;

'limitation direction' has the meaning given in section 45A(3)(b) of the Mental Health Act 1983;

'local probation board' means a local probation board established under section 4 of the Criminal Justice and Court Services Act 2000 (c 43);

'relevant sentence' means any of these –

  (a) a sentence of imprisonment for a term of 12 months or more;

  (b) a sentence of detention during Her Majesty's pleasure;

  (c) a sentence of detention for a period of 12 months or more under section 91 of the Powers of Criminal Courts (Sentencing) Act 2000 (c 6) (offenders under 18 convicted of certain serious offences);

  (d) a detention and training order for a term of 12 months or more;

'restriction direction' has the meaning given in section 49(2) of the Mental Health Act 1983;

'restriction order' has the meaning given in section 41(1) of that Act;

'supervision requirements' means requirements specified in a notice under section 103(6) of the Powers of Criminal Courts (Sentencing) Act 2000;

'transfer direction' has the meaning given in section 47(1) of the Mental Health Act 1983.

(2) For the purposes of sections 35 to 44, an offence is a sexual or violent offence if it is any of these –

(a) murder or an offence specified in Schedule 15 to the Criminal Justice Act 2003 (c 44);

(b) an offence in respect of which the patient or offender is subject to the notification requirements of Part 2 of the Sexual Offences Act 2003 (c 42));

(c) an offence against a child within the meaning of Part 2 of the Criminal Justice and Court Services Act 2000.

CHAPTER 3

OTHER MATTERS RELATING TO VICTIMS, ETC

48 Commissioner for Victims and Witnesses

(1) The Secretary of State must appoint a Commissioner for Victims and Witnesses (referred to in this Part as the Commissioner).

(2) Before appointing the Commissioner the Secretary of State must consult the Attorney General and the Lord Chancellor as to the person to be appointed.

(3) The Commissioner is a corporation sole.

(4) The Commissioner is not to be regarded –

(a) as the servant or agent of the Crown, or

(b) as enjoying any status, immunity or privilege of the Crown.

(5) The Commissioner's property is not to be regarded as property of, or held on behalf of, the Crown.

(6) Schedule 8 (which make further provision in connection with the Commissioner) has effect.

49 General functions of Commissioner

(1) The Commissioner must –

(a) promote the interests of victims and witnesses;

(b) take such steps as he considers appropriate with a view to encouraging good practice in the treatment of victims and witnesses;

(c) keep under review the operation of the code of practice issued under section 32.

(2) The Commissioner may, for any purpose connected with the performance of his duties under subsection (1) –

(a) make proposals to the Secretary of State for amending the code (at the request of the Secretary of State or on his own initiative);

(b) make a report to the Secretary of State;

(c) make recommendations to an authority within his remit;

(d) undertake or arrange for or support (financially or otherwise) the carrying out of research;

(e) consult any person he thinks appropriate.

(3) If the Commissioner makes a report to the Secretary of State under subsection (2)(b) –

(a) the Commissioner must send a copy of the report to the Attorney General and the Lord Chancellor;

(b) he Secretary of State must lay a copy of the report before Parliament and arrange for the report to be published.

50 Advice

(1) If he is required to do so by a Minister of the Crown, the Commissioner must give advice to the Minister of the Crown in connection with any matter which –

(a) is specified by the Minister, and

(b) relates to victims or witnesses.

(2) If he is required to do so by or on behalf of an authority within his remit, the Commissioner must give advice to the authority in connection with the information provided or to be provided by or on behalf of the authority to victims or witnesses.

(3) In this section 'Minister of the Crown' includes the Treasury.

51   Restrictions on exercise of functions

The Commissioner must not exercise any of his functions in relation to –
  (a) a particular victim or witness;
  (b) the bringing or conduct of particular proceedings;
  (c) anything done or omitted to be done by a person acting in a judicial capacity or on the instructions of or on behalf of such a person.

52   'Victims' and 'witnesses'

(1) This section applies for the purposes of sections 48 to 51.

(2) 'Victim' means –
  (a) a victim of an offence, or
  (b) a victim of anti-social behaviour.

(3) It is immaterial for the purposes of subsection (2)(a) that –
  (a) no complaint has been made about the offence;
  (b) no person has been charged with or convicted of the offence.

(4) 'Witness' means a person (other than a defendant) –
  (a) who has witnessed conduct in relation to which he may be or has been called to give evidence in relevant proceedings;
  (b) who is able to provide or has provided anything which might be used or has been used as evidence in relevant proceedings; or
  (c) who is able to provide or has provided anything mentioned in subsection (5) (whether or not admissible in evidence in relevant proceedings).

(5) The things referred to in subsection (4)(c) are –
  (a) anything which might tend to confirm, has tended to confirm or might have tended to confirm evidence which may be, has been or could have been admitted in relevant proceedings;
  (b) anything which might be, has been or might have been referred to in evidence given in relevant proceedings by another person;
  (c) anything which might be, has been or might have been used as the basis for any cross examination in the course of relevant proceedings.

(6) For the purposes of subsection (4) –
  (a) a person is a defendant in relation to any criminal proceedings if he might be, has been or might have been charged with or convicted of an offence in the proceedings;
  (b) a person is a defendant in relation to any other relevant proceedings if he might be, has been or might have been the subject of an order made in those proceedings.

(7) In subsections (4) to (6) 'relevant proceedings' means –
  (a) criminal proceedings;
  (b) proceedings of any other kind in respect of anti-social behaviour.

(8) For the purposes of this section –
  (a) 'anti-social behaviour' means behaviour by a person which causes or is likely to cause harassment, alarm or distress to one or more persons not of the same household as the person;
  (b) a person is a victim of anti-social behaviour if the behaviour has caused him

harassment, alarm or distress and he is not of the same household as the person who engages in the behaviour.

53   Authorities within Commissioner's remit

(1) For the purposes of this Part the authorities within the Commissioner's remit are those specified in Schedule 9. ...

55   Victims' Advisory Panel

(1) The Secretary of State must appoint persons to form a panel, to be known as the Victims' Advisory Panel.

(2) The Secretary of State must consult the Attorney General and the Lord Chancellor before –

    (a)   appointing a person to the Panel, or

    (b)   removing a person from the Panel.

(3) The Secretary of State must consult the Panel at such times and in such manner as he thinks appropriate on matters appearing to him to relate to victims of offences or anti-social behaviour or witnesses of offences or anti-social behaviour.

(4) The Secretary of State may reimburse the members of the Panel for such of their travelling and other expenses as he thinks appropriate.

(5) If the Secretary of State consults the Panel under subsection (3) in a particular year, he must arrange for the Panel to prepare a report for the year –

    (a)   summarising what the Panel has done in response to the consultation, and

    (b)   dealing with such other matters as the Panel consider appropriate.

(6) If a report is prepared under subsection (5), the Secretary of State must –

    (a)   arrange for it to be published, and

    (b)   lay it before Parliament.

(7) The non-statutory Victims' Advisory Panel is to be treated as having been established in accordance with this section.

(8) If the Secretary of State consults the non-statutory Victims' Advisory Panel on a matter mentioned in subsection (3) before the date on which this section comes into force, the consultation is to be treated as taking place under subsection (3).

(9) The non-statutory Victims' Advisory Panel is the unincorporated body of persons known as the Victims' Advisory Panel established by the Secretary of State before the date on which this section comes into force.

(10) In this section 'year' means a period of 12 months beginning on 1 April.

SCHEDULE 9

AUTHORITIES WITHIN COMMISSIONER'S REMIT

Government departments

1.ZA The Department for Communities and Local Government.

1. The Department for Constitutional Affairs.

2. The Department for Education and Skills.

3. The Department of Health.

4. The Department of Trade and Industry.

5. The Department for Transport.

6. The Department for Work and Pensions.

7. The Foreign and Commonwealth Office.

8. The Home Office.

9. The Office of the Deputy Prime Minister.

Customs and Excise
10. Commissioners for Her Majesty's Revenue and Customs.

Police forces, etc
11. A police force for a police area in England or Wales. ...

12. The Serious Fraud Office.

13. The Serious Organised Crime Agency. ...

Criminal injuries compensation
17. The Criminal Injuries Compensation Appeals Panel.

18. The Criminal Injuries Compensation Authority.

Health and safety
19. The Health and Safety Commission.

20. The Health and Safety Executive.

Legal services
21. The Legal Services Commission.

Court administration
22. Persons exercising functions relating to the carrying on of the business of a court.

Criminal justice system
23. The Criminal Cases Review Commission.

24. The Crown Prosecution Service. ...

Maritime and coastguards
30. The Maritime and Coastguard Agency.

NB. Of the provisions set out above, sections 48–53 and Schedule 9 were not in force on 1 June 2007.

As amended by the Commissioners for Revenue and Customs Act 2005, s50(1), (7); Serious Organised Crime and Police Act 2005, s59, Schedule 4, para 200; Secretary of State for Communities and Local Government Order 2006, art 9, Schedule, para 8.

CHILDREN ACT 2004

(2004 c 31)

58 Reasonable punishment

(1) In relation to any offence specified in subsection (2), battery of a child cannot be justified on the ground that it constituted reasonable punishment.

(2) The offences referred to in subsection (1) are –

    (a) an offence under section 18 or 20 of the Offences against the Person Act 1861 (c 100) (wounding and causing grievous bodily harm);

    (b) an offence under section 47 of that Act (assault occasioning actual bodily harm);

    (c) an offence under section 1 of the Children and Young Persons Act 1933 (c 12) (cruelty to persons under 16).

(3) Battery of a child causing actual bodily harm to the child cannot be justified in any civil proceedings on the ground that it constituted reasonable punishment.

(4) For the purposes of subsection (3) 'actual bodily harm' has the same meaning as it has for the purposes of section 47 of the Offences against the Person Act 1861.

(5) In section 1 of the Children and Young Persons Act 1933, omit subsection (7).

SERIOUS ORGANISED CRIME AND POLICE ACT 2005

(2005 c 15)

145 Interference with contractual relationships so as to harm animal research organisation

(1) A person (A) commits an offence if, with the intention of harming an animal research organisation, he –

    (a) does a relevant act, or

    (b) threatens that he or somebody else will do a relevant act,

in circumstances in which that act or threat is intended or likely to cause a second person (B) to take any of the steps in subsection (2).

(2) The steps are –

    (a) not to perform any contractual obligation owed by B to a third person (C) (whether or not such non-performance amounts to a breach of contract);

    (b) to terminate any contract B has with C;

    (c) not to enter into a contract with C.

(3) For the purposes of this section, a 'relevant act' is –

    (a) an act amounting to a criminal offence, or

    (b) a tortious act causing B to suffer loss or damage of any description;

but paragraph (b) does not include an act which is actionable on the ground only that it induces another person to break a contract with B.

(4) For the purposes of this section, 'contract' includes any other arrangement (and 'contractual' is to be read accordingly).

(5) For the purposes of this section, to 'harm' an animal research organisation means –

    (a) to cause the organisation to suffer loss or damage of any description, or

    (b) to prevent or hinder the carrying out by the organisation of any of its activities.

(6) This section does not apply to any act done wholly or mainly in contemplation or furtherance of a trade dispute.

(7) In subsection (6) 'trade dispute' has the same meaning as in Part 4 of the Trade Union and Labour Relations (Consolidation) Act 1992 (c 52), except that section 218 of that Act shall be read as if –

    (a) it made provision corresponding to section 244(4) of that Act, and

    (b) in subsection (5), the definition of 'worker' included any person falling within paragraph (b) of the definition of 'worker' in section 244(5).

146 Intimidation of persons connected with animal research organisation

(1) A person (A) commits an offence if, with the intention of causing a second person (B) to abstain from doing something which B is entitled to do (or to do something which B is entitled to abstain from doing) –

    (a) A threatens B that A or somebody else will do a relevant act, and

    (b) A does so wholly or mainly because B is a person falling within subsection (2).

(2) A person falls within this subsection if he is –

    (a) an employee or officer of an animal research organisation;

    (b) a student at an educational establishment that is an animal research organisation;

    (c) a lessor or licensor of any premises occupied by an animal research organisation;

    (d) a person with a financial interest in, or who provides financial assistance to, an animal research organisation;

    (e) a customer or supplier of an animal research organisation;

    (f) a person who is contemplating becoming someone within paragraph (c), (d) or (e);

    (g) a person who is, or is contemplating becoming, a customer or supplier of someone within paragraph (c), (d), (e) or (f);

    (h) an employee or officer of someone within paragraph (c), (d), (e), (f) or (g);

    (i) a person with a financial interest in, or who provides financial assistance to, someone within paragraph (c), (d), (e), (f) or (g);

    (j) a spouse, civil partner, friend or relative of, or a person who is known personally to, someone within any of paragraphs (a) to (i);

    (k) a person who is, or is contemplating becoming, a customer or supplier of someone within paragraph (a), (b), (h), (i) or (j); or

    (l) an employer of someone within paragraph (j).

(3) For the purposes of this section, an 'officer' of an animal research organisation or a person includes –

    (a) where the organisation or person is a body corporate, a director, manager or secretary;

    (b) where the organisation or person is a charity, a charity trustee (within the meaning of the Charities Act 1993 (c 10));

    (c) where the organisation or person is a partnership, a partner.

(4) For the purposes of this section –

    (a) a person is a customer or supplier of another person if he purchases goods, services or facilities from, or (as the case may be) supplies goods, services or facilities to, that other; and

    (b) 'supplier' includes a person who supplies services in pursuance of any enactment that requires or authorises such services to be provided.

(5) For the purposes of this section, a 'relevant act' is –

    (a) an act amounting to a criminal offence, or

    (b) a tortious act causing B or another person to suffer loss or damage of any description.

(6) The Secretary of State may by order amend this section so as to include within subsection (2) any description of persons framed by reference to their connection with –
  (a) an animal research organisation, or
  (b) any description of persons for the time being mentioned in that subsection.
(7) This section does not apply to any act done wholly or mainly in contemplation or furtherance of a trade dispute.
(8) In subsection (7) 'trade dispute' has the meaning given by section 145(7).

147 Penalty for offences under sections 145 and 146
(1) A person guilty of an offence under section 145 or 146 is liable –
  (a) on summary conviction, to imprisonment for a term not exceeding 12 months or to a fine not exceeding the statutory maximum, or to both;
  (b) on conviction on indictment, to imprisonment for a term not exceeding five years or to a fine, or to both.
(2) No proceedings for an offence under either of those sections may be instituted except by or with the consent of the Director of Public Prosecutions.

148 Animal research organisations
(1) For the purposes of sections 145 and 146 'animal research organisation' means any person or organisation falling within subsection (2) or (3).
(2) A person or organisation falls within this subsection if he or it is the owner, lessee or licensee of premises constituting or including –
  (a) a place specified in a licence granted under section 4 or 5 of the 1986 Act,
  (b) a scientific procedure establishment designated under section 6 of that Act, or
  (c) a breeding or supplying establishment designated under section 7 of that Act.
(3) A person or organisation falls within this subsection if he or it employs, or engages under a contract for services, any of the following in his capacity as such –
  (a) the holder of a personal licence granted under section 4 of the 1986 Act,
  (b) the holder of a project licence granted under section 5 of that Act,
  (c) a person specified under section 6(5) of that Act, or
  (d) a person specified under section 7(5) of that Act.
(4) The Secretary of State may by order amend this section so as to include a reference to any description of persons whom he considers to be involved in, or to have a direct connection with persons who are involved in, the application of regulated procedures.
(5) In this section –
  'the 1986 Act' means the Animals (Scientific Procedures) Act 1986 (c 14);
  'organisation' includes any institution, trust, undertaking or association of persons;
  'premises' includes any place within the meaning of the 1986 Act;
  'regulated procedures' has the meaning given by section 2 of the 1986 Act.

149 Extension of sections 145 to 147
(1) The Secretary of State may by order provide for sections 145, 146 and 147 to apply in relation to persons or organisations of a description specified in the order as they apply in relation to animal research organisations.
(2) The Secretary of State may, however, only make an order under this section if satisfied that a series of acts has taken place and –
  (a) that those acts were directed at persons or organisations of the description specified in the order or at persons having a connection with them, and

(b) that, if those persons or organisations had been animal research organisations, those acts would have constituted offences under section 145 or 146.

(3) In this section 'organisation' and 'animal research organisation' have the meanings given by section 148.

IDENTITY CARDS ACT 2006
(2006 c 15)

25   Possession of false identity documents, etc

(1) It is an offence for a person with the requisite intention to have in his possession or under his control –

(a) an identity document that is false and that he knows or believes to be false;

(b) an identity document that was improperly obtained and that he knows or believes to have been improperly obtained; or

(c) an identity document that relates to someone else.

(2) The requisite intention for the purposes of subsection (1) is –

(a) the intention of using the document for establishing registrable facts about himself; or

(b) the intention of allowing or inducing another to use it for establishing, ascertaining or verifying registrable facts about himself or about any other person (with the exception, in the case of a document within paragraph (c) of that subsection, of the individual to whom it relates).

(3) It is an offence for a person with the requisite intention to make, or to have in his possession or under his control –

(a) any apparatus which, to his knowledge, is or has been specially designed or adapted for the making of false identity documents; or

(b) any article or material which, to his knowledge, is or has been specially designed or adapted to be used in the making of false identity documents.

(4) The requisite intention for the purposes of subsection (3) is the intention –

(a) that he or another will make a false identity document; and

(b) that the document will be used by somebody for establishing, ascertaining or verifying registrable facts about a person.

(5) It is an offence for a person to have in his possession or under his control, without reasonable excuse –

(a) an identity document that is false;

(b) an identity document that was improperly obtained;

(c) an identity document that relates to someone else; or

(d) any apparatus, article or material which, to his knowledge, is or has been specially designed or adapted for the making of false identity documents or to be used in the making of such documents.

(6) A person guilty of an offence under subsection (1) or (3) shall be liable, on conviction on indictment, to imprisonment for a term not exceeding ten years or to a fine, or to both.

(7) A person guilty of an offence under subsection (5) shall be liable –

(a) on conviction on indictment, to imprisonment for a term not exceeding two years or to a fine, or to both;

(b) on summary conviction in England and Wales, to imprisonment for a term not exceeding twelve months or to a fine not exceeding the statutory maximum, or to both; …

but, in relation to an offence committed before the commencement of section 154(1) of the Criminal Justice Act 2003 (c 44), the reference in paragraph (b) to twelve months is to be read as a reference to six months.

(8) For the purposes of this section –

  (a) an identity document is false only if it is false within the meaning of Part 1 of the Forgery and Counterfeiting Act 1981 (c 45) (see section 9(1) of that Act); and

  (b) an identity document was improperly obtained if false information was provided, in or in connection with the application for its issue or an application for its modification, to the person who issued it or (as the case may be) to a person entitled to modify it;

and references to the making of a false identity document include references to the modification of an identity document so that it becomes false. …

(10) In this section 'identity document' has the meaning given by section 26.

26 Identity documents for the purposes of s25

(1) In section 25 'identity document' means any document that is, or purports to be –

  (a) an ID card;

  (b) a designated document;

  (c) an immigration document;

  (d) a United Kingdom passport (within the meaning of the Immigration Act 1971 (c 77));

  (e) a passport issued by or on behalf of the authorities of a country or territory outside the United Kingdom or by or on behalf of an international organisation;

  (f) a document that can be used (in some or all circumstances) instead of a passport;

  (g) a UK driving licence; or

  (h) a driving licence issued by or on behalf of the authorities of a country or territory outside the United Kingdom.

(2) In subsection (1) 'immigration document' means –

  (a) a document used for confirming the right of a person under the Community Treaties in respect of entry or residence in the United Kingdom;

  (b) a document which is given in exercise of immigration functions and records information about leave granted to a person to enter or to remain in the United Kingdom; or23

  (c) a registration card (within the meaning of section 26A of the Immigration Act 1971);

and in paragraph (b) 'immigration functions' means functions under the Immigration Acts (within the meaning of the Asylum and Immigration (Treatment of Claimants, etc.) Act 2004 (c 19)).

(3) In that subsection 'UK driving licence' means –

  (a) a licence to drive a motor vehicle granted under Part 3 of the Road Traffic Act 1988 (c 52); …

(4) The Secretary of State may by order modify the list of documents in subsection (1).

42 General interpretation

In this Act – …

'designated document' means a document of a description designated for the purposes of this Act by an order under section 4; …

'ID card' is to be construed in accordance with section 6(1);

'information' includes documents and records;

'issue', in relation to a document or card, and cognate expressions are to be construed in accordance with subsection (5);

'modification' includes omission, addition or alteration, and cognate expressions are to be construed accordingly; …

'registrable fact' has the meaning given by section 1(5) and (6); …

(5) References in this Act to the issue of a document or card include references to its renewal, replacement or re-issue (with or without modifications).

FRAUD ACT 2006
(2006 c 35)

1   Fraud

(1) A person is guilty of fraud if he is in breach of any of the sections listed in subsection (2) (which provide for different ways of committing the offence).

(2) The sections are –

    (a) section 2 (fraud by false representation),

    (b) section 3 (fraud by failing to disclose information), and

    (c) section 4 (fraud by abuse of position).

(3) A person who is guilty of fraud is liable –

    (a) on summary conviction, to imprisonment for a term not exceeding 12 months or to a fine not exceeding the statutory maximum (or to both);

    (b) on conviction on indictment, to imprisonment for a term not exceeding 10 years or to a fine (or to both). …

2   Fraud by false representation

(1) A person is in breach of this section if he –

    (a) dishonestly makes a false representation, and

    (b) intends, by making the representation-

        (i)   to make a gain for himself or another, or

        (ii) to cause loss to another or to expose another to a risk of loss.

(2) A representation is false if –

    (a) it is untrue or misleading, and

    (b) the person making it knows that it is, or might be, untrue or misleading.

(3) 'Representation' means any representation as to fact or law, including a representation as to the state of mind of –

    (a) the person making the representation, or

    (b) any other person.

(4) A representation may be express or implied.

(5) For the purposes of this section a representation may be regarded as made if it (or anything implying it) is submitted in any form to any system or device designed to receive, convey or respond to communications (with or without human intervention).

3   Fraud by failing to disclose information

A person is in breach of this section if he –

    (a) dishonestly fails to disclose to another person information which he is under a legal duty to disclose, and

    (b) intends, by failing to disclose the information –

     (i)   to make a gain for himself or another, or

     (ii) to cause loss to another or to expose another to a risk of loss.

4   Fraud by abuse of position

(1) A person is in breach of this section if he –

    (a) occupies a position in which he is expected to safeguard, or not to act against, the financial interests of another person,

    (b) dishonestly abuses that position, and

    (c) intends, by means of the abuse of that position –

       (i)   to make a gain for himself or another, or

       (ii) to cause loss to another or to expose another to a risk of loss.

(2) A person may be regarded as having abused his position even though his conduct consisted of an omission rather than an act.

5   'Gain' and 'loss'

(1) The references to gain and loss in sections 2 to 4 are to be read in accordance with this section.

(2) 'Gain' and 'loss' –

    (a) extend only to gain or loss in money or other property;

    (b) include any such gain or loss whether temporary or permanent;

and 'property' means any property whether real or personal (including things in action and other intangible property).

(3) 'Gain' includes a gain by keeping what one has, as well as a gain by getting what one does not have.

(4) 'Loss' includes a loss by not getting what one might get, as well as a loss by parting with what one has.

6   Possession etc. of articles for use in frauds

(1) A person is guilty of an offence if he has in his possession or under his control any article for use in the course of or in connection with any fraud.

(2) A person guilty of an offence under this section is liable –

    (a) on summary conviction, to imprisonment for a term not exceeding 12 months or to a fine not exceeding the statutory maximum (or to both);

    (b) on conviction on indictment, to imprisonment for a term not exceeding 5 years or to a fine (or to both). ...

7   Making or supplying articles for use in frauds

(1) A person is guilty of an offence if he makes, adapts, supplies or offers to supply any article –

    (a) knowing that it is designed or adapted for use in the course of or in connection with fraud, or

    (b) intending it to be used to commit, or assist in the commission of, fraud.

(2) A person guilty of an offence under this section is liable –

    (a) on summary conviction, to imprisonment for a term not exceeding 12 months or to a fine not exceeding the statutory maximum (or to both);

    (b) on conviction on indictment, to imprisonment for a term not exceeding 10 years or to a fine (or to both). ...

8   'Article'

(1) For the purposes of –

    (a) sections 6 and 7, and

(b) the provisions listed in subsection (2), so far as they relate to articles for use in the course of or in connection with fraud,

'article' includes any program or data held in electronic form.

(2) The provisions are –

    (a) section 1(7)(b) of the Police and Criminal Evidence Act 1984 (c 60),

    (b) section 2(8)(b) of the Armed Forces Act 2001 (c 19), ...

(meaning of 'prohibited articles' for the purposes of stop and search powers).

9   Participating in fraudulent business carried on by sole trader etc.

(1) A person is guilty of an offence if he is knowingly a party to the carrying on of a business to which this section applies.

(2) This section applies to a business which is carried on –

    (a) by a person who is outside the reach of section 458 of the Companies Act 1985 (c 6) ... (offence of fraudulent trading), and

    (b) with intent to defraud creditors of any person or for any other fraudulent purpose.

(3) The following are within the reach of section 458 of the 1985 Act –

    (a) a company (within the meaning of that Act);

    (b) a person to whom that section applies (with or without adaptations or modifications) as if the person were a company;

    (c) a person exempted from the application of that section. ...

(5) 'Fraudulent purpose' has the same meaning as in section 458 of the 1985 ...

(6) A person guilty of an offence under this section is liable –

    (a) on summary conviction, to imprisonment for a term not exceeding 12 months or to a fine not exceeding the statutory maximum (or to both);

    (b) on conviction on indictment, to imprisonment for a term not exceeding 10 years or to a fine (or to both). ...

11   Obtaining services dishonestly

(1) A person is guilty of an offence under this section if he obtains services for himself or another –

    (a) by a dishonest act, and

    (b) in breach of subsection (2).

(2) A person obtains services in breach of this subsection if –

    (a) they are made available on the basis that payment has been, is being or will be made for or in respect of them,

    (b) he obtains them without any payment having been made for or in respect of them or without payment having been made in full, and

    (c) when he obtains them, he knows –

        (i) that they are being made available on the basis described in paragraph (a), or

        (ii) that they might be,

    but intends that payment will not be made, or will not be made in full.

(3) A person guilty of an offence under this section is liable –

    (a) on summary conviction, to imprisonment for a term not exceeding 12 months or to a fine not exceeding the statutory maximum (or to both);

    (b) on conviction on indictment, to imprisonment for a term not exceeding 5 years or to a fine (or to both). ...

12   Liability of company officers for offences by company

(1) Subsection (2) applies if an offence under this Act is committed by a body corporate.

(2) If the offence is proved to have been committed with the consent or connivance of –

    (a) a director, manager, secretary or other similar officer of the body corporate, or

    (b) a person who was purporting to act in any such capacity,

he (as well as the body corporate) is guilty of the offence and liable to be proceeded against and punished accordingly.

(3) If the affairs of a body corporate are managed by its members, subsection (2) applies in relation to the acts and defaults of a member in connection with his functions of management as if he were a director of the body corporate.

VIOLENT CRIME REDUCTION ACT 2006
(2006 c 38)

28   Using someone to mind a weapon

(1) A person is guilty of an offence if –

    (a) he uses another to look after, hide or transport a dangerous weapon for him; and

    (b) he does so under arrangements or in circumstances that facilitate, or are intended to facilitate, the weapon's being available to him for an unlawful purpose.

(2) For the purposes of this section the cases in which a dangerous weapon is to be regarded as available to a person for an unlawful purpose include any case where –

    (a) the weapon is available for him to take possession of it at a time and place; and

    (b) his possession of the weapon at that time and place would constitute, or be likely to involve or to lead to, the commission by him of an offence.

(3) In this section 'dangerous weapon' means –

    (a) a firearm other than an air weapon or a component part of, or accessory to, an air weapon; or

    (b) a weapon to which section 141 or 141A of the Criminal Justice Act 1988 (c 33) applies (specified offensive weapons, knives and bladed weapons). ...

29   Penalties etc. for offence under s28

(1) This section applies where a person ('the offender') is guilty of an offence under section 28.

(2) Where the dangerous weapon in respect of which the offence was committed is a weapon to which section 141 or 141A of the Criminal Justice Act 1988 (specified offensive weapons, knives and bladed weapons) applies, the offender shall be liable, on conviction on indictment, to imprisonment for a term not exceeding 4 years or to a fine, or to both.

(3) Where –

    (a) at the time of the offence, the offender was aged 16 or over, and

    (b) the dangerous weapon in respect of which the offence was committed was a firearm mentioned in section 5(1)(a) to (af) or (c) or section 5(1A)(a) of the 1968 Act (firearms possession of which attracts a minimum sentence),

the offender shall be liable, on conviction on indictment, to imprisonment for a term not exceeding 10 years or to a fine, or to both.

(4) On a conviction in England and Wales, where –

    (a) subsection (3) applies, and

    (b) the offender is aged 18 or over at the time of conviction,

the court must impose (with or without a fine) a term of imprisonment of not less than 5 years, unless it is of the opinion that there are exceptional circumstances relating to the offence or to the offender which justify its not doing so.

(5) In relation to times before the commencement of paragraph 180 of Schedule 7 to the Criminal Justice and Court Services Act 2000 (c 43), the reference in subsection (4) to a sentence of imprisonment, in relation to an offender aged under 21 at the time of conviction, is to be read as a reference to a sentence of detention in a young offender institution.

(6) On a conviction in England and Wales, where –

    (a) subsection (3) applies, and

    (b) the offender is aged under 18 at the time of conviction,

the court must impose (with or without a fine) a term of detention under section 91 of the Powers of Criminal Courts (Sentencing) Act 2000 (c 6) of not less than 3 years, unless it is of the opinion that there are exceptional circumstances relating to the offence or to the offender which justify its not doing so. ...

(10) In any case not mentioned in subsection (2) or (3), the offender shall be liable, on conviction on indictment, to imprisonment for a term not exceeding 5 years or to a fine, or to both.

(11) Where –

    (a) a court is considering for the purposes of sentencing the seriousness of an offence under section 28, and

    (b) at the time of the offence the offender was aged 18 or over and the person used to look after, hide or transport the weapon was not,

the court must treat the fact that that person was under the age of 18 at that time as an aggravating factor (that is to say, a factor increasing the seriousness of the offence).

(12) Where a court treats a person's age as an aggravating factor in accordance with subsection (11), it must state in open court that the offence was aggravated as mentioned in that subsection.

(13) Where –

    (a) an offence under section 28 of using another person for a particular purpose is found to have involved that other person's having possession of a weapon, or being able to make it available, over a period of two or more days, or at some time during a period of two or more days, and

    (b) on any day in that period, an age requirement was satisfied,

the question whether subsection (3) applies or (as the case may be) the question whether the offence was aggravated under this section is to be determined as if the offence had been committed on that day.

(14) In subsection (13) the reference to an age requirement is a reference to either of the following –

    (a) the requirement of subsection (3) that the offender was aged 16 or over at the time of the offence;

    (b) the requirement of subsection (11) that the offender was aged 18 or over at that time and that the other person was not. ...

35   Restriction on sale and purchase of primers

(1) This section applies to a cap-type primer designed for use in metallic ammunition for a firearm.

(2) It is an offence for a person to sell to another either –

    (a) a primer to which this section applies,

    (b) an empty cartridge case incorporating such a primer,

unless that other person falls within subsection (3).

(3) A person falls within this subsection if –

    (a) he is a registered firearms dealer;

   (b) he sells by way of any trade or business either primers or empty cartridge cases
       incorporating primers, or both;

   (c) he produces a certificate authorising him to possess a firearm of a relevant kind;

   (d) he produces a certificate authorising him to possess ammunition of a relevant kind;

   (e) he shows that he is a person in the service of Her Majesty who is entitled under
       subsection (6) to acquire a primer to which this section applies;

   (f) he shows that he is entitled, by virtue of the 1968 Act, the Firearms (Amendment)
       Act 1988 (c 45) or any other enactment and otherwise than by virtue of being a person
       in the service of Her Majesty, to have possession, without a certificate, of a firearm of
       a relevant kind or of ammunition of a relevant kind;

   (g) he produces a certificate authorising another person to have possession of such a
       firearm, or of such ammunition, together with that other person's authority to purchase
       the primer or empty cartridge case on his behalf; or

   (h) he shows that he is authorised by regulations made by the Secretary of State to purchase
       primers or cartridge cases of the type in question.

(4) It is an offence for a person to buy or to attempt to buy –

   (a) a primer to which this section applies, or

   (b) an empty cartridge case incorporating such a primer,

unless he falls within subsection (5).

(5) A person falls within this subsection if –

   (a) he is a registered firearms dealer;

   (b) he sells by way of any trade or business either primers or empty cartridge cases
       incorporating primers, or both;

   (c) he holds a certificate authorising him to possess a firearm of a relevant kind;

   (d) he holds a certificate authorising him to possess ammunition of a relevant kind;

   (e) he is a person in the service of Her Majesty who is entitled under subsection (6) to
       acquire a primer to which this section applies;

   (f) he is entitled, by virtue of the 1968 Act, the Firearms (Amendment) Act 1988 or any
       other enactment and otherwise than by virtue of being a person in the service of Her
       Majesty, to have possession, without a certificate, of a firearm of a relevant kind or of
       ammunition of a relevant kind;

   (g) he is in possession of a certificate authorising another person to have possession of
       such a firearm, or of such ammunition, and has that other person's authority to
       purchase the primer or empty cartridge case on his behalf; or

   (h) he is authorised by regulations made by the Secretary of State to purchase primers or
       cartridge cases of the type in question.

(6) A person who is in the service of Her Majesty is entitled to acquire a primer to which this
section applies if –

   (a) he is duly authorised in writing to acquire firearms and ammunition for the public
       service; or

   (b) he is a person who is authorised to purchase a firearm or ammunition by virtue of a
       certificate issued in accordance with section 54(2)(b) of the 1968 Act (certificates for
       persons in naval, military or air service of Her Majesty).

(7) An offence under this section shall be punishable, on summary conviction –

   (a) in England and Wales, with imprisonment for a term not exceeding 51 weeks or with
       a fine not exceeding level 5 on the standard scale, or with both; …

(8) In relation to an offence committed before the commencement of section 281(5) of the

Criminal Justice Act 2003 (c 44), the reference in subsection (7)(a) of this section to 51 weeks is to be read as a reference to 6 months. ...

(11) In this section –

'ammunition of a relevant kind' means ammunition for a firearm of a relevant kind;

'enactment' includes an enactment passed after the passing of this Act;

'firearm of a relevant kind' means a firearm other than a shot gun, an air weapon or a firearm chambered for rim-fire ammunition.

55 Continuity of sexual offences law

(1) This section applies where, in any proceedings –

(a) a person ('the defendant') is charged in respect of the same conduct both with an offence under the Sexual Offences Act 2003 ('the 2003 Act offence') and with an offence specified in subsection (2) ('the pre-commencement offence');

(b) the only thing preventing the defendant from being found guilty of the 2003 Act offence is the fact that it has not been proved beyond a reasonable doubt that the time when the conduct took place was after the coming into force of the enactment providing for the offence; and

(c) the only thing preventing the defendant from being found guilty of the pre-commencement offence is the fact that it has not been proved beyond a reasonable doubt that that time was before the coming into force of the repeal of the enactment providing for the offence.

(2) The offences referred to in subsection (1)(a) are –

(a) any offence under the Sexual Offences Act 1956 (c 69);

(b) an offence under section 4 of the Vagrancy Act 1824 (c 83) (obscene exposure);

(c) an offence under section 28 of the Town Police Clauses Act 1847 (c 89) (indecent exposure);

(d) an offence under section 61 or 62 of the Offences against the Person Act 1861 (c 100) (buggery etc.);

(e) an offence under section 128 of the Mental Health Act 1959 (c 72) (sexual intercourse with patients);

(f) an offence under section 1 of the Indecency with Children Act 1960 (c 33) (indecency with children);

(g) an offence under section 4 or 5 of the Sexual Offences Act 1967 (procuring an man to commit buggery and living on the earnings of male prostitution);

(h) an offence under section 9 of the Theft Act 1968 (c 60) (burglary, including entering premises with intent to commit rape);

(i) an offence under section 54 of the Criminal Law Act 1977 (c 45) (incitement of girl under 16 to commit incest);

(j) an offence under section 1 of the Protection of Children Act 1978 (c 37) (indecent photographs of children);

(k) an offence under section 3 of the Sexual Offences (Amendment) Act 2000 (c 44) (abuse of position of trust);

(l) an offence under section 145 of the Nationality, Immigration and Asylum Act 2002 (c 41) (traffic in prostitution).

(3) For the purpose of determining the guilt of the defendant it shall be conclusively presumed that the time when the conduct took place was –

(a) if the maximum penalty for the pre-commencement offence is less than the maximum penalty for the 2003 Act offence, a time before the coming into force of the repeal of the enactment providing for the pre-commencement offence; and

(b) in any other case, a time after the coming into force of the enactment providing for the 2003 Act offence.

(4) In subsection (3) the reference, in relation an offence, to the maximum penalty is a reference to the maximum penalty by way imprisonment or other detention that could be imposed on the defendant on conviction of the offence in the proceedings in question.

(5) A reference in this section to an offence under the Sexual Offences Act 2003 (c 42) or to an offence specified in subsection (2) includes a reference to –

(a) inciting the commission of that offence;

(b) conspiracy to commit that offence; and

(c) attempting to commit that offence;

and, in relation to an offence falling within paragraphs (a) to (c), a reference in this section to the enactment providing for the offence so falling has effect as a reference to the enactment providing for the offence under that Act or, as the case may be, for the offence so specified.

(6) This section applies to any proceedings, whenever commenced, other than proceedings in which the defendant has been convicted or acquitted of the 2003 Act offence or the pre-commencement offence before the commencement of this section.

APPENDIX

CRIMINAL JUSTICE ACT 2003
(2003 c 44)

280 Alteration of penalties for specified summary offences
(1) The summary offences listed in Schedule 25 are no longer punishable with imprisonment.
(2) Schedule 26 (which contains amendments increasing the maximum term of imprisonment for certain summary offences from 4 months or less to 51 weeks) shall have effect.
(3) This section does not affect the penalty for any offence committed before the commencement of this section.

282 Increase in maximum term that may be imposed on summary conviction of offence triable either way
(1) In section 32 of the Magistrates' Courts Act 1980 (c 43) (penalties on summary conviction for offences triable either way) in subsection (1) (offences listed in Schedule 1 to that Act) for 'not exceeding 6 months' there is substituted 'not exceeding 12 months'. …

SCHEDULE 3

ALLOCATION OF CASES TRIABLE EITHER WAY, AND SENDING CASES TO THE CROWN COURT, ETC

PART 1

PRINCIPAL AMENDMENTS

Magistrates' Courts Act 1980 (c 43)
1. The Magistrates' Courts Act 1980 is amended as follows. …

13. In section 33 (maximum penalties on summary conviction in pursuance of section 22), in subsection (1), paragraph (b) and the word 'and' immediately preceding it are omitted. …

Criminal Attempts Act 1981 (c 47)
52. In section 2 of the Criminal Attempts Act 1981 (application of procedures and other provisions to offences under section 1), in subsection (2)(g), the words 'or committed for trial' are omitted. …

SCHEDULE 25

SUMMARY OFFENCES NO LONGER PUNISHABLE WITH IMPRISONMENT

Vagrancy Act 1824 (c 83)

1. The offence under section 3 of the Vagrancy Act 1824 (idle and disorderly persons) of causing or procuring or encouraging any child or children to wander abroad, or place himself or herself in any public place, street, highway, court, or passage, to beg or gather alms.

2. The following offences under section 4 of that Act (rogues and vagabonds) –
    (a) the offence of going about as a gatherer or collector of alms, or endeavouring to procure charitable contributions of any nature or kind, under any false or fraudulent pretence,
    (b) the offence of being found in or upon any dwelling house, warehouse, coach-house, stable, or outhouse, or in any inclosed yard, garden, or area, for any unlawful purpose, and
    (c) the offence of being apprehended as an idle and disorderly person, and violently resisting any constable, or other peace officer so apprehending him or her, and being subsequently convicted of the offence for which he or she shall have been so apprehended. ...

SCHEDULE 26

INCREASE IN MAXIMUM TERM FOR CERTAIN SUMMARY OFFENCES ...

Criminal Attempts Act 1981 (c 47)

28. In section 9 of the Criminal Attempts Act 1981 (interference with vehicles), in subsection (3), for 'three months' there is substituted '51 weeks'. ...

Public Order Act 1986 (c 64)

37. – (1) The Public Order Act 1986 is amended as follows.
(2) In section 12 (imposing conditions on public processions) –
    (a) in subsection (8), and
    (b) in subsection (10),
for '3 months' there is substituted '51 weeks'.
(3) In section 13 (prohibiting public processions) –
    (a) in subsection (11), and
    (b) in subsection (13),
for '3 months' there is substituted '51 weeks'.
(4) In section 14 (imposing conditions on public assemblies) –
    (a) in subsection (8), and
    (b) in subsection (10),
for '3 months' there is substituted '51 weeks'.
(5) In section 14B (offences in connection with trespassory assemblies and arrest therefor) –
    (a) in subsection (5), and
    (b) in subsection (7),
for '3 months' there is substituted '51 weeks'. ...

Criminal Justice and Public Order Act 1994 (c 33)

45. – (1) The Criminal Justice and Public Order Act 1994 is amended as follows. ...

(4) In section 61 (power to remove trespasser on land), in subsection (4), for 'three months' there is substituted '51 weeks'.

(5) In section 62B (failure to comply with direction under section 62A: offences), in subsection (3), for '3 months' there is substituted '51 weeks'.

(6) In section 63 (powers to remove persons attending or preparing for a rave), in subsections (6) and (7B), for 'three months' there is substituted '51 weeks'.

(7) In section 68 (offence of aggravated trespass), in subsection (3), for 'three months' there is substituted '51 weeks'.

(8) In section 69 (powers to remove persons committing or participating in aggravated trespass), in subsection (3), for 'three months' there is substituted '51 weeks'. ...

Police Act 1996 (c 16)

47. In section 89 of the Police Act 1996 (assaults on constables etc.), in subsection (2), for 'one month' there is substituted '51 weeks'. ...

Criminal Justice and Police Act 2001 (c 16)

56. – (1) The Criminal Justice and Police Act 2001 is amended as follows. ...

(3) In section 42 (prevention of intimidation), in subsection (7), for 'three months' there is substituted '51 weeks'. ...

SCHEDULE 32

AMENDMENTS RELATING TO SENTENCING

PART 1

GENERAL ...

Magistrates' Courts Act 1980 (c 43)

25. The Magistrates' Courts Act 1980 is amended as follows. ...

27. In section 33 (maximum penalties on summary conviction in pursuance of section 22), in subsection (1)(a), for '3 months' there is substituted '51 weeks'. ...

Criminal Attempts Act 1981 (c 47)

33. In section 4 of the Criminal Attempts Act 1981 (trials and penalties), in subsection (5)(b), for sub-paragraph (ii) there is substituted –

'(ii) in section 154(1) and (2) (general limit on magistrates' court's powers to impose imprisonment) of the Criminal Justice Act 2003.'...

PART 2

OFFENCES: ABOLITION OF IMPRISONMENT AND CONVERSION TO SUMMARY OFFENCE

Vagrancy Act 1824 (c 83)

145. In section 3 of the Vagrancy Act 1824 (idle and disorderly persons), for the words from 'subject to' to the end there is substituted 'it shall be lawful for any justice of the peace to impose

on such person (being thereof convicted before him by his own view, or by the confession of such person, or by the evidence on oath of one or more credible witnesses) a fine not exceeding level 3 on the standard scale'.

146. – (1) Section 4 of that Act (rogues and vagabonds) is amended as follows.
(2) In that section, for the words from 'shall be' to the end there is substituted 'commits an offence under this section'.
(3) At the end of that section (which becomes subsection (1)) there is inserted –

'(2) It shall be lawful for any justice of the peace to impose on any person who commits an offence under this section (being thereof convicted before him by the confession of such person, or by the evidence on oath of one or more credible witnesses) –
(a) in the case of a person convicted of the offence of wandering abroad and lodging in any barn or outhouse, or in any deserted or unoccupied building, or in the open air, or under a tent, or in any cart or waggon, and not giving a good account of himself, a fine not exceeding level 1 on the standard scale, and
(b) in the case of a person convicted of any other offence under this section, a fine not exceeding level 3 on the standard scale.' ...

SCHEDULE 37

REPEALS ...

PART 4

ALLOCATION AND SENDING OF OFFENCES

Short title and chapter	Extent of repeal ...
Magistrates' Courts Act 1980 (c 43)	... In section 33(1), paragraph (b) and the word 'and' immediately preceding it. ...
Criminal Attempts Act 1981 (c 47)	In section 2(2)(g), the words 'or committed for trial'. ...
Vagrancy Act 1842 (c 83)	Section 5. ... Section 10.
Criminal Justice Act 1982 (c 48)	Section 70

RACIAL AND RELIGIOUS HATRED ACT 2006
(2006 c 1)

1   Hatred against persons on religious grounds
The Public Order Act 1986 (c 64) is amended in accordance with the Schedule to this Act, which creates offences involving stirring up hatred against persons on religious grounds.

SCHEDULE

HATRED AGAINST PERSONS ON RELIGIOUS GROUNDS

In the Public Order Act 1986 (c 64), after Part 3 insert –

'PART 3A

HATRED AGAINST PERSONS ON RELIGIOUS GROUNDS

29A Meaning of "religious hatred"

In this Part "religious hatred" means hatred against a group of persons defined by reference to religious belief or lack of religious belief.

29B Use of words or behaviour or display of written material

(1) A person who uses threatening words or behaviour, or displays any written material which is threatening, is guilty of an offence if he intends thereby to stir up religious hatred.

(2) An offence under this section may be committed in a public or a private place, except that no offence is committed where the words or behaviour are used, or the written material is displayed, by a person inside a dwelling and are not heard or seen except by other persons in that or another dwelling.

(3) A constable may arrest without warrant anyone he reasonably suspects is committing an offence under this section.

(4) In proceedings for an offence under this section it is a defence for the accused to prove that he was inside a dwelling and had no reason to believe that the words or behaviour used, or the written material displayed, would be heard or seen by a person outside that or any other dwelling.

(5) This section does not apply to words or behaviour used, or written material displayed, solely for the purpose of being included in a programme service.

29C Publishing or distributing written material

(1) A person who publishes or distributes written material which is threatening is guilty of an offence if he intends thereby to stir up religious hatred.

(2) References in this Part to the publication or distribution of written material are to its publication or distribution to the public or a section of the public.

29D Public performance of play

(1) If a public performance of a play is given which involves the use of threatening words or behaviour, any person who presents or directs the performance is guilty of an offence if he intends thereby to stir up religious hatred.

(2) This section does not apply to a performance given solely or primarily for one or more of the following purposes –

    (a) rehearsal,

    (b) making a recording of the performance, or

    (c) enabling the performance to be included in a programme service;

but if it is proved that the performance was attended by persons other than those directly connected with the giving of the performance or the doing in relation to it of the things mentioned in paragraph (b) or (c), the performance shall, unless the contrary is shown, be taken not to have been given solely or primarily for the purpose mentioned above.

(3) For the purposes of this section –

(a)   a person shall not be treated as presenting a performance of a play by reason only of his taking part in it as a performer,

(b)   a person taking part as a performer in a performance directed by another shall be treated as a person who directed the performance if without reasonable excuse he performs otherwise than in accordance with that person's direction, and

(c)   a person shall be taken to have directed a performance of a play given under his direction notwithstanding that he was not present during the performance;

and a person shall not be treated as aiding or abetting the commission of an offence under this section by reason only of his taking part in a performance as a performer.

(4) In this section "play" and "public performance" have the same meaning as in the Theatres Act 1968.

(5) The following provisions of the Theatres Act 1968 apply in relation to an offence under this section as they apply to an offence under section 2 of that Act –

section 9 (script as evidence of what was performed),

section 10 (power to make copies of script),

section 15 (powers of entry and inspection).

29E   Distributing, showing or playing a recording

(1) A person who distributes, or shows or plays, a recording of visual images or sounds which are threatening is guilty of an offence if he intends thereby to stir up religious hatred.

(2) In this Part "recording" means any record from which visual images or sounds may, by any means, be reproduced; and references to the distribution, showing or playing of a recording are to its distribution, showing or playing to the public or a section of the public.

(3) This section does not apply to the showing or playing of a recording solely for the purpose of enabling the recording to be included in a programme service.

29F   Broadcasting or including programme in programme service

(1) If a programme involving threatening visual images or sounds is included in a programme service, each of the persons mentioned in subsection (2) is guilty of an offence if he intends thereby to stir up religious hatred.

(2) The persons are –

(a)   the person providing the programme service,

(b)   any person by whom the programme is produced or directed, and

(c)   any person by whom offending words or behaviour are used.

29G   Possession of inflammatory material

(1) A person who has in his possession written material which is threatening, or a recording of visual images or sounds which are threatening, with a view to –

(a)   in the case of written material, its being displayed, published, distributed, or included in a programme service whether by himself or another, or

(b)   in the case of a recording, its being distributed, shown, played, or included in a programme service, whether by himself or another,

is guilty of an offence if he intends religious hatred to be stirred up thereby.

(2) For this purpose regard shall be had to such display, publication, distribution, showing, playing, or inclusion in a programme service as he has, or it may reasonably be inferred that he has, in view.

29H   Powers of entry and search

(1) If in England and Wales a justice of the peace is satisfied by information on oath laid

by a constable that there are reasonable grounds for suspecting that a person has possession of written material or a recording in contravention of section 29G, the justice may issue a warrant under his hand authorising any constable to enter and search the premises where it is suspected the material or recording is situated. ...

(3) A constable entering or searching premises in pursuance of a warrant issued under this section may use reasonable force if necessary.

(4) In this section "premises" means any place and, in particular, includes –

    (a) any vehicle, vessel, aircraft or hovercraft,

    (b) any offshore installation as defined in section 12 of the Mineral Workings (Offshore Installations) Act 1971, and

    (c) any tent or movable structure.

29I Power to order forfeiture

(1) A court by or before which a person is convicted of –

    (a) an offence under section 29B relating to the display of written material, or

    (b) an offence under section 29C, 29E or 29G,

shall order to be forfeited any written material or recording produced to the court and shown to its satisfaction to be written material or a recording to which the offence relates.

(2) An order made under this section shall not take effect –

    (a) in the case of an order made in proceedings in England and Wales, until the expiry of the ordinary time within which an appeal may be instituted or, where an appeal is duly instituted, until it is finally decided or abandoned;

    (b) in the case of an order made in proceedings in Scotland, until the expiration of the time within which, by virtue of any statute, an appeal may be instituted or, where such an appeal is duly instituted, until the appeal is finally decided or abandoned.

(3) For the purposes of subsection (2)(a) –

    (a) an application for a case stated or for leave to appeal shall be treated as the institution of an appeal, and

    (b) where a decision on appeal is subject to a further appeal, the appeal is not finally determined until the expiry of the ordinary time within which a further appeal may be instituted or, where a further appeal is duly instituted, until the further appeal is finally decided or abandoned.

(4) For the purposes of subsection (2)(b) the lodging of an application for a stated case or note of appeal against sentence shall be treated as the institution of an appeal.

29J Protection of freedom of expression

Nothing in this Part shall be read or given effect in a way which prohibits or restricts discussion, criticism or expressions of antipathy, dislike, ridicule, insult or abuse of particular religions or the beliefs or practices of their adherents, or of any other belief system or the beliefs or practices of its adherents, or proselytising or urging adherents of a different religion or belief system to cease practising their religion or belief system.

29K Savings for reports of parliamentary or judicial proceedings

(1) Nothing in this Part applies to a fair and accurate report of proceedings in Parliament or in the Scottish Parliament.

(2) Nothing in this Part applies to a fair and accurate report of proceedings publicly heard before a court or tribunal exercising judicial authority where the report is published contemporaneously with the proceedings or, if it is not reasonably practicable or would be

unlawful to publish a report of them contemporaneously, as soon as publication is reasonably practicable and lawful.

29L Procedure and punishment

(1) No proceedings for an offence under this Part may be instituted in England and Wales except by or with the consent of the Attorney General.

(2) For the purposes of the rules in England and Wales against charging more than one offence in the same count or information, each of sections 29B to 29G creates one offence.

(3) A person guilty of an offence under this Part is liable –

  (a) on conviction on indictment to imprisonment for a term not exceeding seven years or a fine or both;

  (b) on summary conviction to imprisonment for a term not exceeding six months or a fine not exceeding the statutory maximum or both.

29M Offences by corporations

(1) Where a body corporate is guilty of an offence under this Part and it is shown that the offence was committed with the consent or connivance of a director, manager, secretary or other similar officer of the body, or a person purporting to act in any such capacity, he as well as the body corporate is guilty of the offence and liable to be proceeded against and punished accordingly.

(2) Where the affairs of a body corporate are managed by its members, subsection (1) applies in relation to the acts and defaults of a member in connection with his functions of management as it applies to a director.

29N Interpretation

In this Part –

  "distribute", and related expressions, shall be construed in accordance with section 29C(2) (written material) and section 29E(2) (recordings);

  "dwelling" means any structure or part of a structure occupied as a person's home or other living accommodation (whether the occupation is separate or shared with others) but does not include any part not so occupied, and for this purpose "structure" includes a tent, caravan, vehicle, vessel or other temporary or movable structure;

  "programme" means any item which is included in a programme service;

  "programme service" has the same meaning as in the Broadcasting Act 1990;

  "publish", and related expressions, in relation to written material, shall be construed in accordance with section 29C(2);

  "religious hatred" has the meaning given by section 29A;

  "recording" has the meaning given by section 29E(2), and "play" and "show", and related expressions, in relation to a recording, shall be construed in accordance with that provision;

  "written material" includes any sign or other visible representation.'

POLICE AND JUSTICE ACT 2006
(2006 (c 48)

35   Unauthorised access to computer material

(1) In the Computer Misuse Act 1990 (c 18) ('the 1990 Act'), section 1 (offence of unauthorised access to computer material) is amended as follows.

(2) In subsection (1) –

(a) in paragraph (a), after 'any computer' there is inserted ', or to enable any such access to be secured';

(b) in paragraph (b), after 'secure' there is inserted ', or to enable to be secured,'.

(3) For subsection (3) there is substituted –

'(3) A person guilty of an offence under this section shall be liable –

(a) on summary conviction in England and Wales, to imprisonment for a term not exceeding 12 months or to a fine not exceeding the statutory maximum or to both;

(b) on summary conviction in Scotland, to imprisonment for a term not exceeding six months or to a fine not exceeding the statutory maximum or to both;

(c) on conviction on indictment, to imprisonment for a term not exceeding two years or to a fine or to both.'

36   Unauthorised acts with intent to impair operation of computer, etc

For section 3 of the 1990 Act (unauthorised modification of computer material) there is substituted –

'**3   Unauthorised acts with intent to impair, or with recklessness as to impairing, operation of computer, etc**

(1) A person is guilty of an offence if –

(a) he does any unauthorised act in relation to a computer;

(b) at the time when he does the act he knows that it is unauthorised; and

(c) either subsection (2) or subsection (3) below applies.

(2) This subsection applies if the person intends by doing the act –

(a) to impair the operation of any computer;

(b) to prevent or hinder access to any program or data held in any computer;

(c) to impair the operation of any such program or the reliability of any such data; or

(d) to enable any of the things mentioned in paragraphs (a) to (c) above to be done.

(3) This subsection applies if the person is reckless as to whether the act will do any of the things mentioned in paragraphs (a) to (d) of subsection (2) above.

(4) The intention referred to in subsection (2) above, or the recklessness referred to in subsection (3) above, need not relate to –

(a) any particular computer;

(b) any particular program or data; or

(c) a program or data of any particular kind.

(5) In this section –

(a) a reference to doing an act includes a reference to causing an act to be done;

(b) "act" includes a series of acts;

(c) a reference to impairing, preventing or hindering something includes a reference to doing so temporarily.

(6) A person guilty of an offence under this section shall be liable –

  (a) on summary conviction in England and Wales, to imprisonment for a term not exceeding 12 months or to a fine not exceeding the statutory maximum or to both;

  (b) on summary conviction in Scotland, to imprisonment for a term not exceeding six months or to a fine not exceeding the statutory maximum or to both;

  (c) on conviction on indictment, to imprisonment for a term not exceeding ten years or to a fine or to both.'

37   Making, supplying or obtaining articles for use in computer misuse offences

After section 3 of the 1990 Act there is inserted –

'3A Making, supplying or obtaining articles for use in offence under section 1 or 3

(1) A person is guilty of an offence if he makes, adapts, supplies or offers to supply any article intending it to be used to commit, or to assist in the commission of, an offence under section 1 or 3.

(2) A person is guilty of an offence if he supplies or offers to supply any article believing that it is likely to be used to commit, or to assist in the commission of, an offence under section 1 or 3.

(3) A person is guilty of an offence if he obtains any article with a view to its being supplied for use to commit, or to assist in the commission of, an offence under section 1 or 3.

(4) In this section "article" includes any program or data held in electronic form.

(5) A person guilty of an offence under this section shall be liable –

  (a) on summary conviction in England and Wales, to imprisonment for a term not exceeding 12 months or to a fine not exceeding the statutory maximum or to both;

  (b) on summary conviction in Scotland, to imprisonment for a term not exceeding six months or to a fine not exceeding the statutory maximum or to both;

  (c) on conviction on indictment, to imprisonment for a term not exceeding two years or to a fine or to both.'

38   Transitional and saving provision

(1) The amendments made by –

  (a) subsection (2) of section 35, and

  (b) paragraphs 19(2), 25(2) and 29(2) of Schedule 14,

apply only where every act or other event proof of which is required for conviction of an offence under section 1 of the 1990 Act takes place after that subsection comes into force.

(2) The amendments made by –

  (a) subsection (3) of section 35, and

  (b) paragraphs 23, 24, 25(4) and (5), 26, 27(2) and (7) and 28 of Schedule 14,

do not apply in relation to an offence committed before that subsection comes into force.

(3) An offence is not committed under the new section 3 unless every act or other event proof of which is required for conviction of the offence takes place after section 36 above comes into force.

(4) In relation to a case where, by reason of subsection (3), an offence is not committed under the new section 3 –

  (a) section 3 of the 1990 Act has effect in the form in which it was enacted;

  (b) paragraphs 19(3), 25(3) to (5), 27(4) and (5) and 29(3) and (4) of Schedule 14 do not apply.

(5) An offence is not committed under the new section 3A unless every act or other event proof of which is required for conviction of the offence takes place after section 37 above comes into force.

(6) In the case of an offence committed before section 154(1) of the Criminal Justice Act 2003 (c 44) comes into force, the following provisions have effect as if for '12 months' there were substituted 'six months' –

    (a) paragraph (a) of the new section 1(3);

    (b) paragraph (a) of the new section 2(5);

    (c) subsection (6)(a) of the new section 3;

    (d) subsection (5)(a) of the new section 3A.

(7) In this section –

    (a) 'the new section 1(3)' means the subsection (3) substituted in section 1 of the 1990 Act by section 35 above;

    (b) 'the new section 2(5)' means the subsection (5) substituted in section 2 of the 1990 Act by paragraph 17 of Schedule 14 to this Act;

    (c) 'the new section 3' means the section 3 substituted in the 1990 Act by section 36 above;

    (d) 'the new section 3A' means the section 3A inserted in the 1990 Act by section 37 above.

52   Amendments and repeals

Schedules 14 (minor and consequential amendments) and 15 (repeals and revocations) have effect.

SCHEDULE 14

MINOR AND CONSEQUENTIAL AMENDMENTS …

Computer Misuse Act 1990 (c 18)

17. In section 2 of the Computer Misuse Act 1990 (unauthorised access with intent to commit or facilitate commission of further offences), for subsection (5) there is substituted –

    '(5) A person guilty of an offence under this section shall be liable

        (a) on summary conviction in England and Wales, to imprisonment for a term not exceeding 12 months or to a fine not exceeding the statutory maximum or to both;

        (b) on summary conviction in Scotland, to imprisonment for a term not exceeding six months or to a fine not exceeding the statutory maximum or to both;

        (c) on conviction on indictment, to imprisonment for a term not exceeding five years or to a fine or to both.'

18. In the heading to section 4 of that Act (territorial scope of offences under that Act), for 'offences under this Act' there is substituted 'offences under sections 1 to 3'.

19. (1) Section 5 of that Act (significant links with domestic jurisdiction) is amended as follows.

(2) In subsection (2), for paragraph (b) there is substituted –

    '(b) that any computer containing any program or data to which the accused by doing that act secured or intended to secure unauthorised access, or enabled or intended to enable unauthorised access to be secured, was in the home country concerned at that time.'

(3) In subsection (3) –

    (a) in paragraph (a), for 'he did the act which caused the unauthorised modification' there is substituted 'he did the unauthorised act (or caused it to be done)';

    (b) for paragraph (b) there is substituted –

        '(b) that the unauthorised act was done in relation to a computer in the home country concerned.'

20. In section 6 of that Act (territorial scope of inchoate offences) –

    (a) in the heading, for 'offences under this Act' there is substituted 'offences under sections 1 to 3';

    (b) in subsections (1) and (3), for 'offence under this Act' there is substituted 'offence under section 1, 2 or 3 above'.

21. In section 7 of that Act (territorial scope of inchoate offences related to offences under external law) –

    (a) in the heading, for 'offences under this Act' there is substituted 'offences under sections 1 to 3';

    (b) in subsection (4), for 'offence under this Act' there is substituted, in each place, 'offence under section 1, 2 or 3 above'.

22. In section 9 of that Act (British citizenship immaterial), in paragraphs (a) and (d) of subsection (2), for 'offence under this Act' there is substituted 'offence under section 1, 2 or 3 above'.

23. Section 11 of that Act (proceedings for offences under section 1) is repealed.

24. Section 12 of that Act (conviction of an offence under section 1 in proceedings for an offence under section 2 or 3) is repealed. ...

26. Section 14 of that Act (search warrants for offences under section 1) is repealed. ...

29. (1) Section 17 of that Act (interpretation) is amended as follows.

(2) In subsection (2), after 'such access' there is inserted 'or to enable such access to be secured'.

(3) Subsection (7) is omitted.

(4) For subsection (8) there is substituted –

    '(8) An act done in relation to a computer is unauthorised if the person doing the act (or causing it to be done)

        (a) is not himself a person who has responsibility for the computer and is entitled to determine whether the act may be done; and

        (b) does not have consent to the act from any such person.

    In this subsection "act" includes a series of acts.'

SCHEDULE 15

REPEALS AND REVOCATIONS …

PART 4

MISCELLANEOUS

Short title or title	*Extent of repeal or revocation*
…	
Computer Misuse Act 1990 (c 18)	Section 11.
	Section 12.
	In section 13 –
	(a) subsections (3) to (7);
	(b) in subsection (8), the words from 'commenced' to the end.
	Section 14.
	Section 16(3), (10), (11) and (12).
	Section 17(7). …

ROAD SAFETY ACT 2006
(2006 c 49)

20   Causing death by careless, or inconsiderate, driving
(1) In the Road Traffic Act 1988 (c 52), after section 2A insert –

'2B Causing death by careless, or inconsiderate, driving
A person who causes the death of another person by driving a mechanically propelled vehicle on a road or other public place without due care and attention, or without reasonable consideration for other persons using the road or place, is guilty of an offence.'

21   Causing death by driving: unlicensed, disqualified or uninsured drivers
(1) In the Road Traffic Act 1988 (c 52), after section 3ZA (inserted by section 30) insert –

'3ZB Causing death by driving: unlicensed, disqualified or uninsured drivers
A person is guilty of an offence under this section if he causes the death of another person by driving a motor vehicle on a road and, at the time when he is driving, the circumstances are such that he is committing an offence under –
   (a) section 87(1) of this Act (driving otherwise than in accordance with a licence),
   (b) section 103(1)(b) of this Act (driving while disqualified), or
   (c) section 143 of this Act (using motor vehicle while uninsured or unsecured against third party risks).'

30   Meaning of driving without due care and attention
In the Road Traffic Act 1988, after section 3 insert –

'3ZA Meaning of careless, or inconsiderate, driving

(1) This section has effect for the purposes of sections 2B and 3 above and section 3A below.

(2) A person is to be regarded as driving without due care and attention if (and only if) the way he drives falls below what would be expected of a competent and careful driver.

(3) In determining for the purposes of subsection (2) above what would be expected of a careful and competent driver in a particular case, regard shall be had not only to the circumstances of which he could be expected to be aware but also to any circumstances shown to have been within the knowledge of the accused.

(4) A person is to be regarded as driving without reasonable consideration for other persons only if those persons are inconvenienced by his driving.'

31   Extension of offence in section 3A of Road Traffic Act 1988

(1) Section 3A of the Road Traffic Act 1988 (causing death by careless driving when under influence of drink or drugs etc.) is amended as follows.

(2) In subsection (1), after paragraph (c) insert 'or

    (d) he is required by a constable to give his permission for a laboratory test of a specimen of blood taken from him under section 7A of this Act, but without reasonable excuse fails to do so,'.

(3) In subsection (3), for 'and (c)' substitute ', (c) and (d)'.

INDEX